BOTHAM
MY AUTOBIOGRAPHY

Peter Hayter, who has collaborated with Ian Botham in writing this book, is the cricket correspondent of the *Mail on Sunday*. In 1997 he also worked with Ian on *The Botham Report*, the critically acclaimed analysis of the state of English cricket. His other books include collaborations with Philip Tufnell on *Postcards from the Beach* and Tufnell's autobiography, *What Now?* – the first book to be awarded maximum five stars in the review section of *Wisden Cricket Monthly*; *England's Cricket Heroes* and *Great Tests Recalled*. He lives in Shropshire with his family.

BOTHAM
MY AUTOBIOGRAPHY

with Peter Hayter

CollinsWillow
An Imprint of HarperCollinsPublishers

Published in hardback in 1994 by
CollinsWillow
an imprint of HarperCollins*Publishers*, London
Reprinted 1994 (six times)

First published in paperback in 1995
Reprinted 1995
Revised edition 1998, 2000

A CIP catalogue record for this book
is available from the British Library

ISBN 0 00 218959 3

Printed in Great Britain by Omnia Books Limited, Glasgow

The publishers wish to thank the following for providing photographs:
Allsport, BBC, Benson and Hedges, Kathy Botham, Lincolnshire
Chronicle, Patrick Eagar, Hayters, Graham Morris, Pacemaker Press
and Thames Television

To Kath, Liam, Sarah and Becky and to the
rest of my family, my friends and the cricketing
public all over the world who have supported
me throughout the years

CONTENTS

ACKNOWLEDGEMENTS

My thanks go to my wife Mary and our son Max and daughter Sophie who kept me sane during the close shaves; to Chris Dighton who worked tirelessly in the production of the book, compiling extensive research material and conducting countless interviews; to those we interviewed – Kath, Les and Marie Botham, Jan and Gerry Waller, Alan Herd, Douglas Osborne, Rodney Ontong, Tom Cartwright, Trevor Gard, Vic Marks, David Roberts, David English, Dennis Breakwell, Max Boyce, David Gower, Bob Willis, Chris Lander, Alan Dyer, Viv Richards, David Graveney, Bill Jones and Harry Sharp – and, finally, to my mother Lucy and my father Reg Hayter to whom both Ian and myself owe so much.

Peter Hayter
In Elvino's Veritas

FOREWORD

Say the name Ian Botham to me and the first thought I have is not of 'Beefy' the great cricketer but of a magnificent friend, full of love for people, full of support and ready to give you everything he's got.

That's the Ian Botham I have been lucky enough to know since we first met as youngsters at Somerset back in the early 1970s before travelling around the world and playing cricket for and against each other for more than 20 years.

And that's the same Beefy I'm lucky enough to know today, now that our playing days are over.

As a cricketer, Beefy was a man in a million. In the Caribbean, people are always coming up to me and asking about the man, and it is the same the world over. As an opponent we took him 100 per cent seriously. As a team-mate he was amazing.

Once, playing for Somerset against Essex in a county championship match, he batted with such power that all nine fielders were on the boundary. The singles were there for the taking, but still Beefy kept going for the boundaries. It is a sight I will never forget and probably not see again.

Off the pitch he lives his life to the full, with boundless

enthusiasm and magnificent generosity. I remember during one of his trips to the West Indies when I met him at the airport and we went for a few rum punches. Unfortunately for the jet-lagged Beefy, they were about 150 per cent proof, but all he could taste was the orange juice – so he kept knocking them back. Assuring me that he felt fine, he went back with me to his hotel for a wash and brush-up and we arranged to meet in half an hour. But later when I knocked on the door of his room, there was no answer.

Worried, I searched out the chambermaid and persuaded her to unlock the door; and there was Beefy lying fast asleep on the bed. With one of his team-mates I went and borrowed some women's make-up and proceeded to turn him into Beefy the beautiful drag artist. He never stirred once during this time, nor did he realize we had taken a series of photographs of him in this state!

Those pictures are not in this book – even great friendships have a breaking point – but this is the story of a great cricketer and a great person; a man who lives life in all its forms to the full and, above all for me, a man who has been a great friend.

1
THE END OF THE ROAD

I knew it was all over the morning it took me five minutes to get out of bed.

It was two days after I had played for Durham against Glamorgan in the second round of the NatWest Trophy at Cardiff in the mid-summer of 1993. My left hip had been playing up all season, and my left knee and shoulder ached as well, but to be honest it was difficult to distinguish one pain from another. I was worn out from head to toe. Sitting on the edge of the bed that morning, I suddenly realized that my body was sending me a message that I just couldn't ignore any longer. To borrow Tony Greig's well-worn phrase, it was 'Goodnight Beefy'.

For many sportsmen, coming face to face with irrefutable evidence of their mortality is the moment they dread above all others. How many times have you read of people in all walks of sport going on one season or one match too long? And how many times have you read of the bitter price they have paid for doing so? I had always said that one day I would wake up and just know that this was the end, and that when that day came I would accept it without making the decision any more difficult for myself and those around me than it inevitably is.

From the moment I was given an opportunity to extend my career by undergoing back surgery in 1988, I knew I was playing on borrowed time. In grabbing that time and making the most of it, I will always be grateful for the patience and skill of surgeon John Davies. However, I didn't want to be one of those sad figures who doesn't know when to call it a day and who is consequently ridiculed by his enemies and pitied by his friends. Moreover, it became obvious to me that although my body might be able to take a little more punishment in the short term, the long term effects could be extremely damaging; and the one thing I knew for certain was that I didn't fancy spending my retirement years in a wheelchair.

The bottom line, however, was that after twenty years in the professional game my love affair with playing cricket was over. Not only was I physically wrecked, but the events of the 1993 season meant that I was totally disillusioned with the game. Without the drive, I simply didn't want to go out on the pitch any more. Under those circumstances it would not have been fair on me, my team-mates or the public to carry on.

I had always intended that the summer of 1993 would be my last as a professional cricketer, but I had been determined to go out at the top. So when I said in April that I was aiming to win back my place in the England side and play in the Ashes series against the Australians, it was not just the normal pre-season optimism: I meant it. I was convinced I had plenty to offer, especially after suffering with everyone else the woeful excuse for a performance that England had served up on the winter tour to India and Sri

Lanka, as a result of which they had not only been beaten in all four Tests but thoroughly thrashed and totally humiliated.

Frankly, I had been disgusted by what had gone on out there. Graham Gooch played the best cricket of his career when leading from the front as captain, during which period he passed David Gower's record as England's highest run scorer in Test cricket. I have nothing but admiration for the way he made up his mind to play at the highest level for as long as possible and kept himself fit enough to do so. But I have always found that as England captain what he couldn't come to terms with was that the right way for him was not necessarily the best way for everyone.

When it came to the Indian fiasco, I think his biggest mistake was allowing himself to be persuaded to go in the first place. I would never criticize anyone for missing a winter tour. I've done so myself in the past and I understand completely why other cricketers have as well. As players get older the amount of international cricket played and the pressure involved, as well as the business of leaving your family at home for months at a time, mean that if you don't take an occasional winter break you are vulnerable to burn out. It's not a matter of picking and choosing when it suits you to play for England, it's just that players need time to recharge their batteries and rediscover an appetite that can easily become jaded.

If Gooch wasn't keen enough to take on the job of captaining his country on an overseas tour without having to have his arm twisted, then he really shouldn't have gone at all. Once he had made the decision, he then had the bright idea of surrounding himself with his old mates John Emburey and Mike Gatting, and discarding David Gower for some unknown reason. The omission of Gower was nothing short of a scandal and England paid for it dearly. For my money there were people on that tour who looked and played as though they didn't want to be there. They lacked desire and, what is infinitely worse, they lacked pride; once things started to go wrong they simply gave up. Nothing was ever their fault, and there was always an excuse for their abject failures: if it wasn't the smog in Calcutta, it was the prawns in Madras. And by sending out a 'pastoral counsellor', the Reverend Andrew Wingfield Digby, instead of a team doctor the Test and County Cricket Board proved once again that the lunatics had taken over the asylum. I didn't go along with much of what Ray Illingworth said during his tenure of the job as chairman of selectors, but even he had the sense to see that 'Wingers Diggers' was surplus to requirements.

Even though the Indian tour had been a disaster from beginning to end, I was under no illusions about how hard it would be for me to regain my place. I got the impression after the 1992 World Cup in Australia, where in controversial circumstances which I will expand on later I ended up a two-time loser in the final against Pakistan, that my critics would have been quite happy for me to have disappeared from international cricket there and then. There are people in the game who would have thrown me out years ago after the troubles I went through in the mid-1980s, people who were jealous of my success and who simply could not live with the fact that, through no fault of my own, I was perceived to be bigger than the game. In fact, I really don't believe that the selectors had wanted to pick me for the tournament in the first place, but they were forced to because they couldn't find anyone capable of replacing me as a genuine international-class all-rounder.

Despite losing my place during the following summer against Pakistan, I was still enthusiastic about the possibility of a comeback against Allan Border's 1993 Australians. On the evidence of what had happened in India, I was even more convinced that I could do a job at Test level. I certainly hadn't seen any performance to make me think that the players being picked were so good that there was no way back. If the team had been playing well that would have been fair enough, I would have said 'Thank you very much' and looked back on happy memories. But to see an England team floundering with me as a helpless bystander was unbelievably irritating. I had a lot to offer and it was being wasted.

I was hoping that the selectors would learn from their mistakes and give me one last chance. My record against Australia was second to none. Allan Border knew that, the Australian management knew it and so did most of their players who had played against me at some time or another. The minute my name was down on the scoresheet the team automatically got a psychological boost, and for that reason alone had the selectors decided to pick me, morale would have been lifted and the Aussies would have been on edge from the word go.

So when I enjoyed some success in the traditional opening fixture of the Australian tour, for the Duchess of Norfolk's XI at Arundel in May, I felt confident that the message must get through, particularly as one of my victims was Border himself, the Australian captain and my great mate and rival. In addition, Ted Dexter, the chairman of the selectors, was there to see what I could still do.

Judging by what happened later that day, he must have had his eyes closed.

I had been genuinely keyed-up for the match. A party of us had travelled down from Durham: Kath, my wife, my youngest daughter Becky, and county colleagues Wayne Larkins, David Graveney and Paul Parker. The night before the game we enjoyed a meal at a bistro where all the talk was of producing a vintage performance to stake my claim to the all-rounder's position. There was an enormous amount of interest in the match, as there always is when the Aussies are in town. When morning came it took us about an hour to travel the half mile to the ground because of the traffic. I like to think that many of the 16,000 capacity crowd were there to see me put on a show against the old enemy. Certainly the level of commitment shown by the Australians and the seriousness with which they approached the match were not in doubt. When I was hit for four in my first over some visiting Antipodean shouted out: 'It's '93 now mate, not '81'; I had the greatest delight in silencing him a few minutes later when I removed Damien Martyn cheaply.

However, unbeknown to me, Dexter was at that moment in the process of pulling the rug from under me. When I heard of the content of a radio interview he had given after I had bowled that day, during which he appeared to pour scorn on my performance, I hit the roof.

I was in the bar relaxing after the match when a couple of journalists came up to me and told me what had happened. Apparently Dexter had been asked what he thought of my bowling. 'Are the Australians trying to play him into the side?' he muttered, as if they were purposely trying to make me look good. When the interviewer, Mark Saggers, who was understandably taken aback by what Dexter had said and thought he must have been joking, invited him to say something serious, Ted declined. In fact, he simply said nothing at all, leaving his remarks open to the only interpretation possible – that he thought my efforts weren't worthy of real consideration or comment.

Naturally, I was fuming. But when I got wind that the press, scenting a story, wanted to interview me about what Ted had said – or not said – I decided the best thing to do was to leave, go back to the hotel and try and put the whole matter out of my mind. That evening those of us who had travelled down together went to the disco across the road for an impromptu night out, by the end of which I had more or less forgotten all about Ted Dexter.

Then when I read the newspaper reports of the incident the following morning, that set me off again. Kath said it sounded very much as though Dexter did not want me in the England set-up at all. How dare he imply that the Aussies were trying to con the selectors into picking me by throwing their wickets away? Anyone who knows the slightest thing about them also knows that getting out to me is the last thing an Aussie wants to do, especially Border, for whom the events at Headingley in 1981 still hurt badly. The ball that bowled him at Arundel went through the gate between bat and pad as he tried to push it through the off-side. That was a weakness of Border's which I had probed successfully in the World Cup match in Sydney where I managed to take four wickets in seven deliveries without conceding a run and scored 53. We went on to win the match comfortably, and that was probably the moment when the Australians lost their chance of qualifying for the final stages. *Wisden* wrote: 'The combination of the old enemy, the bright lights and the noisily enthusiastic crowd demanded a show-stopper from Botham, and he provided it'. Did Border give me his wicket that night as well?

By this time I had worked myself up into such a fury that I was determined not to let the matter drop. I demanded an apology from Dexter. Two days later the phone rang at home at nine in the morning. It was Ted.

He mumbled something about what he had said being a throw-away line which he had come up with because he wanted to avoid the interview being all about Ian Botham. It didn't wash. After all, I had just bowled the Australian captain and under the circumstances the first thing any interviewer was going to ask him about was my England prospects. It was the time of year when everyone is speculating on who is, or is not, going to make the team. Dexter went on to offer, by way of some bizarre justification: 'You're the master of the one-liner, Ian – look at what you said about Pakistan being the kind of place you would send your mother-in-law for a paid holiday'.

'Yes, Ted,' I replied, 'and the board fined me £1000 for that one.'

I told him I was not happy about what had been said and I was not going to back down. If someone in Ted's position behaves like that then it is for him to explain, not for me to sit back and let it wash over me. In the end he did apologize and the matter was finished – that was all I wanted. What did amaze me was that the TCCB let the whole episode rest without further comment. If it had been a player who had opened his mouth and said what Dexter had said, there would have been an almighty stink and an apology would not have been enough to calm things down.

In absolute honesty, I never expected to get picked for the first Test that summer. I felt I should have been because, although over the years my all-rounder's mantle had fallen to a succession of pretenders, none of them had really looked up to the job. Players like Chris Cowdrey, David Capel and Phil DeFreitas had all been tried and found wanting. Chris was never in my class as a bowler or batsman, although he was a great trier. Capel was never really fit for long enough to be considered a front-line bowler, while DeFreitas flattered to deceive. According to most observers, the latest one to try his hand, Chris Lewis, had shown an alarming lack of what used to be known as 'moral fibre'. In my opinion, I could still contribute more to the team than he did. Lewis has an enormous amount of talent, but he has a tendency to bale out when the pressure is on, and I don't think anyone who watched the first Test of the '93 series against the Aussies would disagree.

But if instinct told me I was not in the frame and Dexter's performance at Arundel did nothing to ease my fears, the writing was on the wall when Lewis picked up an injury and was ruled out of the third one-day international at Lord's, to be replaced by Dermot Reeve. Not only was I behind Lewis in the selectors' eyes, I was now behind Reeve as well. No disrespect to Dermot, but if you had asked the Aussies which of us they would have preferred to deal with there would only have been one winner. Certainly, the Aussies I spoke to were delighted yet somewhat bewildered to learn that I was being ignored.

In his prime, Ted Dexter was a courageous batsman and a brilliant all-round sportsman. He has also always been considered somewhat of an oddball. People who played under him as captain often said that he would wander about in a world of his own, during a match as well as before and after one, and he was renowned for reacting to moments of high pressure by practising his golf swing in the slips. As far as I was concerned, however, he crossed the line between eccentricity and idiocy far too often for someone who was supposed to be running English cricket.

Ted retired from the game long before I had started. As a youngster, I wasn't really a great spectator of cricket because I was always far more interested in getting out on the local recreation ground to play with my mates. I had obviously heard of Ted; the late Kenny Barrington, his Test colleague and later the manager of England who taught me so much, confirmed that he was a hell of a player. He also confirmed that often Ted lived in his own universe.

The first time Ted made any real impression on me was in his career as a television commentator. The incident happened when he was broadcasting from Old Trafford on one of those typical black, thundery Manchester days. He was sitting under an umbrella doing quick interviews with players when suddenly, in the middle of the conversation, he started hopping around all over the place and began shouting hysterically, 'Oh my God. I've been struck by lightning!'

Years later, when I returned to the Test scene in the summer of 1989, I had my first brush with the wackier side of Ted. He had just taken up his position as the new chairman of the England committee with promises of a more professional approach and a brave new world for English cricket after years in the doldrums. Here he was, the man to lead the charge towards a glorious new dawn, making a complete and utter fool of himself in front of the players.

We had arrived in Birmingham the day before the third Test against Australia and were due to meet in the hotel conference room for the customary pre-match meal, get-together and tactical team-talk. This is the time when the players can exchange ideas about the strengths and weaknesses of opponents and establish a few operational rules. Although those who have played Test cricket with me over the years will tell you that my input was normally minimal and usually confined to 'he can't bat, I'll bounce him out', it's true that what is discussed in these meetings can occasionally make the difference between winning and losing. This time, however, Ted turned what should have been a reasonably serious discussion into a night out at Butlin's. As we filed in, Ted stood in the doorway handing out songsheets.

I couldn't believe my eyes. There in black and white was the score to the hymn 'Onward Christian Soldiers' while underneath was Ted's own version, entitled 'Onward Gower's Cricketers'. It is worth reprinting in full, see page 24.

'Right', said Ted. 'Now look, lads, when you get in the bath tonight, I want you to sing this at the top of your voices.'

I thought to myself 'What the hell is going on? Whatever he's drinking, I'll have a pint!' I had played upwards of 90 Tests and suddenly here was this guy telling me in all seriousness to sit in the bath and sing about knocking the 'kang'roos' flat and not upsetting Ian Todd, the cricket correspondent of the *Sun*. David Gower, the skipper, looked as though he was having a near-death experience. The rest of us just sat there in stunned silence. I can't imagine what the younger players thought. All I do

Onward Gower's cricketers,
Striving for a score,
With our bats uplifted,
We want more and more,
Alderman the master,
Represents the foe,
Forward into battle,
Down the pitch we go.

Onward Gower's cricketers,
Striving for a score,
Don't despair too early,
The lion soon will roar.

From the swing of Botham,
Aussie batsmen flee,
On then Dexter's cricketers,
On to victory,
Border's men shall quiver,
At the shout Howzat!,
Brothers lift your voices,
Knock the kang'roos (sic) flat.

Onward Dexter's cricketers,
We don't mind the Waugh,
Don't despair too early,
The lion soon will roar.

Like a mighty army,
Moves the Stewart squad,
Brothers we'll do anything,
Not to upset Ian Todd,
We are not divided,
All one body we,
For Richie, Illie, Tony and Jack,
We'll rewrite history.

Onward Stewart's cricketers,
Indulgence we emplore (sic),
Don't despair too early,
The lion soon will roar.

Jones and Boon may perish,
Merv may rise and wane,
Marsh won't last till lunchtime,
Though Taylor may remain,
Gates so big can never,
'Gainst Foster's swerve prevail,
We have Gooch's promise,
And that cannot fail.

Onward England's cricketers,
Getting off the floor,
Don't despair too early,
The lion soon will roar.

Onward then the media,
Join our happy song,
Blend with ours your voices,
In the triumph song,
Glory laud and honour,
To David G the King,
Just this once, and hell why not,
Let us his praises sing.

Onward Gower's cricketers,
Our failures please ignore,
Don't despair too early,
The lion soon will roar.

know is that neither I nor any of the other players did much singing in the bath that night.

Just before Ted resigned at the end of the 1993 season, and after his comments about England's poor showing having something to do with the juxtaposition of Venus in relation to the other planets, he complained that every time he opened his mouth he was 'harpooned and lampooned' by the press. It was probably one of the simplest tasks of their journalistic careers.

I am still at a loss to explain exactly what his role in the England set-up was. All I know is that he frequently caused huge embarrassment to himself and others. It is hard to take seriously a chairman of selectors who calls his premier fast bowler Malcolm Devon and then gets all excited about the prospect of picking a batsman called Jimmy Cook, who just happens to be South African.

I recall the time that John Morris and Jonathan Agnew realised they had no chance of going on the winter tour to the West Indies in 1989/90. They had arrived at the Porter Tun Room in the City of London for the Cricket Writers' Club annual dinner on the eve of the NatWest Final to which several past and present cricketers are invited as guests of the members. This is the time when, traditionally, most of the talk is concerned with who will be in the squads for upcoming winter tours. When Morris and Agnew set off for the evening they must have thought they might have been in with a squeak. After their conversation with Ted they knew they had another think coming. 'Excuse me, chaps', Ted called out as he was walking down Chiswell Street in search of the venue. 'You two look like cricketers. Do you know where this dinner is taking place?'

These stories may be amusing in hindsight, but as a professional I find that kind of amateurish behaviour hard to tolerate. Ted might have been a fine player and a lovely guy socially, but as far as I was concerned he was taking money under false pretences, money that could have been diverted to many other projects that would have served the game better.

But my opinion of him is not just based on the obvious gaffes he committed at regular intervals. For it was during that disastrous series of 1989 that I found not only was Dexter a man I could not respect, he was also a man I simply could not rely on at all.

Our performances throughout that series were undistinguished to say the least. Looking back, we had started off on the wrong foot even before a ball had been bowled. After the 1988 winter tour to India had been called off due to the Indian Board of Control's objection to the inclusion of players who had been on the first 'rebel tour' to South Africa in 1982, England were looking for a new captain. The original choice of Dexter and the manager Micky Stewart had been Mike Gatting, but when that was vetoed by the chairman of the TCCB, Ossie Wheatley, who for some reason felt that Gatt had still not served sufficient time for his supposed misdemeanours, they turned reluctantly to David Gower. That meant that England were going into a vital series with a captain who the selectors had not wanted in the first place. This caused problems right from the start.

When Gower won the toss prior to the first Test at Headingley, Ted stuck his oar in straight away by persuading him that the inclement weather forecast (which incidentally turned out to be wildly inaccurate) meant England should ask Australia to bat first. And they did, all day and all the next day, scoring 601 for seven declared before going on to win the match by 210 runs. When I returned to the side after injury for the third Test at Edgbaston, we were already two-down and no one was really sure who was running things – Gower, Stewart or Dexter, least of all the captain himself!

At the same time, one of the worst-kept secrets in modern cricket history was starting to seriously undermine team spirit. The South African cricket authorities, led by Dr Ali Bacher, were in England recruiting players for another 'rebel tour' to be played that winter while the Test side were due to take on the West Indies in the Caribbean. The dressing room, and everywhere else it seemed, was awash with rumours of just how much money was on offer, who was going and who was not. It had reached the stage where the England committee asked players to sign a declaration of availability for the winter tour.

I had been targeted by the South Africans in a big way and was interested in what they had to say. Of course I was intrigued by the possibility; I would be lying if I said otherwise. So when Bacher rang me after the Edgbaston Test, I was definitely listening. The cash on the table for signing up for two winter tours was staggering. Even when I called their bluff by asking for half a million pounds, the organizers did not seem unduly perturbed. Everyone understood that those who did go could more or less kiss goodbye to the thought of playing Test cricket again for a long time and, in my case, probably for ever. Financially, however, it would have made a lot of sense. Although I was also under no illusions as to what would have happened to existing and future commercial contracts, I knew that most of my

Test playing career was behind rather than ahead of me and that, had I accepted the South African money the financial benefit to myself and my family would have been enormous.

By this time, Micky Stewart, on behalf of the England management, was doing his best to persuade me not to go. They wanted me in the West Indies, he said, and he pleaded with me to make myself available. They made it quite clear that if I did so, I was more or less guaranteed a place on the plane.

It took a lot of soul-searching to come to a decision. I discussed the situation fully with Kath and my solicitor and long-time friend Alan Herd and once again, as I had done in 1982, I came to the conclusion that I had more to lose than gain.

The bottom line was pride: professional and patriotic. The West Indies were the one side against whom I felt I still had something to prove, both to myself and to the public. I had never fulfilled my potential against them as I should have done, and I wanted another crack. So I informed Micky of my availability and he accepted the news gratefully.

Then they proceeded to let me down badly. The night before the squad for the tour was due to be announced, Kath answered the phone. Ted was on the line.

'Hello Ian,' he said. 'I'm afraid we're not taking you to the West Indies.'

'You what?' I replied. 'You begged me to make myself available for the winter tour and I told the South Africans where to go as well. And now you are saying you don't want me after all.'

'Er well, I didn't ask you personally,' he replied feebly.

I felt like I had been stabbed in the back. I went berserk and slammed the phone down on him. I don't think I have ever felt so devastated. Seeing what a state I had worked myself into, Kath left the room; she knew I was not going to be fun to be around for a while. I was so enraged that if Ali Bacher had been sitting there with a contract and a pen I would have signed without a moment's hesitation, and to hell with the consequences. I took myself off to the drinks cabinet and emptied a bottle of brandy in an effort to get it out of my system. Then, to really rub it in Micky and Ted later denied that they had persuaded me to make myself available. As far as I am concerned their denials were a lie.

To this day I've never been given a satisfactory explanation. From what I have been told it was Gooch, who replaced David Gower as captain when he was sacked at the end of the series and then also found himself out in the cold, who did not want me. Maybe I'll never find out for certain. What I do know is that it was another phone call from Ted, on quite another subject, which finally removed any doubts that my England career was over.

A few days before the Trent Bridge Test against Australia in early July 1993, I answered the phone and, bearing in mind how he and the other selectors had studiously ignored my performances all summer, I was surprised to hear Ted on the other end of the line. That surprise quickly turned to amazement when I heard what he had to say. He asked me if I would be interested in taking the England A-team to Holland as captain.

I couldn't believe what I was hearing. Trying to avoid a conversation with him because I had heard enough and didn't want to give him the satisfaction of even discussing this farcical suggestion any further, I replied that I had prior engagements and left it at that. But when I put the phone down I was seething. Ted had spent half the summer messing me about and now he had the cheek to ask me to get involved in a clog-dancing mission. All I could think of was that this was supposed to be some sort of peace offering for excluding me from the Test side, or a fancy public relations exercise. Either way, I was thoroughly cheesed off. It was just about the last straw.

The Test side was losing and showing no signs of improving. When they picked the side for the third Test from a position of 2–0 down with four to go, the party of thirteen contained five uncapped players. And then I received this call from Dexter asking me if I would like to waste my time in Holland. I knew now that my last chance had gone forever. If Ted really didn't want me to be part of the new set-up, why didn't he have the decency just to say so, instead of all this messing around? In the back of my mind I can't help thinking that the real reason why Gooch, Dexter and company did not want either David Gower, Allan Lamb or myself back in the picture was that, if we had succeeded, they would have been left with an awful lot of egg on their faces. Against that sort of reasoning I knew my international career was over no matter how well I performed.

Once I discovered where I stood, I started to think about Durham. I wanted to be sure in my own mind that I was doing the right thing by them.

To be totally honest, there was no point in my playing any more championship cricket because we were near the bottom of the table and the county needed to rebuild. Although I had proved to myself that I could still perform with the bat by scoring a century against Worcestershire, my last match had ended with a two-day defeat by Surrey at The Oval. I had batted twice on the second day, faced eight balls, and made eight runs. We lost by an innings and more than 200 runs. I knew I was not going to be around for the following season and started to think about retirement in a positive way. At Durham there were four or five players whose contracts were on the line, and it was not fair that I should take up a place in the team while they were in limbo and likely to have only a handful of games in which to prove their worth.

At that point eight championship games remained, and I reasoned that by leaving there and then those fringe players would get a fair crack at earning contracts for the next season. It would also help the club because it would give them a chance to assess the talents of those players as they planned ahead. With those thoughts in my mind, there was obviously not a lot of point in my carrying on.

There was one significant advantage in getting out of the game at this stage. I'm sure that it is the hope of every father who plays professional sport that he will one day be able to watch his son performing at the same or higher level. I have not proved the exception to the rule, even though I have never pushed Liam to play cricket, rugby, or tiddlywinks for that matter, and have merely made sure that I was available if he needed me.

But no one in the family, least of all Liam himself, was under any illusions about the problems he might have to confront simply because of who he was. The fact that he has always been a naturally gifted sportsman and he is my son, means that he has been prey to the long-lens treatment. To a certain extent there is no harm in that, as long as the photographers and newspapers involved haven't over-stepped the mark (and, by and large, they haven't).

True to form, however, just around the time of my retirement, the thing we feared most happened. Liam, having been selected to play for England Under-15s against the touring South African boys in 1992, had showed enough talent and promise to be offered a summer spell with Hampshire. On his first day at 'work', a 2nd XI match against Worcestershire at Southampton, his club captain Mark Nicholas told me he had never seen so many reporters at the county ground. Liam took the whole thing in his stride, even being relaxed enough to tell the assembled throng that he intended to be even better than his Dad. Cheeky bugger! Liam, being a Botham, then managed to play a good game as well as talk one by taking four wickets.

So far, so good. Then, a couple of weeks later, the inevitable happened. A friend of mine from one of the national papers told me that people had been asking questions about an alleged incident involving Liam and some other Hampshire cricketers in a nightclub. Here we go again, I thought.

Liam had been playing for Hampshire seconds against Warwickshire in Leamington Spa. One evening after the close of play he went with some of the players to a local nightclub. Because he wasn't born yesterday he made sure that he drank only soft drinks, but someone there recognized him and told the manager he was under age. The manager talked to Liam, told him what had happened and informed him, regretfully, that if there were any complaints he would have to ask him to leave. Half an hour later, the same guy complained again and Liam duly left with the minimum of fuss.

Apparently, this non-event was enough to get the *Sunday Mirror* terribly excited and a story duly appeared along the lines of Liam Botham, son of cricketing legend Ian, blah, blah, blah ... being kicked out of a nightclub. What bothered me most was that this kind of thing is actually believed by people who should know better. These ignorant idiots, who for some reason have convinced themselves to believe everything they have read about me over the years, turn around and say 'There, look at Liam Botham, like father like son', and the mud sticks.

The problems of living and working under the scrutiny of the media were only one of the reasons why Liam made his decision to give up cricket in favour of his chosen professional sport, rugby union.

I never had any doubts that Liam was good enough to make a career for himself in cricket. His performance on first-class debut for Hampshire on 28 August 1996, two days short of his 19th birthday, proved the condition known as golden balls was indeed hereditary. Pulled out of a 2nd XI game he turned up for the county's match against Middlesex at Portsmouth after the start of play, dismissed Gatt with his seventh delivery and finished with figures of 5 for 67. Had he been able to operate outside the glare of publicity over who he was and rather just be judged on how good he was, he might even have gone all the way.

But his decision was based as much on how he saw the two sports progressing as much as any feeling over living in the spotlight. Frankly, for a young man equally good at rugby and cricket, by the time he had to choose, there seemed little choice to make.

Of course, I would have loved to have played with or against Liam at county level. And I was delighted when he was brought in as a last-minute replacement for a charity match between the Rest of the World and my own England XI at Hove a few weeks before I announced my retirement. But realistically it was never going to happen in any other way. By announcing my retirement when I did, rather than dragging it out to the end of the season, I felt I could at least try and deflect some of the inevitable attention away from him as he attempted to take his first steps in the game.

I don't regret many things in my life but the circumstances surrounding my final game have left me with a tinge of guilt. Although I was more than happy to be bowing out against the Aussies, it was such a spontaneous decision that I didn't even get an opportunity to tell my parents about it. I didn't exactly know what to tell them and, besides, the telephone did not seem the right way to go about it. As usual, it is the people nearest to you that you think about least. In all likelihood my father Les would have wanted to be there for my swansong; in some ways it was a relief that the game itself was a non-event.

I had decided to keep the news quiet until I had had the chance to talk to Geoff Cook, the director of cricket and David Graveney, the captain, about my plans. Dean Jones was the only one of my team-mates who knew in advance. I have always been very close to him and knew that, in the tradition of a true Aussie, if you tell him something in confidence you can be certain it isn't going anywhere else. I told him on the Saturday morning when I picked him up on our way to the game. Dean said he wasn't surprised. He told me that he and his wife, Jane, had been talking about me quitting only the week before, speculating on when it would happen. When I arrived at the Durham University ground, I saw David and Geoff, told them my decision and swore them to secrecy. At first David was dumbfounded, but when I explained that the body had had enough he accepted it. Mathematically, we still had a chance in the Sunday league competition and I told him that if he wanted me for the last few games, I would be happy to oblige. Once I told Geoff the reasons for my decision, he agreed that I had done the right thing and I appreciated that.

The information was so watertight that none of the other players knew about it until the following day, when the *Mail on Sunday*, who had managed to get wind of the story somehow, let the cat out of the bag. When I reached the ground for the second day's play the place was buzzing. Geoff felt he had to confirm the story, but I was determined not to say anything publicly to anyone until I had fulfilled my newspaper column commitments by giving Chris Lander of the *Daily Mirror* the exclusive to which he and they were entitled. The rest would have to wait.

The third and final day's play eventually started late in the afternoon because of rain, but there had been no sitting around for me. From the moment I arrived at the ground, it was like a circus. First there was a press conference that lasted 55 minutes, probably the longest of my career. Someone asked if I thought the rain would turn the day into something of an anti-climax, but I joked that as I had spent a lot of the last twenty years praying for a cloudburst, in some ways this would be a fitting end. I had hoped that my last day in first-class cricket would end more quietly than it did. I just wanted to drift back into the dressing room, pack up and go. The rain delay destroyed any prospect of a result, contrived or otherwise, but the skies cleared enough for us to play a pretty meaningless three or four hours in the afternoon. If ever there was a case where umpires or captains should be given a little bit of discretion in deciding to end the match, irrespective of the weather, this was it. The crowd was marvellous but nobody gained anything from us going out there except those who had spent so much time in the beer tent that they would have been captivated by watching Humpty Dumpty sitting on the wall. Steady, I wasn't that overweight!

In my final spell of bowling I decided to have a bit of fun to try and cheer everyone up by doing my Jeff Thomson impersonations, among others. Then, after a few overs I turned to David Graveney and said: 'Thanks David, I think that will do'. It was quite a moment. As I turned to take my position in the field, the reality of what I was doing suddenly hit me – no more bowling, no more batting, no more anything. The pavilion clock showed there was still half an hour to go but that was it from me, my time was over. It was the end.

Both batsmen, David Boon and Matthew Hayden, came down the wicket to shake my hand and I cannot remember anything that happened between that moment and the time stumps were drawn. I had, as they say, lost the plot. In fact, the only thing I do recall was my appalling attempt at keeping wicket for the final over of the match, minus pads and gloves. However, I was soon brought back down to earth when at the close of play I went into the dressing room to clear my locker. The bastards had pinched the lot!

On arriving home I threw myself into a small party we

had arranged for close friends. I finally crashed at ten to five the following morning after talking Egyptian into the small hours with Alan Herd. It was only a short nap as I had to leave the house at 7.15 a.m. to catch a plane to Alderney where we have our second home. I have no idea how any of the others got home. It is quite possible, of course, that one or two might still be there now.

2
A BOUNCING BABY BOTHAM

There was a time three months into my mother Marie's pregnancy when the entire Ian Botham story might have been over before it had even begun.

Both my parents had been good at sport, highly competitive and fit as fiddles. Les, who was a keen cricketer, ran for East Yorkshire, had a soccer trial for Hull City boys and played for Combined Services, while Marie had played cricket, badminton and hockey to a reasonable standard. For some reason, however, they had acute difficulties in starting a family.

Marie had suffered four miscarriages before she became pregnant with me. Then, a third of the way through this pregnancy, she went through a particularly rough patch of health, and there were very real fears that she was going to miscarry again. Towards the end she was confined to bed, and it was obviously a worrying time for her and Les. What must have made it worse for her was that Les, serving in the Fleet Air Arm, was stationed in Northern Ireland so he was absent when the time came for Marie to enter the maternity hospital in Heswall, Cheshire. There must have been an overpowering sense of relief when, on a drizzly 24

November 1955, the first shout was heard from a bouncing 10lb 1oz baby Botham and a telegram was duly sent to inform Les he had become a father. In the excitement, when he finally arrived on leave a week later, he managed to oversee a complete muddle in the registering of my birth. My parents had been married in Scotland and for sentimental reasons had settled on the Scottish spelling of 'Iain'. But the birth certificate read 'Ian' – so that was to be my name. It also (thankfully) read 'Terence' rather than the family's traditional second name for boys, 'Herbert' (although some would say I have been a right one ever since). There is a familiar ring about a Botham father being out of town for the birth of a Botham child. I was in Australia on a Whitbread Scholarship in 1977 when Kathy discovered she was pregnant with Liam; I missed Sarah's birth because I was on tour; and I was again missing for the arrival of Becky when I made my first walk for Leukaemia Research from John O'Groats to Land's End.

Once on the planet, it seems I was determined to make my mark from the very start. Soon after I was born the family moved to Londonderry where we were put up in services' married quarters, and it was here that I showed the first signs of the adventurous side of my nature. Mum recalls how she left me sitting with a box of toys inside a playpen in the living room while she was working in the kitchen. A few minutes later she was surprised to find me crawling around her feet. Puzzled, she carried me back to the playpen and convinced herself that, perhaps, after all, she had not put me inside in the first place. When I appeared in the kitchen for the third time she realized something was up and decided to keep an eye on me through the crack in the door. She couldn't believe her eyes. I was lifting the edge of the playpen onto the toy box, crawling out under the gap and then pulling the playpen down to the floor again, leaving everything in the right place. Everything, that is, except me.

Once I had found a way out of my confinement, nothing was going to stop me as I found a variety of ways to get myself out and about and to cause parental palpitations. If I was left outside the house in my pram, brake or no brake, I would bounce it up and down until I eventually succeeded in getting the thing moving. I managed to cover some fairly impressive distances but, luckily, everyone knew who I was and where to return me. By the time my sister Dale was born in Ireland in February 1957 – I have one other sister, Wendy, and a brother Graeme – I was 15 months old, up on my own two feet and walking. Of course, that posed a new set of problems for Mum and Dad who were constantly running around trying to contain my wanderlust. Dad decided to fence in the garden but that was more of a challenge than an obstacle. For baby Botham, if it was there, it was there to be scaled. I regularly managed to escape and often the only evidence of me ever having been in the garden was a pair of dungarees left hanging on the fence.

At one time I even got as far as the driver's seat of a big armed forces' truck, where I was found playing happily with the steering wheel and fingering the hand brake. The cab was so high off the ground that nobody could work out exactly how I got there, and I shudder to think what mayhem might have been caused if I had prised the hand-brake loose.

If these were the first signs of the free spirit that was later to shape my life for good and sometimes for ill, my competitiveness took only slightly longer to manifest itself. After 18 months in Northern Ireland we returned to the mainland and Cheshire. During a toddlers' 20-yard dash at the navy sports day, I hit upon a novel method of dealing with the opposition, which involved me barging into the rest of the field, leaving most of them on their backsides, and consequently finding myself about as far ahead as you can get in a 20-yard race. Surprised, I stopped to look where the rest of the runners were, only to find them all back on their feet and streaming past me. Unfortunately, running was never one of my strong points; distances I could manage most of the time, but sprints and races were not my forté. Years later, a certain tactical naiveté led to my first sporting calamity at Buckler's Mead School in Yeovil. As house captain for the school sports day, I had asked for volunteers for someone to compete in the mile race. Thank you, volunteers, for your vote. I was so determined to do well that if I had to run I was going to win or die trying. When they carried me off, I was about a lap ahead – it was just a pity that there were still another two to go.

Life as a toddler in Ireland had also been significant for the first of my many trips to hospital. A hard crack on the head led to my first stay in a hospital ward as I was kept in the Londonderry Hospital for four nights of observation. No serious damage was done that time, but it caused enough of a scare for the doctors to suggest that I should be fitted with some kind of protective headgear. Just telling me to mind how I went would have done no good at all, so Dad ended up making me a special foam helmet. Inevitably, it was only a matter of time before I was back in casualty. On settling in Yeovil, where Dad took up a position with Westland Helicopters after a year in the North West, Mum virtually had a waiting room chair reserved for herself in the local hospital.

I had my first operation in Yeovil General Hospital at the age of four. I had been out shopping with Mum in town when I suddenly collapsed with a terrible stomach pain. There was a panic, I was rushed to hospital and less than an hour later I was on the way to the operating theatre for surgery on a hernia. To make things easier for me, my parents brought in my teddy bear, Mr Khrushchev, the name inspired by the influence of television in my early upbringing. To make me feel better the hospital staff pretended the bear had been through the same ordeal as me and had undergone the same treatment. On my discharge I gave probably the first and last hint that I might possibly be interested in anything other than sport as a career. Mum told me to thank the doctors for looking after me and, according to her, I said: 'The doctors don't make you better. They just stand there at the end of the bed, say "Good morning" and ask the nurses how you are. It is the nurses who do all the work and make you better. I think I'll be a doctor when I grow up'. By the time I had another hernia operation four years later, I understood more about how the system actually worked and abandoned that idea for good.

For the next six years, home was 64 Mudford Road, Yeovil, a house with plenty of trees and a large garden, although not large enough for my liking. What lay beyond the garden gate still proved an irresistible draw and led to one of my first encounters with the iron fist inside the velvet glove of Marie Botham. It was only the shock of being told that Dale and I were found running across the busy main road that led Mum to administer the spanking, for that had certainly not been the normal reaction to our misdemeanours. When Dad came home at lunchtime to find us in bed, he thought we were ill. Punishments usually took the form of the 'you have nearly pushed it too far' warning movement of Mum's hand towards the wooden spoon she kept in the kitchen as a deterrent. But as I grew older the occasional smack was administered, superseded at my secondary modern school by the cane, a regular adversary, and they certainly did me no harm. Pity there is not more of it these days.

It was about this time that my sporting life began in earnest. The house at Mudford Road backed on to the playing fields of Yeovil Grammar School, where I could often be found watching the older boys playing cricket. I was frequently discovered here by Len Bond, an assistant groundsman at the school, who would cart me back home in his wheelbarrow. My love affair with sport began in earnest when I moved from Miss Wright's private school at Penmount to Milford Junior School in September 1962. The school day worked on the basis that I went home for lunch, until I discovered that if you stayed for a school dinner you could also play football. I managed to persuade Mum and Dad to let me stay on even though I was in my first year and you were not meant to play football until the second. My ally was Richard Hibbitt, the deputy headmaster who was in charge of games. He saw how keen I was, made room for me and was soon asking my parents for permission to pick me for the school team. That was all the encouragement I needed, and by the ripe old age of seven I was already practising my autograph for the day when I would be famous.

I didn't have to wait long for my first appearance on national television, although *Songs Of Praise* from St John's in Yeovil was not exactly what I had in mind. At the time the family attended church fairly regularly, and as the church choir was struggling for numbers I was drafted in. I should point out that my singing talents, which are legendary, had no bearing on my selection. I was so bad that when the big day came I was told politely but firmly to mime. Ironically, when the programme went out, I was the chorister who received the most attention from the cameras. Indeed, my ability as a mime artist was to stand me in good stead in pantomime later on in life.

Considering the number of times I have been called upon to scribble my name since then, all that handwriting practice at the age of seven was of great use. Not that you would ever have convinced my parents or teachers at the time: for them it was another distraction from the real job of inwardly digesting. My form mistress at Milford, Mrs Olwyn Joyce, was heard despairingly telling my parents that she wished the school had been built in a traditional style rather than with modern, panoramic windows. Being easily distracted by the sight and sound of a bouncing ball, I was forever staring out of the window watching other classes playing games and wishing I was out there with them.

There were no such problems with Mr Hibbitt. He even forgave me for breaking a school window since the damage had been caused by a cricket ball. Although I had been bowling daisy cutters at the garage door from the age of six and disappearing into the local park for games of cricket at every available opportunity, Mr Hibbitt showed me that there was money to be made from sport when he placed a pile of coins on a good length on the pitch and told us that if we managed to hit them, the cash was ours. I cleaned up, as I did later when, at thirteen, I made my debut for Somerset Under-15s against Wiltshire. The deal was 6d per run, and my score of 80 ensured a jackpot which my Dad was forced to cough up but did not risk again. Needless to say, my one great sporting achievement at Milford came in the form of a six which Mr Hibbitt reckoned would have carried at either Taunton or Lord's. Then, one sports day I took part in a contest to see who could throw the cricket ball furthest on the playing fields of Buckler's Mead.

I was standing at the throwing line when the teacher doing the measuring in the distance shouted at me to have my go. It had to be pointed out to him that not only had I already done so, but my ball had landed many yards behind the spot where he was standing. Later, incidentally, in the summer of 1968 the same thing happened when I managed a record throw of just over 207 feet in the Under-13 tournament of the Crusaders' Union National Sports Day at Motspur Park in South London. The judges did not believe the distance I had achieved with my first throw and made me throw again. They measured this one and I came home with the Victor Ludorum Cup for my age group and a record that stood for many years.

By the time I moved to secondary school at Buckler's Mead, my sheer bloody-mindedness about getting my own way was well established. In general, I enjoyed myself. My lack of aptitude for an academic life was well-known by my mates who christened me 'Bungalow'. I got into a few scrapes and scraps, but when the punishment was handed out I took it without complaining. The most serious incident came when I walked out of a woodwork lesson and never went back. Woodwork and I never really got on. I would start to make a coffee table and the legs would get shorter and shorter until all that was left was a big tray. My dovetails never dovetailed and I had no interest at all in the subject. The end came when I was in the work-room one day and the teacher, a Mr Black, suddenly turned round because someone had been mucking about behind me. There were no questions asked, he just walked up to me and whacked me on the head with a T-square. I was so angry, I was shaking. I wanted to flatten him there and then. Instead I told him I was going to do him a favour and leave the room. I went straight to the headmaster, explained what had happened and told him I was not the sort of person who would go home bleating about what had gone on in school. I said that I was never going in a class with Mr Black again, and I got my way.

Adolescence brought the usual horrors for me and my family. My ideas about fashion were to cause one or two run-ins. I was a teenager at the time when platform shoes were all the rage – the first time around. Quite naturally I wanted some, whatever Mum said, but shortly after I eventually got hold of a pair, I realized that she might just have been right all along. Mum was always keen to be with me when I bought clothes because she was rightly fearful of the consequences of my colour blindness. This time I spurned her offer and went into town on my own with the inevitable dire results: blue flared trousers, a bright orange shirt with a huge collar, and a pair of immense platform shoes. Mum and Dad were going out that evening to watch some five-a-side football at a local sports centre and I told them I would join them later in my new gear. In the process of putting on this ghastly costume, I managed to trip over my shoes and rip the trousers.

Mum also noticed around this time that I had begun to open my eyes to the possibility that girls might offer more than pig-tails to pull. When I came home one day and announced casually that I required some Lifebuoy soap, Mum's response was immediate.

'What's her name?' she inquired.

'Margaret,' I told her.

'And what is the attraction?'

'She can run faster than me.'

We all have at least one tale from this grisly adolescent period which we pray will be forgotten about on Judgement Day. Mine involved my sister Dale and her pet hamster. My return home for the weekend from the Lord's groundstaff, where I had been taken on as a 'trainee cricketer' following a recommendation by Somerset, coincided with its untimely demise. On hearing the news, I went up to Dale's room, removed the hamster from its cage and, paying scant attention to her grief, proceeded to swing it around by its tail to make sure it really was dead. Dale somehow failed to see the funny side.

I was a real charmer to Dale and my other sister Wendy, putting live spiders in their beds etc., and once I very nearly caused our charwoman, Mrs Whittle, to have a heart attack. I decided it would be great fun to deposit a large plastic snake behind a chair she was about to clean. You could hear the shrieking all down the street.

Every youngster threatens to leave home at one time or another. My big moment came when I announced to Mum I was off to London to see the bright lights. Within ten minutes, there waiting for me in the hall were my bags, packed and ready. When it dawned on me that if Mum did not clean my cricket gear I would have to, I thought better of it. But the real battles at home were over my absolute determination to make a career out of sport. My parents were worried about what would happen if I failed to make the grade or was badly injured, not that the thought ever existed in my mind. When, after I had succeeded in escaping from school at fifteen, Somerset arranged for me to go to Lord's, Roy Kerslake, a prominent member of the county's cricket committee, had to do the hard sell on my Dad who was worried that if it should all fall apart I would be a 16-year-old with no qualifications. What swung the decision for him was being told that those who failed to make it to the county circuit would often use their groundstaff experience to find jobs coaching cricket at independent schools.

As far as I was concerned, however, the only choice I had to make was which sport to concentrate on. I already had an offer to join Crystal Palace football club. The manager at the time, a West Country man named Bert Head, wanted to sign me and I asked Dad for some advice as there were other clubs, five from the First Division as I recall, who were after me as well. Les said 'Right, son. I think you are a better cricketer', and that was the decision made. Had the offer come from Stamford Bridge, things might have turned out very differently because I was a Chelsea fanatic. When my turn to choose the bedroom decor coincided with their FA Cup winning run of 1970, I gave Mum a Chelsea rosette so that she could buy the wallpaper and bed covers in exactly the right colours. She drew the line when it came to the carpet, but even so the name Chelsea was stencilled all over the house, and when they beat Leeds United in the Cup Final replay at Old Trafford, I went up to my room with a piece of chalk and sketched the trophy on the wall as the finishing touch.

If you were to ask a psychoanalyst to explain the awesome significance of all these early experiences (and I can assure you I have no intention of doing so) I suppose that he would conclude that here were the makings of a character that was determined not to be shackled and to have his own way. Certainly, my hatred of confined spaces is well known. In later years, it was very easy for my critics and others to point to my dislike of net practice as yet another sign of a supposed lack of professionalism. 'What, Beefy in the nets? He must be ill', they would jibe.

The fact is that I have always suffered badly from claustrophobia and although some will still take this with a cellar full of salt, nets felt like prisons to me. I genuinely used to suffer acute anxiety from being in them, and I suppose that is why on many occasions my batting practice would degenerate into a slog. As so often with me, it was a case of covering up a genuine fear with sheer bravado. It goes without saying that I am a show-off – I don't hide from that and I'm not trying to excuse it. If I hadn't been, I'm sure I would not have been able to produce some of the great performances I did. But I'm sure it is no coincidence that I felt most fired up when my back was against the wall. That was not simply a Roy of the Rovers mentality: the fact is that when you have nowhere to go, the only way out is to emerge with all guns blazing. Imran Khan, the great Pakistan all-rounder and captain, talked about this when he described how his team had come from the depths of despair to win the 1992 World Cup. After they had been humbled in the initial qualifying matches he told his players 'Be as a cornered tiger . . . Come out and fight', and sometimes that is the only option available.

All through my life I have possessed extraordinary self-belief. Even as a kid, there were no doubts about what I was going to do when I grew up. I was going to be a professional sportsman. When I encountered the careers master at Buckler's Mead this attitude of mine would often lead to a series of pointless rows as I would be summoned to the library to go through the same ritual time and again.

'Morning, Ian. What thoughts have you had since we last met?'

'Nothing new. I still want to play sport.'

'Fine. Everyone wants to play sport. But what are you really going to do?'

I would end up repeating myself, getting angry and saying that there was no point in my attending these advisory sessions because I knew precisely what I was going to do. There were dozens behind me in the queue who had no idea what they wanted to do, and they were the ones who needed a careers master, not me.

Clearly these aspects of my character have been absolutely vital in enabling me to enjoy my career and live life to the full. All sportsmen who make it to the top have to be ultra-competitive, there simply is no other way to succeed. Without the desire to win and the need to be better than the rest, you won't last five minutes. However, as the Americans are prone to saying, 'If you want to talk the talk, you have to walk the walk'. As a kid I simply had to win at everything, and that desire to be No.1 has never left me. I make no apologies for the way I have conducted myself over the years and I have no regrets. Life is too short to be forever wondering whether you did the right thing. But I fully appreciate that there has been a price to pay and that, more often than not, others have had to pay it.

I have always found it difficult to admit to mistakes. I had enough trouble conceding that I might possibly have made an error on the cricket field. My cricketing teammates will tell you that, according to me, I was never, ever, out. If a bowler was lucky enough to take my wicket, I had a never-ending supply of excuses to run through when I got back to the dressing room. As far as I can recall, I don't think I ever came up with something totally ludicrous; there was always a hint of plausibility in the argument I put forward. No, I didn't claim to be distracted by UFOs and there was nothing like 'I crashed the car, sir, because the tree that wasn't in my driveway yesterday was there now'. But I have to admit to serving up some real beauties in my time; like being put off by someone turning the page of his newspaper, for instance. Similarly, when I was bowling, if a batsman hit me for four it was not because he had played a good shot or I had bowled a bad ball. Invariably it was all part of a grand plan and it was simply a matter of time before the poor sucker fell for it. If I dropped a catch it was obviously because the ball was coming out of the sun. If there was no sun in the sky at the time, then a passing cloud would get the blame. If no cloud, then the moon. I would come up with anything rather than admit that I had been at fault. It was a case of protecting my pride, making myself feel invulnerable. Perhaps the most comical of all of these incidents took place during the Old Trafford Test of the 1989 summer series against Australia when, with our first innings total on 140 for four, a moment when the state of the match dictated that a modicum of discretion was required, I aimed a wild swing at the spinner Trevor Hohns in an attempt to hit him out of the ground and missed. That must be classed as one of my most embarrassing moments on the cricket field, alongside the time I went out to bat against Western Australia in Perth on the 1986/87 tour with a throbbing hangover and no bat.

'Sorry about that, lads,' I said, as I slid back into the dressing-room. 'My bleedin' bat got stuck behind my pads.'

'I didn't notice they were strapped to your bleedin' head,' replied John Emburey.

The bottom line was immaturity. For me, the slightest admission of failure or inadequacy was out of the question, and it was the same whatever I did. When, at the age of fifteen I returned home from a school cruise on the Mediterranean having shot up in height on the trip to over six foot, my behaviour was quite extraordinary. Dale and I used to measure ourselves against the kitchen door and it annoyed me intensely that she had always been taller. This time I insisted that Mum measure me and when I discovered how much I had grown, I ran into the garden to find my sister, shouting 'Dale! Come here now. I want to measure you!' You wouldn't have believed my reaction upon discovering that I had finally outgrown her. FA Cup winners have celebrated less. It was pathetic.

If I drove a sports car I had to drive it faster than anyone else, as the men from Saab found out when I managed to write off two in the space of an afternoon's sponsored racing at a cost of £24,000. When I decided to try and raise money for leukaemia research the only way to do it was to walk the length and breadth of the country (or over the Alps with some unenthusiastic elephants), and if I was drinking with mates, I had to drink them under the table as a matter of principle. I would do anything or try anything to show how big I was, and that included drugs.

I won't go into details now because you will read more later, but, yes, of course I have overdone the booze in my time and smoked the odd joint. I may have been depressed, I may have been tempted to do it for kicks – and believe me, on the international cricket circuit during the years I played, there were a multitude of kicks to be had – but the fact is that I did so for no other reason than because they were there. I broke the law. I'm not proud of it and there were occasions when I could have gone seriously off the rails.

But when people ask me what I dislike most about myself, the answers are very simple and straightforward. It has taken me long enough to confront the facts, but I am not afraid to do so now. When it comes to getting myself into hot water, a lot of what you will have heard and read about me is absolute rubbish, but some of it is not. I have been a selfish bastard. At times I have also been aggressive, tyrannical, chauvinistic and hot-tempered.

My only plea in mitigation is that if I hadn't been, none of what you are about to read would ever have taken place.

3
A SMASHING TIME AT LORD'S

I sometimes wonder what would have happened to the career of Ian Botham if Andy Roberts had not smashed my teeth in.

I remember the occasion as though it was yesterday – and who wouldn't? After all, it is not often that you take a ball in the face from one of the greatest and most fearsome fast bowlers of all time, and live to tell the tale.

I only made the final XI for Somerset's Benson and Hedges quarter-final against Hampshire in June 1974 because our pace bowler Allan Jones was ruled out with a leg strain, but I had already made my mark on proceedings in peculiar circumstances when I managed to remove Hampshire's premier batsman, the South African Test star Barry Richards, rated as one of the all-time greats. Our wicket-keeper Derek Taylor used to stand up to the stumps for my bowling in those days (bloody cheek!) and, after I had bowled him, Richards actually stood his ground for a few moments because he was convinced that the ball with which I had beaten him all ends up must have cannoned off Derek's pads onto the stumps (even more bloody cheek!). As a young tyro I was reasonably satisfied with the rest of my performance in the field that day, which brought one more wicket and the chance of some purposeful hurtling around the boundary. In fact, although I didn't know it at the time, my whole life was about to change.

When I came to the wicket, Somerset were more or less dead and buried. Seventy runs were required from the final 15 overs as I marched out to bat at number 9, with only three wickets remaining. Tom Cartwright, my batting partner and the man to whom I owe more than anyone for helping me become a top-class bowler, soon departed from the action, caught at mid-on. And then, shortly after I had been joined by Hallam Moseley, it happened.

Andy Roberts had been terrorizing English county pros all season playing for Hampshire and was about to establish himself as the West Indies' main strike bowler for a decade. With 38 runs needed, hooking him for six seemed like a good idea at the time. But I paid for my foolishness when, next ball, Roberts bowled me the fastest delivery I had ever seen, or, to be more accurate, not seen. I knew roughly from which direction it was coming and my first instinct was to try and hook it. Halfway through getting into position to play the shot the truth hit me – and then, a fraction of a second later so did the ball. These were pre-helmet days, of course, but I did just manage to raise a gloved hand in front of my face, and that instinctive act of self-preservation almost certainly saved me from serious injury. In the event, the force of the ball smacking into my glove which then, in turn, smacked into my face, was still sufficient to knock out one tooth and break another clean in half. Looking back, the worrying thing was that the teeth in question were on opposite sides of the jaw.

By the time I had spat them out, taken a glass of water and had a spot of treatment, I was fully aware that there were some in the crowd who, believing that the game was up, actually wanted me to go off retired hurt to avoid further, unnecessary punishment.

The thought never crossed my mind. In fact, there was very little crossing my mind at that particular moment. The effects of mild concussion meant that it was not until some time afterwards that I had any kind of clear recollection of what followed, but in a curious way I think the incident helped to settle me down. I predicted that Roberts' next delivery would be a yorker, guessed right and managed to get enough bat on ball to clip it away for three runs. From then on, I succeeded in farming as much of the strike as possible so that, after Hallam departed, there were just seven runs needed to win from sixteen balls when number 11 Bob Clapp joined me.

Although those watching must have found the tension unbearable, my total concentration meant that I was in a cocoon. In the penultimate over I played and missed three times before connecting with the winning hit to the cover boundary. As a batsman, Bob was what is commonly known in the game as a ferret – he went in after the rabbits. But I will always be grateful to him for helping me make my name. He finished with one of the best nought not outs in history, I collected the Gold Award and the first chapter of the fairy tale was written.

That evening a couple of old Somerset players, Bill Alley and Kenny Palmer, who later went on to become Test umpires, warned me: 'Today, you are everybody's hero. Tomorrow, they'll have forgotten you'. Needless to say I thanked them for the advice, but what I really felt was more along the lines of 'Give it a rest, you old buggers'. In fact the lesson they were trying to pass on could not have been more apt and, as time passed, that peculiarly English phenomenon they were warning me about – newspaper today, fish-and-chip paper tomorrow – became a recurrent theme. For the moment all I could see were the headlines.

The first produced unexpected results. When I strode into the Gardener's Arms for a celebratory pint of bitter and a spot of mild adulation, I informed the landlord, 'The usual, please'.

I was somewhat taken aback by his response when he turned and asked: 'And just what is your usual?'

'The usual,' I replied, a shade irritated. 'You know what it is, the same as it's been for the last year and a half.'

At this point, the local evening paper was produced and waved under my nose. The headline read: '17-YEAR-OLD SOMERSET YOUTH PLAYS A BLINDER'. Fortunately the landlord was chuckling as he poured out the pint, knowing full well that had he applied the letter of the licensing laws in my case, his profits would have been cut in half over the past 18 months.

When the next day brought my first experience of national newspaper coverage, you could not see my head for the clouds. 'BLOOD, SWEAT AND CHEERS FOR BOTHAM', announced the *Guardian*. 'YOUNG BOTHAM THE SOMERSET HERO' echoed the *Daily Telegraph*. Who was I to argue?

There is no doubt that the whole affair had an enormous effect on my career. Because of the press reaction, people all over the country had been made aware of the existence of somebody who up until that point had been, to almost all of them, a nobody. And it had all happened overnight.

We all want heroes to worship, whether they be sportsmen or women, film stars, actors, politicians, rock stars, brain surgeons or journalists. It may or may not surprise you to learn that John Wayne was mine. Now, because of my exploits on the field, I had set a certain standard for myself that many observers expected me to live up to every time I went out to bat or bowl. (I felt this particularly after the events of the summer of 1981 when the Australians were the victims of the best Test cricket of my life.) This meant that from then on, producing a great performance for Somerset carried extra significance. In terms of national awareness I was still a small fish in a big pool and, certainly in the opinion of good judges, I had nowhere near as much potential as another young Somerset batsman called Vivian Richards. But from that moment on, the name Botham rang a bell.

There is no doubt, either, that at this stage there was a very real danger of allowing the publicity to go to my head. Although my time on the Lord's groundstaff had taught me many lessons in life, I was still young, raw and very naive. In fact, even to get as far as I had done, I was extremely fortunate to have been in the presence of two men who, despite all my efforts to exasperate them, were prepared to keep an eye on me and encourage me.

Brian Close, the man chiefly responsible for turning Somerset from a social side into a successful one, was a hard nut – some would say a nutter. A tough Yorkshireman who was never prepared to compromise, his whole approach to the game was based on absolute belief in his own ability and that there was no point in turning up if you weren't prepared to do everything to win. It was this self-belief that enabled him to play for England and attain the 'double' of 100 wickets and 1000 runs in county cricket at the age of eighteen. However, his abrasiveness meant he was never likely to be a darling of the establishment. It was no surprise to anyone, least of all him, when he was sacked from the England captaincy after the Yorkshire side he was skippering were booed off the field following his decision to use time-wasting tactics to ensure a draw against Warwickshire in 1967.

To others more mindful of personal safety, the call to return to Test cricket at the age of 45, after nine years in the international wilderness, might have been answered with two fingers. But when the England captain Tony Greig decided he needed the physical equivalent of a brick wall to stand up to the West Indies pace attack that had been battering his team black and blue during the summer of 1976, it was typical of Closey that he accepted without a moment's hesitation. No one who witnessed it will ever forget his bravery when standing up to the horrendous onslaught from Roberts and Company in the Manchester gloom. Even Clive Lloyd, the West Indies captain, admitted his bowlers had gone over the top that day. But typical of Closey, he was just as proud of his bruises as he was of his batting. One of the standing jokes in the Somerset dressing room was his insistence that although Muhammad Ali might just beat him over fifteen rounds, he would be damned if the champ would knock him out. This was not just the usual dressing room bravado either, he really meant it. It goes without saying that I loved the guy for his guts. In fact, I would go so far as to say that starting out with Closey was vital for me because he taught me so much about attitude. He was the toughest man I ever played sport with or against and although, at one time or another, every single member of the side had their rows with him, he inspired us because he would never ask you to do anything he was not prepared to do himself and he would never, ever, give up. I'm sure that I had Closey's example in the back of my mind when I was reacting to Roberts' attempt at dental surgery in that Benson and Hedges quarter-final.

Closey was also instrumental in helping introduce into the club the young talent that was required to build for the future. Somerset eventually offered me a one-year contract, and I joined on the same day as Vic Marks, Phil Slocombe and Peter Roebuck, with Viv Richards soon to follow.

Although he was a hard drinker, Closey could also be a fearsome disciplinarian. Once, during a one-day game against Nottinghamshire at Trent Bridge he actually sent off one of his own players. Allan Jones was not bowling particularly well that day, but he was not the only one who was surprised when Closey called him across and made various rather undiplomatic observations about his performance and the size of his ticker. After a short row and amid much scratching of heads and suppressed laughter, Jones was dismissed, even though he had four overs still to bowl and there was no other recognized bowler to put on.

His one and only disagreement with me on the field came in similarly bizarre circumstances, not because I had played a rash shot (though God knows I played enough of them) nor because I had bowled badly or dropped a sitter. My crime was to perform a brilliant run out without due care and attention to what might have happened if I had missed. Although I was innocent on all counts, I have to concede that he did have a point. A few weeks after the game against Hampshire in the B&H, we were drawn against Surrey in the quarter-final of the Gillette Cup. I was bowling to Geoff Howarth, later to captain New Zealand, who proceeded to hit the ball back past me. I turned to my left with my back to the play, fielded the ball and, as I noticed the batsmen attempting a quick single, swivelled and hurled down the stumps. What I didn't know was that there had been a serious communication problem between the two batsmen and, as they were both stuck down the striker's end, I could actually have walked up and quietly removed the bails. Closey berated me at length for, in his eyes, showing off. We were still at logger-heads when the next batsman arrived to take strike. I argued that no one had shouted to let me know what was happening so I had no idea where the batsmen were. His point was that I should have known. That incident taught me the lesson of thinking, even in pressure situations, that I never forgot though I have to admit I didn't always follow it to the letter on the field.

Occasionally I settled for simply trying to intimidate opponents with my presence, particularly when it came to my absolute conviction that I could always bounce bats-men out. Years later in 1984 against the West Indies at Lord's, I overdid the delivery so much against Gordon Greenidge that I managed to concede 117 runs in just over 20 overs as they made 344 to win in less than a day. As far as I was concerned, the next one was bound to get him, but, of course, it never did.

Our success in beating Surrey enabled me to put another of Closey's laws into practice in the semi-final against

Kent. Although we lost by three wickets, I won a personal battle with Colin Cowdrey, then one of the legends of the game. Closey always tried to instil in me a feeling that I should never be overawed by the reputation of whoever might be standing at the other end, whether batting or bowling. He saw things very much in black and white, and if his motto was not exactly kill or be killed it certainly was about imposing your will on your opponent, rather than allowing him to do it to you. People often asked me then how I felt about bowling to a man like Cowdrey. For me, it made little difference. Partly due to my own self-confidence and largely due to Closey's advice, I made a point of treating all batsmen alike, and I'm certain that I took Cowdrey's wicket that day simply because I believed I could.

Tom Cartwright was the other major figure in my early development. Tom was an excellent all-rounder with War-wickshire, Somerset and England, and I think in many ways he saw me as a younger version of himself. It was Tom who was instrumental in helping me get my early chances with Somerset after he watched me in the nets at Millfield School, where he had been coaching. Against opposition from other influential figures within the county who saw me as just an average cricketer, Tom pushed my claims. He also saw how desperate I was to become an all-rounder, and my enthusiasm must have struck a chord. Without his help, my bowling might simply have been ignored, because the majority of judges had hardly considered it worthy of attention.

For instance, I will never forget, and I'm certain my father Les won't either, the occasion of my first opportu-nity to impress at a national level, the English Schools'

Under-15 festival of 1971, staged in Liverpool. I had been selected to represent the South West and, naturally, Dad came with me. In the trial game to decide who would play for England Schools against the Public Schools at Aigburth, I produced what I thought was a telling performance with the ball only to later discover it had been a waste of effort. When I came on to bowl, I set a precise field in accordance with a tactical plan, and I enjoyed my first reward when I did the batsman through the air and had him caught at mid-wicket. When similar hard work earned a further five wickets, I left the field satisfied with my bowling and feeling confident that I would succeed in making the final XI.

Unbeknown to me, not for the first time and certainly not for the last, the selectors and I did not see eye-to-eye. In fact, their perception of what had taken place was entirely different. Les had been sitting close to them to see if he could pick up anything from their conversations, and when I took that first wicket he overheard one of these so-called experts comment: 'Ignore that. It was a fluke'. Against such reasoning I had no chance of making the team and I was duly left out, primarily because they considered me a batsman rather than a bowler. I suppose they hadn't ever heard of all-rounders. In the years that followed, whenever I managed to achieve anything on the cricket field, it gave me the greatest satisfaction to remember those blinkered observers and wonder what they were doing with their lives at that moment.

Les was fuming, and when the selectors added insult to injury by offering me the exalted role of substitute's substitute, 13th man, he and I said 'Thanks, but no thanks' and promptly headed for Lime Street station.

Fortunately, Tom had seen enough to make a rather different judgement. He took me under his wing and taught me the art of swing bowling. He used to hang his head in despair sometimes when he saw me try to bounce people out, but in the end he believed in me enough to persevere. It was Tom who ensured that Somerset recommended me to Len Muncer, the chief coach of the Lord's groundstaff boys, the nursery for young talent from all over the country. Tom also persuaded Somerset to give me a chance in a couple of Sunday league games at the end of the 1973 season. It was in the first of these, a televised match against Sussex at Hove, that I took a skyer in the deep to dismiss Tony Greig, a feat that played a large part in the club's offer of a contract. It was just as well that Tom and Closey put in the effort they did, because, frankly, although it was an awful lot of fun, the education I received at Lord's was mainly concerned with extending my repertoire of ways to skate on thin ice.

I thought Yeovil was a big town, but coming to Lord's and London in 1971 really opened my eyes to the big bad world. When I first arrived in the 'smoke' I was the original yokel, sixteen years of age and totally naive to the realities of big city life. In short, my name was Ian Bumpkin.

The first thing that struck me about London was the fact that everything was still switched on at one or two in the morning. If you went to the West End at that time, there would be thousands of people milling around as if it were the middle of the afternoon. I just could not work it out. The first time I went into a strip club with the older groundstaff boys, I just stood there laughing in amazement at these women dancing about and taking their clothes off.

I really had no idea this sort of thing went on. I had a lot to learn.

My first visit to Lord's took place at the end of August 1971 when I travelled up with Mum for a trial. Marie sat in the rose garden behind the pavilion while I went off to try and prove what I could do. I remember bowling and batting quite well, but I was competing with lads who were considerably older than me. So I was quite surprised when they told me that they wanted me to start on the following Saturday. Before that, there was not much of the season left, but, at the end of it, I was invited back for the summer of 1972. There was still the winter to deal with so I returned to Somerset and the local labour exchange to look for work to tide me over. It wasn't glamorous, but I'm proud to say I never went a week without finding something, and ironically I earned more in that six months than I did in my first cricket season with the county.

I didn't mind the physical work, whether it was as a petrol-pump attendant, brickies' labourer or plasterer's mate, and I wonder how many of those who have since walked along the corridors of Yeovil General Hospital realize they are treading on my handiwork. Perhaps the most important aspect of these odd jobs was that they made me appreciate the cricket season all the more when it came, and made me even more determined that there was going to be more to my life than laying floor tiles.

When I arrived at Lord's full-time, I had my first taste of the kind of ritualistic behaviour that is part and parcel of professional sport – the initiation ceremony. The older boys would come into the junior dressing room, grab the newcomer, pin him down and strip him, then coat his privates in whitewash. All very grown up, of course, but the fact is that your standing within the group was dependent on how well you resisted the assault. Although only sixteen, I was a bit of a handful even then. The first time it happened to me, it took about six of the boys to hold me down. So I was 'in'. There was a lot of larking about, particularly on rainy days, and if any of my playing colleagues or opponents who became victims of my practical jokes later on want to know from where I got the idea of setting fire to newspapers while they were being read, or sticking chunks of fresh (and sometimes not so fresh) fruit or the occasional prawn in their batting gloves just before they went out to bat, they need wonder no more.

My big mate at the time was Rodney Ontong, who had arrived from East London near Johannesburg, South Africa. In many ways his home town was as much in the sticks as Yeovil had been, and as two country boys we immediately hit it off. We also shared the same confident attitude and approached cricket in an identical fashion – our motto was work hard on the pitch, then play hard afterwards. I would provide scrumpy from Yeovil and Onty would arrive with his suitcase loaded with South African brandy. It was a genuinely gruesome combination, but it did the job and the groundstaff Head Boy, Bill Jones, one of whose jobs, would you believe, was to ensure discipline in the ranks, would often be left to pick up the human debris at the end of the night's entertainment. I soon learned all about the drinking games that you had to compete in if you wanted to be part of the social scene: the yards of ale, the boat races and the like. I had sampled beer before coming to Lord's, but it was only when I formed my partnership with Onty that I really started to get the taste.

The only difference between us was that he managed to toe the line better than me when it came to discipline. He would make sure that he stayed on-side with the coaches, Len Muncer and his assistant Harry Sharp. But I struggled with Len, who was one of the military school of cricketers, with razor-sharp creases in his flannels and immaculate shoes. What annoyed me most was that he had decided very early on that I couldn't bowl. That was absurd because Somerset had sent me up as an all-rounder, not just a batsman who could bowl a bit. I wanted to be in the game as much as possible and Len's resistance was a pain in the neck.

Most of my bowling was done in the nets, not only for practice but also because it was the place to escape from some of the more mundane tasks that were part of the job. By falling out with Len, however, I lost out on one of the perks.

At weekends when MCC teams were playing up and down the country, they would more often than not find themselves a player or two short. So they would send to Lord's for a member of the groundstaff who would then not only have his expenses paid but would also enjoy a free lunch and tea. From one match you could end up making as much as the £12 we were paid per week. Len controlled the list of who went where and unfortunately, because of our differences, I was hardly ever selected for one of these trips.

The bottom line was that Len didn't have much time for me because he felt I was too brash and over-confident. He may even have been right. I probably didn't do myself much good in his eyes when on one occasion my desire to prove myself in this fiercely competitive world led to me breaking convention. I was going through a bad patch at the time with my batting and when we came up against a weak side from the City of London school, I failed to follow the normal tradition of giving your wicket away, preferably in a suitably subtle manner, on reaching fifty. I went on to make a hundred instead, and after leaving the field to stony silence I was taken to one side by Len and given a fearful ear-bashing. His attitude antagonised me no end but, to be fair to him, he did tell my parents that he was surprised I was not being called back to play for Somerset seconds during that year.

Harry Sharp, nicknamed the 'admiral' because he had been an able seaman during the war and who became the Middlesex scorer when he packed up coaching, was different and I always made a point of keeping in touch with him. He would stand behind the net when I was batting, with half a fag stuck behind his ear, and deliver his verdict.

'Bloody awful shot, Botham . . . but if you keep hitting it son, you keep playing it.'

The £12 weekly wage did not go far after rent and bills. We were paid on Thursday and by Sunday would be broke. So to stay alive, we got up to the usual tricks like jumping the barriers on the tube, and we soon developed a few key dodges to supplement our meagre income. We never got involved in anything seriously criminal, it was more of an initiative test. One of these, the Great Seat Cushion Scam, was our chief money-maker. It worked like this: Step One – arrive at the ground early. Step Two – divert a number of seat cushions, say 50 to 100 from the normal selling positions to the little booths where we worked selling scorecards. Step Three – when handing over a scorecard to spectators arriving at the ground, offer cushions at 5p rather than the normal 10p hire charge. Call me Al Capone.

The cushiest number was delivering updated scorecards to the offices all around the ground. That meant constant access to the pavilion, and more importantly, to the kitchens where the 'legendary' Nancy Doyle would slip us poor starving waifs the odd bacon butty. Rodney and I even found a way to make some spending money while gargling at the same time. Working behind the Tavern Bar during match days offered excellent opportunities for spirits, not to mention pints, of free enterprise. Basically the trick was that whenever a group of businessmen arrived we made sure they received our undivided attention. Slowly but surely they ended up paying a bit more for each round of drinks, and, of course, the more they imbibed the less they cared. Needless to say, offers of 'and one for yourself' were never knowingly refused. After a couple of hours of this we would be staggering around the place, parrot-faced, making a complete cock-up of the orders and ringing up totals that bore absolutely no resemblance to the actual cost of the drinks. When this exercise in creative accounting was performed once too often, Rod and I were given a new order – of the boot.

Another potential opportunity for cash prizes was the job of bowling at MCC members in the nets. The ones we targeted for special treatment were known as the 'Jazz Hats'. These were the flash harrys who turned up in their sports cars with all the latest gear that always looked fresh out of the wrapper. The call would come through, Bill Jones would ask the name of the member and if he decided the man in question was not a big enough tipper for him to bother with, he would delegate accordingly.

The method for finding out what kind of tip you might pick up was tried and trusted. After bowling for five minutes or so and supplying a comfortable number of half-volleys, it would be time to adjust your aim towards the thigh pocket. If you heard the tell-tale jingle of change, there was not much point in continuing the drudgery for too long and it was the signal to start bringing the session to a close with a few quicker deliveries. If you heard no sound at all, there were two possibilities. You were either breaking your back for a tight bastard who carried nothing, or a gent who carried only notes. As you didn't want to risk missing out on the latter, a lot of players who barely knew which end of a bat to pick up suddenly found themselves middling the ball like world-beaters, hearing exclamations of wonder at their superb strokeplay and astonishment that they were not representing their county at the very least. If the fellow in question turned out to have short arms and deep pockets, however, the next time he turned up it would be open warfare.

The groundstaff team was known as the Nippers, and whenever we played away we would make sure to feed well during the tea interval. It was comical to watch the lads stuffing chicken legs, vol-au-vents, sandwiches, pork pies and anything else they could lay their hands on into their kit bags. The only thing you had to make sure of was clearing out the bag from time to time; sweaty jockstraps and rotting pork pies often made a potent combination. The matches were taken reasonably seriously, but if the opposition was not particularly strong everyone understood that once a decent game of cricket had been had by all, the main priority was to get to the bar as soon as possible. For the home matches we were aided and abetted by an umpire called John Collins. You could tell when the pub doors were opening because his decisions would become more and more outrageous. As the shadows lengthened, any appeals for caught behind or lbw became a mere formality.

By and large I managed to keep out of big trouble during my time at Lord's. The nearest I came to it was an incident involving a water jug and one of the juniors, a lad called Anwar Muhammad who was a cousin or nephew, I can't recall which, of the Pakistan Test player Younis Ahmed. It was a wet, miserable day and I decided the dressing room boredom needed to be lifted with a bit of horseplay. I picked up the jug intending to give the lad a soaking and as I went to throw the water, the handle came clean away and the whole thing shattered. Anwar Muhammad nearly lost a finger and I was cut around the wrist. There was blood everywhere and an ambulance was called for. I think it was only the seriousness of the injuries that saved us from strife.

The pleas of 'accident', however, failed to save Onty and me from being evicted from our digs. The landlady was a classic of the genre, with big thick glasses through which she was not inclined to see the funny side. She scared me witless. The problem arose during one of our regular games of football in the passageway when Rodney let fly with a magnificent unstoppable volley. Dipping and swerving at the last minute, it smashed through the window and into the road outside. Enter the Dragon.

We were well behind with the rent and had received several warnings, so it was bags-in-the-street time. Luckily, it was near the end of the season so we were able to doss down on the floor of some friends and then, once we had outstayed our welcome, we had to resort to sleeping at the ground. Security was minimal so we managed to sneak in and kip in the baths in the juniors' changing rooms.

At this stage little thought was given to the possible consequences of our actions. Although the cricket was taken seriously, we were living for the moment without a care in the world. Soon, however, the attractions of London began to wear thin and I was glad to get away from the place. I was impatient and I wanted to break through into the county circuit.

I was due to return to Lord's for the whole of the summer of 1973, but in the event I spent hardly any time there because during that season I became a regular in the Somerset second team.

The young players were being introduced into the senior team gradually so it was never a case of club cricketer one day, pro the next. There was a definite pecking order and the junior players had to know their place. It amazed me in later years to watch fresh-faced seventeen-year-olds march in on the first day and demand: 'Where's the sponsored car?' In those days you did as you were told and kept your mouth shut. If you failed to observe this simple rule, there was every chance that one of the senior players would take it upon himself to point out the error of your ways, normally by grabbing you by the scruff of the neck and pinning you against the nearest available wall.

I made a conscious decision when I got into the first team to play the part of the dumb country boy. (Hands up those who said it shouldn't have been difficult.) While I was perceived as such I was no bother to anyone, more a figure of fun, and it made me laugh to see some of the other youngsters getting in over their heads. I would think to myself, 'You silly lad, you'll pay for that sometime', and sure enough most of them did. Because the rest of the team thought I didn't have a brain cell in my head, there was never any danger of me being asked for an opinion on club politics, which meant I could just concentrate on playing and going for a beer afterwards – and that suited me down to the ground.

Quietly, though, I had already sorted out my objectives. Priority number one was to get in the team, then stay there. From there, the target was a county cap. And next, even at this stage, was England.

First there was the little matter of finding a place to live. My initial fixed abode was in Greenway Road, Taunton, where I was billeted with Dennis Breakwell, the slow left-arm bowler who had recently joined us from Northamptonshire. It was called a club flat, but there is no doubt that the term 'flat' definitely represented a breach of the Trade Descriptions Act. Not to put too fine a point on it, it was a complete tip: even the cockroaches passed by on the other side of the street because some of its unique features would have tested the descriptive talents of the most imaginative estate agent. First, it was so damp that there were fish jumping out of the wall. Then, due to the fact that the mod cons had been cut off from the previous summer, there was no electricity or water. We did have the luxury of a toilet but it happened to be situated outside, and flushing it could only be achieved by the skilful application of a bucket of water. The only heating we had was created by burning newspapers and old rubbish. There were no cooking facilities so we made sure to get our fill at the ground or to raid the milk float that clattered down the street in the early morning. It was not the sort of place we looked forward to returning to at the end of the day, so more often than not we didn't. We spent most of our evenings in the Gardener's Arms, not just to be sociable but also to have a roof over our heads and a bit of warmth and light.

Here, the most useful aspect of my training at Lord's was put to good use. When it came to the challenge of sinking three pints in a minute, no one could touch me. At closing time it was off to a club, either the Camelot or the 88-400, or back to play cards by candlelight. We kipped in sleeping bags on the floor. Luxury. Fortunately by the start of my breakthrough season in 1974 the situation had improved somewhat. My salary had been doubled – to £500 per annum – and Dennis and I found a new flat, in St James Street, right next to the county ground. We also had a new flat-mate, Viv Richards.

Viv and I had hit it off the first time we met, when we had been selected to play for Somerset Under-25s against Glamorgan at the Lansdowne Cricket Club. The grapevine had already been humming with stories of the young West Indian, and when we bumped into each other I found that he had also heard of me. The moment he dropped his bag on the dressing room floor something clicked between us and that bond has remained ever since. What also helped to break the ice was the fact that our performances in that match represented a spectacular reversal of roles. Viv, the great batting hope, was bowled first ball but then redeemed himself by taking five for 25. Yours truly, who was busy boring everyone to tears with tales of my brilliant bowling, chucked down a lot of old rubbish then scored a century. Afterwards I said to him: 'Listen, Viv. You take the wickets. I'll score the runs'.

Even then, Viv was totally committed to succeeding. He

later said that what struck him about me in those early days was my total belief in myself and the fact that I was always positive. What impressed me was that there was never any danger that he was not going to make full use of his immense talent. He had the best eye of any cricketer I have ever seen, and he said he felt that any moment of the match when he was not batting was wasted. I think that came from his childhood experiences of playing beach cricket on his native island of Antigua. He told me once about his childhood, and how on the beach he would be one of a huge crowd of kids waiting for their turn to bat. If you got out, it was quite possible you would not get another chance for days, so you did everything you could to stay in. I respected his near-obsession, but although I was also single-minded about succeeding I didn't go quite so far as he did in those early days. While he would actually sleep with his bat by the bed, my sleeping companion was a bottle of gin.

These were heady days but things were also close to getting out of hand. The early successes were marvellous, of course, but with them came local fame, and with that some local aggro. I had been in my fair share of scraps at school but the more successful I was on the cricket field, the more the so-called hard men of life wanted to have a pop at me. When I went out to a pub with friends, there would always be the one comedian who insisted on proving to his mates that he was tougher than me, and I had difficulty coming to terms with that. Where some people could just count to ten and walk away, I had difficulty getting past one. I was never one of those who could turn the other cheek; it was always an eye for an eye and a tooth for a tooth.

Although later incidents were to have wider-reaching

implications, and one almost cost me the chance of captaining England in 1980/81, the first I recall clearly took place in Taunton when Dennis and I were returning home after a few pints at a local club. Suddenly, these two youths appeared from nowhere. One of them dived over a wall at me, grabbed a chunk of hair from the back of my head and ripped it clean away. I have no idea why he did this and I wasn't going to waste time asking questions or wait for him to pull a knife or bottle. I knocked seven bells out of him in about 30 seconds while Dennis kept his mate occupied by telling him: 'If you want any trouble, pal, you can have it'.

Viv was also a very handy man in a crisis. I could not bear the kind of racist remarks people would sometimes come out with when he was around. Viv was already a tough person, but I think his early experiences hardened him even more. Later, when on more than one occasion he was abused by idiots in the crowd at Headingley, it still hurt him deeply which was why both he and I were so thrilled by the reception he received when he bowed out from Test cricket in the final match of the 1991 series with England at The Oval. As he walked out to bat in his last innings, the crowd gave him a standing ovation all the way to the wicket. At the end of his knock of 60, during which he had established a career Test batting average of over 50, they did exactly the same thing on the way back to the dressing room. Halfway back he stopped, turned and acknowledged the gesture by raising his bat to all sides and doffing the maroon cap of the West Indies that meant so much to him. It was one of the great moments of cricket, and I consider it a privilege to have been there on the field at the time.

I recall one early example of the kind of man he is. We were in the 88-400 club and Viv was standing at the bar when he overheard two blokes discussing whether it really was Ian Botham they were looking at. Eventually the bet was struck: for £10 one of them was to walk across and stand on my foot. I was blissfully unaware of what was going on even though a man I had never met had come and practically camped on my shoes, but when he returned to the bar to collect his winnings, Viv stopped him and said: 'My friend seems to be a bit dead tonight. How about dealing with a live person?'

As time passed, the closeness of my relationship with Viv caused some problems between Kath and I because she complained, with some justification, that it seemed as though I was closer to him than I was to her. Living, eating, drinking, batting and bowling together over a period of years, it was inevitable that we grew to know each other inside out, better even I think than we knew our wives or our wives knew us. But that was all in the future. At this stage my meeting with my future spouse was still some way off. In fact, it came about as a direct result of Andy Roberts rearranging my teeth.

4
WEDDING BELLS

When Gerry and Jan Waller accepted the invitation from their friend Brian Close to attend Somerset's Benson and Hedges semi-final match against Leicestershire at Grace Road, Leicester on 26 June 1974 and to bring along their daughters Kathryn and Lindsay, little did they know that by doing so they were setting in motion the chain of events that was to alter their lives, the lives of their children and that of Ian Botham irrevocably.

Gerry and Lindsay arrived at the ground first after travelling down from their home in Thorne, near Doncaster, but Jan had not been feeling very well so Kath had stayed behind until her Mum had finished her day's teaching. The pair drove down together, finally turning up at around six o'clock. In fact, Kath apparently had not been too keen on coming at all as she had just returned from a business trip, was worn out and, in any case, was meeting up with her boyfriend over the weekend!

By the time she and Jan arrived, rain had brought proceedings to a soggy halt for the day and the players were sitting around in the bar. Kath already knew some of the Somerset lads through Brian, and I had noticed her presence in a pair of navy blue hot pants and long white boots at a match at Weston-Super-Mare with more than a passing interest. She had never set eyes on me before, however, so when I sat down with the group she first asked me what I did for a living, then enquired as to whether I had watched any of the match before the rain had fallen.

'Actually,' I said, 'I was playing in it.'

After recovering from that slight embarrassment the evening turned out to be fun, and Dennis Breakwell and I duly invited Kath and Lindsay out for a Chinese meal. Kath decided to drive, but as we walked through the gates she suddenly realized she had forgotten where the car was parked. We ended up walking two-thirds of the way round the ground, then sprinting the final section as the rain started to bucket down again before finally diving into the vehicle, which was in fact parked right back where we had started, having been obscured by a large van.

I don't remember much about that evening, but I do recall making every effort to persuade Kath to come to Derby, where we were playing the following Sunday. It was at this stage that I realized I had serious competition as she told me of her arrangements regarding her boyfriend. However, my constant telephone calls, backed up by some helpful encouragement from Jan, appeared to do the trick and a few weeks later Jan, Gerry and Kath all travelled down to Taunton for a match and a meal afterwards with Closey and myself. It was after this that Jan made one of the worst character assessments of all time. 'What a nice, quiet young man' she told her daughter. In any case, it was clear to both of us by now that there was a mutual attraction and the courtship began in earnest.

Kath was doing a business studies course at Lanchester

polytechnic in Coventry and, in between times, working for her father helping to promote high-quality drums and drumsticks used by some of the big name rock stars. Incidentally, in view of the 'Sex, drugs and rock 'n' roll' allegations that were to dog our life together in future years, it was somewhat ironic that Kath was the first to rub shoulders with rock stars like Phil Collins of Genesis and Jon Bonham of Led Zeppelin in this capacity.

As our relationship blossomed, Kath managed to arrange as many business trips as possible to coincide with my county games, and in her trusty Austin 1100 she would appear at cricket grounds in Somerset, Devon, Cornwall or wherever we happened to be playing at the time. And in September 1974, just three months after we met, I proposed.

Kath recalls the moment far more vividly than I for the simple reason that I was drunk at the time. She had been down for the weekend and we ended up at Carnaby's nightclub in Yeovil. Although I enjoy the atmosphere of such places, I am about as expert in soft-shoe shuffling as I am at singing, so while Kath spent most of the evening dancing with one of my oldest mates, John Saunders, I spent all of it emptying the contents of various glasses down my throat. It is just possible that as the evening wore on, the amount of attention Kath was being paid by John and the amount of drink I was consuming combined to create a tinge of jealousy on my part. In any case, shortly before leaving, I took hold of Kath and announced, very matter-of-fact, 'I've decided. We'll get married'. I was eighteen at the time, Kath nineteen.

The next morning Kath sought confirmation.

'Do you remember what you said last night?' she asked.

'Of course I do,' I said.

So our future was set. The proposal was not exactly by the book, I grant you, but we were convinced it was the right thing to do, and as far as we were concerned our age didn't matter.

Not surprisingly, however, the news brought a rather different if wholly understandable reaction from those close to us. My father Les burst out laughing, wondering how on earth I could contemplate such a move on £500 a year. Kath's father, Gerry, humoured us initially; I don't think he thought we were serious. But when it became clear that we were, he helped us enormously by offering me a winter job working as a one of his sales representatives.

When the summer of 1975 arrived news of our plans had to be broken to Closey, who was also Kath's godfather. Showing remarkable courage we left that deed to Jan and Gerry, with predictable results. Closey exploded and gave them both a severe ticking off for allowing us to go ahead. He argued that we were far too young to be making such a commitment and told them that he was very concerned about Kath being married to a man who was going to be away from home so often. He was also worried that marriage might hold back my career. Later he took me to one side and warned me that if I ever did anything to upset Kath, he would be at my throat before I knew it. Then he also gave Kath a talking to along the lines of my having a lot of potential and that she would have to understand that cricket came first.

Undeterred, Kath and I kept to our plan. We had originally intended to wait for three or four years before actually taking the plunge but while attending the wedding of a friend a few weeks later, my impatience and impetuosity got the better of me. 'Let's get married as soon as possible,' I suggested. So we promptly set the date for the coming January!

Having decided to live in the north, Kath found us a tiny two-bedroomed cottage in Mowbray Street, Epworth, opposite the birthplace of the methodist John Wesley, and Jan and Gerry gave us the deposit as a wedding present. Furniture was begged and borrowed and, with the help of another friend, I even managed to install a central heating system.

My only concern about the whole affair was what Kath was going to wear. I am very much a traditionalist when it comes to this kind of occasion, so you can imagine my reaction when I heard the rumour that my bride-to-be was contemplating walking down the aisle in a white trouser-suit. Suitably unimpressed, I took Jan to one side and pleaded with her to make sure that when they went to choose the wedding dress, she should do all in her power to dissuade Kath from picking anything too unusual. She did try. On one occasion, according to Jan, Kath fell in love with something pretty horrible which she had set her heart on. 'Of course you can have it,' said Jan, 'but you'll have to pay for it yourself', and their journey home was endured in stony silence.

In the event, the only real casualty of our wedding day was 'Jerusalem' – the organist murdered it. So there I was, on 31 January 1976, married, housed and established in the Somerset first XI by the age of twenty.

I realized, however, that the real work now had to begin in earnest. This was the make-or-break point for me, the moment when my career could have gone one of two ways: I would either make real progress, or there was a real chance I would end up looking at an uncertain future. I was determined to succeed and, as Closey had indicated when he warned Kath of the consequences of getting married to me at such a young age, that inevitably was going to lead to difficulties in our relationship.

To put it simply, my attitude was that if the Ian Botham story was going to go anywhere, my cricket had to come first no matter what the cost. In fact, the Ian Botham story was lucky to last beyond late May, when Brian Close nearly killed me.

Closey was an appalling driver. I recall one time when he took his car into a garage for crash repairs, collected it on the same day, then returned it for more of the same less than a few minutes later. He had got a lift from Gerry to the garage, signed the papers, said 'Thanks very much' and drove away from the forecourt to a roundabout where, only 50 yards away and in full view of the mechanics who had just finished patching it up, he ploughed straight into the back of a lorry. Within minutes he was recircling the roundabout and limping back to the garage to ask them to mend it again.

Despite his incompetence behind the wheel I normally travelled everywhere with Brian, though one time that I didn't will forever be etched in my memory. The occasion of my narrow escape took place after the close of play in Somerset's match against Surrey at Guildford. After stumps had been drawn, I was sitting in the bar having a pint with my team-mate Pete 'Dasher' Denning. Brian said he was going back to the team hotel and I told him I would get a lift from one of the other players and would see him later, a fortunate decision on my part as it turned out. On his journey Brian went over some oil on a bend in the road and lost control of the car before smashing into a lamp post. When I saw the wreckage later I realized how lucky I had been, as the area around the passenger seat had totally caved in. Naturally, Closey didn't have a mark on him!

At least he was doing his best for me in other respects. Called up to face the West Indies in the 1976 summer Test series, I'm sure he put in a good word for me with the England captain Tony Greig. After I scored my maiden first-class century, 167 not out, to help Somerset beat Nottinghamshire at Trent Bridge at the beginning of August, the calls for my elevation to the international side began gathering momentum.

My delight at being picked for England for the first one-day match against the West Indies at Scarborough on 26 August was understandable. But what I did not appreciate at the time, in fact until years later when it was too late to fully make amends, was the effect my single-mindedness was having on Kath.

She had been warned in advance, of course, that the life of a cricketer's wife is seldom easy. Apart from the long separations, during which so much has to be taken on trust, when a player is attempting to establish himself in a highly competitive environment it is all too easy for him to forget, ignore, neglect or simply be blind to the needs of his partner, and that can lead to big problems. This, regrettably, was certainly the case with our relationship during those early years.

I was so focused on what I was trying to do and so self-centred in that respect that Kath, regretably, often came second on my list of priorities and that affected her deeply. During our initial courtship, I would make a point of looking out for her arrival at the ground and was the first out of the dressing room to see her at the close of play. As I began to establish myself in the Somerset team over the next couple of years, the need to be so attentive seemed to become less and less important. As I mentioned before, Kath often said to me that I was putting the team and the cricket before her. Of course, I reacted as you would expect me to at that stage of my life, by telling her not to be so silly and to cheer up and get on with it.

I know now how hurtful it was to her, for instance, when the following season she was the last to know that I had been called up for my Test debut against Australia at Trent Bridge. She had in fact been informed by my mother Marie.

'Isn't it wonderful news about Ian?' Marie had said.

'What news?' asked Kath.

Marie told her that after their celebratory drink at the ground she had been home for some while and had been certain that I would have rung home by now to tell Kath.

Kath was fuming when I did eventually get round to calling her, particularly as I excused the oversight in typically clumsy fashion.

'Oh, sorry, love. The lads brought me a drink and I got carried away. You know how it is.'

'Perhaps next time you have some good news,' she said, 'you might consider letting me in on it. Although I do realize I am only your wife.'

Looking back on those times, this was not the only example of my thoughtlessness. Kath also got somewhat irritated when I went out with the players and dismissed her by saying, 'Why don't you go and have a chat with so-and-so's wife?' I was not deliberately trying to exclude her, although later on when it came to dealing with the latest tabloid scandal I certainly was also guilty of that. It was just that the merry-go-round was travelling at full pelt – and I didn't want to get off.

I was living for today and letting tomorrow look after itself. I was approaching life like a single man, blissfully unconcerned about marital responsibilities – the original one-eyed jerk. The immediate result was that quite soon after we were married, Kath became very depressed, so much so that she sought medical advice. She went to see our local doctor and told him that she kept bursting into tears. He did not seem to be very helpful, but I was worse. I just couldn't understand what all the fuss was about and so we rowed . . . and rowed. We were both strong-willed characters, and Kath gave as good as she got. The situation was not helped, of course, by the fact that I had insisted that we continue to live in Yorkshire while during the summer I would be based in Taunton. During the season, when the opportunity arose of spending some time at home, I then managed to make things considerably worse by disappearing for games of golf. The problem grew and the tension between us rose to such an extent that on occasions when driving the 28 miles from my parents' house in Yeovil (where Kath would occasionally spend time) to a match at Taunton, the extent of my input into the conversation would be the occasional grunted 'yes' or 'no'.

I'm happy to say that, against all the odds and most people's expectations, Kath and I have managed to stick together through thick and thin, but I have no hesitation in saying that she deserves the lion's share of the credit for that. How she put up with me in those early days, I'll never know. Although this is hardly a valid excuse,

I understand now that my behaviour was a symptom of being totally absorbed in my own career. My whole world revolved around cricket, the team and my mates. So by the time I got into that England side for the one-day match in 1976, I must have been pretty unbearable.

I did not exactly cover myself in glory on the field either, but I got the distinct impression from Greigy that I had done enough to be selected for the upcoming winter tour to India and Sri Lanka and to Australia for the Centenary Test in Melbourne. When I was not, to put it mildly, I sulked. Kath tells me I was hell to live with during the early part of that winter: really awful, a bear with two sore heads. Again, all I could think about was myself. Then, by the time I had settled down again and our life at home had stabilized, a telephone call from Donald Carr, the secretary of the Test and County Cricket Board, threw our lives back into turmoil.

Donald informed me that I had been selected for the Whitbread young player scholarship to Australia. I was thrilled, of course, but it had been by no means certain that I could afford to take up the offer in the first place. The scholarship, clearly intended for young single players, merely covered air fares and living expenses. I had a young wife and mortgage to look after, and although my county salary had been doubled to £1000 it looked as if the trip would be financially impossible. Fortunately for me, when I explained this to Donald, Whitbread came up with a suitable package. Then, five days after I arrived down under with Mike Gatting, Bill Athey and Graham Stevenson to begin the three-month trip, I discovered that Kath was pregnant with Liam.

Before the news broke, my first major cricketing trip

abroad had been more or less purely a social one. One game, against an army side in Melbourne, was typical. After an 11 am start we stopped at lunch for what we thought would be the normal forty-minute break. In the end, after a barbecue had left us fed and watered like Royals, we staggered back on the field fully two hours later. The batting side then declared, we batted for twenty minutes, then stopped for tea. An hour later the game restarted, ran for another ten minutes then we all decided to call it a draw and pack up. I learned far more about surfing than cricket on that bizarre trip.

So while I was busy enjoying myself, Kath found herself pregnant, alone and fed up. She had no idea how to contact me so she telephoned Colin Cowdrey, who had been responsible for selecting those to go on the scholarship, and told him to pass on a message that she urgently needed to get in touch with me. Trying not to appear like the neurotic wife, she explained her reasons to Colin and he made several calls before finally tracking me down. When Kath eventually managed to get through to me on the phone, all she heard on the other end of the line was total silence.

'Ian,' said Kath, 'I'm pregnant.'

No response.

'Ian,' she tried again. 'I'm pregnant.'

Still no response.

'Ian? Are you still there?'

I was, quite literally, struck dumb. Delighted with the news, of course, but I just didn't know what to say.

If the prospect of imminent fatherhood was supposed to subdue my hell-for-leather lifestyle, nobody told me because by the time I returned to England after the Centenary Test, I had managed to get involved in a punch-up, this time with none other than the former Australian captain, Ian Chappell. One evening during the match, I was drinking in a bar with players from both sides when I overheard Chappell giving it the typical Aussie verbals and rubbishing England. In fact, he was getting so full of himself that it would have been impossible for me not to overhear him. I didn't like what he was saying and I told him in so many words, warning him that if he carried on there would be trouble. Once again, it was a case of my simply being unable to turn the other cheek. Furthermore, if there is one thing designed to make me see red it is a loudmouth Aussie, no matter who he is. I don't know if Chappell was aware of my reputation for thinking with my fists or whether he was intentionally goading me, but in any case he went on and on. Three times I warned him and three times he ignored me. Finally, I could take no more so I threw a punch at him. The impact sent him flying over a table into a group of Aussie Rules footballers, whose drinks were scattered to all parts. On recovering his composure, Chappell realized he had better make himself scarce, but before he did he stopped at the doorway, then turned and yelled some insult in my direction.

In a flash, I was off and running, straight across the bar and out the door, chasing him into the street. As he fled I pursued him, hurdling the bonnet of a car in the chase. I was about to catch him when I noticed a police car cruising towards us. I have done some pretty daft things in my life but even I realized that the time had come for a tactical withdrawal.

Over the years this fracas has naturally grown out of all proportion, but one rumour I would like to put right once and for all is that I went after Chappell with a bottle. The day I have to resort to that kind of cowardice is the day I know there is something seriously wrong with me. As far as I'm concerned, Ian Chappell as a human being is a nonentity. Obviously he was a great cricketer and a fine captain, but he is one person I was destined never to get on with. I know others who feel the same way about him.

Meanwhile, Tony Greig was in the process of bringing about a complete revolution in world cricket. The South African-born England captain was a showman and a terrifically aggressive cricketer, but he was also a shrewd man and he knew that for years Test cricket had under-sold itself with the result that cricketers were among the paupers of international sport. He came across Kerry Packer, the Australian television magnate, a man who shared his view that something should be done to make cricket into a high-profile big business entertainment industry. Together they came up with the idea of World Series Cricket to be set up in direct competition to Test cricket, and employing the best cricketers from every country. Once the news got out during the following summer's Ashes series in England, all hell broke loose.

Long-standing friendships foundered as a result of the split in world cricket caused by Greig and Packer. Tim Rice, writing in the *Daily Telegraph*, summed up the mood of the establishment when he commented: 'Is Greig so short of a few bob that he has to go to these clandestine lengths to make a buck? If our handsome ex-captain is prepared to hawk his talents in any market place, would he like a role in *Jesus Christ Superstar*? I may well be able to fix it if he would let me know which part would best suit him'.

There is no doubt that many saw Tony Greig as a traitor. As far as I was concerned, he was doing cricket a great service. The International Cricket Council, the governing body of world cricket, decided that the England players involved, Greig, Alan Knott, John Snow and Derek Underwood, should not be barred from playing in the Tests coming up against Australia, but told the England selectors that Greig should not be considered for the captaincy.

Then, two weeks later, after the ICC had announced a total Test ban on all 35 players recruited to World Series Cricket, Packer and Greig took them to the High Court which then upheld their complaint over restraint of trade.

Pakistan tried to break ranks by picking their Packer players in their team against us the following winter (1978/79), but they were forced to back down once we issued an ultimatum that we would not take the field against them. Those who joined Packer were left out in the cold until he reached a compromise with the ICC and the Australian Board of Control in April 1979. This granted Packer's Channel 9 station exclusive rights to televise Test cricket down under and, superficially at least, the issue was instantly resolved.

The wounds took a long time to heal completely, but one undeniable good thing that did come out of it was that the life of the professional cricketer would never be as financially unrewarding again. In order to discourage another breakaway movement, the TCCB realized they simply had to raise more cash and did so mainly through deals like the Cornhill sponsorship of home Test series. And subsequent innovations that turned the traditionalists purple with rage, like coloured clothing, are now considered commonplace in one-day cricket.

As far as my career was concerned the Packer affair did me more good than harm. I was never likely to be invited to join, but once the England side had been stripped of Greig I was the obvious choice to replace him as all-rounder in the long term. Furthermore, as David Gower will agree, our early days in Test cricket were made somewhat easier by the fact that opposing sides had been deprived of some of their best players.

For the moment however, it was back to England and to Kath. The 1977 season was only a few weeks away. I had enjoyed my first taste of international cricket and experienced the atmosphere in the England dressing room during a Test match. I was now even more determined to become an England regular. It was going to be a hugely important summer for me.

5
THE RISE OF AN ENGLAND STAR

By the time I was selected for my first Test, the third of England's Ashes series against Australia at Trent Bridge on 28 July 1977, I had no doubts that I was ready to make the jump. Nevertheless, in the moments leading up to the first morning of the match, I have to admit I was a bundle of nerves.

The point is that no matter how confident you may be in your own ability, you never really know whether you can be a Test cricketer until you go out on the field and get involved. After all, how many great county players have never made the grade when their ability suggested otherwise?

It was the fear of that unknown which caused me to be uncharacteristically quiet in the Trent Bridge dressing room that morning. I can't really remember much about what went on; everything seemed to be happening so quickly. I've no doubt that a thousand and one people came up to me during the days and hours before the match to wish me luck, but I simply cannot remember a single word anyone said, and that certainly applies to the moments immediately before we went out to play.

I do remember, however, that I was barely capable of speech myself. I had a knot in my stomach as big as a fist and my mouth felt dry. I had arrived in the Test arena, but the question flashing through my mind was: 'What the hell happens now?'

I was lucky to be part of a team where new members were not treated as juniors, an atmosphere which had been created by Tony Greig, who was still a member of the team at this stage, although his involvement with Packer had resulted in the cricket authorities insisting he should not be captain. But Mike Brearley, his successor, made sure that tradition continued. Brears encouraged us to talk about the game, and every single player, whether they were making their first appearance or their forty-first, was asked to contribute. I had sampled the atmosphere of the England dressing room before of course, not only during the one-day internationals at the end of the previous summer, but also during the Centenary Test at Melbourne that winter (rather too energetically, it seems, for the peace of mind of some senior players who were the victims of my practical jokes!). So it was not as if I walked through the door to be hit by a wall of blank faces. What's more, the approach to man-management adopted by Greigy and Brears meant that there was no such thing as a pecking order, even though this was the match when the one and only Sir Geoffrey Boycott was making his long-awaited return to Test cricket after three years of self-imposed exile, following the selectors' decision to award the captaincy for the 1973/74 tour to the West Indies to Mike Denness instead of him.

In some ways, I was also helped in those final minutes prior to going out on to the field by the fact that there were so many small details to attend to: just remembering to put my jockstrap on under my flannels rather than over, for instance. And I do recall that my tenseness was eased somewhat when Mike Hendrick came and sat next to me and started to talk about shooting. Mike was a keen sportsman himself, and just chatting with him about something other than cricket helped take my mind off things. But no matter how hard I tried to remain calm and focused on what I was doing, the nerves simply wouldn't go away.

I remember I was desperate for us to field first. No one could ever accuse me of excessive patience at the best of times, but on this occasion the last thing I wanted was to have to sit around on my backside waiting. I wanted to get in the thick of things as quickly as possible. So when Brears returned from the pitch to announce that Greg Chappell, the Aussie captain, had won the toss and decided to bat, I felt a huge sense of relief.

As time passed, however, the nerves returned. The longer the wait the worse it got, and by the time I was given the ball for my first spell in Test cricket I was like a piece of elastic stretched to breaking point.

I had tried to remember Closey's advice about not being intimidated by anyone or any situation, but the harder I tried the worse it got. I was like an actor going on stage for the first time. You can rehearse your lines until you are word perfect but there is still no guarantee that, when the time arrives to open your mouth and deliver them for real, any of them will actually come out, or even if they do, they will come out in the correct order. However, the moment had arrived; there was nothing for it but to take a deep breath and go for it.

As it turned out, had I been playing in my second Test

rather than my first I might even have taken a wicket with that very first ball. Rick McCosker played nervously forward and edged the ball through the vacant third slip space. If I had been absolutely sure of myself I would have insisted to Brears that I should have three slips. What a start that would have been!

The incident taught me a valuable lesson all the same. Junior member of the team or not, from now on I would insist on getting the field setting I wanted.

The remainder of my first spell in Test cricket was something of a struggle, the problem being that even though I had got the first ball out of the way, I was still trying too hard and the adrenalin was pumping too much; I was almost bursting out of myself. Consequently, I strayed down the leg side too often and was generally wayward. When Brears told me to have a 'blow', I felt disappointed that I had not done myself justice. The question 'Is Botham good enough?' remained unanswered. On seeing how pumped up I was, Brears decided to let me have my head by giving me a second spell immediately after lunch. And then came the moment when everything that had happened in my life so far seemed to make perfect sense.

Greg Chappell attempted to drive a short, widish ball from me which instead nicked the inside edge of his bat and rattled into his stumps. As Chappell returned to the pavilion, I tried to look casual, as though this was the kind of thing that happened to me all the time. In fact, my heart was trying to jump out of my chest. Closey had always told me that I should fear nobody. But Greg Chappell? Of course it was a lucky wicket but to hell with that, I was in the book and Greg Chappell, one of the greatest batsmen of all time, was my rabbit!

EARLY YEARS

HI MUM ... ready to take on the world, at eight months.

HAVE BAT, WILL BAT ... the first swing of the willow for Liam as a toddler (above) and yours truly showing a bit more poise at the age of eight.

THE LADS ... the team from Milford Junior School in Yeovil pose for the camera. That's me, front row second in from the right.

AN EASY PUSHOVER ... for the boy who tried to block me out of this picture, taken during a Buckler's Mead Secondary School weekend camp. I've always liked to have the last laugh!

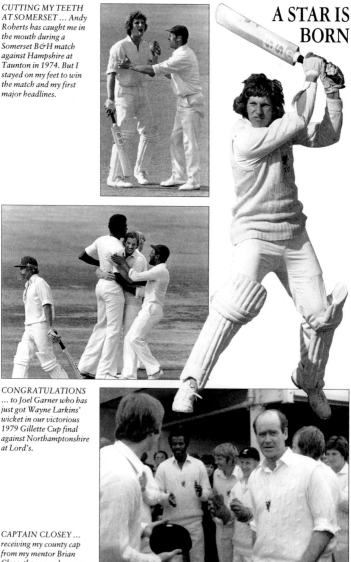

CUTTING MY TEETH AT SOMERSET ... Andy Roberts has caught me in the mouth during a Somerset B&H match against Hampshire at Taunton in 1974. But I stayed on my feet to win the match and my first major headlines.

A STAR IS BORN

CONGRATULATIONS ... to Joel Garner who has just got Wayne Larkins' wicket in our victorious 1979 Gillette Cup final against Northamptonshire at Lord's.

CAPTAIN CLOSEY ... receiving my county cap from my mentor Brian Close, the man who gave Somerset the heart to win.

A WORD IN MY EAR ... 'fiery' Geoff Boycott always has plenty to say on captaincy and any other subject you care to mention, and (below) an informal selectors' meeting with Charlie Elliott, Alec Bedser and Kenny Barrington before the one-day international against the West Indies at Lord's in 1980.

LEADING FROM THE FRONT ... as captain I try to set a batting example (below) during the third Test against the West Indies at the Kensington Oval, Barbados in 1981.

MIRACLE OF '81

AGAINST THE ODDS ... Geoff Lawson (above) got so cheesed off during my innings of 149 not out at Headingley in the third Test that he slipped me a couple of beamers. I didn't forget.

ON A RUN ... Rodney Marsh's middle stump is uprooted (left) on the way to my taking five for one in 28 balls in the second innings of the fourth Test.

IT'S DRINKS ALL ROUND ... the champagne moment on the Headingley balcony (below) after our amazing win.

Flushed with that success I then took the wickets of Doug Walters, Rod Marsh, Max Walker and Jeff Thomson. At one stage my figures were four for 13 in 34 balls, and I finished with five for 74. It all happened so fast that I never really had a chance to savour the moments one by one; all I do recall is that they couldn't find a hat to fit my head for some time afterwards. And what better way to round off that day than being presented to the Queen, who was in the Midlands for the Silver Jubilee celebrations and was visiting the ground on that first day.

Boycott marked his comeback with a century, needless to say, then 80 not out in the second innings, and I managed to make 25 with the bat as we cruised to victory by seven wickets. As for Test cricket, the whole thing seemed so simple! The only negative feature of the match had been Boycott's run-out of his team-mate Derek Randall, something I will come back to later.

There is no doubt that my early success for England was due in no small part to having Mike Brearley as captain. As he proved by trusting me with that second spell at a crucial period of my debut match, he had this great knack of recognizing what made every single player tick and exactly what was needed to bring out the best in them. Technically and tactically, he was as astute a captain as you will ever see. I remember one incident in particular from those early days that made me realize just how he put those qualities to use in the field. Earlier in that season I played under him for MCC against the Australians at Lord's. He noted in that match that I had been bowling too many bouncers. He identified the need for me to use the weapon more sparingly, and then told me so in no uncertain terms at Trent Bridge. An observation on a player had been stored away in his head, and then used to great effect when he needed it. When I helped bowl out the Aussies that day, I hardly sent down a bumper at all. Yet, if Brears had not pushed the right buttons, the combination of my nervousness, my desire to do well and my sheer bloody-mindedness might have had an altogether different result.

The irony of my success in that Trent Bridge Test debut match was that during the game, the man who had done so much to shape my approach to the game, Brian Close, was announcing his retirement from first-class cricket.

Over the years Kath and I have often discussed what might have happened if I had had the benefit of Closey's presence on and off the field for a while longer. He was a wonderful stabilizing influence on me, although he gave as good as he got on the field and in the bar. When he indicated to me that I was overstepping the mark, there was no beating around the bush and I respected him for it. As my career progressed the absence of Brian Close and later Kenny Barrington, at the very moments when I needed a firm hand to guide me, meant that I was left instead to my own devices. My attitude was that Beefy knows best; however, in certain situations, that simply wasn't true.

Of course you have to learn your own lessons in life, but some people are better equipped to do so than others. The early successes I experienced simply reinforced my philosophy that I was going to take everything coming to me even if that meant some people getting hurt in the process. Kath was the one who was hurt most of course, and that is a recurring theme throughout my career. It is easy to say that if I knew then what I know now, things would have been different but I am really not sure that's true either. A few years ago I caught sight of an advertising hoarding in Australia from which I can't recall the product being promoted, but the message was unforgettable. It read 'Life: Be in it'. I was determined to do that, even if it meant being in it up to my neck. If Closey, Kenny or even Brears had stayed around longer than they did, at least on certain occasions, when I was precariously poised on the line separating right from wrong, there would have been someone close to me with the guts to stand up and say: 'Don't be such an idiot'.

In the meantime, the only things that concerned me were reaching the top in cricket and having a good time in the process. My first Test match was a big hurdle cleared: it hardened my resolve to go out and conquer the world, and helped me to reappraise my targets. Closey had taught me there was no point in going out on the field with any other attitude than that I was the best cricketer alive. I wanted to be the best and if that meant Kath and the family were pushed down my list of priorities, then that was the way it had to be.

I could see the possibilities opening up in front of me. Kerry Packer's intervention in the world of cricket meant that the game in the future would offer substantially higher financial rewards than it had done in the past. This was the age of the first million pound transfers in football and the elevation of sportsmen and women to superstar status the world over. It was the time of winner takes all, and I wanted to be one of the winners.

Fortunately, under the sobering influences of Closey and Brears, I was still able at this stage to appreciate that there were other things in life except me.

We brushed the Aussies aside at Headingley thanks to

Boycs, who followed up his Trent Bridge heroics with a massive 191 in the fourth Test at Leeds, thus becoming the first player to score his 100th first-class century in the Test arena. In front of a packed Headingley crowd (the gates had to be closed on the first two days well before play started) Boycs made sure that the Aussies had no chance of coming back in the series. I got a bit carried away by the excitement and my failed attempt to hit Ray Bright out of the ground from the third delivery I faced meant that I had secured my first Test duck in only my second innings. The Aussies, shell-shocked at having to bowl at Boycott for twenty-two and a half hours since his return to the England side, capitulated without much of a fight in the first innings when I took five for 21, and although I was wicketless in the second innings we eventually crushed them by an innings and 85 runs.

During this match an incident occurred that was indirectly responsible for changing my life. Attempting to field the ball in the deep during the second innings, I stepped on it awkwardly and experienced a searing pain in my left foot. It was a particularly daft way of getting injured. My foot hurt like hell, but it was not until after the match that I found out I had broken a bone, an injury that apparently had been aggravated when I continued to bowl. As a result I was ruled out of the last match of the series at The Oval.

On returning to Somerset from Headingley, I went for treatment at Musgrove Park Hospital in Taunton. On my way to see the specialist I walked through a children's ward where there were kids with their arms in plaster, heads bandaged and legs in traction. At the end of the ward, I suddenly came across four youngsters sitting around a small table playing Monopoly.

'What are they doing here? I asked the specialist. 'Visiting, are they?'

'No,' he replied. 'Unfortunately they're suffering from leukaemia. Two of them have very little time to live.'

It was shattering news for me. I couldn't take in what I was hearing. In that moment all those feelings of self-satisfaction over the events of the past couple of weeks disappeared. The specialist went on to explain, in layman's terms, just what happens to the body when a child suffers from leukaemia. I listened open-mouthed. How could these children, who were playing so happily and who looked to the naked eye as right as rain, be about to die? I suddenly thought of Kath and the baby we were expecting, and a shiver went down my spine.

The doctor then told me that a lack of funds meant the hospital could no longer hold the annual party for the children which, for some of them, would be literally the only thing they could ever look forward to again. I had no hesitation in deciding to pay for the party there and then. It was not a huge amount of money; they just wanted to be able to buy sausage rolls, crisps, party hats and the like, but I wanted to do something and it was the only thing I could think of.

Over the years, the seed that was planted that day grew and grew, and I'm proud to say that the leukaemia walks have not only put the disease on the map in terms of national awareness but, through the generosity of people up and down the country, they have also raised substantial funds for the never-ending fight to beat this ghastly disease. To think, all that started because I stepped on a cricket ball.

A few days later I was in hospital again to witness the

birth of my son, Liam. Again, this was only made possible because of that foot injury. Liam's birth was far from straightforward, however; Kath was in labour for over 26 hours in all and had a terrible time of it. It had all started with minimal fuss, when in the early hours of 24 August, Kath announced she had gone into labour. Around mid-morning she told me it was time to head for the maternity ward at Doncaster Royal Infirmary and it was there that the problems began. Originally I had told Kath categorically that I would not be present at the birth because I felt I would just be getting in the way. So according to plan, I dropped her and her mum off, waved goodbye and returned home to wait. But once I was informed that she was really suffering badly, I went back to the hospital and thereafter never left her side, apart from a brief moment when I was advised by the midwife to take a break. When I entered the delivery room for the first time, Kath was in absolute agony, crawling around on her hands and knees and screaming out in pain. My first reaction was shock, then, when I had pulled myself together, I ran off to get hold of the midwife. Unfortunately, because this was a Bank Holiday weekend, the hospital appeared to be short-staffed; the woman who came appeared under stress and clearly made an incorrect assessment of the situation. She told Kath not to make such a fuss, that everything was perfectly normal and that she was just getting hysterical for no reason. At one stage she actually got quite annoyed with Kath and told her 'Stop being silly.' What none of us knew, until much later, was that Liam had been in an inverted position in Kath's womb. No wonder she had been in such terrible pain.

Finally, the doctor arrived and he soon resolved the situation. I was present at the birth, although by that stage Kath was so exhausted that she probably had no idea I was there at all. In the event, Liam was born at 3.50 a.m. the following morning. It was an extremely emotional moment for both of us; indeed the whole experience had been so harrowing for Kath that she went private for the birth of our second child, Sarah. Incidentally, when the gynaecologist reviewed Kath's case notes over Liam's birth, he expressed his amazement that she had not had a Caesarean operation.

Becoming a father changes a lot of men. It is supposed to be the time when the word responsibility becomes more than something you laugh about. That, however, was never going to be the case with me. Despite the difficulty of Liam's birth, it was simply not in my nature to think of anything other than the next day, the next challenge and the next pint. After all, I was not yet twenty-two and there was a lot more of life yet to come.

Having come through one traumatic experience, Kath was soon facing up to another demanding task, this time sewing name tags into the sackloads of kit which I was required to take on my first overseas tour to Pakistan and New Zealand that winter of 1977/78. It was a job she hated but over the years, as she got used to what was needed and learned to ignore the TCCB tour guidelines on preparing for trips, she found ways round the problem. For a while she used a laundry marker and then, later still, simply did not bother at all. Even at this early stage I realized what kind of system I was dealing with at Lord's: my measurements were sent to the TCCB weeks in advance, yet when the kit turned up the trousers would have been too long in the leg for Joel Garner!

This was another particularly difficult time for Kath. Having been away from her the previous winter when I was on the Whitbread Scholarship in Australia, here I was disappearing again only a couple of months after Liam's birth. Everything in my life revolved around thoughts of the tour. I was terribly excited about the prospect, and as Kath told me later, I was like a kid getting ready to go back to boarding school. When the day arrived and I set off on tour with England, I was determined that this was going to be the start of something big. That something big turned out to be a tour round the toilets of Pakistan; but more about that later.

Part of the education process I was undergoing at the time was learning about my team-mates in the England set-up.

The things that make Geoff Boycott tick would give Mike Brearley enough material for a dissertation in his current career as a psychoanalyst, but coming face to face with the man during this formative period of my career, the biggest impression he made on me was just how selfish he could be. Of course all top sportsmen, whatever their level, need to have that quality, but in my opinion and in the opinion of many people who played with 'Fiery' over the years, Boycott simply went too far, too often.

The first time I had seen Boycott's egotistical nature at work on the field had been during my Test debut at Trent Bridge the previous summer.

After we had bowled the Australians out for 243, we slumped to 34 for two in reply. Then Boycott played the ball straight towards a fielder he had not noticed in the covers and set off for a suicidal single, except that he had no intention of committing suicide. Derek Randall, playing at the other end and in front of his home crowd at Nottingham, had to selflessly sacrifice his wicket as the ball came in to the wicket-keeper, allowing Boycott to remain and go on to make what was admittedly a terrific hundred. Boycott's attitude then, and forever after, was that as he was the best batsman in the side; whenever a similar situation occurred it was the other batsman who should be the one to sacrifice his wicket.

The first time that I personally came face-to-face with Boycott's selfishness was on the initial leg of my first tour to Pakistan. It was during this series that Mike Hendrick and I roomed together, or should I say, 'bathroomed' together as that was where we spent most of our time, taking it in turns to crawl between toilet and basin. We had contracted amoebic dysentery, not a pleasant illness to have in the heat of the Pakistan, and although I'm not a whinger, from time to time it got so bad I never thought I would be able to wear light-coloured trousers again. At one point I actually thought I was dying. It didn't help that we were hardly living in the lap of luxury when it came to some of the hotel accommodation. At least we were never lonely, as when we got to our room there were all kinds of pals around to keep us company such as rats, cockroaches and other local wildlife. On turning off the bedroom light, you could often hear them scurrying along the skirting boards, under the floorboards and behind the walls.

However, both Mike and I were determined to give it our best shot to try and establish ourselves in the side, and we attempted to pull the wool over the eyes of the management over the seriousness of our condition. Reporting for duty on the morning of the final warm-up match before the Test in front of the disbelieving selectors and physio

Bernard Thomas, we managed about 50 yards of one lap around the ground before collapsing in a sorry heap.

And then came Boycott. He had got wind of the fact that Mike and I had begged our wives for and had received Red Cross parcels of tinned food to ease our condition. One evening there was a knock on our door. It was Boycott.

'Hello, lads,' he chirped. 'I've got some Dundee cake here and I wonder if you would like to swap . . .'

He was unbelievable! Mike and I were going through hell and all the time Boycs had this little hoard of goodies stored away for his own consumption. Now, when he knew we had something to trade, it suddenly became available.

Being unable to get on the field and give it my all proved a great frustration for me, not least because, despite my successful introduction to Test cricket, I had found out that I still had something to prove to the man who mattered most. Just before going down with dysentery, I had had a private chat with Mike Brearley about my role on tour. I was full of myself and I wanted to be heavily involved yet I felt I was not really getting a fair crack of the whip. Brears simply informed me that he considered Chris Old as his premier all-rounder, and he had chosen to go with him. I told Brears that I didn't agree with his assessment of our relative merits. But he was spared any further confrontation with me as the dreaded belly-bug laid me low.

In fact (and this is somewhat ironic bearing in mind what I have already said about Brearley's influence on my career) it was not until he himself was out of the picture after returning home with a broken arm and Boycott had taken over as captain for the New Zealand leg, that I had my chance to get things moving again.

The first Test at Wellington was one of the strangest I have ever played in, and not simply for the fact that after 48 years and 48 Tests between the two countries it was the Kiwis' first win over England. Strong winds blew throughout the match and these conditions seemed to affect our Geoffrey. After winning the toss he put New Zealand in and they made 228. Then when it came to our turn for a bat, I was witness to one of the most tedious innings I have ever seen in my life. Boycs's 77 made on the third day went like this: 10 runs in the first hour, 12 runs in the second, 6 runs in the third (including a boundary), 12 runs in the fourth, Zzzzzzz. The innings lasted seven hours 22 minutes and he faced 304 balls. Call International Rescue.

As a team we must have been bored out of our minds because although we needed only 137 in the second innings to win we completely fell apart, scoring 64 all out to lose by 72 runs. In fairness, the main factor in the Kiwis' first ever win over England was the brilliant bowling of Richard Hadlee, who took ten wickets for 100 in the match.

Boycott's behaviour in the second Test at Christchurch was even more amazing. We were determined to level the series and I set myself to play a big innings. It was not the most spectacular of my career but my maiden Test hundred was one of the most satisfying. I was given tremendous support by our 'keeper Bob Taylor who had been with me for almost five hours when I repaid him for all his efforts by running him out. I was on 99 when nerves got the better of me and I shouted for a suicidal single. After compiling a big first innings total, we just failed to enforce the follow on. But when we did eventually bowl New Zealand out we desperately required quick runs to give us enough time to bowl them out a second time and win the match.

As captain, Boycs knew more than anyone else exactly what was needed, but he was so wrapped up in his own performance that he singularly failed to get the scoreboard moving. Consequently, we only had about 20 runs on the board after 11 overs. Then things turned ugly after a disgraceful incident involving the Kiwi seam bowler Ewen Chatfield and Derek Randall. (Chatfield had nearly died on the field at Auckland on England's visit in 1975 after being hit on the head by a bouncer from Peter Lever. The ball had smashed into his temple and fractured his skull. His heart actually stopped beating for several seconds and only prompt action by the England physiotherapist Bernard Thomas, who used mouth-to-mouth resuscitation and heart massage on the New Zealander, saved his life.) Sadly, Chatfield at that moment committed one of the cardinal sins of cricket. As he reached the wicket to send down a delivery, he suddenly stopped and nicked off the bails while Randall was backing up. As every schoolboy cricketer the world over knows, this is, as they say, 'just not cricket'. It's fair enough if the batsman is seeking to gain an unfair advantage by racing out of the crease too soon, but even then the normal procedure is to issue a warning before carrying out the threat to run him out if he tries it again.

This time Randall was just backing up in the normal way; the umpire had no option but to uphold Chatfield's scandalous appeal and that was the spark for some bad feeling between the sides. When I got out to the wicket to join Boycott, having been promoted up the order to try and increase the scoring rate, I drew the attention of Chatfield to how we felt about what he had done.

'Remember, mate,' I said, 'you've already died once on the cricket field. Anything can happen.'

But at that moment I also had another purpose in mind. Bob Willis, the vice-captain, had sent me out to the crease with the clearest, if most extraordinary of instructions.

'Go and run the bugger out,' Willis said.

As I arrived at the wicket, Boycs came up to me and moaned about how he was trying his best but he just couldn't get the ball off the square. I told him not to worry and that I would sort everything out. So I did: I sorted him out by about ten yards. I hit the ball into the off-side and called him for a run. He never stood a chance. On being given out by the umpire, he just turned and looked at me blankly. 'What have you done? What have you done?' he mumbled as he walked past me back to the pavilion.

By the close of play, we had a lead of 279, enough to help us push home an advantage the next day. But when I got back to the dressing room, I found Boycs still sulking and sitting on a bench with a towel over his head. He was not talking to anyone, and certainly not to me. This wall of silence remained well into the following day.

The only player he did converse with was his Yorkshire team-mate and ally Geoff Cope, with whom he spent the next morning wandering around the outfield agonizing over the declaration and his position as captain.

In the end, we declared at the overnight total then bowled New Zealand out easily to win by lunch time on the final day. That morning session was perhaps one of the most bizarre of my career. Boycs was still not talking to me, so when I was bowling he communicated with me via the other fielders. Whoever was fielding at cover or mid-off would be sent over to say to me 'Boycs wants to know if you want another slip' and I would respond 'Tell him that would be nice'. The fielder would then trot over to Boycs and pass on the message. It was all so unbelievably petty. After the match was over and won, needless to say Boycs took great delight in informing the press of how well his plans had worked out.

The victory, no matter how it was achieved in the end, was especially sweet for me because of my first Test hundred, an innings that proved to me that as well as learning things about people I was also learning things about the game. In my early career, batting was a very straightforward business. 'Get out there and give it a whack' was my philosophy. But if I was going to succeed at the highest level the time had come to give it a bit more thought than that. It was thinking and learning from my experiences in the first Test at Wellington that helped me make the century in the second Test at Christchurch that proved so decisive. At Wellington, Richard Hadlee got me out twice by tempting me into the hook and getting me caught once at square leg and then at deep backward square leg for 7 and 19 respectively.

When we got to Christchurch I remembered the lesson. This time when Hadlee bowled short to me I just let the ball go. It was still an aggressive innings, but it was controlled aggression. It was a lovely feeling to have reached this milestone, and when it was over I just wanted to go out there and do it again.

Another 50 in the second innings to go with my five-wicket haul and my century in the first proved a vital contribution to our levelling the series at 1–1. It also meant that I was well on the way to establishing myself; and the following summer against Pakistan I managed to do just that. In the first Test at Edgbaston I made another century in our victory by an innings and 57 runs, and it was here that I had my first encounter with the kind of controversy that has cast a constant shadow over all my dealings with Pakistan.

The Pakistan players and management were unhappy at the way Bob Willis had bowled at the nightwatchman Iqbal Qasim as they followed on, chasing our 452 for eight declared. Qasim came to the crease late on the Saturday evening to see out the last over, which he did with ease. Then on the Monday, he survived a number of lifting deliveries from Willis without any fuss. Mike Brearley, back in harness after recovering from a broken arm, commented after the match that he felt Qasim was a competent and able player. When Willis tried another approach, by coming round the wicket, he caught Qasim with a lifter that hit him in the mouth, forcing him to retire hurt.

The Pakistan manager, Mahmood Hussain, accused Willis of using unfair tactics, but as I saw it, the problem was not Qasim's lack of ability but the fact the visitors were heading for defeat by an innings inside four days. The way Qasim had batted up until that point proved he was no rabbit.

Nevertheless in the interests of fairness, a compromise was reached between the two managements, and the teams went into the next match at Lord's with a collective total of five players classified as non-batsmen and to be spared the ordeal of the bouncer. Willis and Hendrick were the English players singled out, while the Pakistanis had preservation orders slapped on Qasim, Sikander Bakht and Liaqat Ali. The protection, however, did not spare them from defeat as I enjoyed my best match yet for England.

I scored my third Test century, 108, as we reached 364. In their first innings Willis took five wickets and Phil Edmonds four to force the follow on, and second time around it was my turn with the ball as I took eight wickets for 34. I had been put on at the Nursery End to allow Willis to change ends and I just needed one sniff to get into my rhythm. I took seven wickets in the morning session as their last eight wickets fell for 43, to complete the best return by an England bowler since Jim Laker had taken nine for 37 and ten for 53 against Australia at Old Trafford in 1956. They tell me that this was the best all-round performance ever by an England player.

New Zealand were our next opponents in that 'split' summer of 1978, and although my batting tailed off slightly, my bowling continued to reap rewards. In the three-match series, I took six for 34 in the second Test at Trent Bridge and followed that up with six for 101 and five for 39 in the final Test of the summer at Lord's as we completed three straight wins.

That marked the end of my first year in Test cricket. The apprehensive debutante had come of age; I could be well pleased with my record from eleven Tests of three centuries, eight five-wicket hauls and one bag of ten wickets in a match.

Off the field, things were going fantastically well too. As far as the public were concerned, the void created by Tony Greig's defection to Packer had been well and truly filled. The Fleet Street publicity machine was working overtime to keep tabs on the new 'superstar'; the sponsorship deals, exclusive newspaper articles, and all the other trappings of success were becoming part of our everyday lives. Helped by my agent, the legendary Fleet Street figure Reg Hayter, to whom I had been introduced by Brian Close, a mutual friend, I grabbed everything with both hands. After all, you never know when it is all going to end and I realized that this was the time to cash in. Unfortunately, these developments simply caused more problems for Kath. We had some great times during this period, but because of my off-field commitments, they were becoming fewer and farther between. Most of the functions to which I was invited, whether cricket dinners, pro-am celebrity golf tournaments or other publicity events, were for men only, while the rest of the time was usually spent enjoying typical bachelor pursuits – rounds of golf or nights in the Somerset pubs, for instance. Kath told me later that she felt very much like a spare part, particularly as she was carrying a nine-month-old Liam around with her at the same time. Looking back, I can't blame her for thinking like that. All I can offer in my defence is that my world was travelling at 100 mph. It was heady stuff and my head was spinning.

When it became obvious that I was going to make the trip to Australia that winter, Kath made it quite clear to me that the prospect of another long separation did not fill her with joy. In fact, when I had returned from Pakistan and New Zealand a year earlier, we vowed we would never again be apart from each other for so long. Kath was pregnant again and after consulting the doctors she had been told that she could only come out to Australia provided she returned by the middle of December. If we were going to have any decent time together, it had to be right at the beginning of the tour. The TCCB have never been keen on wives coming out on tour but we wrote off with a formal request and were told that we would be notified in due course. When the TCCB secretary Donald Carr rang to tell me that the answer was no, I told him that this was not good enough and I urged him to do everything in his power to change the decision. The conversations continued throughout the evening but I was getting nowhere fast. Finally, my patience snapped and I issued an ultimatum. 'If you won't allow Kath to join me I shall withdraw from the tour' and I meant it. The next morning an early call from Donald indicated that the ploy had worked and Kath was able to join me for about two and a half weeks.

Many observers chose to concentrate on the fact that we achieved our 5–1 success under Brearley against an Aussie side badly damaged by defections to Packer, but they tended to forget that we had lost some great players of our own. In any case, you can only beat what's there.

I was lucky to make the tour at all, my part in the proceedings being delayed after I cut my wrist badly from accidentally putting my hand through a swinging pub door at a send-off party. I was kept in hospital overnight but the news from the specialist was good. He told me that although the tendons were severed there was, fortunately, no damage to the nerve and the injury would take about three weeks to heal. The reason I recall this incident so well is that it triggered something which gave me my first taste of the darker side of the newspaper industry. Unbeknown to me, while I was in hospital Kath was about to receive unwelcome late-night visitors at our home in Epworth.

There was a knock on the front door to which Kath responded. On our doorstep were two men who introduced themselves as reporters from a national paper.

'Evening Mrs Botham,' said one of them. 'Can you confirm a report we have had that Ian has been badly injured in a fight in a pub and is out of the England tour?'

Donald Carr had told all of us not to say anything to anyone about what had happened until the TCCB had had time to prepare a full statement. Kath, remembering Donald's instructions, was tight-lipped.

'I'm afraid I've got nothing to say.'

Then the other reporter intervened. 'Come off it, luv. We've got the story and whatever you say, even if you say nothing at all, we are still going to print it. Why don't you come clean?'

Kath tried to be polite and told him there was nothing she could add. Next day, however, a story full of innuendo appeared in the tabloids which suggested that I had been involved in a punch-up. From that moment on, both Kath and I realized we had to be extremely wary of the press.

Kath and I arrived in Australia before the start of November 1978 and although it was still a good two weeks before my hand would heal well enough to allow me to play, my determination and will to be fit meant that I was ready for action a fortnight before the first Test was due to start in Brisbane – a recovery that confounded the medical experts.

It might all have been for nought, however, thanks to a dodgy oyster. The night before the Test was due to start, Kath and I visited a seafood restaurant where I tucked into a plate of Oysters Kilpatrick. I don't know about Patrick, but they bloody nearly killed me. I was up all night going various shades of white until, finally, Kath called the paramedics. They gave me something to ease the pain, but unfortunately the side-effects of the drug were such that I was sent into a slumber which a herd of elephants wouldn't have disturbed. I finally woke at around 10 a.m. on the morning of the match and arrived at the ground twenty minutes before the start of play. I was lucky to have made it there at all.

Brears, now with a full chin of beard and christened the 'Ayatollah' by the locals, lost the toss and the Aussies decided to bat. Disastrously, as it turned out, for they were 26 for six and then 53 for seven before struggling through to 116 all out. I took three for 40 and then scored 49 as we built up a 170 run lead. They did better in their second innings and set us 170 to win the match – a total we reached with seven wickets in hand.

I'm not a superstitious person but the next game, my 13th Test match, certainly didn't go my way. For the first time I came out of a Test without a wicket and ugly match figures of none for 100. Even so, England won by 166 runs.

It was not long before another example of Geoff Boycott's peculiar nature surfaced. In a tour match against South Australia at Adelaide, just before Christmas 1978, he again showed his priorities were Boycott first, the rest nowhere. For that game, Boycs had been dropped down to number 11 below Edmonds, Emburey and Lever, and by the time he arrived at the crease we needed nine to win off the last over with Geoff Miller going great guns with a half-century to his name. That became two for victory off the last ball. What happened? 'Dusty' managed to get the ball away to the point boundary and they ran one to tie the match. Would Boycs turn and go for the second? Not if there was the slightest chance of Boycott being run out.

We went into the third Test at Melbourne fancying our chances of making it 3–0 in the series. It was not to be, however, as Brears suffered his first defeat as captain in 16 Tests and Allan Border started his Test career on the winning side. Our batting had begun disastrously in each innings. I was back among the wickets – three for 68 and three for 41 – but, chasing 283 to win in our second innings, we were soon in trouble at 6 for two and capitulated to 179 and defeat by 103 runs.

This was a big shock for the whole party. We had so dominated the first two games and now here we were battling to regain our supremacy. With the score at 2–1, it was far from easy. In the fourth Test at Sydney, I scored 59 out of a disappointing England total of 141, and by the end of the first day the Australians had reached 56 for one.

On the second day, we dug deep and restricted the Aussies to 283 and a lead of 142 runs, but we were soon in trouble again when Boycs was out first ball in the second innings, leg before to Rodney Hogg. It was Boycs' first duck for England for nearly ten years. Derek Randall then began a salvaging operation with a brilliant 150. The Aussie crowd moaned that our scoring rate of 346 in 146 overs was a mite slow, and, surprise, surprise, they even suggested that Arkle should: 'Ave a go, yer mug'. To hell with them, we were fighting for the Ashes.

The last day arrived with the Aussies needing 205 to win in 265 minutes, certainly a reachable target under normal circumstances, but the wicket was beginning to crumble and our spinners John Emburey and Geoff Miller managed to extract enough turn to share seven wickets and have them all out for 111. We were 3–1 up and back in the driving seat.

Our subsequent 205-run victory at Adelaide meant that Brears became the first England captain since Douglas Jardine in the 1932/33 'Bodyline' series to win four Tests on an Ashes tour down under.

England had never beaten the Aussies by a margin as large as 5–1, but that was the prospect ahead of us as the series reached its finale at Sydney. Brears had a real go at us about commitment, saying that the series may have been in the bag but the job was not done. We responded by winning the match by nine wickets. I had now played eight matches against the Aussies and won seven.

On flying home in mid-February, I met my daughter Sarah for the first time. She had been born two weeks before I returned, and thankfully without any of the traumas Kath had suffered over Liam's birth.

But the wheels of international cricket continued to turn. The first half of the home summer of 1979 was taken up with the World Cup, where I made the first of my two appearances in a final at Lord's. We were well beaten in this instance, Viv Richards taking us apart with an awesome 138 not out and Collis King's late blitz taking the West Indies to 286. Although Brears and Boycott put on 129 for the first wicket we were always behind the clock.

The World Cup was followed by a four-Test series against India during which I got back in the groove, twice taking five-wicket hauls in an innings and making my top Test score to date of 137. Luck and the will to win were paying handsome dividends. That 137 at Headingley in the third Test was a typical Botham knock, with the ball flying to all corners of the ground. The match had been interrupted by the weather, but by lunch on the Monday the century was in the bag, although I was disappointed to miss by one run the chance to score a Test century before lunch.

The victory by an innings and 83 runs in the first Test at Edgbaston enabled us to win the series 1–0 but not until we had survived a thrilling draw in the fourth and final Test at The Oval when the Indians, needing 15 from the final over to square the series at 1–1 could not quite manage it and were forced to settle for the draw. In fact, all four results were possible with three balls to go after Sunil Gavaskar had made a memorable 221 to take his side to within reach of their target of 438. That match also marked my first personal milestone in Test cricket. I began my 21st Test needing just three runs to reach the landmark of 1000 runs and 100 wickets in Test cricket quicker than anyone had ever done before. I soon collected those runs on my way to 38. The least said about my second innings in that match the better. I was run out for nought. No prizes for guessing that my batting partner at the time was a certain G. Boycott.

The winter of 1979/80 should have been feeding time for Beefy again, with a short tour to Australia followed by a one-match trip to Bombay for the Indian Golden Jubilee Test. Sadly, the Aussies had got their act together after the Packer defections and despite my haul of 11 wickets in the first Test at Perth, they won by 138 runs. The next game at Sydney was going to be won by the side calling right when it came to the toss, which the Australians did.

At this point our lack of success was causing a bit of

friction within the camp, and unsurprisingly Boycott was again in the thick of it. The pitch was clearly going to favour the bowlers and Boycs didn't fancy it at all. His reluctance to put himself in the firing line almost provoked the normally mild mannered Mike Brearley into thumping him. The pitch at the Sydney Cricket Ground was in a terrible state: it was saturated after two and a half days of rain and it didn't take a genius to work out that it was going to be a quick flyer. Boycs took one look at it and started complaining about his neck being stiff and how he didn't think he was going to be able to play. Brears had his doubts and sent him off to the nets, where he looked in good enough health to us. Finally, he went up to Brears and announced: 'I'm not playing. My neck's still sore'.

Brears saw red; he was literally shaking with rage and I thought for a moment he was going to belt him. Eventually, Boycott was forced to play but we lost the match and with it the three-match series. Other players on that tour had played on through pain and injury, but it seemed that at the first sign of a pitch he didn't fancy, in my opinion Boycs had tried to jump ship. As far as many of us were concerned, that was the last straw. If Boycs was going to pick and choose his games, he could go and play with himself. I for one didn't go out of my way to talk to him again on that trip. By the time the third game arrived, it was all over for us, even though Graham Gooch hit 99 before running himself out with his maiden Test century in sight and I scored an undefeated 119 in the second innings.

Before flying to India we made a conscious decision to enjoy ourselves come what may. Bearing in mind the difficulty obtaining decent beer on the sub-continent, we dumped as much of our clothing as we could to make room in our bags for supplies, and then we went out and bought up virtually the entire stock of the local Australian grog.

I had never been there before so I was in for a huge culture shock. It may have been a shortish stay but I soon came to appreciate that this was a thrilling and magnificent country. 'Deadly' Derek Underwood, my room-mate, had seen it all before, though there were the odd occasions when even he was taken by surprise. Take, for example, our first night in the Taj Mahal hotel, when he put my smart blue leather shoes outside the bedroom door for cleaning . . . and that was the last I saw of them! I expect they are still in service all these years later.

There was a lot of unwinding to do after the tensions of the previous five months. Off the field, Deadly was collaborating with his ghost writer Chris Lander on a book but not getting very far. Poor Deadly, he wanted some peace and quiet in order to finish it once and for all, but of course if Lander came to our room, we ended up chatting and drinking to all hours with the result that no work would be done. Then they tried to beat me at my own game by going off to Lander's suite, but I soon became bored on my own. So I joined them – with the same result.

On more than one occasion I dragged them up to the French restaurant at the top of the hotel. One evening, Deadly became so intoxicated that he started imagining he was on the dance floor and began gyrating on the table where some unfortunate Indian couple were trying to eat their meal. At this point I decided it was time to make a tactical withdrawal. The following morning I went to see the manager of the hotel and asked him if he knew whose meal we had disturbed. He told me and I immediately arranged for them to be sent tickets for the Test match as a form of apology. It turned out to be one of the best moves of my career, because from then on nothing was too much trouble for him.

This was the trip where I really got to know Lander, who was later to become an essential member of the Leukaemia Walk team. It was also the tour where he picked up the nickname 'Crash', which came about when Deadly and Lander tried another dodge to avoid me and settle down to work on the book. One night they disappeared up to the hotel penthouse suite where a female entertainer was providing the cabaret in the bar. They reasoned that I would never think of looking for them in the bar if I thought they were working. Bad planning, boys. After a few 'soft drinks' (orange juice laced with something a bit special) Lander was flying. Somehow he ended up on the stage, performing the original Karaoke in front of an audience that took a long time to warm up but, once they had, were quite ecstatic. Then, suddenly, the full impact of the drink took its toll.

I've heard of singers like Tom Jones walking into the audience to meet his fans. Crash took rather more direct action: he slipped and fell head first into them. Hence the nickname was born.

I managed to do some more damage to him later on tour. One night during the Test match we went back to his room armed with a couple of bottles of brandy and ordered up some tandoori chicken from the kitchen. Suitably prepared for a memorable feast, we got ourselves comfortable and settled back for an evening in front of the television. But on switching it on and despite fiddling for what seemed like an age with the controls, we couldn't get a decent reception, and in my frustration I hurled a chicken bone at the screen. The bone missed and instead hit the wall behind and bounced off it, before lodging itself in the back of the set, at which point, almost miraculously, the television started working again.

It was a good night and we had a few laughs, but as the television programmes made no sense I decided to take on the job of entertainments officer. I set Crash and Deadly a challenge: standing on the table, they had to drink some brandy, eat the tandoori chicken and read a passage from the Gideon Bible at the same time. Not surprisingly, they failed miserably in this task.

The next morning Crash woke up to find he had spent the night with several pieces of chicken. With head throbbing, he struggled across the room to turn on the television in order to watch the cricket before falling back on his bed. He was meant to be covering the game but was too ill to get there, and this was the best he could do.

He couldn't believe his eyes. For the England bowler he saw running in and taking a wicket with the first ball of the day was yours truly! The next thing he saw was smoke rising from behind the set. He shot across the room to find a plate load of tandoori chicken simmering away gently in the back of the telly. I can't imagine how it got there.

In fact, my performance in the match – a century and 13 wickets – probably secured for me the job of England captain once we returned home for the summer series with the West Indies. Little did the selectors know what had been behind it.

All in all, the events of the past three years had been quite an introduction to Test cricket. One thing for which I will always be grateful is that during those extraordinary times on and off the field, Mike Brearley was around when I needed him. I firmly believe that if circumstances had been different, lessons I learned from him would have helped me become a successful England captain.

As it turned out, I was an unsuccessful England captain.

6
JUST CALL ME CAPTAIN

I didn't go out of my way to get the job of England captain. It was my belief that I was more than capable of rising to the task, but I never really thought I would have a chance of proving it. In the event, I did get that chance and although England failed to win a Test while I was in charge, in my view I did a fairly decent job.

My sadness was that once I had lost the England captaincy I knew I would never get it back again, the reason being that those who wished to prove that the captaincy affected my performance were given all the evidence they needed during my tenure in the job.

To a certain extent my form deserted me during my period in charge, but as far as I am concerned that was pure coincidence. Until that time, my career had been more or less one continuous success story. I was bound to have a poor run of form somewhere along the line; it just happened to be while I was captain of my country.

Although I was an instinctive cricketer, relying more on practice than theory, most of the captains I have played under have thought enough of my tactical awareness to have used me as a sounding-board. That was certainly true of Mike Gatting, David Gower, and to a lesser extent Mike Brearley. During the winter of 1979/80, against an Australian side which had just welcomed back the Packer players, and then against India for the Golden Jubilee Test in Bombay, Brears co-opted me on to the England selection committee, which meant I was in a position of responsibility ahead of more senior players.

When he got back from that tour, Brears had already made up his mind that he did not want to go abroad in the winter with England again. His aim was to concentrate on his training in psychoanalysis, for which he was clearly ideally suited, so it was obvious that a new captain had to be found. I think his preference would have been to carry on as captain for the early part of that 1980 home series against the West Indies. He considered me as his natural successor, and by staying on as captain for the summer he could have helped ease me into the job and kept an eye on me at the same time.

In hindsight, I believe that if this had happened my career as captain would almost certainly have lasted far longer than it did. Brears could have taught me a lot about how to get the best out of players.

Brian Close, who was an England selector at the time, was the only one who saw the danger looming. He was violently opposed to the idea of making me captain: he was convinced that at the relatively youthful age of twenty-four, I was not ready for it yet. Not only would my own game suffer from the burden of responsibility, he reasoned, but I was also far too naive and inexperienced (not to mention headstrong) to be able to cope with the man-management side of the job.

I have to admit that as far as the last point is concerned,

Closey was probably right. Terms like 'man-management' meant little to me. Another word I could never understand when it came to playing for England was 'motivation'. Why should anyone ever need motivating when they are playing for their country? Basically, my approach to man-management amounted to little more than making sure nobody drank alone and everyone got their round in at the bar. In fact, that caused problems later when, during the tour to the Caribbean in 1980/81, I attempted to ban Graham Gooch from going on training runs during the day because he was always nodding off in the evenings. As far as I was concerned, the sound of Goochie snoring when I was trying to tell a joke was detrimental to team spirit. On a more serious note, I felt he was just doing too much and I wanted him fresh where it mattered, on the pitch.

Whatever my failings in that department, when I took on the job of captaincy I was absolutely convinced that I could do it. Whatever misgivings Closey had, there were no doubts in my mind. If you are offered the captaincy of England you don't say 'No' or 'Not yet, but come back and see me in six months time'. The only possible answer is 'Yes . . . anytime, anyplace, anywhere'. There is no greater honour than to lead your country.

What I didn't know at the time, and could never have guessed, was that I had just sustained an injury which, eight years later, very nearly brought my career to a close. During the periods when the severity of my back complaint increased, I often thought back to the moment on that shivering day in April 1980 when, playing for Somerset against Oxford University at The Parks, I felt a slight twinge in my back. I hadn't taken the trouble to loosen up sufficiently before starting a bowling spell and, at first, I put the stiffness down to that. The pain was no bother to begin with in fact – I bowled 25 overs with it – but on the final day it was giving me so much trouble that I reverted to bowling off-breaks. During that summer it got progressively worse, particularly as having given up smoking I put on a little too much weight which exacerbated the problem. I even had to resort to wearing a corset in the first Test at Trent Bridge. When X-rays revealed that I had a deformity of the spine, an operation was considered but the idea was eventually shelved because the experts felt that it might put extra strain on the adjoining vertebrae.

I bowled through varying degrees of pain from that day on. I never knew when it was going to flare up again, and by and large I succeeded in putting it to the back of my mind until, in 1988, the operation became a necessity rather than an option.

My reign as England captain began with the two one-day Prudential matches against the West Indies at the end of May 1980. The first, a rain-affected game at Leeds which ran into a second day, we lost by 24 runs. The West Indies batted first and scored 198 all out in 55 overs. In reply, Chris Tavaré top scored in the match with 82 and I hit 30, but from a position of 38 for four we were always facing an uphill struggle, and we were eventually all out for 174.

The next match on 30 May was at Lord's and I won the toss again, choosing to field. The West Indies made 235 for nine, mainly due to some fine bowling by Vic Marks. Geoff Boycott and Peter Willey laid solid foundations for our reply – 135 for the first wicket in 33 overs – but then we lost four wickets for 25 runs. It was not until I arrived at the crease that we managed to pull the game back our way. Supported by Vic Marks, I scored an unbeaten 42 and hit the winning boundary off Joel Garner with nine balls to spare. The series had ended 1–1 but the West Indies took the trophy on a higher scoring-rate over the two matches.

It was not a bad introduction to the England captaincy, but there is a world of difference between a one-day international and a Test match and I was yet to be appointed to the latter role. The following day, 31 May, Alec Bedser called to let me know that the job was mine. I was obviously thrilled. I had no misgivings, it was *the* job in cricket and I was supremely confident of making a success of it. I was the youngest England captain, since Ivo Bligh in 1882/83. (Incidentally, Ivo's other claim to fame was to lead his side to the defeat that prompted those ladies of Melbourne to burn the bails and present the ashes to him in an urn.)

By a strange quirk of the fixture list, the day I was given the news coincided with Somerset's game against Middlesex at Taunton, where the new captain of England was in opposition to the ex-captain, Mike Brearley. Mike had also been phoned and told the news by Bedser before play began, and he was first to come across and congratulate me.

I could not have been handed a harder introduction to Test cricket than back-to-back series with the West Indies and a Centenary Test against the Australians in between. Throw in the political problems in the Caribbean on the 1980/81 winter tour and you can see that I had my work cut out.

In fact, as a team we did pretty well. I seriously believe that if we had had a little bit of luck we might even have taken the first series. The single result came about in the first Test match at Trent Bridge, a game we came so close to winning, and after that we performed pretty creditably to draw the other four. Obviously the weather helped us in certain situations, but I personally believe it also helped the West Indies to survive at Old Trafford. It was a case of swings and roundabouts.

In those days, England were facing a mighty West Indies side. In the batting department, Gordon Greenidge and Desmond Haynes were the openers, followed by Viv Richards, Alvin Kallicharran and Clive Lloyd. As for the bowling, Malcolm Marshall, Andy Roberts, Joel Garner and Michael Holding made up one of the most awesome attacks ever seen in Test cricket.

My first Test in charge against the West Indies at Trent Bridge was a tremendous match. The rift with the Packer brigade had been healed and both Bob Woolmer and Alan Knott were back in the side for the first time since 1977. I won the toss and decided we should bat. I went on to prove that I could captain the side without losing my natural aggression by top scoring in the first innings with 57 as we made 263.

The West Indies replied by making 308, with Viv Richards and Deryck Murray both hitting 64 while I picked up three for 50 and Bob Willis returned four for 82. Second time around we made 252, leaving them a target of 208 in just over eight hours. It was never going to be easy against our attack of Bob Willis, John Lever, Mike Hendrick and myself as the pitch was doing a bit. When Greenidge was caught behind off Bob by Alan Knott with the score at 11, we felt that another breakthrough would be decisive. Unfortunately, Viv Richards tore into the bowling, scoring 48 in 56 minutes to ease the pressure on the rest of the batsmen. Although I got his wicket just before the close, when the last day started the West Indies needed only 99 to win with eight wickets in hand.

The crowd barely reached 1000 but those that bothered to come saw us win, lose, win and ultimately lose the game. As the day wore on, wickets fell regularly and the tension mounted. When the West Indies were 180 for seven, thanks to Bob Willis' five for 65, we felt a win was within our grasp. They were still 23 from victory and despite two dropped slip catches things were going our way. And then disaster struck.

In those days, if you had to pick a fielder to take a catch to win a Test match, the man you would turn to without hesitation was David Gower. Ninety-nine times out of a hundred he would have snapped up Andy Roberts at cover off Bob without even thinking about it. This just happened to be the hundredth time. No one on the field could believe it, least of all David. You can never say that one catch is the difference between winning and losing; but just how important that particular chance had been to both sides became obvious when, after he was run out for 62 by a direct throw from Peter Willey, Des Haynes ran from the field in tears believing his mistake had probably cost the West Indies the game, even though only three runs were required with two wickets remaining. If only he had been right . . .

The second Test at Lord's was affected by rain and on the last day we managed only half an hour before play ended. At that point we were 133 for two chasing a first innings deficit of 249 runs. Some said we were saved by the weather, but we were playing well enough not to have needed any help from the elements. The highlights of the game were a knock of 123 from Graham Gooch followed by Des Haynes hitting 184 and Viv Richards 145.

The weather dominated again at Old Trafford for the third Test where ten and a half hours were lost to rain and bad light, but again we were fighting back in the second innings after collapsing first time round to 150 all out.

At The Oval our best batting performance of the summer put us in the driving seat as we finished our first innings with 370 on the board. I then claimed my 150th Test wicket, the sweet prize of Viv Richards who was brilliantly held by Peter Willey in the gully. The West Indies finished 105 behind us and but for a battling 61 from Faoud Bacchus we could have been in an even better position. The advantage, however, quickly swung away from us at that point and in our second innings we plummeted to 18 for four. Peter Willey then got us out of jail with 100 not out in an unbeaten last wicket stand with Bob Willis worth 117, and that allowed us to declare at 209 for nine. However, time ran out and our chance of winning the series went with it.

We finished the series with another draw at Leeds where two days were lost to rain. A poor first innings of 143 was trumped by the West Indies score of 245 but we did better in the second innings and were 227 for six when play came to an end. I had finished the series with 13 wickets and 169 runs and was left to reflect on what might have been if David Gower had held on to that catch at Trent Bridge.

There was no break for the team as the Australians were over for the Centenary Test at Lord's, and we warmed up for the game with two comfortable one-day international victories over them at The Oval and Edgbaston.

Once again the weather intervened to spoil the big day at Lord's. Australia, with Graeme Wood hitting 112 and Kim Hughes 117, declared at 385 for five. We struggled and were all out for 205, undone by Dennis Lillee's four for 43 and Len Pascoe's five for 59. The Aussies then made 189 for four declared in their second innings and set us a target of 370. We were 244 for three when time ran out, Geoff Boycott on 128 not out. It was not much of a game and the main talking point was the scuffle on the Saturday afternoon during which two MCC members had a set-to with umpire David Constant.

Constant, Dickie Bird, Greg Chappell and myself had just returned from a fifth pitch inspection and were entering the Long Room when the scuffle began. Chappell and I had to step in to cool down the situation and when the umpires eventually came out to start play at 3.45 p.m. they had to have a police escort through the Long Room.

That said a lot about a section of the MCC membership, as I was to find out a year later when their behaviour and reaction towards me in the second Test against Australia was the straw that broke the captain's back. I still won't forgive them for the way they behaved that day, and I know a lot of players who feel the same. A tame draw marked the end of the season for me and it was back to my home in Epworth for a break and the chance to go fishing and play some football and golf before heading out to the West Indies in the New Year.

What should have been a quiet time turned out to be nothing of the sort.

I have always enjoyed my football and before marrying

Kath I would travel down from Yorkshire to Ilminster Town on the Saturday for a match, returning to Yorkshire for the Sunday fixtures of Moorends Trinity. As Scunthorpe was close and I knew some of the players at the football club, I would train there. Football was a great way of taking my mind off things.

I had a few games for the reserves and the coach John Kaye recommended me to the manager Ron Ashman. I played two first-team games for them, coming on as a substitute a few minutes after half-time in a 3–3 draw at Bournemouth on 25 March 1980. I made another substitute's appearance in the following game, a 3–1 defeat at home by Wigan. I was still a registered non-contract player for the next season and would train with the players because I enjoyed it. I got on particularly well with the goalkeeper, Joe Neenan. Every Christmas the team had a night out in Scunthorpe and I was invited along to join in the celebrations.

The fortunes of Scunthorpe were hardly soaring at the time because they had just lost a second round FA Cup replay against non-League Altrincham. That may not sound like the end of the world, but the crucial point was that if they had won, their next opponents in the third round would have been Liverpool . . . at Anfield!

Joe gave away a penalty and Altrincham won 1–0. You could say he was feeling a touch sensitive.

We went to a nightclub called Tiffany's and had a few drinks. Now earlier in the evening Joe had taken some stick from some troublemakers and on going to the gents there had been a bit of a scuffle, but because I was at the bar I knew nothing about this. Eventually, the time to leave arrived and we moved outside on to the pavement to meet the mini-bus whereupon Joe encountered his friends again, who were still having a go at him. Joe was no push-over. He stuck up for himself and eventually had to be pulled away and you would have thought that would have been a lesson for them. But they refused to leave it alone and stupidly they carried on baiting him. Finally, my patience snapped. If they wanted trouble, they could have it. Joe was a mate of mine and I was going to stick up for him. He chased them down the road and I set off after him. I must have been fit at the time because apparently we had covered 600 yards to catch them. At this point Joe cornered this bloke, Steven Isbister, in a 'ten foot' (the local Scunthonian name for an alleyway) that runs between terraced houses in Berkeley Street.

Joe, who had been severely provoked, thumped Isbister in the jaw and that seemed to settle things. As far as we were concerned the incident was over and done with. The next day, however, all hell broke loose. The newspapers were full of it, running stories along the lines of 'Ian Botham Beat Me Up'.

Eventually, Joe and myself were charged with assault 'occasioning actual bodily harm' and the case came up at Scunthorpe magistrates' court in January 1981. Joe said he couldn't afford to plead not guilty and go to the Crown Court, and he insisted that he would rather take the £50 fine and forget it. That, in my opinion, is a sad state of affairs and says little for justice, but he reckoned he had no choice. In the end, he was fined £100 plus costs, while I pleaded not guilty and elected for trial in the Crown Court.

That posed a few problems to say the least. First, the TCCB were not overjoyed about the England captain facing assault charges in the first place. Second, there was the danger that the date for the hearing might be set while I was meant to be in the West Indies. Meanwhile, there was a third party interested in the events in court, namely Thames Television. Unbeknown to me they were preparing to feature me on This is Your Life and they decided that, if I was convicted, they would have to shelve it. In the end Thames delayed the programme until the case came to its conclusion almost a year later. Had I known beforehand that they were planning this, I would have refused to appear on the programme. I know a lot of people say that, but I mean it. If Eamonn Andrews had come out to me with his Little Red Book I would have told him, politely of course, what he could do with it. The idea of somebody saying 'This Is Your Life' to a 24-year-old is quite ridiculous.

In the event Alan Herd managed to sort out the trial date and I was able to lead the England tour to the West Indies that winter without any problem.

The case eventually went to Grimsby Crown Court later that year where it was revealed that Isbister, a naval rating, had previous convictions for attacking a man of fifty and for criminal damage. Two of his witnesses, who were friends, also had records for theft and criminal damage and one of them for causing actual bodily harm as well. The irony was that the police had described them as typical Scunthonians – if that was the case then God help Scunthorpe. I was eventually acquitted and Don Oslear, the locally-based Test umpire who had come along to give me some moral support, said he was astonished that the case had ever got to court in the first place.

Later, would you believe, Isbister and I almost bumped

into each other again. While in Barbados on the 1981 tour, some of the players were invited by the captain of *HMS Invincible*, which was berthed out in the West Indies, to come on board. I learned later that Isbister had been one of the crew. Just as well they kept him well away from me.

This was the start of the bad publicity, the snowball that soon became an avalanche and at one point in my career very nearly buried me for good.

As for my captaincy on the 1980/81 tour to the Caribbean, my approach was straightforward. I was happy to pick a side, then go out on the field and play the game. I think that caused problems because some of my teammates wanted and expected more from me than I was able to give. As I have said, man-management was never my strong point, and it certainly wasn't at this stage of my life, aged 25. Once for instance, when I told the press if we didn't improve on our performances that 'heads will roll', it took me a few hours to extract my foot from my mouth.

The other aspect of the job at which I was not particularly adept was all the red tape and horse-trading that went on with the selectors. They would sit around the table and say: 'Well if you want to take player X, I'll agree with you providing you back my choice of player Y'. This went on all the time. On this tour, for instance, I wanted to take along Roland Butcher, the Middlesex batsman. I had a gut feeling that he was the man for the trip, with the technique and flair to cope with wickets where there was that bit more bounce. He had also played out in the West Indies before, not to mention the fact that he was a magnificent fielder.

The selectors, however, were pushing for me to take Bill

Athey instead, and it was a real battle to get them to accept my choice. As things turned out, Athey was chosen as first reserve and came out when Brian Rose returned home with eye problems.

The tour was beset by difficulties from the start. In the first seven weeks we managed only 17 days of cricket, the weather turning practice tracks into strips that were untypical of the West Indies, we had the Jackman–Guyana affair and, worst of all, the death of Ken Barrington, the assistant manager and coach, and a close personal friend.

There is absolutely no doubt in my mind that the political pressure of the Guyana situation contributed to Kenny's death. He was a worrier and the tense situation caused him a great deal of stress. It was a stunning and awful blow to us as a team and as his friends.

Kenny was a great influence on me. I used to terrorise him with various practical jokes, like turning up the flame in his cigarette lighter without letting him know, and setting fire to his newspaper. He had a wonderful line in gobbledygook. I'll never forget, for instance, the time when he attempted to explain one of my dismissals as being a result of the fact that I had been caught in 'two-man's land'. The players had a huge amount of respect for him and he was always genuinely concerned with our problems and, unlike so many former Test players, he resisted the temptation to hark back to how things were better in his day.

Kenny was tremendously helpful to me personally. He realized that I was young and inexperienced in some matters and did everything he could to advise and encourage me.

There was no hint of the difficulties we were later to

confront when we started the tour with a 190-run win over the Young West Indian XI at Pointe-à-Pierre in Trinidad, then won two one-day games in the Windward Islands before the first one-day international in St Vincent. Here, we bowled really well to restrict the West Indies to 127 but found the going just as tough when we batted, losing four wickets for one run at one stage. We then dug in and crept close to the total but eventually ran out of batsmen to lose by two runs. Colin Croft took six for 15.

The first Test was at Port-of-Spain in Trinidad where we lost by an innings and 79 runs. The West Indies batted first and though nobody passed three figures there were sizeable contributions right down the order and they declared at 426 for nine. Our first innings subsequently collapsed against the hostility of Garner, Croft, Roberts and Holding and we were all out for 178 and asked to follow-on. Only David Gower and Graham Gooch among the English batsmen scored more than 40.

In the second innings, Geoff Boycott hit 70 but the rest of the side folded and we were all out for 169. I received some flak for trying to hit Viv Richards out of the ground and holing out to Michael Holding for 16, but the ball was there to be hit and I felt I could not shelve my natural game just because I was captain.

One down in the series . . . and our real problems were only just beginning. Our key strike bowler, Bob Willis, had been struggling with a serious knee injury for most of the tour and finally had to fly home. This was a huge blow to me because not only was Bob my vice-captain, he was also a good friend, ally and confidant. Throughout the tour I never really felt I was getting the full support of all the players. Bob's withdrawal made things even more difficult.

On 23 February his replacement, the Surrey pace bowler Robin Jackman, flew out to join us in Guyana. Both Jackman and the person to replace Willis as vice-captain were to quickly become hot issues.

When Jackman first arrived, a Guyanese radio commentator said that his inclusion in our side was in breach of the Gleneagles Agreement – the sporting boycott of South Africa that contributed to the eventual dismantling of apartheid. Jackman's name was on a United Nations blacklist because he had played and coached in the Republic. The British government insisted, however, that the agreement was not relevant in this case because it did not refer to actions by individuals. After all, there were other members of the England team who had played in South Africa and at no time was there any attempt to hide the facts. But that was not good enough in Guyana where Jackman had his visitor's permit withdrawn and was told by the Guyanese authorities to leave the country.

The tour manager, A.C. Smith, and the rest of the England management responded by saying that England would not play the second Test because it was no longer possible for us to select the team of our choice without outside restrictions being imposed upon us. 'AC' did a bloody good job during this fiasco, as he did later after Kenny died. In fact, his input throughout this tour and especially later on during the 'Sex, drugs and rock 'n' roll' trip to New Zealand in 1983/84 was tremendously helpful. I was pleasantly surprised. Before we left for the Caribbean I was under the impression that all the TCCB members were the same – stiff-upper-lip Oxbridge twerps. A.C. Smith proved to be an exception: he saw the players' point of view and, when he could, he backed us to the hilt. Furthermore, he was not one of those egoists who considered himself to be more important than the cricketers under his charge. As far as the press guys were concerned, getting a juicy 'quote' from him was about as easy as getting a drink out of Boycs. They joked that if you asked A.C. whether it was raining, he would go to the window, look out, come back and say 'Yes, but don't quote me on that.' But the players appreciated that he made it his business to keep such a low profile as to be almost invisible.

Things in Guyana were hotting up, and we were up all hours holding meetings and trying to find out what was going on. The atmosphere was very unpleasant; local hostility was being stirred up against us and we were effectively prisoners at our hotel. We couldn't go out in to the town as that would have been far too dangerous so we spent three days hanging about the hotel doing very little. Behind the scenes negotiations were going on, messages were travelling backwards and forwards and everyone was on edge. One evening, I looked across at Kenny Barrington and I could see how tense and uptight he was getting. I told him he had to go off and relax. None of us had been getting much sleep, but I don't think Kenny had slept a wink.

I'm not the type to feel intimidated or threatened by any situation, but this was the one occasion in my life where I felt very unsure about what was going to happen next. We were cooped up in the hotel trying to behave as normally as possible, and although the manager tried to help by providing a stock of videos to help relieve the tedium it was a miserable time. We did manage to get out once, to an official function. From the windows of the coaches transporting us from our hotel, we saw these locals walking the streets armed to the teeth with guns, knives and machetes – and this was just the everyday folk going about their business. Guyana at that time was just waiting to explode.

Everybody was affected by the situation, even the normally unflappable John Emburey. One day we found a gym and I suggested to the players that we go and relieve some of the boredom by playing a game of five-a-side football. But we did not have any bibs so it was to be skins against shirts. 'Embers', who has been a very good friend over the years, was on the skins' side.

'I can't play like this,' he moaned.

It's the only row I can ever remember having with him. I exploded. 'Look Embers', I said, 'we're trying to do something positive here and all you can do is moan. Just shut up and get on with it.'

It seems like a small thing now, but at the time it wasn't. It was a perfect example of how the tension was getting to all of us.

We did manage to play a one-day match at Berbice which is a town in the middle of swamp and jungle country reached by military helicopter. There were two helicopters and all the England team climbed into the first one and headed up country, except for me. I was left to ride with the West Indian side. Given the volatility of the situation this was probably the safest place to be. We played the game, lost by six wickets, and the minute the match was over the helicopters reappeared and we were whisked back to Georgetown.

The second Test match was duly cancelled. We were eventually forced to leave Guyana on the morning of 27 February but the other Caribbean countries were anxious that the tour should proceed. There was a long delay at

Georgetown airport before a highly relieved England party headed off to a warmer welcome in Barbados. Everyone was delighted when the wheels of that plane left the ground and when we reached Barbados you could see the team spirit flood back. Talks on the future of the tour were still taking place, however, and it was not until 4 March, following another round of meetings this time with representatives of the governments of Barbados, Montserrat, Antigua and Jamaica, that it was announced we would continue.

The Guyana escapade had been ridiculous; a case of two-bit politicians gone mad. The whole thing had been blown absurdly out of proportion. Of course Jackman was feeling the pressure, but then we all were and the consensus had been that the sooner we got out of Guyana the better. In many ways, Jackman coped really well. I remember when I first played against him I wanted to knock his head off because he really antagonised me; I thought 'you arrogant, strutting gnome'. But then I got to know him and found he was the life and soul of the party and a brilliant team man. He would bowl all day, bat all day, and do anything a captain could have wanted.

He also had a fabulous sense of humour and when we travelled on coaches he would sit at the front, grab the microphone normally used by the tourist guide and entertain us with his Tony Hancock routine (he was in some way related to Hancock). I'm convinced he was good enough to have gone on the stage.

A further problem we had to confront was who should take over from Bob Willis as vice-captain. The two names I had in mind were Peter Willey and Graham Gooch, and in the end I wanted Gooch only for Lord's to veto me – a decision made from 4000 miles away that proved, not that I needed it, what an antiquated and outdated organization I was dealing with. How could those sitting at Lord's appreciate the circumstances of our situation? How could they understand the requirements of the team? Surely, when a team is on tour the best policy is to take the advice of the captain and the tour manager.

In my eyes the senior professional on the tour was Peter Willey. I had a lot of respect for him because he was tough, he fought fire with fire and would not be intimidated. If you wanted a good and hard true pro, then Peter Willey was your man. He had his moans now and again but when it came to the crunch he was the player you wanted next to you. 'Will' was an essential player in the team and had already played his part: there was no need to make him the vice-captain. One evening in Guyana we were at a reception where we both had a glass of scotch or two. I took him to one side and asked him if there was anything he thought I should be doing that I had not done yet. He made a few sound, sensible tactical suggestions but also said something that made me stop and think.

He pointed out that I was a young captain and had always been one of the boys, which was perhaps not the best thing given my position. Will said it would give me more clout if I could distance myself a little and go off and do my own thing because by mixing with the rest of the lads I was unconsciously undermining my authority as captain. This was hard for me, probably the hardest part of being captain, but Will was right. However, I wanted Will to carry on giving me that kind of input from an objective standpoint, not as my number two.

My mind made up on the vice-captaincy issue, I

approached Graham Gooch to find out how he felt about it, and he was happy to accept. I felt by promoting Graham we could have got more from him and he would thrive on the responsibility as has since been proved. After he had given me the green light, I put my thoughts to A.C. Smith and Kenny Barrington and they supported me. The Board then turned round and said bluntly, 'No, Geoff Miller is the vice-captain'.

I was stunned and argued the point with A.C. and Kenny but there was nothing I could do: Alec Bedser and the selectors had made a decision from London that was non-negotiable.

'But we've still got a problem,' I told them. 'Geoff might not play in all the games.'

I then had to go and see Graham and tell him I was sorry, and although I wanted him, the Board didn't. He took it well and that was one difficult conversation dealt with only for another one to follow: telling Geoff Miller about his new position within the England party.

Geoff was taken by surprise. He actually said that it could be a bit embarrassing because he thought he would not be in the side for all the Tests. This was exactly the point I was trying to make with the Board. We ended up with this ridiculous situation at selection meetings where Geoff was volunteering to sit outside the room until it was decided whether he was in the team or not. I said to him that was nonsensical, we were meant to be behaving as reasonable adults. If the Board's decision defied all logic, the fact they refused to tell me why they wanted Geoff and not Graham was even more irritating, They categorically refused to discuss it and, to this day, I am still waiting for an explanation.

The tour contract meant I had to stay silent, and I was unable to say a word publicly about the Board's meddling. I have often wondered if things might have turned out differently if I had got my way and Graham had been vice-captain.

If these were not problems enough, I was still coming to terms with captaining the side. I freely admit that understanding what motivates the players has always been a difficult area for me. Chris Old was one who tended to be overawed rather than inspired by playing for his country, as one incident in particular demonstrated.

We were in Bridgetown preparing for the third Test on a wicket that could have been tailor-made for Chris, and Kenny said we should have him in the side. I said he did not seem that keen on playing, but Kenny insisted we had to play him and I was happy to agree. On the morning of the match, ten minutes before we were due to toss up, Chris came up to me and said he couldn't play.

'What do you mean you can't play?' I asked him.

'I've been stung.'

'By what?' I enquired.

'I don't know,' he said.

'Where?' I pressed him.

'Somewhere,' he said and walked off. I could think of no other reason for his actions other than he had simply bottled out. I was so incensed that instead of trying to talk him round I bawled him out, leaving him in no doubt as to my assessment of his character.

Now if I had been Mike Brearley, and this was something I would learn later, I would have walked up to Chris and told him that the wicket was ideal for him, that he was the best man for the job and I really needed him in the side. Instead, I was getting myself psyched up for the game, I was winding up the other players and just didn't have the time or the inclination to get involved with this kind of nonsense. 'Chilly' subsequently faded out over the rest of the tour; we ended up playing Graham Stevenson instead and he did a good job for us. The difference between the two players was illustrated in Antigua where Stevo bowled for three hours with a torn thigh muscle heavily strapped.

Looking back, however, I should have bitten my tongue, counted to ten, and tried to coax Chilly back on board because we all knew what great qualities he had as a bowler.

In Barbados for that fateful third Test, we were perhaps not quite motivated by but certainly driven on to play in memory of Kenny Barrington who died suddenly on the evening of 14 March, the second day of the game. The news came as a shock to the whole team.

Kath had come out to join me and we had returned to our room that evening after going out for a meal when the phone rang at about 11 pm. A.C. Smith was on the line.

'Ian,' he said, 'Bad news . . . Kenny has had a heart attack. I'm afraid he's dead.'

I was stunned. AC said there was nothing we could do at that moment, but I was to meet up with him at 7.30 a.m. the next day to decide how we should proceed. We went down to a little jetty on the beach front near our hotel and I asked him whether we should continue with the match. It was decided to break the news to the players first before making a decision.

I thought the team would be in no frame of mind for the rest of the match, but after our meeting we decided to go on because that was what Kenny would have wanted us to do. The players were devastated and when we arrived at the Bridgetown ground on that third day there was no atmosphere, just this sad vacuum. Even the crowd, who had got to hear about it, were drained of emotion and unnaturally silent, having held Kenny in very high esteem after watching his contests over previous years with Charlie Griffith and Wes Hall. They showed the utmost respect for him that day.

Before play started the two teams lined up and stood for a minute's silence along with the capacity crowd of 15,000. Several of the players from both sides were in tears. All were devastated by the tragedy, yet they responded well and gave their all during the game. Although I was affected deeply myself I could not show it; I had to bounce back and go out on that field and lead from the front. I kept saying, 'Come on, let's do it for Kenny, all of us'. If I had let my head drop, I think we could have fallen apart.

It wasn't enough, however, as the West Indies won the match easily. Viv Richards scored an unbeaten 182 in their second innings while Graham Gooch, who had really taken Kenny's death to heart, produced a superb second innings knock of 116 out of our total of 224. My other abiding memory of that match was an extraordinary over bowled by Michael Holding to Geoff Boycott at the start of our innings which is still talked about in hushed tones by those who saw it. The pitch was grassy and hard and Geoff was jumping about like a jack-in-the box. He did well to survive the first five balls even though he never laid a bat on them. I don't think he even saw the sixth which bowled him all ends up. Boycott out for a duck was not exactly the most encouraging way to start against the

West Indies at the best of times, let alone in this situation.

The team held together very well under the circumstances. We went to Antigua for the fourth Test where we lost one day to rain but came out of the match with a comfortable draw. I won the toss for the third time in the series and decided to bat. We scored a healthy enough 271 with Peter Willey hitting an unbeaten 102. The West Indies replied by scoring 468 for nine declared, with Richards scoring 114.

A first-wicket stand in our second innings of 144 between Gooch and Boycott laid the foundations for the draw, and Geoff was 104 not out when close of play arrived with us on 234 for three.

From Antigua we moved on to Jamaica for the fifth Test at Sabina Park. For the first time in the series, I lost the toss and we were put in to bat. Gooch set about Colin Croft and by the time we were all out for 285 he had scored 153 of the total. Once again, the West Indies managed to score heavily all the way down the order as they reached 442 with no one reaching a century.

At 32 for three in our second innings, we looked to be in trouble but when three hours of play were lost to drizzle we were given some valuable time – and David Gower made the most of the situation with a brilliant knock of 154 not out. He shared in a vital fourth-wicket stand of 136 with Peter Willey and batted for almost eight hours to save the game. We returned home, the series lost 2–0. I may have only scored 73 runs in the four Tests but I was England's leading wicket taker with 15 victims at an average of 32.80. What is more, despite all the problems, several of the players had produced excellent individual performances.

The West Indies tour had been a big learning experience and at times there had seemed to be nowhere to hide. Whenever I felt we were turning the corner, another disaster would happen. Even so, I was not too disappointed with my own contribution as captain.

My approach to captaincy has always been very positive. I don't agree with talking about the opposition – it is what you can do as individuals and as a team that counts. When I returned to the England fold for the last time in the days of the Gooch/Stewart regime in the early Nineties, I was really taken aback. There would be long talks about the strengths and weaknesses of each and every player we faced. Not only did I find it very boring, but I also felt it was highly counter-productive.

For a start, issuing this sort of data just baffles the team and undermines confidence in its own abilities. I firmly believed in simply psyching one another up over a beer or two. If you worry about what your opponents are going to do rather than what you are going to do to them, then you may as well pack up before you start. And if you can't get motivated to play for England then you shouldn't be anywhere near making the side in the first place.

But it seemed that my approach was not enough for the critics, and the feeling was growing within me that, slowly but surely, the rug was being pulled from under my feet.

Nevertheless, I was made captain again for the one-day games against Australia at the start of the 1981 summer series. My only look at Kim Hughes' touring side had come in their match against Somerset towards the end of May. Rain, however, ruined that match as they made 232 for eight declared and we replied with 25 for no wicket.

We enjoyed a good start in the first one-day international at Lord's, reducing Australia to 60 for four and a final total of 210 for seven from their 55 overs. An opening stand of 86 between Gooch and Boycott set us up and we reached 212 for four with more than three overs in hand. Two days later we were at Edgbaston for the second match in the three-day series and, left to chase 250 to win, we looked in good shape at 224 for five by the 50th over. Gatting was leading the charge and with two balls remaining looked to have hit Dennis Lillee over deep extra cover only for Geoff Lawson to take a marvellous catch and effectively win the match for the Aussies. We were all out three runs short of the target. The consolation was that Mike collected the Man of the Match award for his excellent 96.

The decider was being played at Leeds, ten days before the start of the first Test, and the Australians made a good showing of it thanks to 108 from Graeme Wood which paved the way to a total of 236 for eight from their 55 overs. Our reply faltered from the start; Boycott was out for 4 and only Gooch, Gatting, Willey and Jackman reached double figures as we were bowled out for 165.

For the forthcoming Test series the England selectors, in their infinite wisdom, then made the decision to let me captain the side on a match-by-match basis.

The first Test at Trent Bridge could have gone either way, but we had only ourselves to blame that it went Australia's. I lost the toss and we were put in on a pitch that was always going to favour the seam bowlers. We had left out John Emburey while the Australians had no place for their spinner Ray Bright. Wickets went down at regular intervals. Bob Woolmer, restored to the team in an effort to sort out the troublesome number three position, was out for a duck (and, as it turned out, halfway towards a pair) and we were eventually all out for 185.

In the Australian first innings, our bowlers hit back well and we had them out for 179. It would never have been anything like that but for Allan Border's 63; indeed, we should have had him out for 10 but he was dropped behind the wicket by Paul Downton. Our second innings was worse than the first and at one point we were 37 for four. David Gower hit 28 and I top scored with 33 as we limped to 125 all out, and a lead of 131. Dennis Lillee had been the destroyer-in-chief with five for 46.

Although conditions had improved for the batting side, we still made the Aussies sweat and it needed a solid knock of 38 from John Dyson to see them home to a four-wicket victory. Like my first game against the West Indies, this was a result which I felt could have so easily gone our way.

I was duly appointed to lead the side for the second Test at Lord's, but by then I had decided that my time was up as captain. I simply did not know whether I was coming or going; I could not plan ahead and, to be quite frank, the uncertainty was demoralizing for me and for the team. At a family lunch on the Sunday before the game, I announced that if the selectors were going to persist with the policy of giving me the captaincy on a match-by-match basis, then I would be forced to resign. Getting out before things degenerated even further looked the best course of action for everyone concerned.

It was not only me who was suffering. Kath had been through a hell of a lot in the past 12 months and more recently during the last two Tests. I was never sure where I stood over the captaincy and that state of affairs caused me to be withdrawn and moody and, as usual, Kath had to bear the brunt of it.

From the outside, situations like this look straightforward enough: 'England captain does badly . . . England captain resigns . . . Long live the new England captain' is how it normally goes. But the pressure that builds up when things are going badly not only affects you but the people closest to you.

Until that point the Ian Botham story had been success all the way. I was more confused than disappointed by my bad run during the early part of that summer, and by and large I felt able to cope with the knocks and the setbacks.

It was different for Kath though. Not only was she in a position where so-called friends and neighbours found it somewhat awkward to be in her company, but the one person with whom she wanted to share her feelings, namely me, had put up a wall. The newspaper criticism didn't bother me that much – I learned from very early on that if you worry about what people write in the press, you will never get out of bed in the morning – but Kath was bound to be affected by it all.

In fact, things had got so bad after we lost the one-day series that Kath had begged me to resign even before the Test series began; it was clear to her that the selectors were holding a gun to my head. When I got back home after dealing with the press she said, 'It's not worth it. Why don't you just give it up?'

She told me later that I was not myself during that period. She was right of course, I had withdrawn into my shell. It was the same old story: I didn't need anyone's help to sort out my problems, not even Kath's. I snapped at her and the kids; even Tigger, our boxer dog, started moping around the house. Whenever Kath asked me how I was feeling I just trivialized her concern by saying 'Forget it, everything is fine', and I became very irritated if she pressed the point. Not surprisingly, Kath was getting fed up with this. She also became quite depressed, so much so that she lost about a stone in weight. So when we walked through the Grace gates on the first morning of that Lord's Test to be confronted by a newspaper hoarding shouting out 'BOTHAM MUST GO', that was more than enough as far as I was concerned.

We were put in by Kim Hughes and Gooch launched the innings with a hard-hit 44, Gatting made 59 and, despite my duck, a typically belligerent 82 from Willey helped bring the final total to 311, which gave us something to defend.

It was pretty much neck and neck in the Australian innings, and but for their tail-wagging we would have ended with a first innings lead. Border top-scored with 64 then Rod Marsh hit 47, Ray Bright 33 and Dennis Lillee an unbeaten 40.

On the second day, the MCC membership showed themselves up again when the umpires, Don Oslear and Ken Palmer, took the players off the pitch when bad light stopped play during the extra hour added on for an earlier stoppage. They were wrongly under the impression that they could not come back despite a considerable improvement in conditions. The crowd started jeering and throwing cushions on the pitch, and the following day the TCCB issued an apology over the misunderstanding. But the natives were restless.

Our second innings started on the fourth day and time was running out, so when I walked to the crease I was prepared to take up the fight. I wanted to score quick runs and turn the screw on the Australians, so I pushed myself up the England batting order in an effort to achieve this. Then, rightly or wrongly, I tried to sweep Ray Bright's first ball and was bowled behind my legs for nought.

As I came back towards the Pavilion not a soul among the Lord's members mumbled 'bad luck', and not a single MCC member looked me in the eye. They all just sat there dumbstruck. Some picked up their papers and hid behind them, others rummaged in bags and a few just turned their backs on me. Ever since, I have treated MCC members with contempt. From that day on I never raised a bat to acknowledge them at Lord's.

The match went into the fifth day and we set the Australians a target of 232 to win in 170 minutes – enough time to tempt them and long enough for us to have a go at bowling them out. They started badly, and we reduced them to 17 for three thanks to two lbw decisions for Graham Dilley and my catch to dismiss Graham Yallop off Bob Willis. However, Graeme Wood then dug in for 62 and the Australians were happy to settle for the draw at 90 for four.

The England selectors may have been dithering over the captaincy question but by now my mind was made up. It was all or nothing. I could see that I wasn't going to get the backing I wanted and thought I deserved, so I handed in my resignation. It was a very low point in my life. Yet even then I was stripped of any dignity when, fifteen minutes after handing in my notice, Alec Bedser, the chairman of selectors, told the press, 'We were going to sack him anyhow'. Why he said that I will never know and why he told this to the press and not me is another mystery. The

TCCB gagged me so I could not publicly react to his statement, and I was left to wonder what point he was trying to make.

The whole family had been at Lord's for the five days of the second Test to give me moral support, but in the end I wanted to be alone. Kath obviously knew something was up as I was holed up in the dressing room for a while before running the gauntlet of pressmen to join her in the car. I told her then that I had resigned the captaincy. Kath was desperate to be with me at this time and I now know how much I hurt her by refusing to let her join me. But I needed space to think things through. She had already arranged with her parents and Diane, our nanny, to look after the children for a few days so she could go down to Somerset with me, but I was emphatic I wanted to be alone. I was rejecting her and she felt spurned by me, left to pick up what information there was about me on the television and in the papers. We drove to the hotel car park where I dropped her off before going my own way, and there was only the briefest of farewells before I sped away. It was selfish and thoughtless of me, and my actions left a scar on our relationship that lasted for a very long time. Kath was angry, upset and confused. As my wife she had wanted to be close to me and to support me, and here was I turning round and saying 'No, leave me to myself'. Fortunately, Gerry, my father-in-law, understood my point of view and he tried to explain it to his daughter as he took her home to Yorkshire while I headed west. I realize now how hurtful that must have been, and how my blinkered vision had not only left her alone but vulnerable too. The situation wasn't helped by a conversation between Kath and my mother the next day. Mum, in all innocence, went into great detail about the reception I had been given by the crowd at Taunton that day. 'It was wonderful, Kathryn,' she said, 'you should have been here'. Little did she realize that Kath's absence was through no fault of her own.

As I drove into Taunton that night and towards the Four Alls pub, I felt down and on edge and had no idea what sort of reception was awaiting me. In the event, I need not have worried because my friends were there to support me. They had guessed this was where I would head for and the place was full to the rafters. I was given a magnificent ovation which immediately helped to boost my spirits.

Armed with a bottle of gin and with Viv Richards as my companion, I left the Four Alls later that evening to talk through the troubles of recent days with him. Suddenly the clouds started to part.

That was not the end of my cricketing summer, but certainly of my captaincy and it had been a rough ride. After the pain and sweat of the West Indies, I had come home to a barrage of publicity questioning whether I should remain as England captain. The BBC's *Newsnight* programme even ran a tasteless piece entitled 'The Trials of Ian Botham'. I had been forced into a position where all I could do was resign, but the irritating thing was it came at the point when I felt that at last I was getting the hang of the job; I was coming to terms with all aspects of it and I was ready to bloom. Not for one minute would I agree that the captaincy affected my form. Everyone has ups and downs and for a while I was in a slight cricketing trough. Given time, though, I'm certain I would have come good as captain.

The following morning I arrived at the county ground and by 9.30 a.m. it was already filling up. I came out of the pavilion to walk across the pitch to the nets and the reception I received from the locals was sensational. They were up on their feet, clapping me all the way across the pitch. It was one of the most exhilarating moments of my career, not only lifting me but the whole Somerset team. I thought of those people at Lord's giving me the cold shoulder and I looked at the Taunton supporters and thought, 'Hang on a minute, these are the real people, these are the people who count. To hell with Lord's and to hell with the selectors'. What a shame Kath was not there to enjoy the moment with me.

If this was an episode of *Question Of Sport*, now might be the moment for David Coleman to ask: 'What happened next?'

7
THE MIRACLE
OF 1981

The safest and easiest conclusion most observers have come to regarding the reversal of my fortunes during the summer of 1981 was that the captaincy had placed such a burden on me that I was simply unable to perform; and that it was only after that burden had been removed that I could do myself justice as a player with bat and ball.

As far as I am concerned, however, this is the wrong conclusion. I honestly felt that I was getting to grips with captaincy after all the problems I had encountered in the West Indies. My return to form at the same time as giving up the job was, I believed, pure coincidence. Nevertheless, it was somewhat of a relief to be able to forget about the one thousand and one things that crowd your mind when leading your country. Now I could be judged solely on my achievements as a player, and I was absolutely determined to prove myself to all those who doubted me.

Those particular thoughts were well to the fore when I was approached by Mike Brearley, the man to whom the England selectors turned to replace me, on the eve of the third Test at Headingley.

I had always got on extremely well with Brears. I

respected him as a player, a captain and a person. People have spoken about our relationship almost in terms of father and son but this was absolute nonsense. He knew what made me tick – he seemed to know what made everyone tick – yet there is no doubt that we treated each other as equals.

So when he posed the question about my availability for the Headingley Test, I think he knew what the answer was going to be.

'Beef,' he said, 'are you sure you want to play? If you don't, I will fully understand.'

'Of course I bloody want to play, Brears. I have a good feeling about this match,' I said.

'That's great,' he said. 'I think you'll get 150 runs and take ten wickets.' In the event he was not too far wrong.

Although I appreciated the fact that he had asked me for all the right reasons, pulling out of the England team had never entered my head. My attitude has always been that you can run from situations but you can't hide, for they only catch up with you in the end. In any case, I was not intimidated by the position in which I found myself. On the contrary, I felt inspired by it. I wanted to go out there and put on a performance against the Australians which would make all the nightmares of the last year disappear. I wanted to show the world I could still play, and what better opponents to prove that against than the Old Enemy.

Once the business of resigning the captaincy had been attended to, Kath and I both felt a huge weight had been lifted from our shoulders. Now, as I approached the Headingley Test it was my intention to remove the misery from our lives once and for all.

Although technically, bearing in mind Brearley's inquiry, there had been a chance that I might miss this match, the other player who would make this one of the most memorable sporting events of all time was far nearer to being merely a spectator.

Bob Willis was that close to missing the Headingley Test. If things had turned out only slightly differently, England's main strike bowler would have been Mike Hendrick instead. No disrespect to Mike, but who knows what may have happened then? Bob had not been well during the second Test at Lord's and his bowling was badly affected. (He served up an astounding 32 no-balls during the game.) After the match he had staggered home and gone straight to bed with a chest infection. His poor performance, allied to doubts over his long-term fitness after he had been forced to come home early from the West Indies with a knee injury, meant that there was a huge question mark hanging over not just his selection for the Leeds Test, but also his international future. Bob had decided to sit out the next championship match for Warwickshire in order to try and get himself fully fit for the Test match, but the selectors saw his absence rather differently. They reasoned that if he was not fit enough to play in the championship he was certainly not fit enough to play for England the following week. During the selection meeting that weekend they made their decision: Bob was out, and Mike was in. They even went so far as to send out Mike's official invitation.

After the meeting Alec Bedser rang Bob to let him know. Bob was flabbergasted by the news. He explained the reason why he was not playing for his county and assured Alec that he was already fit enough but wanted to save himself for the Test match. He told him he would prove it if necessary by turning out for the Warwickshire second XI the following day. With this misunderstanding resolved, Alec then made a desperate call to Derbyshire to ask them to intercept Mike's invitation. The office staff duly weeded through all the post when they came in on the Monday morning and luckily managed to seize the letter just in time.

Wisden recorded the events of the next five days as follows:

At Leeds, 16–21 July, England won by 18 runs. A match that had initially produced all the wet and tedious traits of recent Leeds Tests finally ended in a way to stretch the bounds of logic and belief. England's victory, achieved under the gaze of a spell-bound nation, was the first this century by a team following-on, and only the second such result in the history of Test cricket.

The transformation occurred in less than 24 hours, after England had appeared likely to suffer their second four-day defeat of the series. Wherever one looked there were personal dramas: Brearley returning as captain, like England's saviour; Botham, who was named Man of the Match, brilliant once more in his first game back in the ranks; Willis, whose career has so often heard the distant drums, producing the most staggering bowling of his life when his place again seemed threatened.

My own memories of what took place will live with me forever.

After Kim Hughes won the toss and decided to bat, the Aussies cashed in on some fairly ordinary bowling on a pitch far worse than their total of 401 for nine declared suggested. Hughes later described 400 runs on that track as being as good as a thousand and few disagreed with him. After bowling only three overs on the first day, I had a decent crack on the second day and finished with six for 95.

This was where Brearley's brilliance at mind games came into play. In an effort to try and swing the ball more, I had experimented with a new delivery technique in which I would move sideways just before lining myself up to let the ball go. Brears thought it had taken some of the pace and zip out of my bowling; he wanted me to bring the experiment to a close and just put my back into bowling fast. Once a swinger, always a swinger he reasoned, so why fiddle about with something that worked anyway? He even wound me up about my remodelled action by calling me the 'sidestep queen'. I got the message and reverted to my original, more natural delivery – with pretty decent results, as it turned out.

Still, my success had come too late in the day to stop Australia building what should have been, and under normal circumstances would have been, a match-winning score. Early next morning we lost our first wicket when Graham Gooch was lbw to Terry Alderman and that was the signal for our collapse to 87 for five. So it was 'welcome to the latest crisis' as I walked to the wicket. Bearing in mind the uneven bounce, I decided the best form of defence was attack and I carried this out with some success, making 50 from 54 balls. I was beginning to approach my best form, and it took a bastard of a ball to get me out. I was already committed to a forcing shot as Dennis Lillee managed to extract extra bounce from a delivery just outside off stump, so I was too late to adjust when it reared sharply, touched the glove and Rod Marsh took a great catch high above his head. This was the first of several records broken during that match as Marsh became the top wicket-keeper in Test history (264 victims in 71 Tests).

I was fairly satisfied to be back in the runs again. It was my first fifty in 20 Test innings, and in any case a great improvement on the two noughts I managed at Lord's. But we were still in trouble: on a pitch like this any kind of first innings deficit was likely to be crucial, and the way we were batting the Australian lead was going to be huge. We eventually followed-on and although bad light cut short proceedings, we had already lost Gooch before stumps, out for the second time in the day.

At that stage defeat was a foregone conclusion. The rest of our second innings would be little more than a formality, and even if by some chance we did manage to edge past the Aussies' total, the victory that would have put them in an unassailable position in the series was effectively in the bag. So when both teams turned up at my house on the Saturday night for the traditional Botham barbecue, the mood in the camps could not have been more different. Kim Hughes and his players were on a high; we on the other hand were about as low as you can get. The party helped improve our mood, however, and we ended up in a rugby scrum on the lawn before the Aussies headed off back to their hotel around midnight.

Sunday was a rest day and it would be nice to be able to tell you that I spent it plotting the events of the next two days; that I had lulled the Aussies into a false sense of security and now was the time to put my master plan into operation. In fact, all I did was to go down to the pub for a quiet pint, and when I left that evening for our hotel I told Kath I would check out in the morning and be back home sometime on Monday afternoon, maybe early evening at the latest.

We held out through the morning session, as it turned out, but by 3 p.m. that day, when Graham Dilley joined me at the crease, the match was more or less all over. We were 135 for seven, still 92 runs short of making the Aussies bat again. The ground was nearer empty than full and the bookmakers left no one in any doubt as to the way they saw things. Ladbrokes made England 500–1 and they had very few takers.

When I saw those odds I thought, 'Bloody hell, that's got to be worth a punt'. Unfortunately I soon became too busy to do anything about it. But the price was definitely too seductive for Lillee to ignore. Initially he wanted to put £50 of the Aussies' team fund on us, but they told him not to be so foolish. I wonder how many of them regretted being so hasty as things turned out – £25,000 might have made a nice little addition to their kitty. At least Dennis didn't miss out, as he gave the team bus driver a tenner to do the necessary. And then began the most dramatic passage of play I was ever involved in.

Over the years many people have asked me about the events that followed. What was going through my mind? What did I say to my partners? What did I say to Hughes and his team? When was the moment I knew it was all going to come good? And over the years so many thousands of words have been written about my innings by so many that you would have thought the entire population of Great Britain and the Commonwealth was at the match to see it.

The truth is that it was just one of those crazy, glorious one-off flukes. To be perfectly honest, when I went out to bat I wasn't really interested in the state of the match at all. At the start of the innings, I wasn't particularly concentrating on the score, and I wasn't the only one. By the time Dilley joined me, Brears had given up the ghost. He had actually changed out of his cricket gear, showered and packed up his kit. Diplomatically he chose to put on a clean cricket shirt so that if anyone looked up at the England balcony, his acceptance of the inevitable would not be too obvious. Dilley was playing in one of his early Test matches. No one rated him as a batsman so he reasoned he had nothing to lose and decided to go for the big ones which, at first, the Aussies found very amusing; as far as they were concerned the match was all but over, the Ashes were in the bag and they could stand a bit of light entertainment from a number 9 batsman they were convinced barely knew which end of the bat to pick up. And to be honest I was just enjoying the spectacle without taking it at all seriously. But Graham just kept on hitting and he kept on connecting so I thought I had better join in. Suddenly, and really almost without us noticing, we had edged the total close to, level with, and then unbelievably, ahead of the Aussies. We were still not really in the game but at least we had given them a run for their money and the punters who stayed had something to smile about.

Slowly, the mood started to change. By the we passed their total I was well in the groove and from then on I cannot remember playing another defensive shot. If it was short I hooked, pulled or cut. If it was in the slot I drove and drove hard on the basis that even if I got an edge, more likely than not the ball would carry over the heads of the slips. Some of it was sheer unadulterated slogging – as Mike Brearley said afterwards 'pure village green stuff' – and I remember one inside edge, in particular, that flew for four past square-leg. Now I was playing by pure instinct.

When people recount their favourite moment they often talk about one specific shot off Alderman. The reason it has stuck in the general consciousness is because of Richie Benaud's memorable comment: 'No need to look for that one . . . it's gone straight into the confectionery stall . . . and out again'.

But the shot I remember above all others was a square cut off the back foot off Lillee which was probably the sweetest I have ever hit in my life. It hit the boundary board before anyone even had a chance to move.

By this time Christopher Martin-Jenkins in the television commentary box was close to a nervous breakdown and even I was getting quite excited. For the first time I started to think about the match situation. I told Dilley to keep going and he did his best before finally perishing for 56. Although at that stage we were still in effect only 25 for eight at least we had made sure Australia would have to bat again.

They were clearly becoming rather annoyed by all this. Geoff Lawson lost his rag to such an extent that he actually sent down two beamers. I could accept one as an accident but two had to be more than a coincidence; I stored them away in the memory banks for future reference.

Although irritated by his tactics the good news was it showed that the Aussies were under pressure. There is no doubt they bowled faster as they got angrier, but they also started to lose control. What did surprise me was that Hughes kept the quicks on for so long before trying to tempt me with a spinner. When Ray Bright did eventually get his chance he very nearly got my wicket, and had he done so that would have been the end of the fightback.

Back in the pavilion, on Dilley's dismissal, Chris Old was being urged on by Brears. 'Just hold it together and keep an end up,' he told him.

Chilly did exactly what was required, scoring 29 and helping me add 67 for the ninth wicket. During this stand I passed my century: it had been scored from 87 balls and the second fifty from a mere 30 deliveries. The atmosphere was electric; every run was cheered and every four was greeted with an explosion of noise. But the Aussies had suddenly gone very quiet.

By this time I was seeing it like a football and with Bob Willis, the last man in, making sure I had most of the strike we managed to add another 31 runs to end the day at 351 for nine, 124 runs ahead. I left the field on 145 not out, at that time my highest Test score. Back in the dressing room I took the weight off my feet, lit up a cigar and struggled to come to terms with what had happened. I couldn't make any sense of it so I gave up trying. The press were keen to grab me for some quotes but after the way I felt some of them had been responsible for the way I was hounded out of the captaincy, I was not in the mood to co-operate. In fact, I made my point to them in far from subtle fashion when I refused to attend a hastily arranged press conference and, while being pursued to my car by reporters I wrapped a towel around my mouth.

Having checked out that morning, I checked into the

hotel again along with the rest of the lads, then went off for fish and chips and a couple of well-earned pints. That evening, unlike the previous one, my mind was fully focused on the job in hand. If we could just edge our lead up to around 200, I felt we had a chance. The following morning, not surprisingly, the papers were full of 'BOTHAM'S MIRACLE'. Pat Gibson, the cricket writer for the *Daily Express* summed up the mood when he wrote: 'The amazing Ian Botham had the mourners dancing in the aisles at Headingley last night with the greatest comeback since Lazarus'.

To be truthful, when we reached the ground no one really believed we had a chance. And our hopes of adding 50 or so the following morning disappeared when Bob Willis was caught by Allan Border off Alderman after we had added only five to the total. I finished unbeaten on 149 and we had a lead of 129 which, although nowhere near enough for us to harbour real ambitions of winning, at least meant we were still in the match.

Then Bob – who, don't forget, very nearly didn't make it on to the field at all – stormed in at pace to produce one of the greatest bowling performances ever seen.

He was fully aware of the situation; during the week before the match he had discussed with me and a few other close colleagues the possibility that this might be his last appearance for England. There were a few young bowlers knocking on the door and, after having to pull out of the West Indies tour, he had admitted, 'I never thought I'd play cricket again, let alone Test cricket'.

No wonder he ran in that day like a man possessed, and as though his life depended on it. He knew that his career probably did.

Here again we profited from a spot of Brearley psychology. He held Bob back at first for two reasons. Firstly, he reasoned that as Dilley and I were on a roll he should keep us going. Secondly, he thought it might help to wind Bob up. The events of the next couple of hours were more or less a blur to me at the time, but recalling them gives me nothing but pleasure. First I had Graeme Wood caught behind by Bob Taylor at 13 for one and we were on our way. Then John Dyson, who had made an excellent hundred in the first innings and Trevor Chappell pushed the Aussies to 56 without further loss. Now Brears switched Willis from bowling uphill, which he had not enjoyed, to downhill which he certainly did. The result was the most magnificent spell of sustained hostile bowling it has ever been my privilege to witness. First a bouncer to Trevor Chappell took the glove and went to Bob Taylor behind the stumps; then two runs later, in the last over before lunch, I held on to one at slip off Kim Hughes. Three balls later it was 58 for four when Graham Yallop was caught at short square-leg by Mike Gatting.

As we came out after lunch we looked across the balcony and saw the expression on the faces of our opponents: talk about rabbits caught in the headlights! By now the pitch had made batting a lottery and our adrenalin was pumping. Old bowled Border to make it 65 for five, Bob tricked Dyson into mishooking (68 for six), Marsh top-edged him to Dilley to make it 74 for seven, and then Geoff Lawson was caught behind for one, making the score 75 for eight.

Now it was our turn to get the jitters as this amazing match took on yet another twist. They still needed only 55 to win and although that should have been too many bearing in mind the state of the pitch, somehow Lillee and Bright managed to put on 35 in four overs. Taking a leaf out of our book by going for broke, Bright got stuck into Old, hitting him for ten in one over.

It was all getting a bit frantic; but then came the moment that made all the difference. Bob bowled a ball to Lillee as near to the block hole as he could manage. DK tried to go for the big hit but only managed to spoon the ball up in the air. It looked safe at first because Gatting, positioned quite deep at mid-on to cope with the slog, had an awful lot of ground to cover and, as we all know, even at his fittest Gatt moved with all the grace and athleticism of a supertanker. The ball couldn't have been in the air for more than a couple of seconds but it felt like a lifetime. Everyone just froze on the spot, except Gatt of course. From somewhere he found the pace he needed, and seemingly in slow motion dived and held the catch inches above the ground.

Although we still had one more wicket to take, I think that was the instant we knew the match was ours. We were even able to cope with Old dropping not one but two sharp chances at third slip.

Then came probably the most memorable moment in my career. Bob, who had never run in with more passion, commitment or sheer self-belief, sent down a perfect yorker and Bright's stumps were scattered to kingdom come – unbe-bloody-lievable!

It was a moment that was almost impossible to do justice to in words. The next day Paul Fitzpatrick in the *Guardian* did as well as anyone could as he wrote:

To be at Headingley yesterday was to be part of a drama as gripping as anything the fertile mind of Wilkie Collins could have dreamed of. It was impossible to take the eye away from a single delivery; every run that edged Australia towards their target of 130 heightened the anxiety of an absorbed crowd; every wicket England captured added another heart beat of tension, until by the time that Willis uprooted Bright's middle stump to end the game most nerves could have stood no more.

Not since the golden age of cricket have England won a Test to compare with this . . .

Not since A.E. Stoddard led his side to victory by ten runs in Sydney in 1894, the only previous instance of a Test side following on and winning the game, has an English cricketing public been given quite such cause for celebration.

Coming as it did a week before the wedding of Prince Charles and Lady Diana Spencer, our achievement gave the cricket public and the whole nation an excuse to start partying somewhat earlier than expected.

Most crucially, in the short term, the efforts of Bob and I had created a real mental barrier for the Aussies to overcome from now on. I was now their bogey man, something I exploited against Australian batsmen and bowlers from then even up until the World Cup in 1992. No matter what kind of form I was in, the Aussies always knew that I was capable of turning a match and I'm sure that a lot of my later success against them came about as a result of what happened that day at Headingley.

Certainly it transformed the mood in the England camp

completely. The dressing room was absolute bedlam, swarming with photographers and well-wishers. All the players were mentally and physically drained, with Bob Willis looking about as ecstatic as a man who just realized he had forgotten to post his winning entry on the pools.

The Aussies had bought their victory champagne in advance but, needless to say, it remained unopened. When we sent our dressing room attendant into theirs to ask if we could borrow some, it was suggested to him, in good old-fashioned Australian, that he might consider leaving the room. Eventually the England management succeeded in negotiating a fair price for a few bottles and we downed the lot. Peter Willey, who had only ever tasted winners' bubbly when it had been offered to him by the other side, was enjoying pouring it himself for the first time in his nineteen-Test career and he said simply, 'That's better. All the other stuff I've drunk has made me want to puke'.

All over the country the reaction was extraordinary. Some friends in Glasgow told me that the traffic had stopped in the streets and huge crowds had gathered outside television shop windows. It was even claimed that the Stock Exchange had ground to a halt.

My one abiding memory of the whole affair was of Brearley. Once, during the innings, I scored a streaky boundary and glanced up to the balcony expecting to see him urging me to calm down a bit. Instead, he was grinning and gesticulating that I should have tried to hit the ball harder.

Of course, everyone reached the same conclusion afterwards – that I would never have been able or been in the mood to play that kind of innings if I had still been captain. I don't agree with that for one minute. Even when

I was making a pair at Lord's, I was still convinced that I would get amongst the Aussies and that it was only a matter of time before I ran into form. As far as my captaincy prospects went, I was just sad that time came one Test too late.

So, having levelled the series now it was down to us to push home our advantage. The finale of the next Test at Edgbaston was in its way every bit as dramatic as Headingley had been. For the second successive Test we appeared to be on the way to defeat, and for the second successive Test we managed to turn a match on its head in front of a huge and deafening crowd.

Our first innings was a disaster. We were bowled out for 189 and this time there were no excuses. The pitch was in superb condition, the outfield was fast and we really should have cashed in. Australia managed to make 258 despite some good bowling from John Emburey and then when we made only 219 in the second innings, it seemed that we were there for the taking. Australia needed just 12 more to win than they had done at Headingley with two days to play and we seemed to have exhausted our supply of miracles.

Bob bowled brilliantly again on the fourth morning but with AB batting solidly, Australia reached 105 for four, needing 46 more runs with six wickets remaining. I had not been keen to bowl because I felt the wicket was more suited to spin. There seemed nothing in the pitch for the fast bowlers, so I suggested to Brears that he put on Peter Willey to partner John Emburey. Willey could give the ball a rip and I reasoned he might just get some turn out of the rough outside AB's off-stump. The umpire, Dickie Bird, also thought we should try both spinners, although not for the same reason. When Brears went up to him and asked 'What do you think?' Dickie told him 'It's all over, skipper. The best thing you can do is put on the twirlers so we can get away early'.

In his next over, Embers sent down a ball which lifted off a good length, took AB on the gloves and was caught by Gatt close in. Brears, who had asked Willey to loosen up, then changed his mind and asked me to have a go. And then lightning struck again.

In the space of 28 deliveries I took five wickets for one run. Marsh was the first to go, bowled; Ray Bright fell leg before for nought; Dennis Lillee was caught behind for three; Martin Kent was bowled; and finally, as the noise and atmosphere reached fever pitch, Terry Alderman missed a straight one and was bowled for a duck.

By 4.30 p.m. on that glorious Sunday afternoon we were 2–1 up. I grabbed hold of a stump and whirled it round and round in unabashed joy as I sprinted off the pitch.

Sure, I had bowled fast and mainly straight – but enough to deserve figures of five for 1? No way. The Aussies lost their bottle, there was no other explanation for it. In fact, I can recall the look on the faces of the Aussie batsmen as I ran in. It was exactly the same shell-shocked expression as I had seen at Headingley a fortnight earlier.

By the time we got to Old Trafford for the fifth Test, I really believe that the Aussies were longing for home. No matter how well they did, I think they felt that the fates had decreed that this was to be England's summer, or rather mine. And so it proved to be at Manchester.

People have often asked me to compare the 149 at Headingley with the 118 I scored in Manchester. In truth, there is no comparison. Whereas Headingley was as much a slog as a Test innings, this was something completely different. John Woodcock in *The Times* posed the question: 'Was this the greatest Test innings ever?'

We had batted first and made 231 and bowled out the Aussies for 130. But by the time I went out to bat a second time on the Saturday morning, we had surrendered the initiative and were struggling on 104 for five. I don't know, I just decided this was going to be my day.

In the first innings Lillee had me caught in the gully first ball. So I had something to kick against. From the very start it was one of those occasions when everything clicked. Every shot I tried came off, including a couple of sixes off Lillee which I managed to slap off my eyebrows, and I can only remember one shot which didn't hit the sweet spot, an inside edge that just missed the off stump on the way to the fine-leg boundary.

Many people forget, however, that I probably wouldn't have been able to do what I did without the efforts of Chris Tavaré at the other end. 'Tav' received a lot of stick from crowds and in the press during his brief Test career for batting at a snail's pace. But people forget that he had been brought in to do a specific job at number three, namely to stay in at all costs so that an innings could be built around him. It wasn't pleasant, it wasn't pretty and, for the spectators, it was often as much fun as watching paint dry. It can't have been much fun for Tav either, as his natural game was to play shots. But he stuck to the task brilliantly, and no matter what his critics said there were never any complaints from inside the dressing room. On this occasion, he had already taken four-and-a-quarter hours to make 69 in the first innings and he was even slower in the second when his seven-hour 78 included the slowest fifty in Test cricket (304 minutes). Of the 149 we added for the sixth wicket, Tav made just 28. But the whole point was that in its way his innings was every run and every minute as important as mine. Once I was out, it enabled two more big stands to be built, as Alan Knott made 59 and John Emburey made 57 and we established a lead of 505. In some ways, it might have been more appropriate to ask whether, of its type, Tav's second innings was one of the greatest ever. As far as I was concerned, it was an epic.

The Aussies were not finished. Yallop and AB both scored hundreds as they made a reasonable fight back to score 402, but in the end the task was beyond them and the Ashes were ours. What an amazing sensation and what an incredible transformation from the early part of the summer!

It's safe to say that the despair I felt after bagging a pair at Lord's was the worst feeling I had ever had in my career. As I was warned when I came into the game, you are only as good as your last match, and that last match as captain at Lord's had been pretty awful. Until that point my career, apart from one or two little hiccups, had been one success after another. I thought I could handle failure, but you never really know if you can until you come face to face with it. In reality, I had tried to ignore the possibility totally until the point when it all started to go wrong because, as I had always been taught by Closey and it was always my gut feeling anyway, the only way to succeed at the highest level is to have total belief that you are better than anyone else on the field.

I admit that doubts had begun to creep in. Although

I had felt in good form, there was a certain amount of desperation in my constant refusal to accept that I was having a bad run. As everyone knows, cricket is a game played in the mind as much as on the pitch and although I talked a good game, the longer I went without performing to the standards I had set myself the more the doubts started to creep into my thoughts.

So what happened at Headingley, Edgbaston and Old Trafford left me with not only a fantastic sense of achievement but also an overwhelming feeling of relief. In the dark times, no matter how great your self-confidence, you simply never know for certain whether the good times will ever come back. Now I knew for sure that I was on the way up again.

My next innings proved that everything was back in place. The Sunday after the Old Trafford Test in a John Player league match against Hampshire at Taunton, I made a century in 67 minutes. The official timing for my second fifty was nine minutes (although I thought it was more like seven!).

One thing that period of my life did teach me was that it is the friends that stick by you through the bad times who are the ones that really matter in the long run. It was amazing to me how many of my so-called mates had disappeared during the previous 12 months. As a young man thrust into the limelight I was always going to be the target for those who fancied a spot of reflected glory. As people like George Best and many others have found out to their cost, when you're on the way up there are plenty of people climbing over each other to buy you drinks, but when things start going wrong, more often than not, you drink alone. I think it was the feeling of being deserted which affected me so deeply when I returned to the pavilion after the second duck at Lord's. I've never felt more lonely than I did that day. Now, of course, all the fair-weather friends came crawling out of the woodwork.

If ever there was a lesson I wanted to pass on to any young sportsman, it is this: choose your friends with care. Some of them might not be there when you need them most.

The Oval Test, the last of the summer, ended in a draw and it also brought to a conclusion one of the most significant on-field relationships of my career. Mike Brearley had announced in advance that this was to be his last Test match and, as the match drew to a close on the final evening, he received a standing ovation when he left the field having scored 51 and made his exit from the Test arena for the last time.

Brearley was the fourth in a quartet of major influences on my cricketing career. Brian Close and Tom Cartwright had been the first two, of course, and then came Kenny Barrington. Yet Brearley was different from the others. At a time when a lot of people had been treating me like an idiot, he went out of his way to deal with me as an adult. Rodney Hogg, the Australian fast bowler, summed Brears up perfectly when, on meeting Mike for the first time, he greeted him with, 'Oh yes, you're the fellow with a degree in people'.

He was a marvellous captain to me. He encouraged me when I needed it and restrained me if he thought I was in danger of overstepping the mark. Most important though, he listened to me. His approach to motivation was straightforward: according to Brears the secret was to get everyone to motivate each other. He knew that the success of any team is based on mutual respect. He wanted me to contribute on the field and if ever I wanted to try something different he was always willing to let me have my head.

He was, quite simply, the best captain I have ever played under and it is possible that, as with Barrington, a lot of the problems I encountered in future years might not have arisen if he had been around at the time.

When it came to reining me in, Brears was helped by the fact that he was somewhat older than me. When it came to me being captained by men like Bob Willis, Mike Gatting or David Gower, I think sometimes they had a problem because we were of a similar age. With Brears, because he was older he found it easier to tell me what to do and what not to do. If I overdid the bouncer (perish the thought), whereas David would find it difficult to get the ball out of my hand Brears would just say, 'Get off. You're bowling like a prat'.

The other person I have to thank for the summer of my life is Kath. Obviously, during the lowest points of the summer the whole thing had been extremely difficult for her and there were times when, as I have said, I intentionally shut her out and put a 'Do Not Disturb' sign around my neck. She handled these distressing situations as well as she could, and I was just so pleased to be able to blow the bad times away and make life that much more pleasant for the both of us.

8

THE LURE OF
THE RAND

Three times the gold of South Africa has been waved in front of my nose and three times I have had a hard look at it before deciding to put country before cash. The first time the matter arose was on Keith Fletcher's 1981/82 winter tour to India, and the prime instigator was one 'Sir' Geoffrey Boycott.

That tour very nearly did not take place at all. At the time there were widely differing interpretations of how the Gleneagles Agreement should apply to sport and although Britain was one of the signatories, pledging 'vigorously to combat the evil of apartheid' in the field of sport, the attitudes of the white and non-white cricketing nations seemed some way apart. We had first come across the problem with the controversy over Robin Jackman's presence in Guyana the previous winter. A United Nations committee had blacklisted Boycott and others in contention for tour places due to their sporting links with South Africa, and in October 1981, after the Test and County Cricket Board had reacted to the Indian government's ban on Boycott and Geoff Cook by replying that they were not willing to change their team, it seemed certain that the tour would be cancelled.

In the end, after the personal intervention of the Indian prime minister Mrs Indira Gandhi, the ban was lifted and the tour was allowed to go ahead. I wonder what was going through her mind when, on 28 February 1982, the news broke that Boycott and other top England cricketers had landed in South Africa for a rebel tour that had been secretly planned and organized while they were in India.

Boycs had been up to his old tricks on the field as well. With a hundred in the third Test at Delhi, he passed Sir Garfield Sobers' record to become the highest run scorer in Test history. Having achieved that milestone, within two weeks he was heading home pleading 'physical and mental tiredness'. There were not that many eyebrows raised when he left the ground in the middle of the fourth Test in Calcutta claiming he was too ill to field, then proceeded to spend the afternoon on the golf course. What amazing powers of recovery!

Throughout this trip Boycs had been busy trying to recruit players for the rebel tour. When the offer was put to me I was certainly interested. I was a player at the top of my profession earning only £7000 per annum, and somebody was willing to offer me a staggering £45,000 to visit South Africa for a couple of months. The figures said it all, and of course I was prepared to have a look at the deal – after all, who in his right mind wouldn't be? No professional sportsman has any guarantees over the future; loss of form, or worse, serious injury can happen to anyone and it is up to every individual to do what they consider best for themselves and their family in the long run.

The subject had been raised during the previous winter

tour to the West Indies, but it was just talk, mainly to fill the many idle moments, not least, ironically, when the Guyana Test was called off following objections to Jackman's presence. But so much of what happened on the trip was overshadowed by the sudden death of Kenny Barrington that by the time we got home, South Africa was the last thing on my mind.

Little did I realize that once he got back from the West Indies, Boycott had made himself very busy behind the scenes assisting with the arrangements for the South African pirate tour. He was buying an off-the-shelf London-based company called Oxychem Ltd, which had struck a deal with a firm called RASIP, founded in Scotland by Holiday Inns (South Africa) specifically for the purpose of oiling the wheels of a rebel tour. It worked like this: Boycott's company Oxychem was there to supply cricketers to RASIP, which in turn was providing the contracts to play in South Africa. During the summer of 1981 certain contacts were sounding out players on an informal basis, but it was not until the winter tour to India that the whole project started to take real shape.

It was all cloak and dagger stuff, rather like a John le Carré book, and they called it, would you believe, 'Operation Chessmatch'. The words 'cricket' and 'South Africa' were never mentioned; instead they were replaced by codenames like 'chessboard' and 'pawn'. That led to one hilarious moment in Bangalore when my solicitor, Alan Herd, who had flown out to see me to discuss the situation, was asked by David Gower to offer some friendly advice. At that time, Alan knew nothing about the codename and told David that he would be pleased to help but asked him to come back later because he was dealing with me. A couple of hours later David sidled up to Alan and said: 'I believe it is time we spoke about Spassky'. Poor Herdy didn't have the faintest idea what he was talking about!

All along Kath was dead against me going to South Africa and by pure coincidence she had been in Herd's office when I phoned to ask him to come out to Bangalore along with my agent, Reg Hayter, to discuss the whole deal. I told Herd that a few of the other England boys wanted a word with him on an informal basis. It was so confidential that we couldn't talk on the phone, so I let Kath explain a bit more to him. But before putting down the phone I made sure to tell him to bring a stilton, brandy and some bottles of red wine with him – essential supplies for the overseas troops (or for me, to be more precise).

Flying out Herd and Hayter was proof of how seriously I was considering the offer. After all, the sort of money being talked about was not to be sniffed at, and taken on that basis alone the players were in a similar situation to those who had been wooed by Kerry Packer all those years before. But even as Reg and Alan were on the way out to India I was having serious doubts, because this was not a simple deal. On the one hand, there was the temptation of the money, but on the other hand there were a host of possible repercussions. One thing was clear: whatever decision I made, I wanted to continue playing for England.

Forty-five thousand pounds was a lot of money for playing cricket, but that was virtually all the deal had going for it. Moreover, the series of commercial endorsements that topped up my pay would be under threat if I did decide to go to South Africa. This was a crucial stage in my career following the disappointments of the West Indies tour a year earlier and the loss of the England captaincy. At last things were beginning to go right for me; my profile was sky high, I was in demand and there were plenty of commercial opportunities coming my way.

At this time the issue of South African politics was arousing strong passions worldwide. A lot of very prominent and honourable politicians were very active in denouncing apartheid, and although a few of the more dubious variety were jumping on the bandwagon in order to try and make a name for themselves as well, there was no doubting that the whole political system was creaking under the pressure. I had seen at first hand the trouble that could be stirred up over individuals like Jackman. There was no telling what might happen if a squad of England players went out there.

Herd and Hayter had a fair inkling of what the reaction would be and explained that I was likely to be banned from playing for England if I went, with the inevitable consequence that many of the commercial deals relating to that side of my career would collapse. A major player at that time was the American sports firm Nike, who along with sports equipment specialists Patrick were bidding for my signature. Nike were highly sensitive about South Africa, especially as the Olympic Games were coming up in Los Angeles in 1984, and if an England rebel cricket team was to spark a mass boycott of the games it would not have been good for their business. It wouldn't have been too clever for mine, either.

There were attempts by the South Africans to build an 'insurance' policy into the deal whereby if the individuals who jumped ship were to lose Test status, they could go back on month-long tours to South Africa for the next two years and receive the same fee, adjusted to take into account inflation. Nonetheless, Reg and Alan made it quite clear that if I went, financially I would be worse off and, more critically for me, I would certainly be barred from playing for England. Quite apart from anything else, I did not want to be seen to be doing anything that could be construed as supporting apartheid, a system I was totally opposed to. I would be a liar to say that finance didn't come into it; when you have a wife and family to support you simply have to consider everything. But at the end of the day you still have to look at yourself in the mirror. Did I need any more convincing? After serious consideration, the answer had to be 'no', and as far as I was concerned the matter was closed.

I asked Alan Herd to pass on my decision to Boycott, and good old Geoffrey blew his top. His immediate reaction was that I had jeopardized the whole tour, which of course was just nonsense. In view of my deeds of 1981, I suppose I would have been seen as a big draw, but I was just one of a number of players lined up; and in any case the whole plan was far from sound because of the veil of secrecy surrounding it. The main worry was that there was no direct deal with the South African cricket authorities. Therefore, if news of the plan leaked out and the tour subsequently fell apart, the players would have been left high and dry, blacklisted by the world cricket authorities and unpaid over the winter.

Boycott was desperate to have me on board and when Herd paid him a visit at his hotel room, he was on the phone to Peter Venison, a sports promoter who had brought the draft contracts to India. Boycott handed the phone to him and asked him to talk direct to Venison.

Suddenly the tour fee on offer to me was swelling by the second until it finally reached £85,000. But I was adamant about my decision and I think by this stage the message had got through. My mind was made up and there was no turning back. They could have offered me the moon and still got nowhere.

These furtive talks were taking place in a Bangalore hotel where a few of the team were housed in chalets near the swimming pool. To reach these you had to go down a long corridor, at the end of which Boycott had a room on his own as usual. Although this was away from the main part of the hotel, we had all the mod cons (after a fashion, as is always the case in India) including air conditioning, which came via a long metal ventilation duct that ran through all the rooms.

After Herd had broken the news of my decision to Boycott, the atmosphere became quite strained; the angrier Boycott became, the louder his voice boomed. Suddenly, there was a knock on his door and Graham Dilley stuck his head round. 'I thought this was all meant to be secret,' he said. 'It might interest you to know that every word you are saying is being carried crystal clear down the air conditioning vent to every room in the block!'

As to the deal itself, Holiday Inns eventually pulled out, but, after they were replaced by South African Breweries, Boycott set to work again, undeterred by the fact that I was no longer on board.

Boycs' trip ended in bizarre fashion. After we had a go at him for sliding off to play golf while we were sweating it out in that Calcutta Test match, Boycs quit the tour in a fit of pique. That was the signal for 15 team-mates to grab hold of the nearest piece of paper they could find and get him to sign a resignation note before he had time to change his mind.

Two others who turned the deal down flat were David Gower and Mike Gatting. Going to South Africa was fine for the likes of Boycs and other older players nearing the end of their careers; Gower and Gatting, on the other hand, were quick to say no, realizing that going on the trip could have ruined their England futures.

Apart from all these behind-the-scenes distractions – and the fact that, after India had won the first Test they made sure to produce pitches on which there could be no prospect of a result and little point in attempting to get one – off the field this Indian tour was a marvellous end to 1981 and a good way to begin the new year. My team-mates gave me the royal treatment throughout the tour, simply because I managed to keep them supplied with copious quantities of English bitter.

In those days India was not on the list of holiday destinations for a real ale enthusiast and we had struggled on throughout the tour with the local brew, the delightfully named Rosy Pelican London Lager. Unfortunately, you didn't get much you could drink in a bottle anyway because you have to pour half the stuff away to get rid of the glycerine before you could reach the lager. My elevated status among my peers came about when I won the BBC Sports Personality of the Year award and during the interview, a live link-up with London, I was asked if there was anything I was badly missing. I said we would give anything for a good pint of beer, and the next thing we knew there were umpteen cases of Webster's Yorkshire bitter on the way out. There were problems getting the drinks through customs, but a little bit of bartering smoothed things over. The load was broken up and re-distributed by Govind, the man who has looked after England touring teams for years and whose main claim to fame is that he has never lost one piece of luggage – which, as anyone who has been to India knows, is an achievement worthy of a medal. Because of this, hero status was accorded to myself and Govind for the rest of the trip.

The Indian crowds on that tour were absolutely incredible. To begin with, there were just thousands of people camped outside our hotels. It was unreal, and I found it hard to come to terms with the fact that all these people wanted was a glimpse of me, although occasionally one or two of them wanted a little more than that.

There was an amazing moment at the end of the tour in Kanpur where we found a colonial club close to the hotel with a snooker table and Worthington bitter. One day I visited the place with Geoff Cook, and as we were coming out of the hotel and walking behind a barrier manned by police, suddenly one of the locals burst through the cordon and ran across to me, whereupon he grabbed me where I keep the family jewels and tried to plant a kiss on me.

My eyes were starting to water and I didn't know how to get rid of this guy who was screaming, 'Iron Bottom, Iron Bottom, I love you, I love you', so I thumped him. The poor bloke was lying there helpless on the ground while the crowd cheered and the police laughed. The name 'Iron Bottom' stuck in the memory, although my teammates decided to call me 'Tin Arse' instead.

Then there was another time when I met a family who had left their village 40 miles away and travelled for two days with their horse and cart simply to hand me a garland and take a few photographs. They were there and gone within five minutes, having spent at least the previous 48 hours on the road.

Early on during that tour we had a day off coming up in Nagpur so we decided to make the most of our evening. Eight of the players hired two motorized rickshaws and headed downtown to a local strip club. The place was in a basement down two flights of stairs; to describe it as dingy would be taking flattery to the extreme. In the company of the local Nagpur mafia, who were there having a few beers, we ordered several gallons of the local brew, siphoned off the glycerine as usual, and settled in for the evening's entertainment. After a while the stripper came on, swathed in what looked like bandages. She peeled off a few layers and the excitement level rose as the lads yelled for her to 'Get 'em off'. Then, suddenly and without any warning, she stopped, bowed to the audience and promptly disappeared off stage . . . even though she still resembled a well-padded Egyptian mummy.

We decided to revert to Plan B: shake off the body-guards and invite some of these girls back for a party. A couple of the lads were despatched backstage to negotiate a deal. Ten minutes had elapsed and there was no sign of them, so we went round the back to find out what was going on. There we discovered one of the boys pinned to the wall by a huge rabid Rottweiller trying to tear out his throat. The only thing restraining the dog was a chain around its neck attached at its other end to a post. The trouble was, this post looked as though it was on the point of being pulled out of the ground, so in the nick of time we managed to rescue our tortured team-mate and scarper.

Not allowing ourselves to be distracted from our attempts to spice up the evening, we then hit upon Plan C:

a rickshaw race back to the hotel with 100 rupees to the winner. How nobody got killed as we carved up the streets of Nagpur that night, I'll never know.

One of my best days on the tour was when I went duck and goose shooting with Keith Fletcher and a party of very wealthy Indian businessmen who drove us up to the source of the Ganges from where we took rafts downriver. Being a sacred water, one of the many traditions surrounding the Ganges is that it is used as a burial place. The whole atmosphere was somewhat eerie, to say the least.

Fletch and I had bagged some ducks and were sitting on the raft enjoying the ride when suddenly a large fish, almost the size of a fully grown dolphin, broke the water right where Fletch was sitting. It was like a scene from *Jaws*. Poor old Fletch, until this moment he had been the very model of decorum and politeness, but now here he was jumping up in the air as though someone had put a firecracker in his shorts.

'Cor, f-----g hell!' he shouted. 'What was that?' It took me about ten minutes to persuade him that it hadn't been a corpse rising from the dead.

Of course, certain aspects of being an English cricketer on tour are a little less exciting. I lost count of the number of official functions we would have to go to where we would be forced to sit through endless hours of speeches in Hindu without understanding a word that was said. All I can say is thank goodness we had our hip flasks with us.

All in all, the Indian experience was absolutely wonderful and I regret never returning there with England.

At least we had put the South African business to the back of our minds for a while. But when we returned home we found that the warnings from Herd and Hayter over the rebel tour had proved to be deadly accurate. The TCCB had decided to ban those involved from playing Test cricket for three years. It was a hard punishment but not unexpected, so there could be no complaints. The 'rebels' certainly could not claim that they had not been forewarned of the consequences. Back on 4 August 1981 the Board had sent letters to many leading players warning that 'any cricketer who takes part in any such international and/or representative matches in South Africa could, thereby, make himself ineligible for future selection for England'. Boycott, in fact, never played Test cricket again. For those who went, it was a matter of taking the money and taking their chances.

Boycott later had a go at me in his autobiography, accusing me of hypocrisy for saying I wasn't going on tour because 'I could never look Viv Richards in the eye again'. These were stirring words and Boycs would have had a point if I had said them. The problem was that I didn't. The quote came about for all the right reasons when news of the tour blew up and the Fleet Street crowd were running around like lunatics, desperate for a story of the latest player to sign up. That comment, made in perfectly good faith and sent out to all the newspapers, was attributed to me in a statement prepared on my behalf by Reg Hayter but which I never saw. Boycs said that because of it he could never trust me again, and he claimed Graham Gooch was of the same opinion. I was hurt by these accusations; it would have helped if the press had checked with me beforehand to find out exactly what my position was on the subject.

I never discussed that tour with Viv although we had talked about South Africa in general and about me joining

ON TOUR

THE WORLD AT MY FEET ... cricket has taken me to countries I might not have otherwise seen. With Geoff Boycott (right) in India during an X'mas party in 1981, the numbers on my chest indicating Boycs' achievement in becoming England's leading Test runs scorer. Whitewater rafting in New Zealand (below) with David Gower, Allan Lamb, Robin Smith and Graeme Fowler, and the crowds gather in India (bottom) for a duckshooting trip.

DERRING-DO

RUNS, WICKETS, CATCHES ... the Aussies (right) are on the receiving end again as I smash the ball over mid-wicket for six at Old Trafford in the Texaco Trophy in 1985. Five slips and a gully (below) for my bowling against India in the first Test in 1982 at Lord's, and taking a sharp catch at slip off Richard Ellison (bottom) to dismiss Larry Gomes at The Oval in 1984.

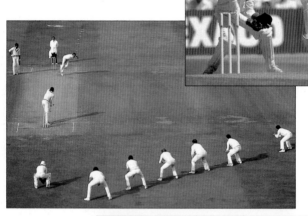

RECORDS GALORE ... launching into a straight six (above) on the way to my highest Test score of 208 against India at The Oval in 1982. Two years later, I'm celebrating my 300th wicket (right), that of Jeff Dujon in the fifth Test against the West Indies.

THAT'S THE ONE ... third Test, England v New Zealand, The Oval 1986. Jeff Crowe lbw b Botham for my 356th Test wicket, overtaking Dennis Lillee's world record.

GOODNIGHT BEEFY

OVER AND OUT ... *trying to hook Curtly Ambrose at The Oval in 1991 (above left), I clipped the bail as I lost my balance. It led to Jonathan Agnew's memorable observation: 'He couldn't quite get his leg over'. But a moment to savour (above), a catch for Durham that dismissed my old mate Viv Richards, then playing for Glamorgan.*

GOODBYE AND FAREWELL ... *it's thanks to the Durham crowd during my final match for them (right) against the Australians in July 1993. A less happy departure (above) as Wasim Akram celebrates the end of my World Cup final in March 1992. I was not a happy man.*

the second rebel tour captained by Mike Gatting in 1989. 'Go and talk to them,' Viv had said. 'You can't play forever, man'.

Before that second tour, there had been one other offer presented to Viv and I a couple of years after the 1981/82 rebel tour. But that never got off the ground because of the offensive way in which the deal was presented to us. Two South African businessmen came to see me at Taunton with the idea of taking a multi-racial side out to the Republic. Viv said, 'See what they have to say'. After 20 minutes from them about all the wonderful things on offer, I asked what would happen if Viv and I wanted to have a drink, sit on the beach or play a round of golf together. One of the businessmen replied: 'That's easy. We'll make Viv an honorary white man'.

At this point negotiations ended and I just laughed in their faces. What did it mean? When I go to Antigua to visit Viv, do they have to make me an honorary black man? In the end it was a good job that these guys only talked to me and didn't get to Viv, judging by his reaction when I told him what had happened, I think he might have given those men more than just the benefit of his opinion.

Needless to say the meeting with these two businessmen ended the moment they came up with those words. My view is simple and clear-cut: the idea of discriminating against a man simply because of the colour of his skin is totally alien to everything I have been brought up to believe. The fact is that if Viv and I had been brought up in South Africa we could not have shared a house, and one of the great and most enduring friendships of my life would almost certainly never have existed. In fact my relationship with Viv was one of the reasons why I took such exception when years later Imran Khan accused me of racism and I decided I had to defend myself against the allegations in court.

Funnily enough, I really do believe that all the cricketers who either went on rebel tours themselves or travelled there to coach were of the same opinion. There is no point in denying that the real reason most of them went was for the money; the amount being offered was huge in comparison to the average county wage. The simple truth is that in cricket, as in any sport, you've got to make your bundle while you can and, within reason, however you can.

Money, however, was not the only thing on Mike Gatting's mind when he accepted the offer to captain the second rebel side to South Africa on the ill-fated 1989/90 tour.

Gatt had been an excellent England captain and hugely popular among his team-mates. He led by example but also understood that all players are different and need to be treated as individuals. It was this approach that had brought out the best in the side on the 1986/87 Ashes trip after which Gatt had looked set to be England's captain for as long as he wanted the job.

He was also fiercely proud of representing his country – a real Union-Jack-underpants merchant, even if he could rarely find a pair to fit him. So when he made the decision to turn his back on England in 1989, there had to be more to it than hard cash. There was and the full story dated back to 1987.

Gatt was not the only England player irritated beyond breaking point by the umpiring they suffered on the 1987 winter tour to Pakistan. Chris Broad, for instance, was severely reprimanded after standing his ground when given out in the first Test and, as the comments that were picked up by a television microphone implied, the England players felt that there was 'one rule for one team and one for the other'. But as captain Gatt should not have allowed himself to be provoked into showing his and his players' feelings so publicly. What made his stand-up row with umpire Shakoor Rana at Faisalabad even more serious was that the whole thing was picked up by the television cameras and broadcast over and over again in Pakistan and at home.

Gatt simply lost his temper. There were extenuating circumstances for his behaviour, yet he shouldn't have made that outburst and he knows it. What he should have done was bite his tongue and then had a word with Shakoor Rana in private at the end of the session. But we are all human and we all make mistakes.

When Shakoor Rana's ridiculous posturing even went as far as him delaying the restart of the match until he had a written apology from Gatt, the affair descended into farce. Gatt had no intention of agreeing to this and saw no reason why he should. Back at Lord's, however, the TCCB saw it differently and forced Gatt to back down. At least the players were behind Gatt all the way. If the Board had not stepped in, I'm sure the match would never have been completed. But then they made themselves look utterly stupid when, after reprimanding Gatt publicly, they awarded him and every other player a £1000 hardship bonus at the end of the tour that looked suspiciously like a sweetener.

By the time England returned home there had been more trouble on the field. During the Bicentennial Test against Australia in Sydney, Chris Broad, having made a century, flattened the leg stump with his bat on being given out and was fined. Then in New Zealand, Graham Dilley was also hit in the pocket when after he had an appeal turned down, the stump microphone picked up something along the lines of 'Oh, dear me'.

None of the above was ultimately considered serious enough for Gatt's position as captain to be in jeopardy for the forthcoming series with the West Indies. After winning the Texaco Trophy 3–0, England then earned a creditable draw in the first Test at Nottingham. And then it was Gatt's turn for the treatment.

When Micky Stewart picked up his copy of the *Sun* in the breakfast room at the Rothley Court Hotel that fateful morning to read the back page story about the Test match, he was blissfully unaware of the headline on the front page. It read: 'GATTING MADE LOVE TO ME – BLONDE TELLS OF ROMPS AT STAR'S HOTEL'. When it was pointed out to him by a helpful reporter, the message brought his breakfast to an abrupt end. Soon afterwards it was the end of Gatt's captaincy as well.

Peter May, the chairman of selectors, issued a statement insisting that the TCCB believed Gatt's version of his alleged misbehaviour with a local barmaid . . . and then proceeded to sack him anyway. I couldn't believe how unfair and preposterous the allegations were; after all, anything that goes into Gatt's room after 10 p.m., he eats.

After England had run through the A–Z of county captains, appointing John Emburey, Chris Cowdrey and finally Graham Gooch, and the 1988 winter tour to India had been cancelled due to objections over the inclusion of Gooch and others with South African links, it was Gatt to whom the new chairman of selectors Ted Dexter and

Micky Stewart turned as their choice of captain for the 1989 Ashes series. Gatt was told the job was his.

Now at that stage ninety-nine per cent of the cricket-watching public, and most of the players for that matter, wouldn't have known Ossie Wheatley from Ossie Ardiles. But it was later revealed that Wheatley, as chairman of the TCCB cricket committee had put the block on Gatt's appointment by exercising his right of veto. Apparently, he represented powerful voices inside the establishment who were still not satisfied that Gatt had done his time. I have heard it suggested that they also feared a reaction from the Pakistan Board who were still fuming over the Shakoor Rana affair. In any case the book was closed on Mike Gatting, who subsequently made his decision to go to South Africa on that 1989/90 tour out of sheer frustration and anger as much as anything else.

Indeed for reasons of my own, when the South Africans came calling that final time in 1989 I was definitely interested. I talked to a lot of the players who had been out there lately, people like Graham Dilley. I asked all the relevant questions about conditions in South Africa and they said they were very impressed with the substantial changes that had taken place during the last five years. Reassured on that front, I then decided that if I was going I wanted to be involved in the coaching and promotion of the game in the black townships.

Clive Rice and Mike Procter were making enquiries on behalf of Dr Ali Bacher, the chief executive of the South African Cricket Board, regarding the availability of certain English players. The money on offer was again huge. This time I was asked to name my price and I said it would have to be a minimum £500,000, tax-free. I had still not fully recovered from the back surgery and I simply didn't know how long I could go on playing for England – it could be a week, a month or a year.

It got to the stage where I sat down with Ali Bacher at home to discuss a proposed deal. He went to great lengths to explain how things had changed in South Africa, and how there were cricket contacts in the black townships and developments in the pipeline for encouraging black cricketers. He even admitted that it had been right for the South Africans to have been kicked out of world cricket at the time when he was captain.

At the end of this meeting with Ali there was an offer on the table for two tours. But though I felt more positive about the prospect of going there than I had ever done before, I was still some way from being convinced. The political position might have been improving because of the changes taking place, but South Africa was still some-thing of a political hot potato and there remained concerns about the stability of the country. If I decided to go, con-tracts and endorsements would again be put at risk, and one of my main priorities was sorting out some proper compensation for the deals I might have lost. The talks with Ali were meant to be top secret but when he heard that I had checked out a few things with several South African contacts, he went mad and threatened to cancel any potential deal on the spot.

Once that storm had blown over, it was back to the negotiating table where all sorts of bartering went on. Progress was being made, and we had reached the stage where the London accountants of the South African Cricket Board, Touche Ross, wanted to meet with my accountants to sort out precisely how much they would have to cough up to compensate me for lost contracts. Ali Bacher finally found himself in a position to offer me a three-year deal, the first two years of each visit made up of five-week rebel tours and the last year playing for a South African provincial side. The finer points of the deal were left for Alan Herd to examine.

Although I had made sure that I had registered my interest, I still saw the trip as very much the option up my sleeve. I was keen to be part of the England set-up on the winter trip to the West Indies, and I suggested as much to the management. Throughout that summer in the dark corners of laundry rooms and other unlikely venues, they had been trying to get me to confirm my availability for the Caribbean. Micky insisted that they were going to pick a new side for the tour, that they wanted Gatt to lead it and they wanted me as the experienced senior player.

The rumours circulating about who was going to South Africa and who was not were gathering such momentum that they were having a detrimental affect on the England team. It did not help that during the summer we were being slaughtered by Allan Border's Australian side, of course, but by the time we arrived in Manchester for the fourth Test there was a clear split in the dressing room. The whispering in corridors had reached its peak, and the atmosphere was dreadful.

Finally, the news broke and the initial squad for the rebel tour was released. My name was not on the list, but neither was Gatt's at this stage. Then, during the lunch interval on the Saturday of the fifth Test – we were 37 for four at the time – I received a phone call from Herdy about the three-year South African offer during which I ended up saying 'No' to the deal. I told him that I felt this was my last chance to really prove myself against the West Indies and, considering the state of play at the time the call was made, the other England players could do with some good news. I had no worries about being up to the job, and my ambition was as strong as ever because the West Indies were the one side I had not scored a Test century against, nor had I really fulfilled my potential against them.

The decision made, I told Micky I was available while also giving Kath a call so she could set to work re-arranging my diary. At this stage I wasn't expecting to go off on tour with England – I knew I was going. So when Dexter later informed me that I was not wanted on voyage I was more than bewildered.

As I have said, had the South Africans come back to me then I might have reacted the same way as Mike Gatting and signed up there and then.

The irony of the situation was that while I had turned down the South African money in order to represent my country and was now out of the picture, two players who had done exactly the opposite by signing up for the first rebel tour, Gooch and Boycott, were on the point of joining the England tour to the Caribbean – the former as captain, the latter as his batting guru. What price loyalty?

There are a lot of similarities between Graham and Geoffrey, not least their single-mindedness. Boycott was Gooch's batting mentor; no one knows more about the skill and technique of batting than 'Fiery'. The problems arose because at the same time as moving freely among the players in the nets and elsewhere as Gooch's batting coach, Boycott was also earning his living as a television commentator and newspaper pundit, criticizing the same players at the same time as he was supposed to be helping them.

It was a situation that caused plenty of resentment among the rest of the players, especially during the trip to New Zealand in 1991/92, just before the World Cup, when Boycott's influence was terribly counter-productive. I just couldn't see how he could join the ranks of the media and at the same time stick his oar in with the England camp. If a player who had received the 'benefit' of Boycs' hands-on approach went out and had a good game, Boycs would pop up grinning on the television to tell the world 'Well, I spent half an hour with him in the nets yesterday and sorted him out'. Having taken the credit for those who did well, you could bet your bottom dollar that, according to him, the main reason behind any other batsman's failure was that he had not sought out Boycs for help.

Not only that, but we had this ridiculous situation where one minute Boycott was in the nets and the next he was on television identifying a player's specific weaknesses. Our opponents New Zealand just loved it. They had their twelfth man and coach tuned in to all this on the television in the dressing room. And who knows, the odd message might just have made its way out onto the field.

We felt as a team that this was unhelpful. If Gooch wanted to use Boycs for batting coaching that was understandable, but he should have gone to a quiet corner of the ground to do it. You have to remember that Boycs' presence around the party was as a journalist – first and foremost. Everyone was uneasy when he was about: some of the younger players even felt obliged to talk to him because of his relationship with Gooch. In truth, they would have rather told him to get lost. His meddling was not doing the side or team spirit any favours and, in the end, it was raised at a team meeting. The message must have been passed on because eventually he disappeared from sight, but not until after he had done his damage.

As a player my last brush with Boycs left me with a rather sour taste in the mouth. I arrived in New Plymouth to join my colleagues on that 1992 trip to New Zealand several weeks after the rest of the party. Prior commitments had meant I was unavailable for most of the New Zealand leg of the tour, but that was a perfectly satisfactory situation as far as Gooch and the management were concerned. They wanted me out there primarily for the World Cup, due to start after the New Zealand leg. Because I had not done as much training as the rest of the lads, I obviously needed to knuckle down and shed a few pounds before the action started. Before that, however, I first needed to recover from the long flight. I asked Micky if he wanted me in the nets the day after I arrived but he said that the best thing for me would be rest and relaxation, so I took the opportunity of a round of golf on the local course. When the *Sun* was sent a photo of a less than svelte Beefy whacking a golf ball around immediately after stepping off the plane, Boycs piled in with some comment about me being 'unprofessional and letting the side down'. Coming from the man who left his team-mates during a Test match and went off to play eighteen holes himself, I found it very hard to take, and I made the paper pay for it later as I took legal action against their allegations.

The whole thing might not have been so bad if Boycs' influence could and would have been beneficial had his criticisms been more constructive, but he never seemed to have a good word to say about anyone apart from Gooch and Alec Stewart. As a result he managed to make himself just as disruptive an influence out of the team as he had been in it.

Having said all this, if ever I was asked to pick a team to save my life, Boycs would be the first name down on the list (in fact, as you will read later, he was). All discussion of his personality aside, he was the one batsman I played with or against who could be relied on to never ever give his wicket away. He wasn't just committed to batting: he was obsessed by it. He ate, drank and slept it. He lived for cricket and couldn't understand why everyone did not feel exactly the same way as him.

He was also the only man I ever came across who succeeded in re-inventing himself as a player. In the early days he had all the shots in the coaching manual and he was not afraid to use them. One innings in particular, when he made a hundred and smashed the ball to all parts for Yorkshire in the 1965 Gillette Cup final, has achieved almost 'legendary' status.

But as time went on I believe he saw batting as more important than anything else. Any time he was not doing it meant he was somehow less alive, and for that reason he hated getting out more than any batsman I ever knew. The problem was that this meant he became a selfish batsman, always playing for himself rather than for the team, and this self-absorption expressed itself in other ways which soon became obvious to others, even his fans. The last time I was in the West Indies, for instance, some guy approached me in one of the rum shops and asked me 'How's the eye specialist?' I didn't know what on earth he was on about at first. Then he explained: 'You know, Geoff Boycott . . . the "I" specialist'.

The frustrating thing is that when he is in the mood,

Boycott can talk a lot of sense about the game. As I have said, he was one of the best opening batsmen I have ever had the privilege of playing with; what a pity that too often the selfishness that enabled him to succeed in the first place seemed to take over him completely.

I just wish somebody had got hold of him at an early age and said simply: 'There's more to life than batting, Geoffrey'.

9
SEX, DRUGS, AND ROCK 'N' ROLL

It is impossible to gauge the exact moment when I became fair game in the eyes of the guardians of social morality. I'm not just referring to the media, but also to those who make it their business to pry into, examine and pass judgement on the lives of people they know nothing about and care for even less.

To some extent, I had created a rod for my own back with the heroics of 1981. The hundreds I made at Headingley and Old Trafford and the bowling at Edgbaston set the standard by which all future exploits would be judged. My performances in 1982, in particular my highest Test score of 208 against India at The Oval (during which, incidentally, I managed to dislodge some tiles from the pavilion roof) and some quickfire hundreds for Somerset kept the pot boiling, but when I suffered the inevitable downturn in form, many refused to believe it was as simple as that. There must be a more sinister reason, they intimated, and during the miserably anti-climatic tour to Australia in 1982/83 the bloodhounds were let loose. Those newspaper editors who believed their job entailed knocking people down as quickly as they built them up in order to maintain interest and, more crucially, circulation, had decided that Botham was to be the next target. I certainly got the feeling that they were waiting for me. It seemed I was the flavour of the month, caught in the middle of the tabloid war that was raging at the time.

Because I had signed an exclusive contract with the *Sun* to transmit my thoughts to paper via a ghost-writer, or 'ghost' as they are known, the other tabloids then felt they were entitled to have a go at me. Eventually, the *Sun* joined in too in an attempt to rival the more sensational stories that were appearing about me elsewhere, and things reached such a state of confusion that on one occasion, when replying to criticism over something that had appeared under my name, I managed to come up with the memorable line: 'My ghost is writing shit'.

Looking back on 1983 now, Kath and I went through a pretty dismal time all round. The year began on a happy enough note with the news that she had become pregnant again. But the first sign of the troubles to come had appeared on the very first day of 1983 when, midway through the England tour down under, the *Sun* printed a pack of lies about myself and Rodney Hogg. I had always got on splendidly with the Aussie fast bowler whom I first encountered on the 1978/79 tour when we bet each other a bottle of any drink for the one who took the other's wicket more often, and to anyone who knew us it was obvious we were mates. But it seems the *Sun* was looking for a good story and they were not going to let the truth get in the way.

The facts were that as Rodney and I passed by each other at a Sydney restaurant and nightclub named Pier One on New Year's Eve, we indulged in the usual knockabout banter, no more, no less. The *Sun* story read: 'BOTHAM IN NEW YEAR'S EVE BRAWL WITH AUSSIE TEST STAR' which was total, utter rubbish. Eventually, the paper printed an apology which took up about three lines on page 17, but I could sense the way the wind was blowing. At this stage, Bob Willis, the England captain and a man with whom I had developed a firm and trusted friendship that has withstood the test of time, advised me to sever all ties with the paper. My attitude, however, was that the money was good and that no one took the tabloids seriously anyway. How wrong I would be proved as time progressed.

I am the first to admit that my bowling on that 1982/83 tour was a disappointment. Although I did not realize it then, the back problem that originated in 1980 and which almost ended my career during the 1988 summer was starting to take effect, and my lack of mobility led to some less than penetrative spells. I didn't want to admit it to anyone in case it affected team morale, but I was struggling to find rhythm and my timing was all wrong. I was not releasing the ball with any certainty and, despite finishing as our highest wicket-taker in that series, I knew (and so did the team) that I was not the force I should have been. Consequently the Aussies, over whom I should have had the Indian sign after the events of 1981, grew in confidence and were able to win the series without really dominating it. I kept trying to persuade Bob Willis that my bowling would come right in the end, but in the event it never did. I think he felt I let him down, and to be honest I couldn't argue with that assessment even allowing for the mitigating circumstances. In fact, my only real success with the ball came in the dramatic Melbourne Test. There, despite a last-wicket partnership between Allan Border and Jeff Thomson that had all but won the game for the Aussies, I managed to conjure up victory by three runs when Thommo drove at a wide half-volley and the ball went into and then out of the hands of Chris Tavaré in the slips before Geoff Miller clung gratefully onto the rebound.

To make matters worse, I had also caused problems for myself by criticizing the Aussie umpires. After we drew the Sydney Test finishing the series 2–1 losers, I was quoted as saying in the English newspapers: 'We have had one poor decision after another. I hate to lose and, even less, I hate to moan after being beaten. But it has to be said the umpiring on this tour has not been very good. In fact it was so bad at times that you felt we had to get fourteen of their wickets and they only had to get seven of ours'.

Although the comments were made in private and were not for publication, as far as I was concerned I was stating an honest opinion and one that I shared with Doug Insole, the manager and Bob Willis, the captain. I genuinely thought the umpiring was dreadful. On reading my comments, the Australian Cricket Board complained to the TCCB and I was fined £200.

Meanwhile Fleet Street, encouraged by a less than flattering photograph of me sitting with Dennis Lillee by a pool on the rest day of the Adelaide Test, had already made up their minds as to the real cause of my poor showing. According to them, I was too fat.

Things went from bad to worse during the 1983 summer. I had a poor World Cup, during which all of the other leading all-rounders performed conspicuously better than me, particularly Kapil Dev who helped his side achieve an unlikely victory over the West Indies in the final. Then, after another indifferent display in which we lost the Headingley Test against New Zealand, Bob Willis was hounded by press reporters who insisted I should be dropped. When he asked them which two players they suggested should be brought in to replace me, the names of Trevor Jesty of Hampshire and Surrey's David Thomas were thrown back at him. When Bob pointed out that neither player was likely to be able to do the all-rounder's job on their own, one of the tabloids immediately contacted the two players, told them the England captain said that he didn't rate them and printed a story accordingly.

But all this was nothing when compared to the next bitter blow. For it was during this match that Kath and I went through the worst experience of our marriage thus far.

Our ordeals at the hands of the press had been causing Kath much suffering. She took the criticism to heart, although mainly in silence, and it was obvious that it was having as much, if not more of an effect on her as it was on me. Until that evening, she had kept to herself the news she was about to tell me because she was desperate not to overburden me in what she understood was already a pretty tense situation, but when I walked through the door on the eve of the rest day, she decided she simply had to get it over with.

During a routine antenatal check on the baby Kath had been carrying, she was told by the gynaecologist that no heartbeat could be heard in the womb. She was informed that this was not particularly unusual but was advised to come back after the weekend for a scan. She tried to put a brave face on things, as she always did, but I could tell how worried she was. I attempted to reassure her by playing down the situation, saying 'Don't worry about it, love. I'm sure the scan will show everything is okay'. I tried not to show my feelings and attempted to carry on, publicly at least, as if nothing was wrong, but deep down I was distraught. I felt utterly helpless. I also felt guilty, as all fathers do at a time like this, wondering whether there was anything I could have done to have prevented this situation from arising. Should I have been more attentive? Had I allowed the pressure of my own situation to affect her well-being? Had my reaction to the pressure been a factor? All kinds of questions were buzzing around my head. I just didn't know what to say to her.

When the Test finished early, I accompanied Kath to the hospital for the scan. The results confirmed our worst fears. The baby was dead and Kath was admitted immediately. We both just sat there, completely numb and unable to express our emotions. After the initial shock, I tried to comfort Kath. You never really know what to say in this kind of situation, but I tried to emphasize to her that life goes on, and that we had to face it together.

There was nothing more I could do there and then, and we decided that in order not to draw attention to what had happened I should carry on as normal. As far as we were concerned it was our business and nobody else's; if the story got out it would only lead to more unwelcome press intrusion. So I managed to organize a plane to get me to Somerset's one-day match against Sussex and told Kath I would be back as soon as humanly possible. I didn't really know what I was doing that day; I was playing as if in a trance. But our wicket-keeper Trevor Gard, a long-time friend in whom I had confided, later told me that he had never seen me bowl as fast. In the event, the game finished in double-quick time and I flew back to be at Kath's side that evening.

Whether the suspicions of the press had been aroused by the fact that I had flown in and out again, or by my half-crazed performance, the news spread somehow or other. It made the lead story on the BBC's Nine o'clock News and the next day was all over the front pages. Kath and I were devastated and angry, and it took Kath in particular an awfully long time to get over the loss.

As the summer progressed, my relations with the media plummeted to an all-time low. At the next pre-rest-day press conference during the Lord's Test, Bob Willis, who had been as incensed as I was with the intrusion into our private grief, decided to answer all questions with a blunt 'Yes' or 'No'. After I scored a century on the first day of the Trent Bridge Test, I refused to talk to any of the press. I just couldn't take any more. Then one evening at Taunton, I lost control in spectacular fashion. I was strolling around the outfield with some mates from the opposing team when I suddenly spotted an opportunity that was too good to resist. The press box was empty and there was no one else around, so I picked up one of the deckchairs scattered along the boundary perimeter and hurled it through the closed window, and I was ready to do even more damage before my colleagues restrained me and dragged me out of the ground.

Ironically, my fortunes on the field improved from then on until the end of the season. Perhaps that gesture had helped me to get something out of my system. Apart from the century at Nottingham, I played one of the most treasured innings of my career to help Somerset reach the final of the NatWest Trophy. Brian Rose, the current club captain, was injured and so I led the side against Middlesex at Lord's in the semi-final in his absence. I made somewhat of an arithmetical cock-up with the bowling arrangements which led to Joel Garner, then probably the best fast bowler in the world, not having the chance to complete his full twelve-over stint. Then, when we slipped to 52 for five in response to Middlesex's 223, the game appeared lost.

Cynics have suggested that the motive behind the captain's innings I set myself to play was the opportunity to use the occasion to stake my claim for the Somerset captaincy on a full-time basis, as the first step on the road back to the England job I so desperately wanted to try again. Certainly, I was concerned with playing a mature, responsible innings but not for that reason. I simply wanted to win the match for myself and for my county. The ability of some people to twist things to suit their own theories never ceases to amaze me. When the last over came I was still there on 90 and the scores were level. What happened next baffled many observers, but I had conferred with the umpires beforehand and established that, as long as we did not lose more than one wicket, we would win. I decided to try and block out the final over from John Emburey, and with close fielders all around the bat, I did just that, although I must admit my heart was in my mouth when I padded up to the final ball which must have been perilously close to trapping me leg before. To this day, Embers remains convinced that he had me. The match was over by then anyway but I desperately wanted to carry my bat. My answer to him is 'Look in the book'.

When we beat Kent comfortably in the final and I raised a trophy as captain for the first time, Kath and I believed that at last we were starting to emerge from the long dark tunnel.

After a long and stressful tour to Australia in 1982/83, something told me that England's 1983/84 tour next winter to Fiji, New Zealand and Pakistan would be a good one to miss. As things turned out, I should have listened.

I was determined that whatever criticisms might come my way on the winter tour, no one would ever again be able to accuse me of being too fat, so I threw myself into my football training with Scunthorpe United and even got myself into their first team. I was delighted with this, of course, but the TCCB clearly weren't. They contacted me to say they were unhappy that I was risking injury by playing Fourth Division soccer so close to leaving on tour. Why they singled me out in this way was beyond me: after all, Allan Lamb and David Gower were off skiing somewhere and Mike Gatting was also playing local football in London. Why weren't the Board concerned enough to talk to them? I was so irritated by their heavy-handed treatment that I played on beyond the time when I had originally intended to stop. I had decided in advance to pack up before Christmas but after they rang to try and bully me into not playing, I told Scunthorpe I would be available for the Boxing Day game against Hull City after all. The match was played in front of a crowd of some 20,000 and I managed to prevent the Hull centre-forward, Billy Whitehurst, from barely having a kick all afternoon. Then I played the following day against Preston, before flying out with the England party for a warm-up match in Fiji two days later.

Then the fun and games really started.

The cricket played by the England side in New Zealand

was poor throughout but the worst performance of all came in the second Test in Christchurch. We collapsed twice to be all out for 82 and 93 and lost by an innings in just twelve hours of actual playing time. I bowled a pile of filth and, in the second innings, managed to get out first ball when Martin Crowe caught me at short leg. My wry grin as I walked back to the pavilion indicated that I felt we were caught up in one of those situations which was beyond our control. I had in fact hit the ball smack off the middle of the bat, only to be denied a certain four by a brilliant catch. The press, with their pens already poised over bucketfuls of vitriol, saw my facial expression in a different light: to them it looked as if I simply didn't give a toss about losing my wicket.

They came to the conclusion that our poor showing, and mine in particular, had nothing to do with bad cricket and everything to do with wild living. Slowly but surely the rumours started to spread. From a personal point of view, what happened on the New Zealand leg of the tour was no different to the kind of behaviour seen on every England tour I have ever been on. There are times during the long separations from family and friends that the pressure of touring catches up on you. It is during these low periods that players need a release. Some find it in drink and, on occasions, some find it in female company. With the rise in the worldwide popularity of cricket, it is hardly surprising that by this time the 'groupie' had become a common sight on tour.

I found my escape in the occasional joint. And although I have always denied the specific allegations about what was supposed to have taken place, I am now quite happy to admit that, from time to time, I did take dope on this tour. Dope was merely a way out of the pressures; it is not something I condone, it just happened. I can't justify my actions, but there were times when I hid in my room, had a joint and totally switched off, otherwise I think I might well have gone round the bend. The fact was that I had reached breaking point: it had got to the stage where I felt I could no longer go down to the hotel bar for a drink without being branded an alcoholic. If I sat down for a meal and passed the time of day with a waitress, immediately she would be jumped on by reporters subjecting her to the Spanish inquisition and asking 'Did he ask you for sex? . . . Did he ask you for drugs?'

These scum of the earth who had flown out to join the cricket correspondents but were in the main operating separately from them, got up to such amazing tricks in search of their stories that they would have been funny if they weren't so serious. People would be hiding behind pot-plants trying to pick up on bits of conversation, or in lifts where they would pose as tourists and try and engage you in conversations from which they might be able to glean titbits of scandal. It was bizarre, almost like being in a film. It was not until we had moved on from New Zealand to Pakistan that the allegations began to appear back home, but when they did, the shit really did hit the fan. One paper printed a story saying that almost the entire England team had been high on drugs at a concert given by the rock group, The Pretenders. Well, there was an awful lot of dope being smoked at that gig, something that was a typical occurrence at rock concerts in those days, but it was not being smoked by us. What we had done was smuggle in a large quantity of tequila mixed with orange juice, the same rocket fuel that later got me through so many of the most painful moments on the Leukaemia walks.

Stories started to appear about players and other women; and then came the heroin accusations. It was actually alleged by the *News of the World*, although not printed for about another three years, that I had shared a night of heroin-induced passion with the wife of a cricket journalist. Sex, drugs and rock 'n' roll – the tabloid writers were taking their pick.

Just as absurd was a story printed there and then that was nothing but a total flight of fancy. It was stated that during the second Test in Christchurch the England dressing room resembled a modern day Sodom and Gomorrah. According to one local paper, it was like an 'opium den'. The rumour was that the players had smoked pot in the dressing room during the game and that we had stuffed damp towels into the crack at the bottom of the door in order to stop the smoke and the distinctive aroma from spreading. The fact that this was supposed to have taken place when rain had stopped play with the usual crowd of people knocking on the door, moving in and out and asking for bats to be autographed, not to mention others appearing like tour manager A. C. Smith, did not dissuade the reporters in question from having a field day. It was all cobblers and even the *Mail on Sunday*, who had their own team of news reporters follow us around for the whole tour trying to dig up dirt, admitted: 'Investigations by Mail on Sunday journalists have failed to substantiate this allegation'. But when they alleged that an incident took place involving myself, Allan Lamb, two women and a couple of bags of cocaine in a hotel bedroom, the situation got completely out of hand. What had not helped (and this was no fault of his) was the presence on tour of pop star, cricket fan and my good friend, Elton John. We had first met in Sydney on the previous tour and got on well. Elton and I both had a lot in common at this time. Elton knew all about media hounding and helped me put things in perspective, and our friendship grew as a result. Later, on the 1986/87 tour down under he even baby-sat for Kath and I when we wanted to get away from it all. But the press, in their flights of warped fantasy only saw him as the rock star whose image hardly fitted into the MCC coaching manual and whose relationship with the players clearly proved that we were a bunch of debauched, drug-crazed maniacs.

All these allegations were investigated by the New Zealand police authorities and found to have no basis in truth. They issued a media release in which they stated the following:

Police have published the findings of their detailed investigation into the allegations of drug misuse associated with the English cricket team's summer tour of New Zealand.

No charges are to be laid as a result of the investigation.

We have found that much of what was reported seems to have been founded in rumour and speculation which upon proper investigation has evaporated in the mishmash of contradictions and uncorroborated allegations. There was a need for caution to be exercised because some 'witnesses' had allegedly received offers of money and other inducements, for their information.

They spelled out their findings over five specific allegations as follows:

1. *Allegations that members of the England cricket team were smoking cannabis at the Elton John concert in Wellington.* The England media claim to have a statement supporting this allegation from a professional woman living in Napier. This person was spoken to by detectives and she categorically denies having seen anyone smoking cannabis at the concert.

2. *Another allegation related to a person claimed to have supplied drugs to England cricket players in Dunedin.* This was also denied. The alleged supplier told police that he thought the allegation may have been based on a 'boozie fantasy' which just got out of hand. As his story goes, he and others had been responsible for dreaming up a fanciful plot about supplying a particularly potent variety of cannabis to England cricket players with the intention of adversely affecting their performance. Police were told that the story was pure fabrication, and re-told many times.

3. *A statement obtained from a woman by the English newspaper.* This was found to contain many false statements.

4. *Another incident at the Wellington Hotel, where a certain member of the touring team was alleged to have been looking 'spaced out'.* This lacks corroboration. In fact, another person in the room at the same time denies the allegation.

5. In another incident members of the England cricket team were in the audience at a rock concert at Christchurch. There was an allegation that some were smoking cannabis. Police enquiries have revealed that cannabis was offered to one member of the England cricket team but witnesses stated that he specifically turned the offer down.

The statement concluded by insisting that 'there is insufficient evidence to charge any person with an offence'.

According to the Deputy Assistant Commissioner Brian Davies, Head of Crime and Operations: 'As it could be seen from these examples, the police had been left with only "shadows" after investigating the allegations'.

But that was of little comfort to those suffering the latest scandals back home.

By the time we arrived in Pakistan, the knee injury I suffered in the Test match at Wellington had flared up to such an extent that I had to return home for immediate surgery.

In the days leading up to my return, things at home went from bad to worse. One of Liam's school friends had been banned from playing with him by parents who told him to 'stay away from Liam Botham, his family are all drug addicts'. Kath was inundated with reporters camped outside the front door and trying to force her to respond to the stories, so she left home with Jan, Gerry, Liam and Sarah, to stay with Christine Garbutt, a friend and feature writer on the *Daily Mirror*. However, the hounds would not be put off the scent. Because the *News of the World* could not reach any of the immediate family, they decided Kath's grandmother should be the next target, and they put her under intense pressure through repeated telephone calls. They told her that the *Mail on Sunday* were printing a ghastly story about me and that she should do everything in her power to persuade Kath to talk to them and give her response. At the very least, they insisted, she must tell them where Kath was staying.

I didn't know quite what to expect when I got into Heathrow. Certainly I knew from Kath and Alan Herd that stories had been printed, but I was blissfully unaware of how sensational they had been. When the plane landed I was left in no doubt. The scene at the airport was unbelievable. I passed through customs and pushed my trolley up the walkway as usual; then, before I knew it, there was a massive crowd of humanity surging around me. Somewhere in amongst this hurricane made up of camera men and reporters were Kath and the kids, but I simply never saw them as bodies swarmed around me like flies. They were pushing and shoving and obviously cared nothing for the intense distress they were causing. Liam was subjected to a terrible battering in the crush and my daughter, Sarah, was in tears. I was in such a state that I passed right by them before I realized I had missed them. I didn't know what to do and all I could think of was getting the hell out of that madhouse as soon as possible. Every moment and every gesture was eagerly snapped up by the hordes of photographers, so that even when I was being reunited with those closest to me all I could feel was blind rage.

It was then, at the moment of greatest chaos, that I did something I would live to regret: I told reporters that I had never smoked dope in my life. Years later, when I confessed to having done so as part of my agreed compromise with the *Mail on Sunday* to end my expensive libel action against them, this comment came back to haunt me. When the TCCB banned me from all cricket at the start of the summer of 1986, one of their complaints was that I had revealed in the newspaper that I had used drugs after previously denying it.

That was all in the future. For the moment, as we piled into the car for the journey back to Epworth, the tension was broken for a moment by the absurdity of the situation, and we fell into fits of laughter. But then the mood began to change as Kath ran through some of the stories that had appeared in the papers. As she did so, I became more and more angry. These people seemed to have nothing better to do than put me under the microscope without the slightest concern about how much damage they might be doing to my family in the process. When we reached home, Kath's father, Gerry, gave me a copy of the *Mail on Sunday* with the latest allegations. As I read them so my rage reached bursting point. I rang Alan Herd and told him I wanted him to come up for a meeting the very next day.

I've spoken before about how my single-mindedness has affected Kath on occasions, how at certain times I have not been able to see further than the end of my own nose, and how I had excluded Kath from my life at the very moment when both she and I needed her to be involved. I have never forgotten, or forgiven myself, for instance, for sending her packing from my troubles when I resigned the England captaincy in 1981. This was another one of those times. What I should have done was to include Kath in everything Alan and I discussed. She could have been a formidable ally, but instead I shut her out completely. While Alan and I pored over the reports in minute detail, Kath was reduced to fetching cups of coffee. She told me later that whenever she entered the room the conversation would immediately stop and not start again until she left. This was quite unforgivable of me, but by that time I just wasn't thinking straight. At the end of the day I was so self-centred that I totally forgot about her feelings. In a way I thought I was doing the right thing by her in trying to protect her feelings and not wanting her to have to go through this ordeal but, on reflection, it would have done her so much good to have sat with us, heard what was being said and been able to contribute. At the very least, it would have done wonders for her peace of mind.

This heralded the start of the most difficult period of our marriage. From then on, whenever things went wrong I retreated into myself; whenever the latest sensational allegation appeared, I shut her out of my life. I was being a selfish bastard really, but it was a matter of me reacting to these stresses by putting up the barriers. Deep down I was saying 'I'm Ian Botham, I don't need any help from anyone'. It was unfair of me, but I was simply incapable of making rational judgements at those moments. I don't know how she put up with me because it must have been sickening for her to be shut out like that. She was not the only one who suffered either; I became so paranoid that I would treat other, equally innocent characters as though they were sworn enemies.

I ranted and raved with Alan Herd for the best part of a day and insisted he fly out to Pakistan to get affidavits from the players, which he did. I was determined to sue the *Mail on Sunday*, whatever the cost. Then, while he was out in Lahore gathering the statements, I managed to get myself into even more hot water on a totally different subject.

Sitting in my hospital bed following surgery on my return to England and not exactly feeling at the top of my spirits, I gave a radio interview to the BBC's Pat Murphy during which I attempted to pass a light-hearted remark about the trials and tribulations of touring Pakistan, which, as everyone who has been there knows, can be arduous enough at the best of times. During the interview, which lasted about half an hour, I had talked widely about a whole range of subjects, including one that was particularly dear to my heart at this stage – the pressures of touring. I had also told Pat that I believed the England players were capable of buckling down to the task and putting some pride back into their performances. What the editor of the programme decided to highlight, however, was the following, not very convincing attempt at a joke. 'Pakistan,' I said, 'is the kind of place to send your mother-in-law for a month, all expenses paid.'

It was an off-the-cuff remark and I shouldn't have said it. Certainly the Pakistan authorities believed so and they found a willing spokesman in Sarfraz Nawaz, the former Test bowler, who subsequently branded me 'a drug-crazed opium pusher'. Years later, the joke came back to haunt me when I was given out at the start of our reply to Pakistan's match-winning total in the 1992 World Cup final in Melbourne and one of the Pakistan fielders taunted me by saying 'Send in your mother-in-law. She couldn't do any worse.' And it even had repercussions for my nearest and dearest at the time. More than once, my mother-in-law Jan, with whom I have always got on extremely well, was approached in the local high street and asked what she had done to upset me so much. These people were being deadly serious!

All in all, the joke backfired in a big way. The hotel staff back at the Hilton in Lahore had got to hear about the interview and threatened to go on strike. Even the Pakistani solicitors who were typing the affidavits got the hump. All of a sudden they forgot how to spell words like 'the' and 'it' so that the work slowed almost to a halt. Meanwhile, Herd had sent a telex from Lahore to his London office which read simply: 'Tell our client to keep his bloody mouth shut'. To finish things off the TCCB, reacting to the outcry, set up a disciplinary hearing and I was duly fined £1000. The perfect end to a perfect tour.

As I set about recuperating from the operation and making sure I was fully fit for the summer visit by the West Indies, I hoped that the worst was now over. Little did I know. For although I got my wish of captaining Somerset in my benefit year and did reasonably well in the Test series on a personal level, despite the fact that we were thrashed 5–0, the worst was still to come.

Just as the season was about to begin I lost a dear friend, Peter 'Jock' McCombe who died suddenly from a heart attack. Jock had been a trusted friend to both myself and Viv Richards, although certain members of the Somerset committee resented the fact that he was closer to us than any of them and he was, to all intents and purposes, our personal confidant. They were even more aggrieved when Jock was appointed liaison officer at the club, a role which meant he made sure Viv and I wouldn't be bothered by potential hangers-on. In hindsight, it may have started the petty jealousies that later resulted in the rift which caused the sackings of Viv and Joel Garner and my decision to leave the county at the end of 1986.

The immediate problem caused by Jock's death was that

certain functions which I had agreed to attend during my benefit season somehow escaped my attention. On more than one occasion, Reg Hayter had to apologize on my behalf to those who felt they had been slighted by my non-appearance at an event neither he nor I actually knew anything about. The press smelled blood again, and after I arrived a shade late at a benefit match at Sparksford in Somerset, having been delayed by appalling road works, the *Sunday People* set to work with a vengeance. They carried a story saying that I had behaved rudely, refused to sign any autographs and deliberately got myself out so I could leave early. It was all nonsense of course, but by that time the cumulative effect of all the bad publicity was unstoppable. Not only did it lead to the cancellation of some events, but I'm certain that the eventual sum amassed of £90,000 would have been far higher were it not for all the rumours about sex, drugs and rock 'n' roll that had been flying around.

On another occasion, the day before I was due to appear on Terry Wogan's television chat show, someone's idea of a sick joke came near to making me seriously ill. I had hosted a day's shooting that involved traipsing over the hills and dales all day, following which I was relaxing in the pub where a dinner was to be held as the grand finale. Halfway through a pint of the local brew, I started to feel queasy. I had no idea what was wrong, but I knew I was struggling. As everything became a blur, I grabbed hold of Andy Withers, Jock's successor, and told him: 'For Christ's sake, you've got to get me out of here'. In fact, we got as far as the car park before I keeled over, face-first, physically out of control. To be honest, I was petrified. It was only later when the organizer of the shoot appeared that we managed to piece together what had happened. Apparently, some comedian had spiked my drink. Andy got me to bed as soon as he could and stayed up all night to make sure I was all right. He was loath to call a doctor in view of the drugs-related publicity that would no doubt ensue, but fortunately I recovered sufficiently for the programme to go ahead the following day. Needless to say, it was a long time before I had a drink in public again.

People have often asked me what is at the root of the kind of character assassination I was being subjected to at the hands of the media. I happen to believe it is a peculiarly English phenomenon. For some reason, we distrust winners. Look at recent examples of sportsmen and women who have achieved the greatest popularity in our country, and you are almost always looking at failure. With all the respect in the world to a true gentleman, the best thing Henry Cooper did was to knock Muhammad Ali down and then lose against him in the same fight. Frank Bruno finally achieved his ambition of winning the world heavyweight crown, but the public loved him just as much for his ability to take defeat like a gallant loser. In terms of the true standards of the sport in which he attempted but hopelessly failed to compete, Eddie 'The Eagle' Edwards was the greatest nonentity of all time. Yet he was a hero in the eyes of millions of British television viewers.

When it comes to success stories like Nick Faldo, Steve Davis and Nigel Mansell, all the media want to do is find ways to bring them down a peg or two. The 'experts' among the general public, having soaked up the latest scathing attacks from the tabloids, then take great delight in indulging in the usual bar-room blathering about Steve 'Interesting' Davis and how Mansell and Faldo are surly, boring and, quite possibly, mad. In the end it all comes down to jealousy.

People say that once you walk into public life you have to accept the kind of interest and intrusion that always follows. That is certainly true. But I have yet to be convinced by any argument that says it has to be like this. It certainly doesn't happen in quite the same way in other countries. It used to be rock stars who suffered from this kind of treatment; then, during my period at the top, it was sportsmen until now, more recently, the attention has turned to politicians. When will it ever end?

My disaffection with certain sections of the media contributed to the decision I made at the end of the 1984 series against the West Indies, not to make myself available for the upcoming winter tour to India. I felt I owed it to Kath, the kids and myself to take a complete break. At last, I thought, we would all be able to enjoy a winter at home together out of the spotlight and away from the publicity machine that had so disastrously disrupted our lives twelve months earlier. That decision having been made, we settled down to our first winter at home together as a family, relaxed in the knowledge that at least nothing more could possibly go wrong.

At least that's what we had hoped.

The first indication that there might be trouble ahead came shortly before Christmas. During a chat on the phone, Alan Herd told Kath that a partner of his who was working on a case with a solicitor from Grimsby had been told by him that some of the local Humberside police were out to get me. After what had happened years ago when they appeared to be somewhat miffed that I was acquitted after the incident involving Joe Neenan and Steven

Isbister, this added up in my mind and when I spoke to an ex-Scunthorpe United colleague, Vince Grimes, who was now working closely with the force in community relations, it appeared that my worst fears were confirmed.

I started looking for signs and sure enough soon found them. Over a period of a few days leading up to the holiday, I became convinced that I was being followed. I never caught sight of those on my tail, but I was certain it was happening and I was sure that I knew who was doing it. I told Gerry, Kath's father, and we decided not to tell Kath because it would only upset her. Because I was so concerned about what I had heard, I decided to make absolutely sure not to drink even a drop. I intended to drive, so that if I was stopped there could be no reason for the police to have a go at me.

My fears meant that I took it very easy over Christmas and I was beginning to forget about the warning when the fun began. On New Year's Eve at around six in the evening, as Kath was preparing food for a small family party, the doorbell rang. It was the police and they wanted to speak to me, so I showed them into the lounge.

I was stunned by what I heard next. The police said that a small packet of drugs had been found in the pocket of a pair of my trousers that had been sent to the dry cleaners.

I didn't know what to say. I checked with Kath that she had in fact sent clothes to the dry cleaners and when she asked why, I told her.

'They must be joking', she said.

They then said that they had a warrant to search the house.

'Go ahead,' I told them. 'I've got nothing to hide. Search away.'

So they did and I went upstairs with them. After a few moments rifling around in my bedroom drawer, one of them showed me what he had found and looked at me.

'Excuse me, Mr Botham. Do you happen to know what this is?'

I did. It was dope, and in the moment the police officer displayed it to me I suddenly remembered exactly how it got there. After a Test match at The Oval a few years back, some bloke came up to me and offered me something to smoke. Thinking it would be rude not to I was happy to have a puff and when I got home I stuffed the remainder in the draw. I then proceeded to forget all about it, until now.

'Yes,' I replied. 'I do,' and repeated the story.

Meantime, unbeknown to me, another police officer was busy in the kitchen with Kath asking her seemingly innocent questions. I knew I was in trouble and was quite happy to go down to the police station with them and face the music. For me, the worst part of the business was that once I had done so it was also necessary for Kath to come down to the police station to be questioned as well.

I have never made any secret of the fact that I smoked dope in my younger days. In fact, I first tried it at the age of eighteen when it was given to me at a party, and I did so for the same reasons that school kids sneak off for a fag behind the bike shed. I did it for the kick. At the time there were strong moves to legalize cannabis. What's more, I have even shared a joint with a vicar in the vestry of his country church! Although this doesn't excuse anything, I have seen many people, including former Test cricketers, render themselves more senseless through alcohol than I have ever been on dope. And the one thing I have always made sure of is that I have never tried to involve Kath. I know she never approved. In fact, she positively disapproved and still does. To her the argument is very straightforward. Cannabis is illegal, end of story and, knowing how she felt, I made sure I never put her in a compromising situation by smoking in front of her.

Yet here she was in the police station having to undergo the pressure of a formal police interview. Finally, we were released on bail and arrived home separately, and although no action was taken against Kath (quite rightly, as she had done absolutely nothing wrong) they later charged me with possession of 2.19 g of cannabis. The next day, the papers were full of the story and, of course, they went over the top as usual.

BOTHAM AND WIFE IN DRUG RAID DRAMA

This made it sound like a wild orgy rather than the quiet family gathering it had actually been, but it was, as they say, a fair cop and I had no one to blame but myself.

Again, however, it was Kath who had to bear the brunt of the problem, and again Alan and I tended to shut her out of what was going on. At one point she insisted that Alan should demand an apology in view of her treatment by the police, but we felt it would only stir things up. She was at her wits' end what with having to cope with this incident and its effect on the children as well as herself. Sarah had come home from school one day and told her that there had been problems with the other kids, and she was convinced that by extension her reputation had been

HUMBERSIDE POLICE
Form 101 *(Revised June 1984)*
*Delete as applicable

NOTICE OF CHARGES TO THE ACCUSED

Sheet No. ......1............ of ....1.......... sheets

Name ....Ian Terrence BOTHAM................................ Date of Birth ..24.11.55...... SEX M/F*

Address ....'Grasmere', Blow Row, Epworth, Humberside

.... Occupation ...Self employed.... Married /SINGLE*

JUVENILE YES/NO* Name of Parent/Guardian ....

To appear at ....Scunthorpe Magistrates' Court.... on ...14.2.85.... ON BAIL/IN CUSTODY*
                        (Court)   (Date)

NOTICE TO ACCUSED OVERLEAF

CHARGES

You are charged with the offences shown below. You are not obliged to say anything unless you wish to do so, but whatever you say will be taken down in writing and may be given in evidence.

Precedent Code 656 - Unauthorised Possession of Drugs

That you, on Monday 31 December 1984, at Epworth in the County of Humberside, contrary to s.5(2) of the Misuse of Drugs Act 1971, had in your possession cannabis, a controlled drug, without lawful excuse or authority, namely ....

Place Charged ...Scunthorpe Police Station... Time and Date ....

Officer Charging .... Officer accepting charge ....

Officer in case ..Mr FOWLER.. Rank ...DS... No. ...126... Station ..SCUNTHORPE

I have received a copy of the above document .... (accused)

as badly damaged as mine. On hearing this, Kath hit the roof. She came into the sitting room where I was stretched out on the sofa. I had no idea what was coming. She went straight to the glass-topped table, picked it up with both hands and hurled it at me. Luckily for me, her aim was somewhat affected by her state of mind and it missed its intended target, but the message was clear.

Over the next few weeks we went through a very rough patch. I was determined not to be brought down by what had happened and tried to act as if the whole thing was a storm in a teacup. Kath, whose very strong views about drugs have never changed, just couldn't see it that way and whenever I tried to lighten the atmosphere or change the subject she felt I was not taking the issue as seriously as I should. In the end it was something of a relief when on 14 February 1985, Valentine's Day, I pleaded guilty to the charge of possessing dope at, of all places, Scunthorpe Magistrates' Court, as a result of which I was fined £100.

I was now officially 'convicted on a drugs charge', and even to this day that label causes me problems at customs and immigration all over the world. I was a shade aggrieved at the ticking off I received from the magistrate, who got on his high horse and had a go at me about setting the right example. As far as I was concerned, I took my punishment fair and square and I didn't need him telling me how to set an example to kids.

The bad publicity that had surrounded the court case had immediately damaging effects, with the car manufacturers Saab cancelling a lucrative deal I had with them. Despite their insistence that the decision had nothing to do with the court case, it didn't take an Einstein to figure out the reality of the situation. Then another deal set up for me by Reg Hayter with a stationery firm went down the drain and they signed up David Gower instead. At least Duncan Fearnley, my cricket equipment manufacturer, stayed loyal, a fact I took into account when later signing for

Worcestershire after the Somerset affair exploded. And Nike were also very understanding of the situation.

The episode also served to stoke the flames of indignation among those who had been moaning for some time that I had grown too big for my boots, to the extent that pressure was being put on the TCCB at Lord's to act against the first professional cricketer convicted on drugs charges. There were even suggestions that I might be thrown out of the game altogether. Eventually, I was relieved but not surprised to be cleared to play by a disciplinary committee, allowing me to get back to what I do best and prepare myself for the arrival of the Australians.

I was taking nothing for granted, of course, but, although somewhat depressed by recent events, I was itching for the chance to get back into the fray. Then I started to hear whispers that my recall to the Test arena might be in danger, not from administrators but from the players. Stories had been filtering back from the England tour party in India that it had been a far happier ship without me on board. Certainly, David Gower's side had done what no other England team had ever done, coming back from 1–0 down to win a Test series out there, but the implication was that my absence had been a contributing factor and I resented it. Those who were trying to stir it up for me gave unattributable quotes to the press along the lines that morale had been higher without me around and that I was too big a personality to be accommodated in the new team.

Denis Compton gave a particularly 'helpful' interview on radio when he talked about the 'disruptive influence' I had on the England dressing room. 'Botham,' he said, 'is a very great cricketer. But he is not a team man.' Compton implied that the only reason the team had been able to come back to win from 1–0 down was because there was no Botham on tour to mess things up. Personally, I found his comments laughable.

The fact was that the players chosen to replace me as the all-rounder in the team, Chris Cowdrey and Richard Ellison, had failed to do the job. Nevertheless, fuelled by what these other, anonymous players had fed them, the press started to come up with major pieces along the lines of 'BOTHAM AT THE CROSSROADS', which, as you might have guessed, merely made me even more determined to prove them wrong. As a result of everything that we had been through during the previous couple of years, I admit I was feeling at my lowest and most vulnerable for years. As Kath said to me at the time, we just seemed to be lurching from one crisis to another, and although I was still as keen as ever to perform on the cricket field for England, there were times when I wondered if I shouldn't just pack it all in. I hated all the aggravation; it had changed me and changed my relationship with those closest to me. I wasn't myself anymore.

So when a man called Tim Hudson came into my life and offered me the world, the universe and everything, I was ready to listen.

10
HUDSON AND
HOLLYWOOD

An awful lot of you out there have heard the voice of 'Lord' Tim Hudson, but are almost certainly blissfully unaware of it.

According to the man himself, Hudson was a Manchester-born ex-public schoolboy who had once played cricket for Surrey 2nd XI, making 1 and 0 against Kent 2nd XI at Canterbury in 1962, then made millions during his years on the West Coast of America as a disc jockey, property developer, child of the Sixties, inventor of flower power and bosom pal of rock superstars. Unconfirmed reports indicate that he has, at various times, discovered the whereabouts of the Lost City of Eldorado, devised a formula to turn water into wine and unearthed incontrovertible evidence that the moon is made of green cheese.

He was also, and this is true, the voice behind one of the vultures in the Walt Disney cartoon version of Rudyard Kipling's *The Jungle Book*. Next time you or your kids are watching it, listen out for the line: 'He's got legs like a stork, he has'. For when you hear it you will be listening to the voice of the man who promised to make me (a) a fortune and (b) an international film star, and who instead very nearly succeeded in (a) ending my marriage and (b) turning me into an international joke.

I first came across Hudson at the end of the 1981 season when I was on a benefit tour in the States. You needed a crash helmet to avoid serious injury from the names he dropped from dawn until dusk, but he came across as a larger-than-life character with a capacity to dream. I have always had a soft spot for likeable nutters.

By the time we collided again in 1984 he had set himself up, with the help of his wife Maxi, in the stately splendour of Birtles, a big country house in the Cheshire countryside, with its own cricket pitch which he named Birtles Bowl. It was here that he arranged for a match to be played between myself and Geoff Boycott as part of our benefit arrangements. When Hudson next got in touch, his telephone call from the States coincided with my lowest ebb. The drugs case had only just been settled and the future remained uncertain. He had ideas he wanted to discuss and, as I was ready to hear anything positive, we arranged that Kath and I should meet him at Birtles immediately after we returned from a family holiday in the Lake District. It was then that he started to weave his magic spell.

In hindsight what happened shortly after we arrived should have set the alarm bells ringing. Certainly, Kath was somewhat puzzled by the reaction when I asked: 'Have you got any champagne? We have something to celebrate. Kath's expecting'.

The faces of Tim and Maxi dropped alarmingly and you could have cut the atmosphere with a knife. I thought nothing more of it at the time and instead proceeded to lap up Hudson's yarn about what a hero I was and how he was the man who would help me cash in.

After all the bitterness Kath and I had been through, it was sweet music. Hudson had plans, big plans. He had a vision of me as the perfect English gentleman, with a touch of swash and buckle thrown in for good measure. The names he mentioned in connection with the image he had in mind were impressive enough – Errol Flynn, Winston Churchill, Cary Grant, Horatio Nelson – and as I let all this wash over me, it sounded like perfect sense. What I could not see at the time, and did not for some time to come, was that it was all perfect nonsense.

Some of the other ideas he mentioned that night were so mad that I should have seen through them straight away. The entire domestic cricket scene needed to be blown away, he said: Let's have matches between teams captained by Eric Clapton and Elton John. We could put them on telly, he insisted, and the crowds would come flocking in. Start the day with a brass band, have Pink Floyd playing throughout the match and then a calypso band from close of play until the early hours.

I looked around at the impressive surroundings and thought to myself, 'I don't quite know what's going on here, but the guy has made a success of his life so he must have something going for him. Let's ride this torpedo to the end of the tube'. And so we did.

Until this moment I had been looked after by Reg Hayter, one of the great Fleet Street characters. Reg had been the cricket correspondent for Reuters after the Second World War and, in the days when cricketers and journalists were more likely to have their hands wrapped around each other's shoulders than around each other's throats, he developed friendships with star players like Denis Compton, Bill Edrich, Godfrey Evans, Keith Miller, Ray Lindwall, Fred Trueman and Sir Len Hutton which stood the test of time. At one time or another, after setting up his own agency, he had acted for a whole host of sportsmen including Compton, Evans, Miller, Trueman, Basil D'Oliveira, Tony Greig, Henry Cooper and Malcolm Macdonald, and the number of reporters trained by him in the old ways of fairness and accuracy is legion.

Reg was more than a Mr Ten Percent to me, he was a good friend, and I was sad that I was unable to attend his funeral service at St Bride's church in Fleet Street, after his death in March 1994. At the end of the service attended by some of the greatest names in English sport and sports journalism, they carried him out to the tune of 'Teddy Bears' Picnic'. His love of life and sense of fun will be sorely missed.

At the time Hudson walked into my life, Reg, along with Alan Herd, was one of the few people around me not taken in by the bluster and the hype, while those who were included Colin Cowdrey and Brian Close. In fact, Hudson was to set Closey up as his cricket manager at Birtles in the months to come. It had been hoped that Reg and Tim could work together, with Reg looking after the press while Hudson set about earning for me the promised megabucks.

It's true that while I was grateful to Reg for all his advice and the fact that he was genuinely as interested in me as he was in making deals for me, I felt I had been missing out financially. It was my view that a younger man than Reg, who had just turned seventy, might be more able to cash in on my behalf. (As it turned out, Hudson hardly made me a bean other than through existing contacts made by Reg and, in fact, when it came to re-negotiating my contract with Somerset at the end of that season, he actually settled for less than they had been prepared to pay.)

Initially, I was enthusiastic about Hudson and I hoped Reg would be too. But Reg insisted that he simply couldn't work with the man: he feared Hudson's motives and did not believe that his grandiose schemes and dreams were suitable for a top sportsman. It's hardly surprising that, to put it mildly, they never hit it off – they were from different planets. Apart from a moment of horseplay during a benefit event in La Manga when someone stole his clothes, I never saw Reg wearing anything but the regulation grey suit, white shirt and club tie. His only concession to 'fashion' was a pair of brown suede lace-ups which he slipped on when he was feeling really 'way-out', and only a major cash incentive would have persuaded him to wear corduroy in public.

Hudson, on the other hand, was nothing if not outrageous in appearance, deed and word. One of his more outlandish claims was that he had had regular conversations with the millionaire recluse Howard Hughes and that these meetings had been instrumental in fashioning his business ideals. The fact that Hudson would still have been in nappies when Hughes became a recluse was not allowed to get in the way of a splendid tale.

The final straw for Reg came during a visit to Birtles when he went to spend a penny and found himself in what he described as a 'porno toilet'; the walls were covered in photographs of naked women and in the middle of this bloody great montage was a picture of me playing a cover drive! On another occasion when Reg was staying there, he went up to his room to prepare for dinner and all he could hear were voices emanating from Tim and Maxi's room crying out: 'Hotter, hotter. More hot'. Reg gave it the old slap on the forehead and decided he'd had enough. The parting of the ways was not pleasant and I was glad when, some years later, he and I re-established a friendship that had been badly damaged by the whole business.

At the time, though, I was thoroughly taken in by Hudson's banter. His first big idea was to use me to market a range of clothes. The concept was country house cricket and the predominant colours were red, yellow, black and green – something to do with 'peace, love and understanding'. You'll get the idea from the following press release he sent out.

> Super sportsman Ian Botham is planning to hit the fashion industry for six. He is teaming up with millionaire businessman Timothy Hudson to become the image behind a new concept of unique and classic clothing. Fans will be bowled over by the English public schoolboy look that will carry the label 'By Choice, Botham'. Ian Botham is joining the company of Hudson's Hardware as a director. It is to invest £1 million to promote a new line of fashion wear that will range from brothel creepers to bowlers.

I must make an admission at this point: I actually liked the clothes. It may have had something to do with the fact that I am and always have been colour-blind, but I thought the blazers were great. And I liked a lot of the other paraphernalia: the Rolls-Royce in which Tim used to ferry me around, the parties thrown for me at Birtles, and the sound of his voice telling me and the world that I was a superstar and that Hollywood producers were falling over themselves to put me on the silver screen. Not only did I allow myself to be persuaded to have highlights put in my hair, but I wouldn't hear a word said against the man.

When Kath started to have her doubts as the 1985 summer series against Australia progressed, I was in no mood to listen. I didn't realize until later that Tim and Maxi wanted Kath out of the picture because a wife and family did not fit into their grand plan for me; as for Kath's resistance to them at the time, I put this down to jealousy at all the attention I was getting. In fact, I was so taken in by Tim that if anyone dared suggest he was anything other than the answer to all my problems, they were putting their place on my Christmas-card list in dire jeopardy.

As far as my cricket was concerned, the winter off had done me a power of good. A couple of quick hundreds for Somerset at the start of the 1985 season meant that by the time I was picked for the one-day international series I was in prime form, making 70-odd at Old Trafford. However, this was still not enough to appease certain sections of the press who, after the tour to India, had been hoping for a quieter life – a life without Botham. I got out at a crucial stage of the innings, and as a result we did not make a large enough total to win the match. More than that, it was the way I got out that allowed the vultures to tuck in.

Greg Matthews the Aussie off-spinner sent down a ball which pitched around off-stump and in an attempt to play the reverse sweep, I missed the ball completely and was bowled. It was a favourite shot of mine, but, as Peter May (who had succeeded Alec Bedser as chairman of selectors) diplomatically pointed out to the ravenous pressmen, not one that you will find anywhere in the MCC coaching manual.

Fortunately, neither this nor the earlier rumblings about 'better off without him and his kind' got in the way of my performances. At Headingley in the first Test, I took seven wickets, while going in at 264 for four in our first innings I decided I was going to have some fun, and in one hour of mayhem I smashed 60 from 51 balls. (*Wisden* described it as 'a golden hour of explosive batsmanship'.) I hit 85 in the second innings during the second Test at Lord's, where Allan Border made a fantastic 196 to help the Aussies square the series, and I was enjoying a real purple patch that was enough to silence the critics. But then, at Trent Bridge, I ran into trouble again.

To my mind, what happened on the Saturday afternoon was a real storm in a tea cup. But by the time every moment and every gesture of my altercation with the umpire Alan Whitehead had been replayed, analysed and dissected by all and sundry, even members of parliament were climbing aboard the highest horses they could find. Perhaps the most outspoken of all was John Carlisle MP, who ranted: 'People are getting tired of the petulance and histrionic behaviour of some players. This disgraceful behaviour by Botham brings shame on the good name of sportsmen and cricket. It sets a terrible example to the crowd and could be a contributory factor to crowd misbehaviour'. What a load of rubbish.

The following represents the sequence of events. Because Arnie Sidebottom was out of action with a split toe and Paul Allott was also off the field with a stomach upset, I was the only pace bowler available as the Aussies had reached 300 for five in reply to our 456, of which David Gower, who captained the side excellently all summer had made 166. David had just brought me back into the attack and told me to have a real rip with the new ball. It was time to give it everything. I can't remember having bowled faster, and as the back problem was beginning to become quite serious I certainly never did again. The adrenalin was pumping, the crowd was buzzing and it was all or nothing. In an atmosphere crackling with excitement, and in spite of the fact that normally I was too wrapped up in what was going on in the middle to notice these things, this time I could sense that everyone inside the ground was willing me on.

From the first ball, to Graeme Wood, Mike Gatting put down a chance at slip. Then I had Greg 'Fatcat' Ritchie absolutely stone cold dead leg before, only to have the appeal turned down by umpire Alan Whitehead. The only way it could have been given not out was if Ritchie had got an inside edge on the ball, and that was the indication I got from the umpire. Next ball Ritchie got a top edge which flew towards third man where Phil Edmonds pulled off a great diving catch. As the other players ran towards him to offer their congratulations, I noticed out of the corner of my eye that Whitehead's arm was outstretched to signal a no-ball: in the noise and excitement I had not heard the call and neither had anyone else. Now I'm not saying Whitehead was wrong, but the fact is that I have bowled about a handful of no-balls in my entire career and two of them were called by him. I had big problems with my run-up on the tour to Pakistan in 1977/78 and resolved to eradicate them. A no-ball is just a waste of effort and bowling is hard enough work as it is without having to send down any extra deliveries. When I asked Whitehead to tell me how far over the line my front foot had gone, normal practice in cases like this, he refused point-blank.

As the batsmen had crossed, and Ritchie was now up at my end of the wicket, I asked him whether he had, in fact, got a touch on the ball that had trapped him in front. He said 'no' and I let fly with a barrage of words which you wouldn't find in The Bible, continued to curse my luck as I walked back to my mark. Perhaps Fatcat, who went on to score 146 and make the game safe for them, should have waited until we had got back to the dressing room to impart this information, as the former Australian skipper and television commentator Richie Benaud suggested. In any case, the area around the wicket became expletive city. Although I was not having a go at him in person, Whitehead's ears were obviously burning.

My mood was not improved when Ritchie then smacked my next ball over the slips, so I let go with a bouncer, partly to get rid of my frustration and partly because it was the right ball to bowl. The whole episode had set everyone's nerves on edge and I felt I might have a chance of unsettling him with a short one. In the event, Whitehead decided that this was the time to pull me up for bowling too much short stuff, a decision I found bizarre to say the least as both men at the crease were established, recognized batsmen. Then, when he warned me for deliberately running on to the pitch on the line of the stumps, I completely lost my temper. Again, there was no way I was swearing at Whitehead, but the television cameras zoomed in on me and it was obvious that I was not reciting poetry.

I called Gower over to see if he would have a chat with Whitehead since I did not want to get involved. However, the cameras and the occupants of the press box made sure that I was already, right up to my neck. David calmed things down, told me not to let what was going on affect my concentration and, for the moment, the steam evaporated.

This didn't stop the newspapers from wading in. True to form, the TCCB could not rouse themselves for the disciplinary hearing they insisted on having for another forty-six days, until the eve of The Oval Test. The whole thing was quite ludicrous and need never have got out of hand. I was in the wrong in as much as I allowed myself to get carried away. I have to say that for some reason, Whitehead and I have never really hit it off. In my view, he appeared to be more concerned with the letter rather than the spirit of the law and I have always reacted badly to that approach to authority. That is why my favourite umpire was and always will be Dickie Bird.

Dickie is a complete nutcase, of course, but a hugely loveable one for the simple reason that you can always have a laugh and a joke with him, as he proved by his reaction to the catalogue of classic practical jokes to which he has been subjected over the years. My great mate Allan Lamb was quite expert at winding him up. I'll never forget the time we placed firecrackers on Bob Willis' run-up during a Test match. When Bob's lumbering strides set them off one by one, Dickie almost had a heart attack. He was convinced he was under attack from a deranged sniper.

Certainly Ritchie and the other Aussies thought all the fuss over what happened at Trent Bridge was just laughable. They play their cricket hard down under, and over the years the Aussies have become past masters at putting their umpires under pressure.

However, I was determined not to let this one incident spoil the series. I was still enjoying my cricket immensely and after another draw in the fourth Test at Old Trafford, further huge scoring by us at Edgbaston allowed me to play perhaps one of my most relaxed Test innings. Tim Robinson and David Gower had put on a large second wicket stand and in the process David had gone past Denis Compton's record for the highest number of Test runs scored by an Englishman in a home series against Australia, so when I came in at 572 for four I was given a free hand from the start. I had been in great form all summer and clearly the crowd were sensing that I would try something special. So I did: I hit my first ball, from Craig McDermott, back over his head for six and then, after clubbing him for four next ball, repeated the trick from my fourth ball. Over the years some kind observers have described my ability to empty bars at cricket grounds; this was the first time I was actually aware of doing it. People were streaming back into their seats. It was just a pity that although the innings was very sweet, it was also very short. The crowd didn't seem to mind much, they loved every minute of it. In fact, hitting sixes had become something of a habit for me during that year as I hit 80 in all, a record for an English first-class season and an indication that, on one level at least, Hudson's dreams were helping me relax on the field.

A huge slice of luck, when David Gower caught Wayne Phillips off a ricochet from Lamby's boot at silly point just when the Aussies looked odds-on to save the game, helped us win that fifth Test at Edgbaston, and so we approached the final Test at The Oval in high spirits. Before that, however, I was up before the 'beaks'. Summoned to Lord's for the hearing over the Whitehead incident, I was unsure what to expect. Ritchie had offered to speak on my behalf but had been refused permission by the Australian management, while Whitehead clearly expected that I would receive the big stick. In the end it took the committee four hours to conclude that I had been 'guilty of dissent, likely to bring the game into disrepute' and was warned about my future conduct. In other words nothing happened, and the reception of the crowd when I took the field at The Oval showed exactly what they thought of the whole business.

We wrapped up the series in fine style. Gooch made a magnificent 196 and Gower's golden summer continued in an exquisite innings of 157. Needless to say, his golden curls got the champagne shampoo treatment on The Oval balcony after the match. I was well pleased to have made a big contribution on the field at the end of a series which my critics would gladly have seen me miss altogether.

By this time, however, my relationship with Hudson was putting an immense strain on my marriage. In fact, it was during this summer that, for a few days at least, it actually did come to an end when Kath walked out on me.

Kath had become increasingly irritated and frustrated that I seemed to be spending more time with the Hudsons at Birtles than I was with her and the family at our new home in Ravensworth, North Yorkshire. She was right, though. Tim would ring me up and say he had some fantastic new deal in the pipeline and that I had to get to Birtles immediately to discuss it. Then when I arrived, of course, there was no deal. The call would have just been an excuse for Tim to indulge in his fantasies of becoming my guru.

During the season Tim and Maxi had come to all the

Test matches and made a point of letting everyone know just how important they were in my life. They would hang about in the dressing room and generally make themselves the centre of attention. Then one day during The Oval Test, Maxi seriously embarrassed my mum Marie and Kath's mother, Jan. In those days, players' wives, families and guests of the TCCB were invited to take lunch and tea in the dining rooms of the Archbishop Tenison's school across the road from the ground. All three of them were there and had finished lunch when Maxi, cool as a cucumber, took out some cigarette paper and started rolling a joint in front of them.

But the crunch came at a party Tim threw at Birtles. By this stage Kath and I were having regular arguments over what was going on. In fact, we had more rows over the Hudsons than over anything else. She was becoming increasingly sceptical about Tim's promises, which never seemed to amount to anything, and she was growing increasingly concerned about the amount of time I was spending in their company. She was also becoming very worried that Tim and Maxi were doing their best to pull Liam into the 'magic circle'.

Tim had arranged a celebrity cricket match and at the party afterwards the usual Hudson hospitality was in full flow. Quite a few of the England players were there and some of the Australians as well: it was turning into a major bash. Kath, almost at the end of her tether, came up to me.

'Ian, this just isn't my scene. This man is sucking in all these intelligent people and you are being made to look silly. Can't you understand what is happening here?'

'Come off it Kath,' I said, 'You're making a fuss about nothing.'

'Right. That's it. I won't be a part of this. Either come with me now or we're finished.'

I decided to stay. Kath left with Jan and Gerry and told them what had happened. Until that point I had simply not been aware of how much Kath was suffering. She did not actually carry out her threat, thank goodness, but she told me later that the only reason she pulled back from the brink was for the sake of the children. Although I didn't really know how to react at the time, the incident really shook me up. Looking back on it now, it was the beginning of the end of the Hudson saga. I hadn't understood it fully until that point but the truth of what was happening finally started to hit home. Then, when Brian Close told me of a conversation he had had with Tim, I got the full picture at last.

It was at this point that Hudson let it slip to Closey that Kath had no place in his grand scheme. If I was to be marketed properly in Hollywood, he insisted, it had to be as a sex symbol; and sex symbols are only marketable if they're single. Some years later I was given an insight into his assessment of the possibilities when I read what he had to say on the subject in his unpublished diaries.

Being a lover of ladies I have been accustomed to feeling the sexuality in the air most of my life.

But with Both it's all so different from rock and roll. It's real heavy macho man ... watching the ladies squirm in his presence ... particularly in a night-club atmosphere ... subdued lighting ... hot music etc.

Women certainly become uncomfortable ... he becomes like a Roman gladiator at the feast of something or another. Women find it more than difficult not to cross and uncross their legs under his gaze. They seem to breathe much quicker and their chests begin to heave as the nipples push against the soft T-shirt fabric or the silk blouses. He's definitely every woman's piece of rough . . . in the long, long grass . . . by the lake . . . under a full moon.

Of course.

All this would have been quite hilarious if he had not been so serious. What he was saying in effect was that Kath and the kids had to be dumped. A suitable financial arrangement would be made, he insisted, and Kath would be well looked after so long as she drifted away with the minimum of fuss. The fact is that Hudson came within a whisker of destroying my marriage. It was, metaphorically speaking, the classic dealer/junkie thing. Fame was the drug he was peddling and I was very close to becoming hooked for good. Quite apart from anything else, the expected deals were not actually materializing: he had promised to organize a Jaguar car for me; then when Jaguar made it quite clear they didn't want to know, Tim bought me one out of sheer pique then later claimed that instead of it being a gift to me, he expected to be reimbursed out of expenses. He had insisted all along that he did not want a penny from me, but these claims for expenses were becoming more and more outrageous.

Furthermore, he had made it quite clear to me that he considered my proposed Leukaemia walk from John O'Groats to Land's End a waste of effort. Hudson believed that time would be better spent trawling the Hollywood bars and rubbing shoulders with the producers who, according to his fantasy, were queuing up for me to sign on the dotted line but were, in reality, almost certainly completely unaware of my existence.

There were more problems on the horizon. Under my captaincy, Somerset were having a terrible season: although Viv and I were scoring heavily I was not contributing as I should have been. I had played in fewer than half our first-class games due to Test calls and a toe injury, and the club were understandably getting a little upset that I appeared to be spending more time with Hudson than concerning myself with county business. In September I decided to relinquish the captaincy and Peter Roebuck took over the reins. (Little did I know at the time, but that was the beginning of the end of my Somerset career. A year later, after Roebuck had got rid of Viv and Joel Garner, I walked out in protest.) I asked for a one-year contract for the following season and Hudson's part in the negotiations showed just how incompetent he really was. Firstly he insisted that he was far too busy to travel to Taunton to discuss the matter and they would have to come to him. Then shortly after they arrived at Birtles, he promptly demanded £35,000 for the season. But as the Somerset delegation rose to leave in disgust, Hudson backed down instantly and finally settled for a figure way below that which the club had expected to pay!

My relationship with Kath was on more of an even keel by the time I agreed to go with Hudson to Los Angeles. Something in the back of my mind told me that if he did indeed know all these contacts in Hollywood and I did not go with him to meet them, I would never forgive myself for letting the opportunity slip by. Although Kath was clearly unsure about the venture, she agreed that I should give it a go.

In the meantime, the Leukaemia walk had been a wonderful success, with the public responding magnificently and the money raised way beyond expectations. Kath had also produced bonny bouncing Becky. The BBC had tried to arrange for a helicopter to airlift me to Doncaster Royal Infirmary the moment the day's walking was over but didn't quite pull it off and I had to settle for a ride in a old hired white Daimler which roared up the motorway at a stately 50 mph. Fortunately, Kath was well enough to join me for the final steps to Land's End. So when I kissed her goodbye four days after the walk was over and set forth on the great Hollywood adventure with a reporter and photographer from the Sun on board to record my triumphant entry into Tinseltown, my spirits were high.

Three days after we arrived Hudson marched me into the offices of the one producer he did actually know, Monachem Golan. Before we left for the trip Golan had been quoted as saying: 'He's got the looks, the build and the accent to be the next James Bond. I know they are looking around because Roger Moore has hinted that he won't be in the next 007 film. And Ian would be a genuine candidate if he takes my advice and puts his name forward'.

Golan welcomed us and got straight down to business. 'All I want you to do,' he said, 'is put me ten cents on every seat.'

Hudson replied enthusiastically: 'Botham will give you ten cents; he'll give you a million kids in Britain, a million in Australia and even more than that in India and Pakistan.' India may not be so sure about Pakistan though.

'Well, I'll tell you,' Golan responded, 'he's better looking than Tom Selleck.' And then the bubble burst well and truly. All I had to do, he explained, was stay in LA and take acting lessons for six months.

'Er . . . excuse me,' I said. 'What about the tour to the West Indies?'

Golan looked at me as though I was completely mad. 'What tour to the West Indies?'

'Well, the one for which I have been picked to play for England. You know, the one that starts in about three weeks time.'

When it became obvious that I had been expected to give the game up in order to follow my new career, the interview came to an abrupt halt. By this time, the boys from the *Sun* were getting a bit twitchy. 'When exactly are you doing the screen tests, Ian?' they would ask casually, '. . . only our editor would like to know'. When it became clear that there weren't going to be any screen tests, Hudson had a brainwave.

I had been on the Universal Studios tour several times as a holidaymaker and enjoyed it immensely. One of the most popular features of the tour, available to all punters young and old, is the Wild West Shoot-Out. You dress up as a cowboy and walk into a mock-up of Boot Hill, the OK Corral or whatever takes your fancy and slug it out face to face with a gunman wearing a black cowboy hat and muttering 'This town ain't big enough for the both of us'. We ended up staging this pathetic pantomime solely for the benefit of the photographer and the paper, and anyone who wants to see for themselves just what I thought of it need only look at the resulting pictures. I've seen dead hedgehogs look more interested. It was a total, utter shambles.

Although I enjoyed the two-week holiday, it was

obvious to me that the whole thing had been a complete waste of time and I was more than happy to get on a plane home as quickly as I could. Apart from anything else, I realized that Tinseltown was not for this country boy at all. To cap it all, soon after I returned, Hudson began making grandiose statements insisting I was on the brink of a major film deal. That did it for me. It confirmed what by then I already knew deep down: the guy was away with the fairies.

Over the years I have had a chance to analyse the relationship in detail. Some of my friends believed that Tim was in the grip of a kind of obsession over 'Mr' Botham. There were some pretty strange things going on, for sure. For instance, Kath became convinced that Tim would time his phone calls to me at home, during which he would insist that I should come to Birtles for top-level talks straight away, at the very moment he knew I would just be arriving back after a trip.

Tim may have started off with the best intentions but I think the whole thing just took him over and eventually he would have wanted me to be totally dependent on him. He revelled in the celebrity status that accompanied my presence. At one stage, when he was re-negotiating my contract with the *Sun* he even tried to persuade the paper that it should take a regular column from him as part of the deal.

The break was not long in coming. In fact, Kath, Alan Herd and I had been biding our time and awaiting the opportunity to bring the whole fiasco to a conclusion. Then, on the eve of the fourth Test match against Viv Richards' West Indies in Trinidad at the beginning of April 1986, Tim provided it in typically bizarre fashion. Kath had just returned from the annual Easter holiday in the Lake District and had her attention drawn to the front page of the *Daily Star*. There in black and white under the headline 'BOTHAM DRUGS SHOCK' were quotes from Hudson saying: 'I'm aware he smokes dope. Doesn't everybody?'

Apparently the quotes had been taken from a conversation Hudson had with a group of English journalists based in Los Angeles, during a party thrown at the King's Head Pub in Santa Monica. It was typical Hudson, no doubt getting carried away by the sound of his own voice. Of course I smoked dope, but that was hardly the issue. My libel case against the *Mail on Sunday* over their allegations of what took place in New Zealand in 1983/84 was still pending, and I needed my manager to discuss the subject in the presence of reporters like I needed a hole in the head.

When Kath told me what had appeared, I simply couldn't believe it. How could anybody be so bloody stupid?

Tim was due to arrive in time for the Test match but his plane was cancelled and I managed to track him down via a phone in Miami. I went berserk.

'Hudson,' I began, 'What the f--k did you say? If you do not issue a story through your lawyer threatening to sue the *Daily Star* I will have no alternative: I will either have to sue you or sack you. Maybe both.'

He mumbled something about the conversation having been off the record. Off the bloody record! How naive can you get? There I was trying to get my act together to prove myself against the one opponents I felt I still had something to prove to, and this lunatic decides to inform the world that I smoked dope and it was all okay because the conversation was 'off the record'!

So the sorry saga came to an end. And what did I get out of it? Not a lot. All Hudson actually did was re-negotiate existing contracts, and his success with the Somerset deal showed how good he was at that. At one stage, when he was attempting to do the deal with the *Sun*, the sports editor got so fed up with his ravings that he rang up Herdy and pleaded with him to handle the matter instead. He said he just couldn't deal with the guy.

Funnily enough, that was not how Tim and Maxi saw things at all. And a letter Maxi wrote to me in those final mad moments showed how convinced she and Tim were that they had given me the world.

Dear Ian

From the horse's mouth. Exactly one year ago today, your world and life went crashing around your feet. Now, one year later, you are a national hero. Magic? No. Witchcraft? No. Blood, sweat and tears? Yes. During this past year without so much as a signature on a piece of paper, we, Tim and Maxi, have put our ideas, money, home, life, energy, talent and creative abilities at your disposal. Tim has given up his own writing and radio interests to pick you up off the ground and elevate you to the stature which he truly thought you deserved. He has hawked your talents to whoever would listen because he believed in you as a cricket super-hero and a super person.

He and I have argued a number of times about the invasion of Ian Botham into our private lives, as well as completely redirecting our business energies in your direction. Our office deals with your mail, phone calls, contracts, public image, etc., etc. We have scrapped all other business interests in the UK to concentrate on I. T. Botham. We have turned our creative energy into designing a line of clothes, 'The Public-Schoolboy Look', into a company which existed before you were on the scene and welcomed you and your image into it, also making you a 20 per cent partner and director. We have shared our flower power colours and logo with your image. Tim has turned the media completely around and today there is hardly a bad word written about you.

Maxi and Tim Hudson have withstood the hounding of the press at Birtles and tried with all our power to keep them off your back. We organized to have your favourite sports writer (Frank Keating of the *Guardian*) hired (to collaborate on the book *High, Wide and Handsome*) just for you. We have opened the doors of Birtles to you and your friends and family, and closed the gates behind so that you could have privacy.

Maxi and Tim Hudson bought a car for your use when no other English company would do so. We constantly fought your adversaries with words and actions so that today you have become the super sports hero you deserve to be.

We have tried to look after your interests with kindness, consideration and love, and still no signature on the dotted line. Maxi and Tim Hudson purchased contracts (from the previous manager) and we have not even seen very much of their value because we have no I. T. Botham signature.

You, also, have worked hard for the company. You have been a superb model. You have exposed

Hudson's Hardware at every opportunity. You have grown in self-confidence and became the Pied Piper of children. But you have forgotten that the road this year was travelled by us all. I think we have created a Frankenstein, bigger than life. We have disregarded those who said it would be so. We have disregarded the warnings of conceit, selfishness, rudeness and self-gratification. Yet today, one year after our association began, you don't want to share. You don't want to give us credit for our concepts, our ideas and advice. I heard you say more than once that you trusted us and our judgement, and yet you are questioning our ability today. We are a cohesive unit only if we respect our individual talents and creative abilities. You are a star cricket player. We are the creative and business mind. You play cricket. We make the deals. You are a star who is being managed by a star in his own right, who has shelved his personal creative talent to promote a man he believes in; so much so that he has convinced the whole country, and now America, that you are worth money.

If you want to play cricket, negotiate contracts, do your own PR, enter the entertainment world and continue to have a personal life, I wish you luck.

You could be on your way for the rest of your life or you could screw up, as you have done in the past.

It is up to you. We love you, but cannot give our business and talent free. We can pursue our other interests. You can pursue cricket. Make up your mind.

Whatever, good luck.

Maxi.

Excuse me, but where did this rainbow end?

The central point of this appalling piece of drivel appears to be that it was only due to the 'creative energies' of Tim and Maxi that anyone still had a good word to say about me – nothing to do with me being part of an England side that had won back the Ashes or the Leukaemia walk that had raised near to a million pounds and which they both had been so dead against me attempting in the first place.

Some time later I even discovered that he was trying to cash in on the walk himself. A specialist cricket magazine, *Cricket World* carried the following advertisement:

> Hudson's Hollywood XI Rugby Jersey as Worn by Ian Botham on his Great Million Pound Walk for Leukaemia. Available in small, medium or large, £35 + £2 p &p. Write to Dept. CW, Hudson's Hardware, Birtles Old Hall, Cheshire.

The Hudson/Botham liaison did produce one thing that will last forever, although if I had my way it would be put on the nearest bonfire tomorrow, namely my portrait that Hudson commissioned to be painted by John Bellany that still hangs in the National Portrait Gallery in London. Unfortunately, or rather fortunately as it turned out, I could not attend the official unveiling as I was on tour in the Caribbean at the time, but Kath went along in my place. Later she told me of Liam's reaction when the masterpiece was let loose on an unsuspecting public. One of our friends asked him what he thought of it, adding: 'I think it's bloomin' awful.'

'You mustn't say that,' Liam replied. 'Mummy told us that if anyone asks we should say we think it is very interesting.'

It is bloomin' awful. In fact, to this day I think it is the worst picture I have ever seen of myself and not a patch on those spider and splodge jobs that the kids used to come up with on the playroom floor. If an alien landed on the planet with explicit instructions to find Ian Botham and the only thing he had to go on was this picture, he would never find me in a million years. I'm not one of those who goes in for vandalism but in this case I would make an exception. In my opinion, anyone wishing to slash the canvas would be more than justified.

Many years later our youngest daughter Becky was taken to London to see the monstrosity. When it was pointed out to her, she took one look and said simply: 'That's not my Daddy'. She was talking about the painting, of course, but she might just as well have been talking abut the subject because during the period when I was modelling for it, I was as near to losing my identity as I have ever been.

If Hudson was the worst agent I ever had he was certainly not the last. With varying degrees of success my affairs have been handled over the years by a whole host of others. Looking back on the episode, I recall the thoughts of Trevor Gard, my old Somerset buddy, who saw straight through Hudson the moment he set eyes on the man. Trevor often said to me that he could never understand why I ever left Reg Hayter in the first place. Well, the answer is that if we all possessed hindsight in advance the world would be a pretty dull place.

If I thought dumping the clown was going to be the end of my problems, however, I was sadly mistaken. In fact, there was even more turmoil waiting just around the corner.

11
1986 AND ALL
THAT

I set off on England's winter tour to the West Indies in early 1986 determined to put the nightmares of the past couple of years behind me. And I succeeded – those nightmares were replaced by even bigger ones. During two pretty hideous months, I came close to giving up the game as well as giving up on my marriage.

Having just won the Ashes during the summer, we departed for the Caribbean optimistic that at last we might be able to compete with, and even possibly beat the West Indies on their patch for the first time in nearly twenty years. David Gower, the captain, Graham Gooch, Mike Gatting, Tim Robinson, Allan Lamb and myself had all scored heavily against the Aussies earlier that summer, we had what we thought was a well-balanced bowling attack, and the party was full of genuine experience.

As it turned out, our high hopes were somewhat misplaced. The tour started badly and got worse ... and worse. The results spoke for themselves: we won two out of fourteen matches in all and our record in the Test series was played five lost five – a 'blackwash' in other words.

In mitigation it has to be said that we came up against

the best side in world cricket performing at the very peak of its collective ability. Even if we had played out of our skins we would have done extraordinarily well to avoid defeat against a team that included four world-class batsmen at the top of their form – Gordon Greenidge, Desmond Haynes, Richie Richardson and Viv Richards and a bowling attack that was the best of its type I have ever seen. Just running through the names brings back some painful memories. First came Michael Holding and Patrick Patterson then, once you had seen them off, Malcolm Marshall, Joel Garner and last, but not least, Courtney Walsh.

Furthermore, try as we might to find the right kind of practice – short-pitched, horrible quick stuff on uneven surfaces – against which to try to discover and develop ways of coping with the exact same treatment being expertly dished out to us in the Test matches, it proved quite impossible to do so. Geoff Boycott, covering the tour for the *Mail on Sunday*, took great delight in informing his readers that he had no trouble at all in finding suitable net facilities and that he was, of course, available for selection in England's hour of need. All I can say is that facing these bowlers is a bloody easy game from the press box, Geoffrey! His comments were hardly helpful because all they did was increase the pressure on us out on the field and stir things up back home. As soon as things started to deteriorate, the obvious answer as far as the folks back in the UK were concerned was that either we weren't practising enough or that we weren't trying hard enough; if Sir Geoffrey could find a net, they reasoned, why couldn't we? Of course, Boycott had no trouble at all in finding nice, flat, easy-paced pitches on which to practise boring everyone to death, and even if he couldn't he could always claim to have done so for the benefit of the story. We went to see one of Geoff's 'ideal' practice wickets. It was worse than useless: when we arrived a herd of goats were crapping all over it.

When Gower first used the phrase 'optional nets' he did so in all innocence, but, as things progressed, the term took on more sinister connotations, and was used by our critics as clear proof that instead of giving our all, we were enjoying a pleasant, relaxing holiday. 'Nets today?' 'No I don't think so. Certainly not if they're optional, old boy.'

As if these on-field problems were not enough to have to deal with, the issue of South Africa had also reared its head again. Protests against Graham Gooch and others who had been on the rebel tour in 1982 reached such a pitch that by the time we arrived in Trinidad for the second Test, our hotel, the Port-of-Spain Hilton, had to be patrolled by armed guards day and night.

Gooch, who as captain of that touring party was the main target, felt under so much personal pressure that at one stage he actually had to be talked out of going home by David Gower. Goochie never really liked touring in the first place, as his behaviour some years later demonstrated. Early on in the tour he was incensed by an article written in a local newspaper by Lester Bird, the Deputy Prime Minister of Antigua, which savaged Gooch and made it clear in no uncertain terms that he was a less than welcome guest. Gooch took it personally and extremely badly. Instead of just shrugging it off as we all hoped he would, he allowed it to get him down to such an extent that he kept on muttering about wanting to pack it in and go home. To be honest, Goochie's non-stop moaning was a right pain in the neck. The situation got so bad and he became so depressed that the TCCB even flew out a representative, A. C. Smith, to try and talk him out of it. It was only an appeal by Gower that stopped him from disappearing on the next available flight home. Who knows what might have happened to Gooch's career if he had taken that plane? Appearing to have deserted the sinking ship almost certainly would have counted against him when, three years later, he was considered for then offered the captaincy for the aborted 1988/89 tour to India (called off, incidentally, because of the Indian Board of Control's protests at the inclusion of Gooch and his fellow rebel tourists) and then, a year after that, when he was given the job for the 1989/90 West Indies trip.

I wonder what David Gower was thinking when Gooch took over from him after the disastrous Ashes series of 1989 and promptly left out both him and myself for the 1990 West Indies tour and whether, during those years when Gooch treated him as *persona non grata*, Gower didn't allow himself a wry smile over the affair. In hindsight, he probably regretted not packing for him and giving him a lift to the airport.

It goes without saying that the media also played their part in stirring things up. As a result of all the allegations of what had gone on during previous tours, the press contingent had swelled to a ridiculous size. There were an awful lot of editors to be satisfied, most of whom knew nothing about the game and cared even less: what they wanted were stories. In order to justify the large sums of money being spent on sending them out there for the tour, the reporters had to provide them, and sure enough they did so from the start.

It had been decided that Gower and I should miss the first match of the tour, a warm-up game on the beautiful island of St Vincent against the Windward Islands, at that time regarded as the weakest side in the Caribbean. David had been under an awful lot of stress in the period building up to our departure. On the day he was due to return home from a skiing trip he heard that his mother had died, and his pre-tour preparations were totally disrupted by his having to make the arrangements for the funeral. He was mentally exhausted when we eventually arrived in the Caribbean and a day away from it all seemed just what the doctor ordered.

We met up with an old acquaintance of David, a chap called Bjorn, who invited us on to his yacht for a relaxing trip around the island. Fred Rumsey and his wife Colleen, along with the actor Robin Askwith, another mate of ours, were also asked along. Following the antics of Monty Gower's Flying Circus on the 1990/91 Ashes tour, when David and John Morris hired a Tiger Moth to buzz the ground during England's match against Queensland in Carrara, it was Robin who responded by chartering the plane that flew over the Adelaide Oval during the fourth Test bearing the message 'Gower and Morris are innocent'. Gower thought the incident was hilarious – needless to say that Gooch and the England management took a rather different view and used it as more ammunition in their war against the 'Golden Boy'.

Meanwhile, back to the proposed yacht trip. Instead of sitting around doing nothing, and because we knew there would be very few R & R opportunities as the tour progressed, we gladly accepted the invitation. In the event the excursion was something of a disaster. When we arrived alongside the boat, Bjorn was having a lot of trouble getting any one of his three engines to work and even more problems getting any of his crewmen interested in a day's labour. One of them in particular had a somewhat eccentric attitude to the job. Being rather partial to the Jamaican Woodbines, he spent the whole time either wandering around in a cloud of smoke or sleeping, and sometimes both at the same time. In the end we set off hours later than planned. What should have been a chance to unwind and recharge our batteries for the battle ahead became more or less once round the bay and back. The whole trip ended up lasting about forty-five minutes.

Let's just say that from the point of view of public relations, our timing could have been better. We happened to switch on the radio to hear that events at the St Vincent ground were definitely not going according to plan. One of the cricket photographers, Graham Morris, who over the years had developed such a close relationship with David that he was the best man at Graham's wedding, and someone with whom I had also spent a lot of time socially, had come along with us to take the usual Caribbean-style shots. Unfortunately, his 'happy' snaps arrived on the picture desks of the newspapers in England at just about the same time as cricket correspondents were filing reports that suggested we might have been better employed on the field of play rather than just playing around. At the same time as Morris was taking pictures of us sipping cold beers on board a yacht against the paradise background of the Grenadine Islands, our team-mates were being bowled out for 94, until that point the lowest score by an England team on a Test match tour of the West Indies. Here was an instant story for the ravenous tabloid reporters, one which fitted perfectly into the scheme of things pre-ordained by their editors.

The team managed to get things back on a more even keel during the next two matches, as we drew with the Leeward Islands in Antigua and beat Jamaica in Kingston. We were all encouraged by the fact that Mike Gatting, who made 71 in the first match and 80 in the next, looked capable of living up to pre-tour expectations. So we approached the first one-day international in Jamaica in a reasonably positive frame of mind.

Then came the first real disaster of the tour. Although we did not realize it at the time, the incident would have hugely damaging long-term repercussions.

I don't know if you have ever seen the effects of a ripe tomato being squashed into someone's face. It looks a bit like the result of being hit on the nose by a bouncer from Malcolm Marshall. And that is exactly what happened to Gatt.

With England on 47 for two, Marshall was bowling to Gatting, then on 10. As the ball flew up to his head from just short of a length, he rocked back, attempted to hook it and missed. Although he was wearing a helmet, the one he was using had no protective grille to cover his face. The ball smashed into his nose, spreading it all over his face. It was one of the most sickening sights I have ever seen on a cricket field. They were still picking bits of bone out of the ball and off the pitch some overs later, and when Marshall picked the ball up and found part of Gatt's nose still attached to it he went a peculiar colour, dropped it to the ground and nearly threw up for good measure.

I had been rested for the match to protect a slight injury prior to the first Test due to start later that week, and I remember helping the physio Lawrie Brown look after Gatt in the dressing room.

Gatt has always been a brave player, and he is one of those you would definitely want alongside you in the trenches. Although clearly shaken up by the blow, after a couple of buckets of ice had been applied to the affected area he asked casually: 'When will I be able to go out to bat again?' He was quietly informed that this would be impossible for two reasons. First, in the immediate aftermath of the blow he had clipped off his leg bail and was therefore out. Second, his nose was such a mess that he would not be going anywhere for some time except to the hospital.

'You're kidding,' he replied, 'it doesn't hurt that much. What does it look like?'

He went to the mirror to find out. Then he made a crucial error: he attempted to blow his nose. I will spare you the gory details but suffice to say that the dressing room attendant was kept busy for several minutes clearing up the debris. Lawrie and I took him straight to hospital and during the journey I attempted to put a smile back on what was left of his face by telling him: 'Cheer up Gatt. You're so ugly that no one will notice the difference anyway'. But the situation later became distinctly unfunny. Not only did we lose the match by a big margin, but, after Gatt had been stitched back together, he spent a terrible night back in the hotel suffering acute breathing difficulties. He said at one point he felt like he was drowning; he was sure he was going to die. Two days into the Test match he flew home for further treatment. When he arrived back in the UK he was treated to one of the most ridiculous press enquiries of all time: 'Where did the ball hit you, Mike?'

Although Gatt managed to return just after the second Test in Trinidad, within twenty-four hours of getting back he broke his thumb batting, missed the next four weeks and was only, finally, fit enough to play in the final Test in Antigua, where he made 15 and 1.

Not only did the blow mean that the side was weakened for the first Test but also the confidence of the team was badly dented. Subsequently, during the three days it took the West Indies to win the match by ten wickets, it was shattered.

That Sabina Park pitch was fast as lightning and the bounce horribly uneven. It was undoubtedly one the most difficult and dangerous surfaces I have ever played on. John Woodcock, one of the few cricket writers whose views I have always respected, wrote in *The Times*: 'I never felt it more likely that we should see someone killed'. We were not helped by the notorious problem of the sightscreen in front of the George Headley Stand. It was simply too low to be of any use at all when batting against bowlers who were delivering the ball from a height of nearly twelve feet. We had had problems with it against Holding and Walsh in the match against Jamaica and had asked the Jamaican Cricket Association if they could have it raised. They said they couldn't because doing so would have obscured the view of around a couple of hundred spectators who had already paid for their tickets. So, as it turned out, the only people whose view was obscured were the batsmen.

During that first Test we came up against a West Indian who started the match as more or less an unknown quantity and ended it a matchwinner. Before making his Test debut in this match, Patrick Patterson was described by local experts as the fastest bowler in the Caribbean, after

Malcolm Marshall. By the end of it, we all knew that the correct order was the other way round. 'Patto' was murderously quick and I doubt whether we would have had much joy against him even if the sightscreen had been twenty feet high. As it was, he was absolutely devastating.

Although I believe I approached the tour in the right frame of mind in terms of my desire to prove myself against the one team I had thus far failed to do so on a consistent basis, looking back there is no doubt that I was on the edge of exhaustion. The Leukaemia walk had taken its toll mentally, as well as physically. I know that during the Christmas period immediately prior to flying out I had been hell to live with. The achievement of actually completing the walk had lifted me to such a high, such a high, that it was immensely difficult to return to earth and to normality. Then, forty-eight hours before I was due to fly off, Becky, now two months old, was rushed into hospital for an emergency hernia operation.

Kath, the kids and I had just returned from a trip to Hong Kong which was part holiday, part business, and on the car journey from Heathrow to home we put Becky's fractiousness down to exhaustion after the long flight. When we arrived, Kath asked our nanny Diane to give Becky a bath. Moments later, Diane called out for Kath to come to the bathroom, where she said she had felt a lump in Becky's stomach. We took her to the local doctor in Thirsk and straight away she diagnosed the problem. Becky was rushed to hospital and operated on that same evening. Although it had been an alarming incident, there was no question of me delaying my departure for the tour. Becky recovered so quickly that she was as right as rain again within days.

The events of recent winters had made me question whether I actually ever wanted to go on tour with England again. However, having made myself available I made the decision that if I was going, it would be on my terms. The media hounding to which I had been subjected had left me sour, bitter and paranoid. So when I left Kath with the parting words 'The papers won't be getting any headlines about me this time, because they won't even see me', I meant it.

Our bad start to the tour and the reaction to it helped the siege mentality spread throughout the rest of the party. For one thing the press group had swelled to about sixty, many of whom the players would not have recognized from Adam, and there seemed no way of escaping them, particularly as they stayed in the same hotels as the players for most of the trip and almost always travelled on the same flights from island to island. The atmosphere was pretty poisonous to say the least. Back home the merest whiff of a scandal was being lapped up. On one occasion ITN's News At Ten broadcast a story sent back by one of their correspondents describing an incident in which bottles were smashed on the tennis court of our hotel, after which the manager had received several complaints of drunken debauchery. In reality, it had nothing at all to do with the players and the reporter had no evidence to suggest otherwise, but the story was presented in such a way as to invite the viewers to put two and two together and make five.

The press were following me from the start. I am convinced that there were people on that tour whose sole aim was to get Botham. Everywhere I went there was a camera being pointed at me. Every little gremlin from Fleet Street was out there hiding under a rock somewhere. It was unreal: it almost reached the stage where you would spit on the field during a match and a couple of these blokes would run out and take it away for analysis. To this day, I don't know how I stopped myself from getting hold of a couple of them and battering their heads together. It wasn't a particularly helpful situation for the other players either, who I think were all affected by the increased media presence. I certainly got the feeling that everyone was looking over their shoulder. Quite naturally, although they never showed it or said so to my face, some of the players blamed me, and indeed some even went so far as to complain to David about the situation. Luckily, the England captain was extremely supportive throughout.

To be honest, I was pretty messed up mentally. All the pressure certainly affected my game. Only a part of me was actually able to concentrate on the cricket; the rest was worrying all the time about who I was talking to, and who I was being seen with. I knew full well that the moment I exchanged words with a waitress or barmaid that the press would have a field day. 'BOTHAM BONKS WAITRESS ... BOTHAM BONKS BARMAID ... BOTHAM BONKS MOTHER THERESA', I could just see the headlines. So I went out of my way to avoid people: I decided to live like a bloody hermit.

I just didn't know who to trust. New acquaintances would be treated with deep suspicion and even old friends suffered. It was not the way I like to behave because I am not, never have been and never will be a loner. However, with reporters and photographers appearing out of cracks in the wall and the constant danger of some clever bastard setting out to trip me up, I couldn't see any alternative. I hated this isolation – I resented it – but I had had enough of the press. I shut myself away completely, not only from their prying eyes but also from most of my colleagues.

It was a desperate time. I would lock myself up in my room with a pile of videos and gorge myself on room service food. The less contact I had with my fellow human beings the better. Wherever we went and in whatever hotel we stayed, my room was always the same. As far as I was concerned it didn't have a number, just a name: 'The Batcave'. Absolute paranoia had set in to the extent that I was even checking my room for concealed tape recorders and bugs.

My room-mates had to suffer the brunt of my moodiness. John Emburey was so concerned about my state of mind that he mentioned the situation to his wife Susie, who, in turn, asked Kath: 'Is anything wrong with Ian? The players are very worried because he never seems to leave his room'.

As Kath will testify, I rang home almost every night, not common practice on tour and not something I had ever been accused of in the past. These were the worst of times and from the frequency and tone of my calls Kath was becoming worried that something was seriously wrong.

The only moments of light relief involved my mate Allan Lamb and, later, David Gower. We had all heard rumours that a certain Sunday newspaper had been paying girls to get close to some of the players, close enough for sneaky photographs to be taken. Lamby became conscious of the unwanted attentions of a girl who had been lurking around him for no particular reason. He remembered the rumours and during one incident involving some harassing photographers Lamby decided to take evasive action by leaping headlong into the nearest available bush – out of sight, out of mind so he thought. Unfortunately, in the process he injured his leg. (He actually missed the match against Barbados although not, I hasten to add, as a result of this injury.)

An incident involving Gower was similarly bizarre. At the press conference on the eve of that first one-day international in Jamaica he was asked, in all seriousness: 'Is it true that you are having an affair with Paul Downton's wife and if so, does this explain why you are looking tired on the field?' Gower was somewhat taken aback, although he later admitted to me that he did once plant a kiss on her cheek . . . at their wedding!

These were rare shafts of amusement in what was becoming an increasingly nightmarish experience. As far as I was concerned, these incidents completely vindicated my reclusive behaviour but I have to admit that my brooding did little for team morale. After getting out again cheaply in one match I returned to the dressing room, hurled the bat on the floor and complained: 'How the hell are you supposed to play against that bowling on these wickets?' Gatt gave me a severe bollocking, telling me in no uncertain terms to quit moaning. 'What sort of example was that to set before the other players?' he asked. He was dead right, of course. But I just couldn't see or think straight and, as I have mentioned before, one of my great failings is my inability to admit to being in the wrong. I was not covering myself in glory on or off the field and was digging an even deeper hole for myself.

It was because of all the aggravation on this tour that I decided, even if I was going to stay in the game, that there would have to be a very good reason for me to consider touring with England again. On the next trip, to Australia in 1986/87, I solved part of the problem by taking Kath with me for the entire four months, but after discussing the situation with Allan Border on the phone an alternative solution was at hand; namely, that from 1987 onwards I would spend my winters playing for Queensland in Australia. We kept the story quiet for the time being. In any case, there were other stories just about to break that would have put that one in the shade.

I was extremely lucky in those dark moments that Gerry Waller, Kath's father, flew out to join me in Barbados (just how lucky would not become clear until later). Gerry, my room-mate Les Taylor and I spent a lot of time playing dominoes with local fishermen in the rum shops of Oistins, a particularly lively but unspoilt region of the island. It was not exactly the high life of the jet-set international cricketer but at least it was better than staring at the four walls of a hotel bedroom.

And then came Lindy Field.

One of the great clichés which runs through the enter-tainment industry is that there is no such thing as bad publicity. I can tell you from first-hand experience that this is absolute rubbish. For the bad publicity machine that was about to roll into action very nearly ruined my life.

By the time we reached Barbados, where we were due to play a four-day match against Barbados followed by the third Test, my state of mind had improved thanks to the presence of Gerry and his insistence on getting me out of the hotel for a drink from time to time. So, during the Saturday of the Test match when I popped up into one of the stands for a word with Mick Jagger and Eric Idle, I was only too happy to accept Mick's invitation to dinner at his house after close of play that evening.

Mick is an absolute cricket fanatic and loves coming to watch Test matches whenever and wherever he can. I recall an amusing incident involving Mick and Reg Hayter during the early Eighties, when, after Reg managed to provide him with a couple of tickets for a Lord's Test, Mick's office responded by sending Reg an appropriate gift as a gesture of thanks. As far as pop music was concerned Reg believed that Bill Haley and the Comets were about as far out as it got, so I would have paid money to see the expression on his face when he opened up the envelope delivered by motorcycle messenger to his offices behind Fleet Street and found inside a copy of the Rolling Stones' new album, *Emotional Rescue*.

Sitting behind us in the stand that fateful day in Barbados were Gerry, Bob Willis, his brother David, David's wife Caroline and an acquaintance of her's, Lindy Field, an ex-Miss Barbados. As Mick suggested I should bring a few friends with me, I passed on the invitation to those behind.

After getting back to the hotel and ringing Kath to tell her of the dinner party, David, Caroline and I were collected by Miss Field in her car as arranged while Les Taylor and Gerry drove behind us. I should have known from the eventful journey that Miss Field had an active imagination. Although she claimed to know Mick and Eric and that she knew exactly where the house was, she quite clearly had no idea where we were going. We passed the same landmark on three separate occasions and the journey took at least half an hour longer than it should have done. She seemed quite unable to concentrate on the task in hand and spent almost the entire journey chattering away about nothing in particular. Sometime after that fateful evening, information reached me that Miss Field was a friend of Vicki Hodge, the lady who had claimed to have had a passionate fling with Prince Andrew. At this stage, however, there was no reason to suspect her motives. I spent most of the evening chatting with Mick about the cricket.

As events unfolded I came to thank my lucky stars that Gerry had been around all evening. It's one thing denying the kind of lurid allegations later made by Miss Field when there is nobody around to back you up. It is quite another matter when your father-in-law is your prime eye-witness.

In the event, he was not actually called upon to reassure his daughter for another fortnight, but by then the *Sunday Mirror* had dug up another so-called story. The following weekend, towards the end of the Easter holiday, which Kath and the rest of the family were enjoying in traditional fashion with Alan Herd and his family in the Lake District, I got wind of a story the paper was about to publish. A reporter named Mark Souster wrote that he had interviewed Gerry in the hotel and quoted him as saying: 'Ian is on the point of giving up the game. He has never had any support from the TCCB'. Even if the content of what he said was not a million miles from the truth, Gerry was fuming because he had never spoken to the reporter and, in any case, he would never have publicly stated any such thing.

Alan Herd digested the piece and then rang the editor to complain on my behalf. At first he insisted that the report was true, then later, after speaking to Souster, he admitted that the paper had gone over the top. The fact is that Souster had never even met Gerry but had based his report on a conversation with a 'mutual' friend. The editor agreed to print an apology and arranged to send a reporter to see Gerry with a view to setting the record straight the following weekend. For reasons that were about to become only too apparent, that article never saw the light of day.

The first headline of the following week, which appeared on the front page of the *Daily Star* a couple of days before the fourth Test in Trinidad, was bad enough:

BOTHAM DRUG SHOCK

This turned out to be the result of Tim Hudson's 'off the record' chat with reporters in the Santa Monica bar.

I worked myself up into such a fury over the incident that David Gower was quite rightly concerned about whether I would be able to do myself and the team justice in the next match, the fourth Test. Rumours were flying around that the selectors were on the point of dropping me for the first time in my career. Peter May, the chairman of selectors, had watched us lose the third Test in Barbados by an innings and 30 runs, and just before returning home after his holiday in the sun he gave a press conference in which he was certainly less than complimentary about the team's efforts. According to Wisden: 'May called for greater resolve, questioning the team's attitude'.

It was, of course, a thinly veiled attack on yours truly.

In his autobiography, David Gower summed up his feelings about that and about my performance on the tour. He wrote:

By the time the fourth Test came around in Trinidad, the other selectors became serious about dropping Ian, but I was loath to be without a player who was still capable of winning a Test with either bat or ball, and managed to hold them off. However, I saw this as an opportunity to get him fired up, so I called him into my hotel room and told him that he had more or less scraped into the team on a split decision. Nothing heavy, just a quiet word. Which is how I think these things should be dealt with. He still didn't get any runs, but he certainly bowled with a lot more zip after that. To a certain extent, we were all guilty of over-rating ourselves when we arrived in the West Indies and were physically underprepared, but I think this applied to Ian more than anyone else. He is a fiercely proud man, and an extraordinary competitor, but just occasionally these are qualities that can work against you. For instance, here he was early on the tour bowling filth, but still clinging to the view that the long-hop disappearing in the general direction of Bridgetown Harbour was the best delivery in the world – that some incompetent slogger, by virtue of possessing a good eye, a heavy bat and an outrageous degree of luck, had somehow managed to hoik over an absurdly short boundary.

In his mind, he was still racing in and taking wickets. Both's self-belief is such that he could shuffle off to slip with figures of 1–0–36–0 wondering what cruel hand of fate had prevented him from doing the double hat-trick. This trademark of his, that he is in his mind always doing, or about to do, great things, is a mixed blessing. When it is going right, everyone knows what remarkable things can happen. When it is going wrong, he doesn't always step back and look closely enough at himself from the outside. The rest of the team were looking closely at him all right, and all they could see was someone who hardly bowled in the nets, and was disappearing for five an over. No wonder they got disgruntled, and however much I might not have cared for the way they got it across to me, I failed to find the right way to get Ian firing as he can.

In hindsight, it was a pretty fair assessment. The conversation we had at the Port-of-Spain Hilton lasted two minutes. That was all that was needed. I thanked David for his support and sound advice and, momentarily at least, the discussion did help me to refocus on the job in hand.

Unfortunately, it was only temporary. When I first heard the rumours of the story that was about to appear in the *News of the World*, my heart sank. All my efforts to live the life of a hermit had been to no avail. I did not know the full details of the story's content but a friend of a friend had told me that Miss Field had returned to London with a view to selling a story about a supposed night of passion, broken beds and cocaine. I was not at all worried about what she was going to write, but I was desperately concerned about the effect of these kinds of lurid allegation on Kath and the children. Gerry had returned home by this stage and at about the same time the story was due to appear Kath was at Jan and Gerry's house being interviewed for *Woman* magazine. After they had finished their chat, Kath joked: 'Possibly at this very moment someone somewhere is dreaming up another Botham fairy-tale. We've had drugs. They've had a go at his cricket, his weight, him sitting alone in his hotel bedroom. The next one's got to be another woman'.

Little did she know that the curtain was just about to go up on the most harrowing black comedy of our lives.

Shortly before going out to field on the Saturday morning of the Trinidad Test, I got hold of Chris 'Crash' Lander, my ghost writer for the *Sun*, and took him into my confidence over what was about to happen. I then asked him to ring Kath from the press box.

According to Kath, the first in a series of increasingly tense conversations went something like this: 'Hi, Kath. Crash here. How are you?'

'Hello, Crash. I'm fine. What are you ringing for? Is everything OK?'

'Yes, yes. Everything's fine. Ian has just asked me to ring you to ask where you will be in about four hours' time.'

'I'm staying here for the weekend,' said Kath. 'Why? What's the matter? Ian's not injured or anything, is he? Is he all right?'

'Er, yes, er, well, yes, yes. He, er, just wanted me to pass the message on. He's bowling well. Er, must go. Someone else needs the phone, Love to everybody. Bye.'

Half an hour later, Crash rang again. This time the message was different. Kath was already due to come out to join me for the final Test in Antigua, but I had decided that I wanted her and the kids to come out early so that she would be with me and I could protect her as much as possible when the inevitable happened.

'Er, hi, Kath. Crash here again. Ian's just sent me a note to pass on. He wonders if there is any chance that you could fly out sooner than you had planned.'

'Well, when exactly?'

'Er, well, tomorrow, with the children of course.'

'Crash. What the hell is going on?'

'Er, nothing, nothing. It's all under control. Don't worry. Must go. Bye.' Kath, understandably, was confused and worried. She rang Alan Herd and asked him if he knew anything. Well, he did, he had already been spoken to by David Willis who told him he thought that Miss Field might have tried to sell a story to the papers.

I was frustrated that I couldn't speak to Kath direct but there was no way I could simply walk off the field and into the press box and pick up the phone, so I asked Crash to ring again and reiterate my request for her to fly out as soon as possible. During this call Kath asked Crash a direct question: 'Is it another woman?'

The next call she received was from me, at last.

When Kath answered she came right to the point. 'So, it's finally happened,' she said. 'This time it's another woman. We've been expecting this one.'

'Yes,' I said, 'you won't believe the story.'

I proceeded to fill her in and told her that I wanted her and the kids to come out immediately. Of course, that proved impossible. All the arrangements had been made well in advance and she simply couldn't rearrange them in time. She also did not want to give the media the satisfaction of seeing her appearing to fly out in an emergency measure to try and save the marriage.

By the time she did arrive in Antigua, the story was out.

I LAID OUT COKE . . . BEAUTY QUEEN'S NIGHT OF PASSION WITH BOTHAM

TEST ACE IN SEX AND DRUGS SCANDAL

We had decided that the kids should stay at home to protect them from the media circus, and needless to say the Beastie Boys were out in force at the airport. Kath was whisked off in an electric buggy to a place where we could meet privately, but when she first saw me she was so dazed that she didn't seem to recognize me even though I was standing right in front of her. I gave her a kiss and the airport became a sea of flashbulbs. Viv Richards had arranged to have a car waiting and led us to a back exit where we could slip away without any more intrusion. He then engaged the press in conversation so we could make good our escape.

The journey to the hotel was spent in total silence. I just couldn't think of anything to say to ease the tension and neither could Kath. Of course, she wanted to hear my side of the story and, after the hotel door closed behind us I told her. The conversation, which basically amounted to me telling Kath it was all a pack of lies, lasted five seconds and that was that, or so I thought.

One of the most spectacular exhibits in the case for the prosecution was the broken bed. In the article in question, the *News of the World* had even dug up a maintenance engineer by the name of Philip Barrett who was quoted as saying 'I didn't fix the bed myself, but all the guys were talking about it'. In fact, as he later revealed to my solicitor Alan Herd in a statement, it had been Les Taylor, my room-mate, laid up in the room for much of the time while he recovered from a virus, who had caused the damage by flopping down on that particular piece of furniture while attempting to get some kip.

Gradually we tried to return to some kind of normality. The final Test match was occupying most of my attention but it was obvious to me that Kath was fighting hard to avoid slipping into a state of depression about the whole affair, and no matter how much I or others attempted to reassure her, she clearly felt under enormous pressure. I was up to my eyeballs in it, what with the *News of the World* story, the hounding by the press and trying to play Test cricket on top of all that. Naturally, I was also very concerned about Kath. It was an extremely volatile period. Although we were doing our best to behave as if nothing was wrong, it was simply impossible.

I was particularly worried by her mood at one stage, so much so that one of the thoughts buzzing around my over-crowded brain was that she might even do herself serious damage. It was ludicrous, of course, but it showed just what a mental state I was in. One day she went off, with-out letting me know in advance, to have a look at a holi-day villa that we had been offered for a week or two after the Test match was over. I got back to the hotel after the day's play in the Test match and there was no message and no sign of her. No one knew where Kath had gone. I didn't know what to think, but my thoughts were all bad. I rang every number I could think of, then went out looking for her all over the island. I found nothing, not a trace.

I had worked myself into such a state that I was frantic with worry. Finally, that nightmare ended when she walked into the room, without a care in the world. However, the respite was only temporary.

We decided to have dinner in the room. I suggested that

we should go down to the bar for a drink to cheer ourselves up. A few of the boys were there and we had a pleasant time. Bob Willis offered to go out and get a pizza, then one of our friends took me to one side to impart some information about the infamous Miss Field. It was hot news along the lines of her having a very expensive cocaine habit, with more evidence to prove what kind of character she really was. I was delighted to hear it and thought Kath would be too.

To say that was a misjudgement is a masterpiece of understatement. In hindsight it was foolish of me but I simply didn't realize what the effect of telling her would be. When I did she broke down sobbing, saying she never wanted to hear another bloody word about the woman and couldn't I understand that. Then I really blew it. 'For God's sake,' I said, 'what's the matter with you? Cheer up.' It was the worst thing I could have said. Kath got up and stormed out of the bar with tears streaming down her face.

She had calmed down somewhat by the time I got back to the room and, shortly afterwards, Bob brought in the pizza. After he left we attempted to behave normally but it was useless. The tension was so great that it was like a volcano waiting to erupt. I can't remember exactly what triggered the explosion but when it came it was pretty devastating. I grabbed hold of the pizza and promptly sent it flying. It ended up on the ceiling, on the walls, the bed, everywhere. The room was one bloody great pizza! By now I was totally out of control, and I went round picking up anything I could find and hurling it anywhere and everywhere. The ice bucket holding a bottle of wine went flying as did the bedside lamp. It was total, utter devastation. Looking back now, it was frightening. This insane rage had taken over and possessed me; it was as though I was looking at another person doing all this. I stormed off, slamming the door behind me, with no idea where I was going or what to do when I got there. I was in a blind rage, and if anyone had got in my way at that particular moment I dread to think what would have happened.

In the end I finished up in the first beach bar I could find. The next couple of hours are a bit of a blur. All I can remember is pouring my problems into a couple of bottles of rum and rendering myself an ex-human being.

Finally, Bob Willis found me, calmed me down and walked me around a bit to try and clear my head. Then he dragged me back to the hotel. When I returned to the room I was absolutely paralytic. I told Kath: 'That is it. The marriage is finished. We have been trapped by the headlines', and then fell unconscious on to the bed.

The next thing I knew it was daylight and Kath was in fits of giggles. Emerging from sleep and into an incredible hangover, I looked up and saw what she was laughing at. Lodged on the curtain rail was a piece of pizza with melted cheese hanging down from it in long streaks. We both laughed our heads off. I lifted Kath up and she retrieved it. The sight of the pizza had left us both in hysterics and the atmosphere of tension had been broken. In that moment, I think we both realized that if we could go through such a terrible night and wake up laughing then, at the very least, that was something to build on. Indeed, the events of the previous night were never mentioned again.

Meanwhile, the Test match proceeded in a more orderly fashion with us being thrashed again by 240 runs and Viv Richards helping himself to the fastest Test match century of all time, from 56 balls in 83 minutes. It was awesome and if anyone has ever played a better innings I would like to have seen it. *Wisden* did Viv the great honour of reprinting the full sequence of deliveries:

0–0–3–6–1–2–6–1–4–1 (24 off 10 balls); 0–2–1–1–0–4–1–2–0–1 (36 off 20); 1–1–2–0–2–1–1–1–0–0 (45 off 30); 0–1–0–1–6–2–4–4–4–1 (68 off 40); 1–2–0–0–6–6–4–6–1–2 (96 off 50); 0–0–2–1–0–4–6–1 (110 off 58).

It was an incredible feat, one which I shall never forget.

Thankfully, with the match over, I was at last able to concentrate fully on Kath. While the rest of the tour party was heading home, Viv found us a place on the island where we could relax by ourselves and unwind with no press, cameras or anything else to disturb us. It was such a load off our minds to be free of all the parasites and leeches. Within twenty-four hours of being away from the centre of the turmoil, Kath and I felt things coming back together. We spent time walking along the beach, I would go out scuba diving and Kath would sit in the boat sunbathing. It was like going from hell to heaven in an express lift. As we saw the plane carrying all the press and the rest of the party head off into the distance, suddenly Antigua became a completely different world and the support we got from the local people was fantastic.

Kath and I had a long talk about things. I couldn't understand why I had been such a target. She hit the nail on the head straight away. 'Look, I'll be quite honest with you,' she said. 'It is because you are larger than life and people just don't know how to handle it'. I suddenly realized how wrong I had been all those times when I had intentionally excluded her from my personal problems. She was magnificent and that was the moment I think I really understood just how fortunate I was to have her as a wife. It's funny how it needed something so traumatic for that to become clear.

There is an awful lot of truth in the old saying that you just don't appreciate what you have got until you are in danger of losing it.

I had been in real danger of losing Kath, I know that now. I understand how horrific the whole thing must have been for her. How she had the guts, the patience and the courage to see things through during that two-year period, I'll never know.

Viv made sure there would be no hassle. He recruited a couple of his mates to keep an eye out for us for the first few days, and I will always be grateful to him and to Bob Willis for the part they played in helping to save our marriage. Viv was like a big brother to us and Bob had always been there when he was needed.

By the end of the holiday our mood had improved so much that the next set of exotic headlines were like water off a duck's back. The *News of the World* printed a story based on allegations made by Vivien Kinsella, a self-confessed heroin addict and the now deceased wife of cricket writer Steve Whiting, who had, at one time 'ghosted' my column for the *Sun*.

I SAW IAN BOTHAM TAKE HEROIN

POT, COCAINE, HEROINE AND PETHADINE – TEST STAR TOOK THE LOT

Alan Herd succeeded in persuading the Attorney General to ban the paper from publishing the story, which was about incidents that were alleged to have taken place on the 1983/84 tour to New Zealand, on the grounds that it would prejudice my court case against the *Mail on Sunday* for which we were still in the process of preparing.

However, the Appeal Court overruled that decision and off went the *News of the World* again. All I will say about the article is this: if a newspaper has to print what amounts to a disclaimer about an article at the same time as printing the article itself, then they must be struggling.

On the same page as the article appeared, this is what they had to say about the woman whose story they had based it on:

Vivien Kinsella comes from a wealthy Australian high society family . . . But she freely admits that her drug addiction has landed her in trouble with the law.

She says: 'I started taking pot at fifteen, heroin at nineteen and cocaine at twenty-three.'

Our investigators realized, when they interviewed Vivien, that she was sometimes unable to remember specific dates and became confused about minor details.

Like the truth, for instance.

Alan Herd, Kath and I came to a decision. With all this dirt flying around some of it was bound to stick. We considered that in those circumstances the case against the *Mail on Sunday* could turn out to be a nightmare. Although I wanted to proceed and to sue them, there was simply no way the trial could be a fair one. Alan pointed out that if we did go to court a lot of other allegations could be made and that others, apart from myself, would be subject to painful scrutiny. What is more the legal costs were becoming exorbitant. So we decided to drop the case, get it over and done with and out of our lives so that I could just get back to concentrating on the cricket. Kath and I had been through too much. I never give in without a fight, but in this case we had fought and fought and were worn out with all the fighting. It was time for me to hold up my hands and say 'Enough'.

12
THE BAN AND THE COMEBACK

On 18 May 1986, the *Mail on Sunday* ran a front-page story concerning a certain England cricketer. It reads as follows:

BOTHAM: I DID TAKE POT

This is one of the most difficult days of my life. I have decided that the time has come for me to be honest with myself, with the game I love, with my friends and with all of those who through thick and thin have helped and supported me down the years. Over the years an awful lot has been written about me. Some of it has been true and some of it has been ludicrous. I have had to accept, however reluctantly, that these days a Test cricketer or anybody who becomes a major sporting personality, has a very high price to pay for all the adulation and the monetary rewards which go with success.

But there was one article published by the Mail on Sunday on 11 March 1984 which was, in its way,

the most shocking of all. It alleged that during the New Zealand tour, which had just been concluded and which had been something of a cricketing disaster for the England team I had smoked 'pot'.

The Test team had actually gone on to Pakistan for the second stage of the tour when I first heard what it was the *Mail on Sunday* was proposing to print.

I was in the Hilton Hotel, Lahore, when I first got wind of the allegations that were being made against me. I remember that occasion as if it were some sort of nightmare.

My reaction was one of horror. It was a bolt from the blue and I had no one around me to whom I could properly talk. I was a long way from home and it seemed to me that, because of the proposed article, everything I had fought for and worked so hard to achieve would be at risk.

I did something that I have regretted ever since because I have had to live with the consequences of that decision. I denied that I had ever smoked pot at any time in my life and started legal proceedings against the *Mail on Sunday* for what it had said about the New Zealand tour.

I know what I am now saying will shock many people, particularly those who have stood by me for so long.

The fact is that I have, at various times in the past smoked pot. I had been with a group of people who had been doing it and I went along with it.

On other occasions I have smoked simply in order to relax – to get off the sometimes fearful treadmill of being an international celebrity, trying to forget for a moment the pressures which were on me all the time.

I was only a casual user and not an addict or anything like that. I was always in control of myself. I hope this article is a warning to others – particularly the young – of the risks which can be involved.

It would have been so easy for to get 'hooked' and to get on to the other – much worse – drugs.

I came into first-class cricket in 1974. I was 19 years old, wise in the ways of sport but naive beyond all measure as to what the world was really all about. Two years later, at the mighty age of 21, I was playing for England.

The scene was Trent Bridge. The weather was marvellous, the ground was absolutely packed out for the first four days because England were playing Australia. It could not have been a more perfect debut. In Australia's first innings I took five for 74. Suddenly I had become a national figure.

The next Test at Leeds I had another five wickets. That year I became one of *Wisden's* Cricketers Of The Year.

But miserably for me, though at that time I rarely properly appreciated it, on my first day of Test cricket Brian Close, captain of Somerset and then in his forties announced his retirement from the game. My mentor, a man I could respect and when necessary, lean upon, someone I could go to for advice, and receive it straight from the shoulder with no holds barred, was going out of my daily life.

Fortunately, Brian and I remain firm friends and, indeed, he has done everything possible to help me.

I don't think many people realize what it means when one is in one's early twenties and one becomes a national celebrity. One is expected to grow up very fast indeed. It takes time to realize that nearly all those people apparently anxious to be seen in your company are there because they might just be after reflected glory. It takes times to realize that all those invitations, all those splendid parties and the like are there for the Test cricketer and not for the man himself. It takes time to realize who are real friends and who are 'hangers on'.

I was a celebrity. My wife had given me a son and everything I had dreamed about was now laid out before me.

Of course things are never quite what they seem to be on the surface. Among all those people who were suddenly clamouring for my attention and whom I, in my initial innocence, assumed to be men of goodwill, were some who had more dubious intentions. You may think I should have seen through them but I did not and neither do I believe was it possible for me to have done so.

These days I am harder and more cynical. I have become suspicious about people's intentions towards me. I don't make friends as easily as once I did. That is what my so-called status as a celebrity has done for me. But does that make me a better man than when I was 21, fresh-faced and innocent? I think not.

The first temptation was, as it has always been for a lot of sportsmen, alcohol. Wherever I was, there was always someone wanting to buy me a drink. Constantly to decline would have seemed petty. I throw myself wholeheartedly into everything – including a drinks session.

I have been to many functions where some of the great cricketers of the past have been present – people who were my boyhood heroes, people who are to this day talked of in reverential tones whenever cricket is discussed.

To see some of them sink their drink is to witness performances as awe-inspiring as any of them displayed on the field. I have heard some great cricketers of the so-called 'Golden Age' speak now of carousing the night away in the middle of a Test match.

I don't make any criticism. I understand completely. Drink must have been to many of these great men the only way to release tension.

What has changed, not only in the world of sport but everywhere, is the arrival of drugs of all kinds on the market.

I was only 18 when I had my first marijuana joint. It was given to me at a party. I suppose my feeling then was not dissimilar to the feelings of earlier generations puffing an illegal cigarette behind the bicycle shed.

I take a different view today and I will come to that later. But the mood of those times – and I'm talking about the early seventies – was that soft drugs of this kind were completely safe. After all, distinguished men were signing advertisements which were published in *The Times* suggesting that marijuana should be made legal!

On one occasion, when I was in my early twenties, I attended an afternoon garden party at a well-known country-house in Southern England. I was astonished to see people, including many guests from the elite of society right down to one of the barmen serving champagne, openly smoking and enjoying marijuana joints. I was introduced to well-known barristers, journalists and even senior officers of the local police force, many of whom were openly smoking and sharing joints. I even remember one occasion when, about ten years ago, I shared a joint with a vicar as we sat together in the vestry of his Church.

In the level of sport I have got used to, the adrenaline flows in and keeps on flowing. Whether batting or fielding, you can't afford to relax for a moment when you are on the field in a Test match. You have got to be keyed up to a degree which would appear to be intolerable to most people. No wonder then, when the day's play is over, it is difficult to come down to earth.

One's whole mind is buzzing. It is simply impossible, in my book at least, to live for eight hours of the day in a state of heightened anxiety and then, when one comes off the field, to put one's feet up before the fire and watch the telly.

In my case, to cope with it all, I began living it up. Of course this is part of my character, too, but I don't believe that anyone has the right to expect me to have a totally split personality.

The Ian Botham who walks out to the crease at the height of a Test match and hits the first ball for six is, if you like, something of an outrageous cricketer, taking risks that other cricketers might not.

Sometimes I have been criticized for being too 'outrageous' on the field and sometimes I suppose I have been. But I can only point to the record books to show that, by and large, the risks I have taken have proved justified.

I have lived my private life with the same sort of attitude. I have taken risks. I have lived life to the full. There are some things which I am proud of – the fact, for example that I have never knowingly let down friends or family.

When I first took pot it was because I was young and keen to try anything. I wanted to show that I was afraid of nothing. Pot never, thank God, took over my life but I have to admit that it could have become an important factor in it if I

had not realized what was going on.

Occasionally pot helped me to relax and to come to terms with being the kind of public figure that I was. It is no accident that so many people who become famous when they are young start indulging in drugs. This is not just because, as some people say, we have more money than sense but because most of us have come from ordinary backgrounds. If you are a famous cricketer, for example, you have got to get used to hearing yourself praised to the skies but only minutes later reading about how you are a disaster. There never seems to be a middle ground. In a very real sense you become public property.

The *Mail on Sunday* is not a paper which prints scandal for the sake of scandal.

This does not, of course, mean that all Fleet Street reporting is of the same order. Some of the things I have read about myself have not only been ludicrous but vindictive and vicious as well. I do believe that I am entitled to a private life, that I should be allowed to live some part of the day outside the glare of publicity and particularly, that I should be protected from those journalists who simply make up stories in order to get their salacious headlines, hoping to sell more newspapers.

I have, however, decided that I am not going to bother suing everybody in sight. Life is too short. I need to get on with my life and my cricket and to give some peace of mind to my long-suffering family and my children in particular.

What then of the future? I said at the beginning that it was going to be a difficult day for me but it is also going to be one of the most important.

I want to continue playing cricket at the highest level, in spite of what I have said today. I did not have to say what I have said in this article. I did so because I thought it was right and I hope that will be held in the balance when people come to consider my actions.

I hope and trust that all of those who have supported me down the years will stand by me now. With the backing of all my friends – personal and those thousands upon thousands who have turned out to watch me play cricket – I hope to continue to entertain as I have done in the past.

My ambition is to continue to represent my county and my country.

The new Ian Botham is determined to take on the world and win!

So that was it; over and done with. An agreed compromise had been reached with the *Mail on Sunday*. The mental, emotional and economic burdens of litigation had been lifted. Having decided that carrying on with the court case would have been more trouble than it was worth, it had been agreed that I would write an article to get them off my back and now it had been published at last the worst was over.

I knew full well that the TCCB would have to react, but as the article contained nothing new in terms of drugs admissions from what I had said in an interview with Frank Bough on breakfast television during the West Indies tour from which I had just returned, I just hoped against hope that the whole thing might be quickly cleared up. Sure enough, the Board acted immediately. They withdrew me from the squad for the one-day internationals against India and announced an investigation into the drugs charge.

Needless to say, this was just the signal required by Fleet Street to begin their own trial-by-tabloid. Everyone and anyone was dragged out and invited to express an opinion, and each one vied with the other to come up with a more outrageous punishment. The suggested measures ranged from a fine and a one-year ban to Denis Compton's insistence that they should ban me for life!

The disciplinary hearing was set for 29 May at Lord's and it lasted seven hours. The atmosphere in the 'court' room was very strange. Those present were Peter Lush, the Board's new marketing man, David Graveney (at that time the captain of Gloucestershire), his uncle Ken, and Alan Moss, both former players; but as for some of the others I had never seen them before, nor have I seen them since! Alan Herd did the talking for me; I uttered about ten words and only then to contradict Donald Carr, the secretary of the TCCB, for his error over the number of one-day internationals I had played. Although Herdy did his usual professional job it was obvious that they were after blood. Finally, the committee retired to consider their verdict and Alan, his colleague Neil Macdonald (brother of footballer Malcolm) and I retired to a nearby room.

To kill time we decided to play a game of brag. We started off playing for 1p stakes and I soon got bored. After about ten minutes I sent Alan off to try and find some change.(I should imagine Donald was quite surprised to be asked by Alan if he could let him have a fiver's worth of 10p pieces, but the petty cash box was raided and more supplies duly brought in.) While we were playing, I looked out of the window and noticed an intrepid photographer attempting to scale a tree in order to take pictures of the condemned man waiting for his sentence. We carried on playing as if we hadn't spotted him and then, when he finally reached the summit after about half an hour of life-threatening effort, I went to the window and pulled the blinds.

I can't have had my mind very firmly on the card game because by the time we were called in for the verdict I was down to the tune of about £375.

Then came the real blow: I was found guilty of bringing the game into disrepute by using cannabis, and for admitting in the *Mail on Sunday* that I had taken the drug after denying it previously, without clearing the article with the Board in advance.

I found it all difficult to comprehend. Of course I had smoked, and I had admitted it before. Why should the fact that I did so in a newspaper mean that I was now bringing the game into disrepute? Yes, I had been guilty of not informing the Board of the article in advance, but I was legally bound by the terms of my agreement with the paper. What they failed to take into account was that part of the reason for my agreeing to the compromise with the paper in the first place was that I wanted to protect a lot of others – players, cricket officials and even journalists – from what would have been a pretty damning court case. The game really would have been bought into disrepute if that had happened, and the officials in question know who and what I am talking about.

Apparently the first suggestion by one of the committee was indeed a life ban and the next, a ban for ten years, which amounted to the same thing. In fact, the eventual sentence was that I should be suspended from all cricket until 31 July and, although not as harsh as those who wanted me suspended from the neck would have wished, I thought it was ridiculous. It was almost the final straw.

I seriously considered packing it all in there and then. The hypocrisy of some of the cricket writers was unbeliev-able. I have seen the state that some of them get into on tour, and I can tell you that some of them do not confine themselves to tobacco when it comes to smoking. I have even been approached by one or two and asked if I knew anyone who could help them find some drugs. Now the same guys had turned around and stuck the knife in.

There is no doubt in my mind that the bottom line was that it had been decided in advance that this was the time to make an example of me. Even some of my fellow cricketers pitched in with anonymous quotes in several newspapers about how I was getting too big for my boots and too big for the game, and that I deserved everything that was coming.

I stopped myself from throwing it all away for one reason: I was determined not to let the press have the satisfaction of driving me out of the game. I thought: 'I'll be the one who decides when I'm going, not them, and I'll go in my own good time'.

But that day at Lord's was one of the worst of my career: I was at an all-time low. Fortunately, John Emburey had been waiting for me in the car park and when I emerged, he drove me out the back exit to avoid the press. While he had been waiting, he had an illuminating conversation with none other than Denis Compton, which started off badly and steadily got worse.

'That Botham,' said Compton, 'is a useless idiot. They should ban him for life.'

John said that he thought he ought to know that I was a friend of his and he did not share that opinion. It made no difference to Compton who was by now in full swing.

'In fact,' he insisted, 'they should lock him up and throw away the key.'

Charming. I cannot imagine what I may have done to

upset Compton but over the years he said and wrote many damning criticisms of me. Fair enough, if he had taken the trouble to get to know me, but the fact is that unless I am very much mistaken, I never actually met or spoke to the man in my life. Denis was a great player, rightly regarded as a huge star in his own right and a hero to many, but in general I find it very sad when former greats seem to have to resort to cheap shots in newspapers to keep their egos alive. If I felt that was ever starting to happen to me, I think that would be the time to blow my brains out.

Embers drove me back to his house where Kath and the kids were waiting and it was here that I started one of my great binges. After a couple of drinks, we went over the house of a friend, Alan Dyer, where I really got going. By the time Alan and I had settled in at the local pub I was dancing; by the time we got back I had lost the use of my legs. I have never been so drunk in my life.

The next morning I woke up in bed having no idea how I got there. Liam, who was eight going on nine at the time, walked in.

'Daddy,' he said, 'I had to put you to bed last night.'

'Why?' I asked.

'Because you were drunk.'

It was not the proudest moment of my life.

There was no alternative but to take my punishment. Instead of moping around, I decided that I was going to do something positive. So that is exactly what I did: I learned to fly a helicopter, in three weeks, from scratch. The makers of the BBC's *Forty Minutes* programme hit upon a bright idea. They realized I would have some time on my hands in the weeks ahead and asked me if there was anything in particular I would like to do to fill it. They blanched somewhat when I told them, but ended up supporting the venture and making a film of the whole business from start to finish. Sadly, the pilot who taught me in double-quick time, Harry Knapp, later lost his life in a training accident.

I almost managed to avoid further trouble before the ban was lifted. Almost, but not quite. For, as a result of some light-hearted mickey-taking at the expense of the selectors at a fund-raising lunch in Manchester, I hit the headlines again.

I had established in advance that everything I said in a question-and-answer session would go no further than those four walls, but some clever bastard decided to smuggle in a tape recorder, and soon my description of the men who pick the England team as 'gin-slinging dodderers' was all over the front pages.

BOTHAM ON FOUR CHARGES

BOTH'S BACK IN DOCK

I immediately sent a letter of apology to all four selectors, Peter May, A. C. Smith, Phil Sharpe and Fred Titmus which set out my position:

Dear Peter,
    I know you will have read in the Press about the remarks I have made about Test selectors at a private

dinner in Manchester last Friday. I am obviously very upset that what I said has been reported and, taken out of context of the atmosphere of the dinner, could look offensive.

I only meant to make a light-hearted remark in the most general way (but which has backfired on me) in the same way as people make jokes about umpires having white sticks.

I assure you that I have total respect for you personally and the way in which you carry out your job as a selector, and, of course, I have every reason to be grateful to the selectors over the years.

I apologise if what I said has caused you any offence and ask you to accept that none was intended.

I have, of course, written to the other selectors.

Regards

Ian Botham

In spite of this written apology, I was duly summoned to a meeting with Raman Subba Row, the chairman of the Board who had issued a statement 'deploring the comments attributed to Ian Botham' and was asked to explain myself. Fortunately, my account was accepted and the way was clear for my return – if selected by the gin-slinging dodderers!

An awful lot happened to David Gower and England in my absence, most of it pretty dreadful. David simply couldn't get the response he was after from the team and when at the beginning of the 1986 international season his own form deserted him in the first Test against India – which turned out to be the sixth successive defeat for the side since regaining the Ashes little more than nine months earlier – the selectors decided it was time for a change. The problem was not simply that England were losing, but that, in their eyes, David's on-field demeanour suggested he just didn't care. This was nowhere near the truth, of course, but such accusations have been levelled at David ever since he came into the game and some labels stick whether they are true or not. The selectors wanted someone who would leave the field after getting out looking like he was heading straight for the nearest cliff. So they turned to Mike Gatting. Just after he was told he had been fired, David presented his successor with a T-shirt whose message read 'I'm in charge'.

Gatt certainly got the message but England were again hammered in the next Test at Headingley where they were bowled out for 102 and 128 to lose within three and a half days, and despite Gatt's 183 not out in the third Test at Edgbaston that game ended in a tame draw.

If it had been up to the public, I'm sure I would have been back in the Test side as soon as I had served my ban, yet there was still some way to go. Notwithstanding this, at last the future looked full of more promising possibilities. The aggravation of the past two years was all but forgotten, and I had a real chance to go out and enjoy my cricket without my concentration being affected by a million and one distractions. What helped was that so many of the press, and others behind the scenes at Lord's, were writing off my chances of making the 1986/87 winter trip to Australia. That gave me something to fight against and something to prove; there was every incentive for me to show what England had been missing.

Moreover, I was still eager for the wickets to bring me

level with and then beyond Dennis Lillee's all-time record of 355 Test wickets.

First, though, I had to prove my form and fitness. The form was no problem. When I walked out to bat in my comeback game against Worcestershire, I decided it was time to take matters by the scruff of the neck. Urged on by Viv Richards, who said 'Beef, you're the man, now show them you're the man', I made a century off 65 balls to help Somerset win only their third county championship match of the season. Then, six days later, while England were sliding to defeat against the Kiwis at Trent Bridge, I served up something special. On the rest day of the Test match, Somerset travelled to Wellingborough School to play Northants in a John Player league match. It was one of those occasions when everything went right for me. We were 18 for two when I went in with just 26 of the 40 overs remaining. When I left the field unbeaten at the end of our innings, I had made 175 not out and hit thirteen sixes, a record in the competition. Now those who wanted me out of the picture just couldn't close their eyes and forget about me no matter how hard they tried. I wouldn't go away.

Gatt pushed very hard for my return to the Test side with the other selectors and after the new England manager, Micky Stewart, had sounded me out about my feelings towards going on tour the following winter to Australia, I was duly invited back into the fold for the final Test match of the summer at The Oval.

Looking back now, there are some moments in my career which I simply cannot explain in normal cricketing terms. Batsmen of all counties and countries I played against often talked about the 'Golden Arm' (or other parts of my anatomy) – referring to my capacity to take wickets with deliveries that, had they been bowled by anyone else but me, would have been either ignored or dispatched to the boundary with the minimum of fuss. My first Test wicket, when Greg Chappell dragged a wide long-hop onto his stumps was a classic case in point, they said. As far as they were concerned it proved just what a lucky so-and-so I was. Naturally, I take exception to that line of thinking!

Conditions were somewhat in my favour that day at The Oval. The atmosphere was heavy and this, added to the cloud cover, meant that the ball was swinging a lot. I'm not saying that the first ball of my first over in my first match since returning after the ban was the worst I've ever bowled, but it certainly wasn't the best. Unkind observers have described it as a wide half-volley that the batsman had no need to play at; it goes without saying that, according to me, it was all part of a cunning plan.

In any case, it was good enough for the New Zealand opener, Bruce Edgar, who edged the ball to first slip where Graham Gooch juggled with it, then held onto it. I thought it quite amusing when Goochie came up to congratulate me saying: 'Blimey, Beef. Who writes your scripts?' So that wicket meant I was level with D.K. Lillee. I turned to the pavilion and gave it the typical victory gesture, then looked towards the selectors to see their reaction. The only one with a smile on his face was A. C. Smith, my long-time ally behind 'enemy' lines.

Next ball, I almost pulled off something that even I would have found difficult to believe. Jeff Crowe came forward and edged the ball low past John Emburey at third slip. Just imagine what might have happened had it gone directly to him.

As it turned out, I didn't have to wait long for the record because in the very next over Crowe shuffled across his crease to a ball of fullish length and was out plumb lbw. Up went the finger from the umpire, up went the crowd and for an instant neither my scriptwriter, nor Goochie's, could think of anything to say at all.

It was unbelievable. After all the horrors of the previous two years, the sense of elation mixed with relief was overwhelming. The reaction of the crowd said it all: they were absolutely marvellous and I will never forget their support. They had stuck with me through thick and thin, unlike some officials, press men and even personal friends who had deserted me during the most harrowing period of my life.

As I had known all along, but sometimes failed to appreciate fully while the madness was going on, these were the people who made it all worthwhile; the ordinary cricket fans up and down the country who, whatever the newspaper editors might have thought, didn't give a toss what clothes I wanted to wear, what dreams my erstwhile agent had about making me the next James Bond or what allegations the newspapers were printing about me at any given time. They simply wanted to see Ian Botham and England do well on the cricket field.

During those dark periods one of the things that stopped me from giving it all away and turning my back on the game was the amount of heartfelt support that I received from the man and woman in the street. The public's response to the leukaemia walks was amazing enough. Now the reaction of the crowd that day at The Oval put their support in a cricketing context as well.

It should have been one of the happiest days of my life. Then I received a phone call in the dressing room that soured everything.

13
THE SOMERSET
MUTINY

All these years on and still what happened at Somerset in the summer and autumn of 1986 reeks of betrayal and disloyalty. I cannot forgive or forget what went on during that most traumatic period in the club's history.

During the late 1970s and early 1980s the county had enjoyed a level of success that hitherto had been the stuff of dreams. Trophies that previously had seemed beyond the club's modest ambitions were suddenly being swept up, and that in part was down to a tremendous team spirit and a real bonding amongst the players. But success demands a greater input than sheer bloody-mindedness and effort; you need flair and magic, and these qualities shone out in abundance from our West Indian pairing of Viv Richards and Joel Garner. Time and time again, Viv played huge innings and Joel bowled sides out to win us games. The couple spent so long at Somerset that they ceased to be considered overseas imports and became as much part of Somerset as any of the local players. It was simply unthinkable to me that such great servants of the club could be sacked – yet that is precisely what happened.

Loyalty is a virtue I place at the very top of my list and

under no circumstances could I continue at a club where honour and respect were treated so flippantly. It was an act of the vilest treachery, and I hit back on behalf of my mates as only I knew how. As soon as I realized that Viv and Joel were being sacked from the club, I didn't have to wait to be asked: I had no option but to follow.

To my mind, the man who deserved all the blame for what happened was the captain, Peter Roebuck. I can confess now that I was the person who pinned the Judas note above Roebuck's peg in the dressing room after the sackings, because to me that was what he was – a traitor to the people who thought they were his friends. I have no regrets about doing it; in fact I am proud of my actions.

There had been trouble and unrest simmering beneath the surface from the time we reported back in April and it was, looking back, just a matter of time before events came to a head. The catalyst for the impending developments was Martin Crowe, the New Zealand Test batsman who had been Somerset's overseas player in 1984 while Viv and Joel were touring England with the West Indies. Essex had originally showed an interest in Crowe because Allan Border, who had signed a two-year contract with them, was asking to be released towards the end of his first season with the club. Although AB had long harboured the ambition to play English county cricket, he was finding it a bit of a strain on his family life; in addition the Aussie selectors were putting pressure on him to quit early because they wanted their captain fresh for the coming tour to India. By agreeing to AB's request, Essex now had a hole in their ranks which could be filled by an overseas star. Consequently, they made an approach to Crowe.

With one offer tucked away in his pocket, Crowe then went back to the Somerset committee and spelled out his position. At the same time the registration rules were changing; only one new overseas player was being allowed in a county side at any one time and for Somerset to take Crowe that would mean that both Viv and Joel would have to go. (It is important to mention here that had Viv and Joel been allowed to stay at Somerset for the following season, they would have been treated as English registered players by virtue of their length of service with the club, so both would have been eligible to play.) Committees being what they are, there were no further developments at Taunton until late in the season.

That left the players to get on with the business of playing the game – not an easy task given the undercurrents at the time. It was clear that the whole business had to reach a head and certainly the unease shrouding Taunton was reflected in our results. From a golden era of winning trophies Somerset were suddenly an easy pushover and managed just three Championship wins that season.

Weeks of sitting on the fence suddenly ended with the terse announcement at the end of August that they had decided to dump the West Indians – and that was the end of the matter, or at least that's what the committee thought. 'Farewell Viv and Joel, thanks for everything but don't bother coming back' in other words. The irony was that if Border had stayed at Essex this disaster might never have occurred in the first place. Crowe would not have had an offer from them and then, in 1988, Viv and Joel were going to be unavailable for Somerset for the season because the West Indies were touring England. That would have given Crowe a full season of first-class cricket and pushed the moment of decision back to 1989. By that time Joel would have come to the end of his career, and who knows how Viv would have viewed things? I found it quite amazing that they could be thrown out and, try as I might, I could never find any real logic behind the decision.

As things turned out Joel only wanted to play another season, mainly the one-day matches, because his shoulder and knee troubles were bringing his career to an end. Viv, on the other hand, had so much more left in him, as he went on to prove by playing for another seven years and helping Glamorgan win a Sunday League trophy. You can put that into perspective by looking back at the Welsh side's history and seeing how many big prizes they have won: one thing's for sure, no cleaner ever got worn out polishing the trophies in their cabinet! And it shouldn't be forgotten that prior to Viv's arrival, it had taken Somerset 104 years before they even needed a trophy cabinet.

That was what might have been. Instead we were faced with the most despicable behind-the-scenes machinations. Viv, who had already been told by Brian Langford, the Somerset chairman of cricket, that he could have another year's contract, was summoned to the club where he thought he was going to sign this deal. Joel was called in too, and neither of them could have anticipated what happened next. Joel went in first and was told he was no longer wanted, and then Viv was called through to hear the same.

Looking back, it doesn't surprise me that the Somerset committee waited until I was out of the way before doing the dirty deed. In fact, I was out of the way making my Test comeback at The Oval.

Until that Friday afternoon, capturing the record

number of Test wickets had made it a triumphant few days for me.

But those moments of great pleasure and achievement were sullied by the phone call I received from Viv on Friday 22 August 1986, a date that will be etched in my memory forever.

Viv asked: 'Have you heard?' I said I didn't know what he was talking about and I understood less and less as he explained to me the awful truth that both he and Joel had been sacked.

I was fuming. I couldn't believe what had happened. I said there and then that even if Somerset had reinstated Viv and Joel, I was never going to play for the county again. My rage was so intense that it ended up with Viv calming me down on the phone and telling me that I did not have to sacrifice myself for their cause. Viv was saying I had to go on and there was no point in me being side-tracked over something that did not directly concern me.

Noble words, but Viv and I go back a long way. There is trust in the friendship, and I know that when I have been in trouble he has put himself out to help. He would stand up for me and I would do the same for him. That is the bond between us and if the limits of the friendship were to be tested, then this was the moment. As far as my involvement was concerned and in spite of everything Viv said, it was a clear-cut issue. I had to leave the club in protest, and nothing was going to stop me.

As I saw it Roebuck had been planting the seeds for the coup for nigh on 18 months. Whatever he claimed subsequently, it was very well planned.

I believe Roebuck's motivation was the desire to have sole charge of the Somerset dressing room as some kind of guru figure for the team. To do that he needed all real and potential opponents, as well as anyone else who would have stood up against him, out of the way. His desire was to have a young, impressionable side that he could easily control, and the removal of Viv and Joel was a fundamental part of this master plan.

Viv told me that throughout 1986 he felt as if he was on quicksand; suddenly there weren't so many smiling faces around the dressing room, and as time wore on that miserable state of affairs grew worse. He felt there was little support for him in certain quarters, particularly among the younger players, and while you can keep smiling for so long there comes a point when it starts to affect you. Even in the darkest moments, however, neither Viv nor Joel surrendered their dignity. They walked out of Somerset tired and confused perhaps, but with their heads held high and their reputations intact.

Of course, the impressionable younger players were easily taken in by the whispers going round that Viv had given up on Somerset. I actually believe that some players were supporting the sackings because they saw it as a way for them to make it into the side; I heard youngsters actually say they were not getting a first-team chance because Viv and Joel were blocking their way. That was simply ridiculous. Viv was a world beater and so too was Joel. Let's be clear about this – if you are not good enough to be in contention for one of the other nine positions in the team then it is you who should be the one looking for another job, not the players who have done such sterling service for the club.

What happened to raw hunger? To get into the team and make it a winning outfit you need to show that you are prepared to battle for a place on merit. When I heard the excuse being trumpeted that Viv and Joel were blocking the path of the younger players, I knew the county were in a big hole and that this was now a club which had lost its backbone. What happened to the never-say-die spirit which Brian Close had fought to cultivate all those years ago?

Returning to Somerset after that Oval Test had fizzled out into a rain-affected draw, I faced my team-mates with my mind firmly made up. 'Look lads, as it stands you leave me no option,' I told them. 'I am shocked at what has been done and I'm resigning.'

For some reason a few of them thought I was bluffing. There were certain people in that room, like Roebuck and Nigel Popplewell, who had failed to grasp what I was saying. I had never been so serious in my life, and if it had to be spelt out in large letters for them, I had no hesitation in doing that.

Strangely, in the beginning, I don't think Roebuck wanted me out. I think he thought I might make a big fuss when the news of Viv and Joel's sacking was announced and then back down. That he dared put this theory to the test proved to be a serious miscalculation. Peter Roebuck is a very clever man, a very deep thinker, and I would never underestimate him. It is even possible that he calculated he would win either way; that if I stayed I would be bound to throw my hat in with him, but if I didn't want to support him he would have me out of the way anyway.

The season was not over yet, so the two sides in the camp still had to go out on the pitch together to present a united front, which was far from easy. Just before the dismissals came out in the open, Viv and Roebuck had a public squabble at Taunton after Roebuck ordered the groundsman to shave the pitch for the game against Surrey. Viv accused Roebuck of being afraid to face Sylvester Clarke on a quick track, and the argument was a sure sign of the serious trouble brewing.

A few days later, Roebuck went round to Viv's house to try and find out how things stood between them but Viv threw him out. He told me he could smell the man's ambition.

Viv, Joel and I tried to carry on as normal through the fraught final few weeks of that season, because we were not going to run away from the situation. I still think the club thought I was calling their bluff as we went into the last championship match against Derbyshire at Taunton. However, as I waved to all four corners of the ground on being given out before returning to the Somerset dressing room for what would be the very last time, the public, at least, knew this was the end.

I've mentioned the poisonous atmosphere within the club that season and it was certainly not eased by the fact that Viv had started the season as vice-captain. Not only did you have this bizarre situation of the team's two leaders not getting on at all, but once the deed had been done to remove Viv and Joel, there was also the prospect of the sacked player leading the county in the absence of the captain who had been behind the dismissals in the first place! Fortunately, that changed when Vic Marks took over the vice-captaincy job, but an unreal air continued to pervade the county.

Viv and Joel took their sackings very honourably; I think they were both in a state of shock for the remaining few weeks of that season and imagined it was a bad dream. I just knew it had been all planned from the start, so by putting the accusing note on Roebuck's peg in the dressing room, I was stating the facts as I saw them. In my eyes he was a Judas. The plaudits that have come his way in the game have been the result of being in a successful side, built around great professionals like Viv Richards and Joel Garner, yet here he was prepared to stab them in the back in order to achieve his ambition of gaining total control of the dressing room.

Throughout my career with Somerset, I had always thought that there was something a bit odd about Roebuck. As an illustration of his often strange behaviour, I only need to look back at a game at Hove. Roebuck had been going through a period of bad form and it was starting to get to him. The ball was not coming on to the bat and he had collected several ducks in a run of low scores. After failing yet again in this match, he trudged back to the pavilion and proceeded to rummage through his blazer pockets for his car keys. On finding them he lobbed them to Nigel Popplewell, telling him to take the car back to Taunton. Roebuck announced he was walking home. He set off from Hove to Taunton (a distance of some 130 miles as the crow flies) in his ordinary shoes, and ended up being rescued on Salisbury Plain the next day.

And this was the man who was going to take over the running of the club! He was a hard person to understand, and it always struck me that his biggest problem was an identity crisis. He wanted people to look up to him, yet he did not really know who he was, where he wanted to go and what he wanted to do apart from this fanatical desire to rule Somerset. And he was a very hard man to talk to – unless, of course, it was he who wanted to do the talking.

When I look back through conversations I had with him, I find evidence to back up this conclusion. He once told me that he wanted to fulfil his life by having 'disciples'. He envisaged himself as some sort of Messiah, sitting there preaching to followers, and I think he expressed this curious wish to quite a few colleagues.

One night I went to Roebuck's house to talk to him about some team matter. I banged on the door and on getting no reply decided to go round the back as I thought he might have been in the kitchen. I presumed he was home as I saw a light on. The back door was unlocked, so I let myself in and went on through into the living room. There was Roebuck sitting in the middle of the floor, legs crossed . . . and with a rug over his head! For a moment I thought someone had broken in, tied him up and burgled the place, but then I realized he was all right. Trying desperately to keep a straight face, I asked him what he was doing. 'I'm meditating,' he replied.

Such was my anger when the storm blew up that I could have quite happily watched Roebuck being hung, drawn and quartered, but now I feel quite sorry for the man. He is a bit of a sad case. He wanted to be a great leader but unfortunately he did not inspire many of those around him, and to be perfectly honest he did little to change this. Not being exactly a flamboyant extrovert, though it would be unfair to castigate him for that, he made no effort to bridge the gap with others; he never went out of his way to mix with people and, in my view, that would certainly be one reason he was always going to be a failure as a captain. Because he would not go down to the bar and have a drink with the players, he never really got to know them, and consequently could not pick them up when they needed it. The sacking, the unrest and the failure of his leadership to motivate people all combined to make his reign pretty disastrous, and Somerset were back in the familiar groove of, at best, mediocrity. As for Martin Crowe he played one full season and four championship matches the following year before a back injury forced him. That was the last anyone ever saw of him at Taunton.

I may have been certain of my decision to leave and what course my life was going to take, but let me put the record straight by saying this: I never wanted to leave Somerset. The club had been a huge part of my life and, not only that, I had been there when it took off. I had been part of a great team and it meant an awful lot to me. Now the mist has cleared, let's hope the good times return. I had fifteen good years at the club and it would be foolish to let the events of a few weeks, notwithstanding their seriousness, spoil all that.

Prior to those halcyon days at the start of the 1980s, the closest the county had come to success was reaching a Lord's final where they lost to Kent in the Gillette Cup of 1967. It was lovely to come up through that group of players led by Brian Close and know that you had achieved something.

Somerset's outstanding success was down to the way the team gelled. In the beginning there were all these youngsters from various backgrounds: the public school crowd, the good local players, one or two of the old guard, plus Viv and Joel. It was a peculiar mix, but the thing that made it work was our individual and collective ambition. For years it was a very positive dressing room; Closey had shown us the way to win, a legacy that every one of us wanted to follow. All criticism was constructive and despite the differing backgrounds we were all mates together. We were a real team – eccentric, I grant you, but a real team.

Nobody was selfish.

The lads quickly learned that one of my problems was, or perhaps still is, a low boredom threshold. I believe a good spirit in the dressing room lifts the team and being able to play and take a joke was all part of it. If someone was sitting reading a newspaper they knew they were asking to have the bottom of it set alight by a certain I. T. Botham. Even the Deep Heat in the jockstraps and cream cakes in batting gloves and shoes were all part of the fun. And I may not have been to either Oxford or Cambridge, but I could still talk on level terms to people like Roebuck, at least in the early days, and Vic Marks.

Away from home the team got on well and there were plenty of high jinks. Whenever we arrived at a hotel there would be a wild rush as all the players tried to collect their room keys, because once they had the key in the door it was locked and nothing could be disturbed. Lose sight of the key and you were in trouble. Playing in Derby once, I made that fatal mistake. I went up to my hotel bedroom after a night in the bar, walked in and, on seeing the room was completely devoid of furniture, walked straight out again thinking it could not have been my room after all. Little did I realize at the time that Dennis Breakwell and some of the other lads had got in there and managed to reposition every single item of furniture around the rest of the hotel. The bed, for instance, was in a bathroom down the hall!

Fortunately, I got my revenge at Worcester when we

were staying in the Diglis Hotel. One night Dennis returned to his room to find, to his surprise, no bed. He searched the hotel from top to bottom. Still no bed. If he had gone outside and looked up at the building, however, he would have found what he was looking for. Suspended by sheets from his bedroom window, the missing piece of furniture was just hanging there in the wind!

On another occasion, Keith Jennings was the victim of my over-exuberance. I was desperate to go out for a few pints and insisted he came with me. He refused, saying there was something good on the television that he wanted to watch. All my efforts to persuade him fell on deaf ears, and in the end I had to resort to threats. 'Jennings,' I said, 'you are coming out to play, and if you don't open that door now I'm going to take it off its hinges.' Jennings' response from what he believed to be the sanctuary of his hotel bedroom was laughter. So I took two steps back in the corridor, steadied myself ... and threw my body weight against the door. There was a huge crash as I sent it bursting off its hinges and falling into the room. All you could see of Jennings were two feet and two hands sticking out from under the door, which had flattened him against the floor.

Because we were successful as a team, everyone could take it and joined in; the whole thing seemed to mushroom and team morale was at its peak. The club had been in existence for 104 years before it won a trophy, and then in one dizzy weekend in September 1979, first we beat Northamptonshire at Lord's by 45 runs to win the Gillette Cup and then everyone, players and supporters alike, invaded Trent Bridge for our final Sunday League game of the season, where Peter Roebuck's excellent first half century in the competition helped us to a 57-run victory and the title. The party could start at last.

In five glorious years we landed five trophies; Taunton had seen nothing like it. In fact there could have been more prizes, but however successful you are there are always some ready to do you down. We won the NatWest Bank Trophy final against Kent in 1983 and the following day needed to beat Worcestershire for the Sunday League title as well. When we lost the game by 55 runs it led to accusations by some county members that we had drunk too much of the celebration ale after the NatWest victory.

That was certainly untrue, as the time scale of that weekend made partying impossible. The NatWest game finished around eight, then came the presentations and a glass of champagne. But we were all professionals and had a big game the next day. By the time we had packed up at Lord's and driven in a convoy of half a dozen cars over the Cotswolds to Worcester, it was too late for high jinks. We arrived at the Diglis Hotel, ordered some sandwiches and were in bed just after midnight.

We knew we had played badly in that game but it was not from want of trying. The simple truth is that we were washed out: the build-up to that final Sunday had been constant cricket for each of the previous 15 days, and there was nothing left for us to give.

During this period I and the team were at the height of our powers and could seemingly turn it on at will. By 1986, that great spirit was all gone. To hear some juniors moan later that Viv didn't do this or that for them, made me see red. In truth his mere presence should have been a huge boost for them. Look at it this way. If you are a young player at Somerset and you come into the side and are batting at the other end to Viv Richards, isn't that going to help you? If Viv was there in the middle he intimidated other sides and gave his colleagues a lead and an example that nobody could better. His record in big matches was second to none, and there can be no better learning process than being on the same field and in the same dressing room as a master craftsman at the peak of his game.

So that was it: Viv, Joel and I had gone for good. I went on the 1986/87 tour of Australia bitter at what had happened and I was down under when a special meeting was held at the Bath and West Showground at Shepton Mallet to consider a vote of no confidence in the committee. The result was a split vote. Seven of the general committee resigned, including David Challacombe and Peter White who had joined forces with the pro-Richards and Garner faction headed by Roy Kerslake and supported by Peter Denning. The surprise package was Nigel Popplewell, who spoke at the meeting and accused Viv and Joel of a lack of commitment. That was a stunning attack because he was another player who had enjoyed so many good times with Viv and Joel. He had been to their houses and had been a part of that team, yet here he was breaking a long silence to turn against those he referred to as 'friends'. Never to this day have I worked out why he turned on them; in actual fact I think this attack hurt Viv and Joel the most because it was so unexpected. With Roebuck at least we knew what he was up to; but as for Popplewell, he has never explained why he suddenly came out and said what he did.

So Viv and I would not be team-mates again, although we would be rivals for a few years to come. Much has been made of this battle between us – the idea that we went to the wicket determined to outdo one another – but as far as I am concerned this was a misconception. Unlike a lot of batting partnerships we were both attacking players so if we were both at the crease you never had one man holding an end down and the other one playing the shots. Viv, as we all know could tear any attack apart and turn bowlers to jelly; and if I was at the other end with him while this was going on, I would try and do the same because it was my natural game. Our behaviour was not that of a batting contest between two men; it was two players trying to maximize an advantage for the benefit of the team. Viv and I are both winners, we never thought about losing. Because of that we were able to motivate each other. People often mistook that for rivalry, but I didn't think about it in that way and I'm sure Viv feels the same.

When we came up against each other in Test matches it was a different story. Viv wanted to get out to me less than anyone else in the world, and, frankly, I wanted his wicket more than anybody else's. On these occasions the rivalry was intense and razor sharp, but never nasty or bitter. We were both big enough to walk away at the end of the day and have a laugh and a beer together.

Once I had him lbw to a very dubious decision and felt pretty bad about it all day. Even the umpire Barry Meyer knew he had made a mistake and admitted later that he almost called Viv back to the wicket. In the event he only stopped himself because, by the time he had realized his error, Viv was already back in the pavilion, lbw bowled Botham (bad luck!).

Viv was still steaming about it when at the close of play

I went into the West Indies dressing room for a beer and a chat. He was sitting on the bench and just looked up at me with blazing eyes. He didn't blame me for what had happened and I didn't need to say anything. All I said was 'Shocking' . . . and we both burst out laughing.

Yes, it did rile me that I never scored a century against the West Indies in a Test match, but it was some consolation when Viv told me I was always the guy they really wanted out of the way. Malcolm Marshall, Michael Holding and Joel Garner knew what I could do because they had seen it first hand in the county game, so when it came to batting against them I was always their main target.

As a general rule I never wanted any opponent I played against to do well against me or England, but when it came to the emotional moment of Viv's last Test match in England I made an exception. I was recalled for the fifth Test of the 1991 series against the West Indies at The Oval. It was my first Test appearance for two years, and it was to be Viv's last in England and also his last as West Indies captain.

Before the match I took him to one side and said to him: 'You know what I would like, Smokey? You to score 100 and we to win the match.'

It didn't quite work out like that, but almost. Viv scored a second innings 60, and when England batted again it was left to me to score the winning runs from the only delivery I faced in the second innings, striking Clayton Lambert towards the gas holders for four. Of course, Viv would have liked to have won, but even so his disappointment at the defeat that squared the series for us was tempered by knowing he had been in a great final match. He was happy that the series had been so harmonious, and that the cricket had not only been enjoyable but had been played in great spirit. After all, four result matches for a 2–2 series draw was a tremendous advert for the game. This was an important match in another way because it was my first Test win over the West Indies in more than 20 matches!

I think that match brilliantly summed up Viv's love of the game. He was happy with the result, he was happy for me, and we in turn were happy for him. Everything was fair and right, and that is the way it should be. In many ways, our friendship is built on this mutual respect for fair play.

The Somerset split ended an era but could not break a friendship that had been forged from our first meeting. Over the years we had roomed together and shared accommodation on and off for almost nine years in Somerset. At one stage we probably knew each other better than we knew our wives. In international cricket at that time, we were travelling around the world and bumping into each other for round-robin competitions, Test series, one-day matches in Australia and so on. We were good for each other, of that I am sure. If I had a problem with my cricket, it was hard to find someone to talk to, particularly when I was at the peak of my career. But Viv was always the one with whom I could sit down and talk and vice versa, not only because he was a friend but because he was playing at the same level as me and understood the pressures from his own career experiences.

Viv's greatest quality is his honesty. Sometimes he is too honest for his own good. He tends to speak his own mind; if he has anything to say he says it regardless of the consequences and there are some people who cannot take the plain truth spoken so bluntly. But that is the man he is: strong-minded and strong-willed.

As a player Viv had enormous belief in his own ability, and because of the strength of his faith in his own talents, he was able to sustain a high level of performance over a very long time. The bridge between having great ability and actually using it is positive thinking, and Viv had it in abundance.

He's been a fine friend to me and the family. He is god-father to Liam which shows you how close we have become over the years. In my eyes there is probably very little he can do wrong, and I have nothing but admiration for him. He is proud and very loyal and it would not surprise me to see Viv going into Antiguan politics very soon. He has strong beliefs and ideas, he wants to do things for the island, and knowing the man as I do, the Antiguans could do a lot worse.

Being proud of his roots, and rightly so, Viv is fully prepared to deal with the mindless bigots he has come across from time to time. The worst treatment came from a few ignorant idiots at Yorkshire. They got to him very early in his Somerset career, in 1975 to be precise, and the memory of it never left him. Viv had only been in England a couple of seasons and was at this stage extremely sensitive to the slightest suggestion of racism. In a county match against Yorkshire at Harrogate, he had scored a fine double-century and was coming off the field when he passed an old boy who had spent his free time following Somerset to all four corners of the country. He was standing up and applauding Viv's magnificent innings when suddenly some-one in the crowd moved forward and tipped a pint of beer over his head.

Then in the second innings of the same match Viv was struggling with a torn hamstring, and when he was run out another spectator yelled out to him on his way back to the pavilion: 'Get a move on, you black bastard'.

Viv exploded, dashed towards the group of spectators from which the abuse had come, held his bat aloft and shouted: 'Whoever said that, stand up!' Needless to say, no one did and Viv, shaking with rage, had to content himself with taking out his revenge on a dressing room door. This sort of behaviour used to make Viv so angry simply because he could never understand why people did it.

Although, from time to time, the same kind of thing happened in other parts of the country – once even at Weston-Super-Mare, where Viv, Joel and myself marched straight into a crowd of half a dozen drunken yobs who had been shouting racist insults – Yorkshire has the worst reputation for it thanks to the behaviour of a tiny minority. I am not saying all of the Headingley, Scarborough or Harrogate crowd are the same, but there is a small element that follows the county which is undoubtedly racist. When I was captain of Somerset I was particularly aware of it and felt that it was something the home county should have sorted out. You can't tell me the Yorkshire committee were not aware of it. I'm certain they simply closed their eyes and hoped it would go away.

But following one game up there years after the original incident at Harrogate, the abuse was so bad that I decided to take the matter into my own hands. After the match I spoke out on the subject to a gathering of reporters, because quite frankly I was disgusted by some of the comments I had heard. I think there comes a point when you have got to stand up for what you believe in.

One Yorkshire committee man, instead of backing what I had said and promising some sort of action, started jumping up and down at the press conference and complained that I was out of order for raising the issue. His attitude was absurd, and thankfully there were enough people around with the sense to see it. They forced him to back down, but that was hardly the point. In fact that particular incident proved how apathetic the Yorkshire club were about the problem. It should never have got to the stage where I had to speak out in the first place; yet when I did, I still had opposition from one of the committee!

I can see no reason for racial abuse, although I know what causes it. It is often a couple of 'jack the lads' who have had a few pints of beer and who think they can take on the world. Over the years it was, I am glad to say, a relatively rare event but when it was reported one of the first clubs you immediately thought of was Yorkshire. If you ask any of the West Indians about playing at Scarborough or Headingley, they will tell you the same.

My strong beliefs concerning racial equality made it imperative for me to defend myself against Imran Khan's allegations in later years.

As I see it Viv and I are very much the same sort of people, only he was left in the oven a bit longer (and I've got hair). That's my philosophy and the view of most sportsman who are simply not interested in skin colours and could not care less if a person is green, pink, orange, yellow or blue. What matters is what you are, not what colour you are.

Time has a way of healing even the deepest wounds. Viv, Joel and I are now all honorary members of Somerset and proud to be.

I moved on to Worcestershire via Queensland, the deal to join the club being concluded on my behalf by my solicitor Alan Herd. I had links with Worcestershire through their chairman, Duncan Fearnley, who provided me with my bats. The Carphone Group were sponsoring me as well as Graham Dilley, who moved to New Road at the same time. Our arrival provoked huge interest: membership at Worcestershire rocketed and I ended up signing the contract a second time in Australia, in January of 1987, for the benefit of the BBC cameras.

Part of the deal involved Worcestershire finding me a house in a remote location. This turned out to be a country cottage close to some angling waters. It was so off the beaten track that it took several attempts to find the place, but it was ideal; nobody was going to be an uninvited pest there. What's more, I was joining a club that was full of hope for the future and with some big stars to back up that belief. The likes of Graeme Hick, Steve Rhodes, Neal Radford, Phil Newport, Tim Curtis and Richard Illingworth were players heading for the top, and they had a marvellous motivator in their captain Phil Neale. Here was a man who knew how to handle his players and understood enough about their personalities to get the most out of them.

If I had to leave Somerset then I could not have found a better place to land on my feet. Worcestershire won the county championship twice, the Sunday League twice and the Benson and Hedges Cup during my five very happy years with the club.

What will surprise many people is that initially I was nervous about the move. It is easy to forget that despite my travels with England, I had only ever had the one base, my home county in Somerset. I was so keen to do well for my new county that during a spell when I was not getting as many runs as I thought I should, I actually had two days of net sessions! That certainly took my critics by surprise.

In the build-up to me joining Worcestershire for the start of the 1987 season, Warwickshire had been mooted as another possible destination along with a few other clubs. But there was only one club I really wanted to go to. Just look at the Worcestershire team; the quality of the players was obvious. Business was booming at New Road, only a dozen or so season-ticket holders failed to renew their memberships for the following season and the intake of new members soared, so much so that the club ran out of car-parking space.

As for the committee, well they were amazing. After the back-stabbing at Somerset, I was at a place where I knew more committee men at Worcester than I ever did at Taunton, even in the good times. The great difference was that I could go into a committee room and we could talk about things other than cricket, and those who had played in the first-class game did not go about ear-bashing you with rubbish of the 'in my day' variety. Even when we did talk about cricket the conversation with men like Duncan Fearnley, Basil D'Oliveira, the coach, and Mike Jones, the chairman of the cricket, was worthwhile and constructive (at least until the third bottle of wine was opened!).

I thought it would take about a year to settle in, but I was wrong; I felt perfectly at home within a fortnight. I had never been happier in county cricket because I was surrounded by a great set of lads, I was in a lovely part of the world and the beer was good (and cheap).

In all the fuss surrounding my arrival at Worcestershire,

much had been made about how they were going to be the unstoppable side in the county championship, but as it turned out, myself and Graham Dilley were only available for eleven championship matches because of England call-ups, and Dilley missed another five games because of injury. The one-day competitions were our best hope for that season, and how I enjoyed myself in the Sunday League. The rib injury I had suffered in Perth during England's tour of Australia was still niggling me and that combined with the worries about my back meant I never really ran in and gave it the works because I was scared something would give. Instead I relied on line and length, and it worked a treat because I managed to put in some miserly spells. The boys even started to call me 'Tommy' after my mentor Tom Cartwright.

I knew we were going to win the Sunday competition a month before the end of the season. I had moved up to open the innings with Tim Curtis, who, would you believe, managed to outscore me primarily because having been to university he could count up to six and he knew when to take a single to keep the strike! It worked well because we shared a succession of hundred-plus stands. Finally, on beating Northants in the last game of that Sunday programme the title was ours.

They were great years at Worcestershire and the county built on that Sunday League success. My contributions were limited by injury and the back operation that forced me to miss most of the 1988 season, but that didn't stop me from enjoying my cricket greatly. The atmosphere was such that it rekindled my appetite for the game. A winning side is a happy side, and how it showed.

Throughout my time at Worcestershire the one thing

I enjoyed above all else was the tremendous spirit in the dressing room. And looking back now, the decision to leave the club to join Durham, where I played out the last two seasons of my career, was one of the worst mistakes I ever made. There were of course great attractions in going to Durham. It was a new county apparently full of ideas and ambition, and the prospect of playing home matches only an hour's drive from where I lived was extremely appealing. That amounted to the chance to play 'at home' for the first time in 20 years. But I should have known better. Quite early on I became aware of major problems behind the scenes.

I was actually offered the captaincy of Durham as one of the inducements to join the county in the first place. I had met with Don Robson, the chairman, Paul Tappenden, a representative of Durham's sponsors Scottish and Newcastle breweries, and Matty Roseberry, one of the main backers of the club. During our meeting in a local pub, the Durham men insisted they wanted me as captain.

However, when later I met Geoff Cook, the Director of Cricket, to confirm the details of my move, he told me that he had already promised the captaincy to David Graveney. I was not happy but there was nothing I could do about the decision, so I shrugged my shoulders and accepted the fact, but during the time I was there it became more and more obvious to me that Cook had never wanted me at the club in the first place. I even learned that when the idea of me going to the club was first mooted, Cook intimated privately that not only was he not in favour of signing me up, but it was a case of him or me. To this day I still don't know why.

Although he backed down over that, his other big idea

was that there should be no star system at Durham. It was his dream to build a kind of socialist cricket republic where all players would be equal. If he had had his way we would have stood up before the start of each match and belted out a couple of choruses of 'The Red Flag'. It was his idea that there should be no such thing as the county cap system that exists everywhere else in the country. To my mind that is absolutely essential. When I first came into cricket the prospect of winning my second XI cap was a great motivating force; to win the first team cap meant you had really achieved something.

Generally speaking, I got on well with most of the playing staff, sharing some good times with the likes of Dean Jones, Simon Hughes and David Graveney, but my real problems were with members of the committee. Initially, promises were made that were never kept and the level of in-fighting grew and grew.

Indeed, if I needed any more evidence that all was not well in the state of Durham, I was given it in a phone call just a few weeks before my retirement. It came from Roseberry. He told me that a number of influential figures behind the scenes were unhappy with the chairman, Don Robson, and wanted him out. He asked me if I would be prepared to be the figurehead for their campaign.

I was certainly not going to fall in with his plans. It seemed to me that Roseberry was asking me to be some sort of stool-pigeon. He wanted me as a frontman to enable him to gain control, but if the coup had failed it would have been me who took the flak. I didn't bother to ring Roseberry back. I felt sorry for the players, but if I needed any further persuasion that the time had come to get out, this was it.

When it came to leaving Durham, the petty-mindedness of the club appalled me. It was verbally agreed that I would be paid until the end of July rather than September and that I could keep my club car until the end of August. That was fine, as I already had a car sponsorship sorted out with Volvo. When I rang the club to tell them that I had not been paid, they told me that the last cheque would not be released until the car had been handed back. They got quite nasty about this, and I couldn't believe they would treat me in this way. In the end I was so furious with their attitude that I decided to stoop to their level. I told them I could only hand over the car keys if they came round to the house and handed over the cheque at the same time. The whole thing was so ridiculous, but it summed up how what should have been a great finale to my career turned into a sorry ending.

14
IN THE OUTBACK

They are the old enemy, the lot I wanted to beat more than anyone else in the world. The Australians – nothing gave me more satisfaction than putting them to the sword. Yet for all that desire to give them a good thrashing, always I felt a certain kinship with the Aussies. We talked the same language and played bloody hard on the field, but at the end of the day we're still mates willing to share a joke and a beer in the bar afterwards. That's why I am so worried about the spate of sledging that stemmed from them in recent years and threatened to snowball out of control.

The practice of sledging destroys that special bond between players and if something is not done about it soon the game will be damaged beyond repair. I am no saint, and I've 'exchanged' a few words with opponents in my time, but there is a line beyond which players know they shouldn't go. I was horrified with what I saw of the Australian trip to the West Indies on television in 1993, then during the Ashes series with England that summer and against South Africa in March 1994, when Shane Warne and Merv Hughes were fined for on-field misbehaviour that went way over that line. It simply demonstrated the unacceptable face of Australian cricket.

Sadly, this is nothing new. Even during Ian Chappell's period as Australian captain in the early 1970s, rivals had been on the receiving end of many a verbal outburst, but there is no doubt that under Allan Border sledging was getting out of hand. Some of the things that went on were totally unnecessary.

Why did Merv Hughes think he had the right to run up to batsmen and give them the snarling, spitting routine, and what on earth got into Shane Warne in the first Test in Johannesburg when he had to be physically restrained from chasing after the South African opener Andrew Hudson after he had got him out? I read somewhere that Warne said he had been possessed by demons. That's alright then. And what about Alec Stewart deliberately barging into Roshan Mahanama of Sri Lanka in the infamous one-day international at the Adelaide Oval in 1999.

If this is what the modern player thinks being professional is all about, then he needs his head examined. A load of verbal abuse doesn't make you tough: it just shows how ignorant you are.

But I have no hesitation in saying that the Aussies are responsible for persuading the world that sledging was not only acceptable but a vital part of any team's armoury. Down the years the Aussies have certainly produced some great cricketers who never felt they needed to resort to foul-mouthing their opponents. Indeed, I have come up against quite a few of these talented men face to face.

Jeff Thomson was one of the greats. I never batted against Thommo in his prime, but I am told by no better judge than Viv Richards that he was the quickest and most hostile bowler of them all until he was injured following a collision with team-mate Alan Turner in the first Test against Pakistan in Adelaide in December 1976. After that he was never the same again. But watching the tapes of him when he was in his prime in 1974 makes me realize that the man was not only brilliant but also a freak, a Mr Elastic.

You only need to look at his action. If anyone tried to copy him I'm sure they would break in half. At least when facing Michael Holding the batsman could focus on the ball at all times because you could watch it from the moment he started his run up; but Thommo never let you see it until the last moment. He would run in and then twist himself so far round that the first time the ball was visible was when it left his hand. That made him not only hostile but also made his bowling almost impossible to 'read'.

It was stunning to see the lift he could extract. He could get the ball to rear off the pitch in the same way as Joel Garner, but the difference was that Joel, with a delivery point twelve feet in the air, was expected to do that regularly. With Thommo, it was a big surprise.

But even Thomson could not compare with Dennis Lillee who, for my money, was the best of them all. I find it very hard to believe there has been a more complete quick bowler. When he needed to he could bowl fast on any surface, any time and anywhere. And there was more to him than that. A lot of quick bowlers come charging in, let go and don't really know what they are doing or where the ball is going to pitch. 'DK' knew exactly what he wanted to do, and his control was complete. He has been a great competitor, fierce rival and also a big mate. DK was one of the first to call me at home and wish me the best after I announced my retirement from the game. He also got me out of jail once, but I will come to that later.

One of my main rivals down the years has been Allan Border. But although I regard him as a tremendous cricketer and a great personal friend, I have to say that you can trace the resurgence of sledging back to the moment, halfway though his captaincy, when his attitude to the job changed radically.

I rate 'AB' alongside David Gower, Clive Lloyd and Brian Lara in the top bracket of left-handers, and I have enjoyed playing against him immensely. I admire his guts and fighting qualities; out there on the pitch he doesn't give or take an inch, and he is a typical Aussie in that sense. Sometimes, when under pressure he has fully earned the nickname 'Captain Grumpy', but anyone who has captained his state and country for as long as he has is bound to have ups and downs.

There have been moments of great humour as well. I'll never forget him telling the tale about the time he ended up confused and lost when we played Australia at the WACA during the 1979/80 series down under.

AB was pretty new to the Aussie side, and very unsure over keeping his place. When his turn arrived to bat, he came out and scratched and prodded around in very untypical style before I got him out for four, whereupon off he trudged, fuming all the way back to the pavilion. He pushed open the boundary gate and stormed up the stairs to the dressing rooms, where he saw the door was ajar. He banged it open and hurled his bat across the changing room, ripping off his gloves and letting out a tirade of expletives about the bloody Poms and how they had done for him. Having got that out of his system, he then looked around and suddenly realized he was in the England dressing room! To make matters worse, the England tour manager was sitting a few feet away staring in disbelief!

There is no doubt AB has changed over the years. When he brought his team to England in 1985 he was pretty relaxed and very outgoing; in fact, some of his team-mates complained that he spent more time in the England dressing room having a beer with me, Gower and Lamby than he did with them. But by 1989, AB and his team presented a very different face. As he put it, the Aussies had lost the last two series in England and he was not going to become the first captain of Australia to lose three. His new approach was obvious from a conversation he had with David Gower, who had mentioned to him that some of the England boys had been moaning about the fact that he never exchanged one civil word with them, either on or off the field, throughout the tour.

Robin Smith had been particularly surprised and disappointed by AB's behaviour after having heard so much about what a great bloke he was from his friend and mentor, Allan Lamb. Robin couldn't believe how the Australians went out of their way to be positively obnoxious, and he was certainly not prepared for the fearful abuse he received from Merv Hughes and others. Once, in the middle of a long innings, he asked AB whether it would be all right to send for a glass of water. The Aussie captain's response was short and not very sweet. 'What do you think this is,' he asked, 'a bloody tea party?'

AB told Gower that he had taken a long hard look at the way he had approached the last tour and decided it was going to be 'no more, Mr Nice Guy', and if that meant friendships would be put in jeopardy, it was a price he was prepared to pay. On that tour his single-mindedness meant that even the players' wives were barred from the team hotel and there was a very grim, almost missionary zeal about the way the players went about their business.

AB had not changed by the time Australia came out to England for the 1993 tour. In a warm-up match against Somerset at Taunton he publicly berated his fast bowler Craig McDermott, who he believed was not giving him 100 per cent, and warned him that if he didn't pull up his socks he would be on the next plane home. 'And don't think I don't mean it,' he insisted.

Sean Fitzpatrick, the great All Black rugby captain, once said that to be a good winner you have to be a good loser. But AB didn't see it that way. He was not a good loser; he had no time for it at all. In fact, I'm sure it was his absolute hatred of coming second that was at the root of him allowing his players to go over the top on the field.

Sledging is out of order. I make no bones about that. But I think AB's attitude is a symptom rather than a cause. If umpires, captains and cricket authorities the world over got together and decided to punish the offenders severely at all times, the problem would soon be eradicated and, although it pains me to say so, if the Australian Cricket Board had jumped on AB from the start, the situation would not have been allowed to get out of hand. (Incidentally, the most appalling example of how players get away with it involved Peter Kirsten of South Africa. After he was fined for misdemeanours on the field during a one-day match against India, a local radio station actually organized a phone-in which raised enough money to pay the fine and a little more besides.)

The bottom line is that AB was only really guilty of stretching the laws as far as they would go. For that reason, I found his treatment by the Australian Cricket Board, who more or less forced him into a position where he had no option but to resign, peculiar to say the least. The only justification AB needed for his actions were the runs he scored and the success Australia have had under his captaincy. Since 1989 he has turned the Aussies into a major cricketing force again, and while they were enjoying the financial rewards that resulted from that success, the Board were happy to go along with AB's on-field approach. If they were really unhappy with what his team were getting up to on the field, why wait until now to get rid of him?

But back to happier times and happier memories. When I toured Australia with England in the winter of 1986/87, AB was still in the process of rebuilding his team's shattered confidence after the thrashing we gave them in 1985. It was taking time and things were still not fully in place at this stage. In the end we beat them comfortably and, after all the nightmares Kath and I had been through during the previous three years this was the tour that really got me back on the road. From a conversation I had with Micky Stewart prior to returning to the Test side against New Zealand the previous summer, I was convinced that, contrary to some people's hopes, this was not the time for me to quit touring.

Micky made it clear to me that as far as he and captain Mike Gatting were concerned, everything that had happened to me in the past would stay there. However, I had come to one decision about touring: I was never going anywhere without Kath again. The cost of taking the family out to Australia for the whole trip was enormous, but you cannot put a price tag on peace of mind. It turned out to be one of the best things I ever did. Not only Kath, but all my team-mates saw how relaxed I was on that tour, and I'm sure that helped me produce some excellent performances, particularly the 138 I scored in the first Test in Brisbane.

We had not covered ourselves with glory at the start of the tour. In fact, our performances had led Martin Johnson in the *Independent* to comment: 'There are only three things wrong with this team. They can't bat. They can't bowl and they can't field'.

So the Aussies really fancied their chances of getting a firm grip on the series from the start. But we turned the tables at the Gabba by making a big first innings score which gave us the advantage we needed to secure a vital win. During the innings I shared a century stand with David Gower and he could see how much I was enjoying myself. At one point he came down the wicket and said: 'I should be telling you to calm down, but I'm having too much fun'.

That result set us off on the winning trail and we never looked back. In fact we won everything in sight. Little did any of us realise that in winning the Test series 2-1 we would become the last England team to beat Australia in a Test series in the 20th century, and that the Old Enemy would go on to win the next six Ashes encounters.

A lot of credit for our success has to go to Mike Gatting and Micky Stewart for that because, unlike what happened later when Micky and Graham Gooch joined forces and imposed a strict, almost robotic regime on the players, at least here each player was treated as an individual.

Gatt's man-management was brilliant: he understood we were all different and that we all had our strengths and weaknesses, and he found a way of bringing out the best in us. For example, he didn't mind the fact that in the build-up to the real action, we took the occasional opportunity to enjoy ourselves.

During that tour I had one of my booziest nights of all time, one which led to a most embarrassing moment. The night before we were due to play Western Australia in Perth in a special match to mark the occasion of Australia defending the America's Cup, a group of the senior players – Gatt, Gower, Lamby, John Emburey, Chris Broad and myself – were invited to a party at the headquarters of the White Crusader team in Fremantle. It turned out to be a fantastic night. I had tucked into a bottle of brandy and when it was time to leave I found I could hardly put one foot in front of the other.

I was carried back to the limousine for the ride back to the hotel, crashed out, and woke up nursing one of the biggest hangovers of my life. I found out later that Gower had been through an interesting experience of his own on his return journey. He and a couple of the other lads managed to hitch a lift with one of the other guests at the party. As they drove out of Fremantle along deserted streets, the driver went straight through a Stop sign and, as luck would have it, a police car pulled them over. Poor old David was cowering in the back seat, praying he wouldn't be recognized but the driver jumped out, walked up to the policeman and announced proudly: 'You'll never guess who is in the back of my car!' In the circumstances, David was more than happy to oblige the officer's request for an autograph!

The first thing I did on arriving at the ground the following morning was to plunge my head into a basin of cold water and ice. I was so dehydrated that I actually started to drink it. The world was spinning around and I was desperately trying to grab hold of something solid to keep me upright. What I needed more than anything was a good few hours' sleep. Unfortunately, we won the toss and I was due in at number five, so it looked unlikely that I was going to be able to rest my weary head. Fortunately, Lawrie Brown, the physio, came to my rescue. He saw what a ghastly state I was in, and realized that I would be totally incapable of tying up my bootlaces let alone playing cricket. After telling the management that he was taking me away for some treatment on a dodgy ankle, he led me to a quiet back room and set to work to try and revive the living corpse. From time to time, as wickets fell, there would be a knock on the door and an inquiry from the captain or manager as to how the treatment was going. 'Well, he'll be at least another half hour. The ankle needs a little bit more work', Lawrie would say.

Later, these fictitious ailments spread to my knee, my shoulder, or anywhere else Lawrie could think of to keep them at bay. Finally, when we were 69 for six he and I ran out of ideas. I made it out of the dressing room, struggling but just about managing to walk in more or less a straight line. Once past the gate on to the field, I thought the worst was over. If I got out cheaply, bearing in mind what the other players had done, it wouldn't look too bad and then I would have the chance to slip away into a corner of the dressing room and die quietly.

Halfway out to the wicket I got the shock of my life when someone tapped me on the shoulder. For obvious reasons, the identity of the twelfth man remains a mystery to me. I do recall exactly what he said, however. 'Beefy . . . I think you might need this.' He was holding my bat in his hands.

By this time some of the crowd might just have suspected something, so I prepared myself for the inevitable. I have to say that it wasn't so much a case of keeping an eye on the ball in the first few moments of that innings but more a case of actually finding a ball to keep an eye on. I devised a cunning plan: I decided, of the three balls coming towards me, I would hit the middle one. Somehow the strategy worked, and I made 48 from 38 deliveries before returning to the dressing room none the worse for the experience. I have to say, however, that I don't recommend this as the ideal way to prepare for an innings.

It was important that we were able to have a few laughs on that tour because it was, as usual, a long and arduous trip down under. And if you don't get away from the cricket to unwind from time to time you are liable to end up climbing the walls.

Bob Willis recognized the need for this kind of extra-curricular activity on the previous England tour in 1982/83 when we spent a memorable night in my room demolishing every bottle of booze we could lay our hands on. At about four in the morning, I happened to glance over at a couple of the lads sitting on the sofa, their eyes wide open and staring at the television. Intrigued, I went over to have a look at what I thought must have been a riveting film only to discover they were watching a small white dot in the middle of the screen; not only that but their hands were wrapped around a bottle of Chivas Regal. On the shelf above the bed one player was fast asleep, while another was wrapped around the lamp, snoring away contentedly.

When we came round the next day (a day off I must add) we were rather taken aback to find the room was full of bits of uneaten cheeseburger. Somewhere along the line we had ordered up a couple of dozen from room service but had actually eaten none. They were everywhere. Willis had one enmeshed in his hair and when I woke up, someone politely inquired 'Beefy, are you aware that there is a cheeseburger stuck in your ear?'

But on that tour of 1986/87 another helpful diversion was the presence of pop superstar, Elton John. Once the serious cricket had started, professional responsibility put an end to the wild nights. To make up for that, I rented a suite in the hotel and used that as a base camp where we could all get together after a day's play and have a few beers with people we could trust. Elton certainly fell into that category. He would come up and play the role of disc jockey, and we nicknamed him EJ the DJ.

Apart from the contribution he made to team spirit as a whole, he was wonderful for me. I was able to discuss fully with him all the problems I had suffered at the hands of the media knowing that his experiences with the tabloid press meant he knew exactly what I was talking about. We were kindred spirits in a way and he was like a big brother to me and Kath. One time he even babysat the kids for us when we wanted to go out for a quiet night. On our return we found that he had been feeding them jelly and ice cream, reading them stories, and had even tucked them up in bed. Elton was magic, he had plenty of problems of his own yet he still found time to help me.

My next experience in Australia was less happy. When I

joined Queensland in the winter of 1988 (a deal that I had discussed with AB two years earlier during England's tour of the West Indies) the interest in my arrival was enormous. I was looking forward to playing Sheffield Shield cricket, and hoped that the Australian public would take to me and get a lot of enjoyment from seeing me play.

The cricket turned out to be fantastic – tough and uncompromising – and I really believe we could learn a lot in this country from the way the game is structured in Australia. The top three states could easily live with any of the counties in this country, and when you think that the population of Australia is equivalent to that in Greater London, what they achieve from a much smaller base than us is remarkable.

The state teams run three, four or five sides which means the percentage of the population actually playing cricket far outstrips that in England, and the players have ambitions to play at a better and better standard. In England the weekend cricketers by and large are just wanting to get away for a day and have a few beers. I don't mean to be disparaging, but the game at grass-roots level in this country is more social than seriously competitive. As I see it, the biggest advantage the Aussies enjoy is that they don't play nearly as much cricket as us, and therefore there is little danger of succumbing to the disease most prevalent among English professionals, namely, burnout. Cricketers in Australia still have time to do other jobs; take Andrew Hilditch, for instance, who played for South Australia when I was with Queensland and spent his winters working as a solicitor. So there is little likelihood of staleness creeping in.

Following England's great success down under the

previous winter, my popularity with Australians was at an all-time high. I was prepared for some media interest; what I had not bargained for was that following the lead of their British counterparts, some sections of the Australian media seemed determined to have me on a plate and, what is more, some influential members of Queensland who resented me being there in the first place were quite prepared to assist them.

I should have realized what might lay in store when, on arrival at Brisbane Airport to start my three months' winter employment, I walked straight into a scrum of reporters and photographers who virtually pinned me against the wall in the arrivals lounge and wouldn't let me go until I had given them a few words of Beefy's wisdom.

I didn't notice at the time, but sitting in the far corner of the same room was Lindy Chamberlain, the woman at the centre of the dingo baby murder case. One of the reporters told me afterwards that it was extraordinary, bearing in mind her notoriety and all the controversy surrounding the case, that a pack of Aussie journalists should completely ignore her in this way, while concentrating instead on me.

Tom Byron, my Australian agent at the time, had fixed up some excellent deals for me including one to publicize Jack-In-The-Box fast-food restaurants, and when I was introduced to the spectators in the middle of an important basketball match, I was given a standing ovation. In response to my arrival, the crowds for those early games for Queensland were substantially higher than they had been in previous years; and as the season progressed, my popularity among the people of Queensland rose as a result of our successes on the field.

The fact was that Queensland was the only state never

to have won the Sheffield Shield. It had been the same old story ever since the competition first began in 1892/93. 'This is going to be our year' the supporters would say. But of course it never had been; that is, until now. What the dissenters in the background were starting to mutter was that I was behaving as if I felt this was not going to be Queensland's title, but Ian Botham's. This was sheer non-sense. Of course I put myself about in the dressing room, but that was no different to how I behaved everywhere else during my career; after all, I saw it as part of my job to raise the players' spirits. It was a natural thing for me to do.

As we approached the final, however, things started to get a bit tense. By the time we arrived in Launceston to play Tasmania, for some reason Allan Border had slipped into one of his moods. He barely said a word to anyone.

Against all expectations we lost the game and Dennis Lillee and I ended up with a massive bill after being accused of smashing up the dressing room. In reality, all that happened was we broke a few glasses, but as DK said later, 'You could have driven two steamrollers through the place and ended up with a smaller bill than we did'. I didn't realize at the time, but this was the signal for the snipers to take aim and fire.

BOOZED-UP BOTHAM WRECKED OUR CLUB

Defeat by 94 runs brought a dark cloud over the camp, particularly as Tasmania's David Boon scored a century in each innings (having been dropped by AB at slip off the third ball of the match). It was a defeat, but not the end of the world and if we could go to Melbourne and beat Victoria we would have home advantage in the Shield final. But AB's mood was dragging everyone down, and when we reached Melbourne he turned round and said to me 'There's a curfew on – no drinking'. I told him to forget it; if I didn't have a drink I couldn't get to sleep and if I didn't sleep I would be no good for the team. As far as I know the other lads obeyed AB's orders, but I just left him to it and carried on as I always had done. I needed a drink and was going to have one. Besides, if I had changed the habits of a lifetime so suddenly, I'm convinced there would have been an adverse effect on my game.

This was the start of the fall-out between us, and I picked up vibes from the senior figures at Queensland that the knives were out for me. I also got the feeling that petty-mindedness was creeping into the way things were being handled. Having dealt with AB, I now had Greg Chappell calling me at my hotel room and wanting to know why I wasn't attending nets.

He knew full well that I rarely went into the nets under any circumstances.

Slowly but surely, the feeling grew within me that the club was preparing for failure and had decided that I was going to be made the scapegoat. We had lost a game and it was all being pinned on me. We then lost the next match against Victoria when we were all out in the second innings for 168, chasing 376 off 64 overs, and just to add more insult to injury I was hauled before the Australian Cricket Board and fined the equivalent of £200 for swearing. They told me that had I not been provoked by the crowd the fine would have been higher.

Just for good measure, my back was playing up with the injury that was to nearly cost me my career.

We had lost home advantage in the Sheffield Shield final after two successive defeats which meant that Western Australia, as the leading side, would host the match in Perth. But if we could beat them we would give the Queensland club the prize they had craved for almost a century. The pressure was on us because as holders, Western Australia only needed a draw to keep the title.

Having lurched from one disaster to another on the cricket field, the prevailing unrest in the camp worsened as we took the plane to Perth. AB's state of mind had not improved and he and Greg Ritchie were at each other's throats during the flight. Ritchie was complaining about not being picked for the Australian side. I tried to tell him to stop moaning and take a look at his situation. All he had to do, I told him, was lose some weight, and he would get back in the side. It was all down to him.

After changing planes at Melbourne and about ten minutes into the last leg of the flight to Perth the row boiled up again. All the players told Ritchie to put a sock in it – and as you can imagine with a bunch of Aussies, the language was not exactly delicate. Some of the other passengers started to get even more agitated. Ritchie went to the toilet and while he was gone I tried to reason with AB. Perhaps, with hindsight, I should have left well alone for all I managed to do was fan the flames again.

The next thing I knew, someone in the row of seats in front of me had turned round and started complaining about the language we were using. I put my hands on his shoulders, redirected his gaze so he was facing the front again and told him to mind his own business. On reflection, I shouldn't have touched him. I realize that now, and maybe I knew it at the time because as soon as we disembarked I went up to the man and apologized for what had happened because I had clearly been in the wrong. And as far as I was concerned that was the end of it. He seemed quite happy to leave well alone.

When we arrived in Perth we booked in at the Merlin Hotel and soon afterwards and completely out of the blue, the police arrived. They had received a complaint and had come to arrest me! I ended up being taken to the Sheraton Hotel in Perth, where strangely the Federal Police Headquarters is on the top floor of the building. AB came with me but we were kept in separate rooms until the police decide to charge me under the Australian Civil Aircraft Act.

For some reason Australian law demands that you are formally charged at a State jail which meant I was taken to the East Perth 'lock-up'. I was escorted out of the Sheraton Hotel by two uniformed policemen who had a car waiting at the front. It was all very dramatic. Then, who should come round the corner just as I'm being bundled into the back of this police car, but Chris Lander – at the time ghosting my columns for the *Sun* newspaper.

It just so happened that was the day my solicitor Alan Herd arrived in Perth with Kath. Unfortunately for him, he walked straight into this mess. Herdy was desperate to get it sorted out because he could imagine the headlines back home: 'BOTHAM ARRESTED BY AUSTRALIAN POLICE'.

We arrived at the station and before a word was said the duty officer presented us with a cricket bat which he asked me to sign. He then charged me with assaulting a passenger on the flight. The whole affair was starting to run out of control . . . but worse was to follow. It had been a minor incident and it seemed that I would be given bail without too much trouble. AB was happy to stand surety. But the laws in Western Australia state that two people, both of them landowners within the state, are needed as witnesses to stand bail. I was left sitting there watching telly with the duty officer while Herdy went off to arrange bail. While he was away it all started to get a bit rowdy as the Friday night boozers were being brought in, each one apparently more inebriated than the last. You can imagine their reaction when they walked in to see Ian Botham being held on a charge.

Alan's first task was to find a local solicitor to help him with Australian law, while he also needed two citizens of the state to stump up the cash to get me out. On top of that he was not allowed to speak to me. Becoming pretty paranoid by this time, his condition was not helped by the fact that he had finished his last Hamlet cigar. The desk sergeant offered him a roll-up cigarette, but Herdy was in his own nightmare scenario and had visions of being locked up himself if he accepted it. 'You're trying to fit me up with a dodgy fag,' he said.

On returning to his hotel Herdy first of all tried to get in touch with Rodney Marsh before finally tracking down Dennis Lillee who enquired 'What's the old boy been up to now?' DK came down to the jail with his son and a six-pack and managed to get me out. The actual time spent in the 'lock-up' was not too disconcerting. The main problem was that, on the eve of the most important match in the Australian domestic season and possibly the most important match in the history of Queensland cricket, here I was in jail and about to hit the headlines again in a big way.

In the end we lost the game by five wickets, Graeme Wood's knock of 141 in the second innings proving decisive. The season had ended with the wheels really coming off the Queensland cart. We couldn't leave until after the case had been heard by the Perth Magistrates' Court. My main witnesses were Ritchie and AB. Here are their statements to the court:

Allan Border: 'I don't recall Ritchie returning to his seat but I recall a passenger in front of Ian asking for them to keep their voices down. At this stage Ian leant forward from his seat, placed his right hand on top of the passenger's head and I saw Ian turn the passenger's head, turned it around to the front, saying: "It's f--k all to do with you".

'Ian did not pull or lift the passenger from his seat. The passenger did not suffer any harm or discomfort. After Ian spoke to this person I did not pay any further attention to him. After landing I recall Ian apologising to the passenger in front of him. Apart from the brief argument Ian had with me and the incident with the person in front of him there was nothing disorderly about his conduct on the plane.

'I've known Ian Botham for ten years professionally and socially and our families are close. I know him to be a good fellow. I would describe him as a likeable rogue. I've noticed his character has changed in the past few years because "superstardom" has exposed him to a good deal of public attention and accordingly he has become somewhat reclusive. He is very highly regarded for his sportsmanship. I've known very few people in sport who play as hard or as well and with such honour. By reason of his personality he is not a person who enjoys a confrontation and I have never known him to manhandle anyone. I would describe the incident on the Ansett flight as very minor and I am utterly surprised it has led to criminal proceedings.'

Greg Ritchie: 'I got up to use the toilet and returned to see that Ian was very upset. I heard him use very strong language. The passenger sitting immediately in front of him turned round and over his shoulder used words to the effect: "Keep your language down".

'I saw Ian lean over and put his hands on the head of the passenger and turn him to the front and Ian said words to the effect "Turn round. It's got nothing to do with you".

'Ian did not lift this person out of his seat and the person suffered no apparent harm or discomfort. I then saw a passenger in the opposite window seat in our row lean forward and say "pipe down". Ian told him to shut up and mind his own business. Apart from that very small incident I saw nothing untoward in the behaviour of Ian or any other person on that flight that could be described as disorderly. Nor do I believe the words used to the passenger in the opposite window seat amounted to an assault.'

Nor did one of the other passengers, a 67-year-old grandmother named Myrtle Edwards, travelling to visit her grandchildren, who later wrote: 'I was absolutely amazed that these incidents alleged to have occurred led to criminal proceedings against Ian Botham'.

Ritchie had been charged initially himself and was ready to plead guilty. But I told him that, as he was in the toilet at the time the incident happened, there was no way he should accept the charges, let alone plead guilty, and eventually those charges were dropped. Because I had laid a hand on the man who complained, I was technically guilty of assault so I had no option but to plead accordingly and I was fined £400.

When Ansett Airlines then announced they would not fly me, or any of the Queensland party, anywhere, Ritchie told them 'In that case I'll walk back. We'll all walk back'. After much haggling, Ansett relented and as I was due to head off on the Hannibal Leukaemia Walk they gave me VIP treatment.

As far as I was concerned, a trifling little matter had grown out of all proportion. I knew that I had powerful enemies at Queensland but I left Australia safe in the knowledge that I had done enough to encourage people to believe we could win the Sheffield Shield the next time round.

Then, shortly after arriving in Perpignan for the start of the Hannibal Walk, I was informed that there wasn't going to be a next time. The Queensland Cricket Association had met and decided I was out.

The news, passed on to me by my bodyguard Andy Withers on the eve of the walk, came as a complete shock. My contract with Queensland had been for three years and I was being sponsored by the Carphone Group. The company had produced a letter of support for me when I faced the Perth magistrates saying how much I had done for them, but now, behind my back and not to my face, they announced they were withdrawing their sponsorship on the pretext that they had not been able to use me for promotional work in Australia in the way they had envisaged.

Queensland then followed this up by terminating my contract and my days in Australian state cricket were over.

It was a sad ending and, at first, I found it difficult to come to terms with. I had really enjoyed my cricket – it was just the bits and pieces around the game that went wrong.

The house that I was meant to live in was not available for me when the season began and, in fact, never actually became available at all. I bought all the furniture for the place but as I moved from hotel room to hotel room and then to rented accommodation, it remained in storage. As time went on I started to miss so much of what England had to offer that I was actually a bit homesick. In fact, in the circumstances I had considered calling it a day after one season anyway. It would have been nice to have been given the option.

Perhaps someone was trying to tell us that the whole thing had not been meant to work when I turned up the following winter on Worcestershire's pre-season tour and it came down in buckets for almost the entire trip!

I still find it hard to work out why Queensland were so keen to get rid of me because I did good business for them at the turnstiles; they had not attracted such large crowds in years. I also went out of my way to encourage the younger players and build up team spirit.

What Queensland appeared to forget was how close we had actually come to winning the precious Sheffield Shield. It's all very well believing that the law of averages, when there are only a handful of sides playing in the tournament, must turn in your favour at some point, but you have got to do something to make it happen. That is what I was there for and I feel that, on the field and off it, I succeeded. I gave them the belief and the buzz, and my figures for that season speak for themselves – I made 646 runs, including seven 50s, and took 29 wickets. On that score alone the club were more than satisfied with my all-round contribution.

What really bugs and hurts – and yes, I was hurt at being so easily dumped – was that I received double punishment for everything I did.

The court fine settled the plane trouble, the fine was paid for the damage in the Launceston dressing room and again I paid the money for swearing on the pitch. But then all these incidents were repackaged and used again as a justification for my sacking.

It was all so sad. However, one good thing did come out of it – the termination of my contract with the *Sun*. They had complained that they had been unable to get hold of me to do a piece on the comings and goings at the East Perth lock-up. As far as I was concerned that went way beyond our arrangement that I should give them my comments about cricket, and, in any case, at the time they were trying to reach me through Crash Lander, the matter was all sub judice. Alan Herd very quickly organized a deal for me with *Today* and later I joined forces with Lander again on the *Daily Mirror*.

I'll never fall out of love with Australians and the great outdoor lifestyle. Before I arrived in Queensland all those years ago it had honestly been my intention to explore the possibility of settling there for six months of each year – enjoying the English summer then spending the rest of the year down under. I know many people who have thrown themselves into that kind of lifestyle and my many Aussie friends assured me that there would be plenty of welcoming faces to help me, Kath and the kids feel at home.

I did have one last chance to put the Queensland nightmare behind me when I went out there to play my part in England's 1992 World Cup effort. That ended in disappointment on the field, but overall my memories of Australia remain good ones.

And I hope there will be plenty more to come.

15
THESE FEET WERE MADE FOR WALKING

The seeds for the Leukaemia Research walk had been sown in 1977 when I went to the Musgrove Park Hospital in Taunton for treatment to a broken foot which had been aggravated in the fourth Test against the Australians. What was meant to be a routine hospital trip in many ways changed my life and back then there was no way I could have guessed at how my involvement in the fight against the disease would mushroom over the years. It is something that is very important to me, and my efforts on behalf of the Leukaemia Research Fund will not stop until the disease is beaten. Although I have now hung up my walking boots for good, without question raising more than £4 million for the charity is the most satisfying and worthwhile thing I have ever done in my life.

When first I started pounding those roads there was roughly a 20 per cent chance of survival from the disease but now, in some cases, that has risen to 80 per cent. But there are still some very deadly strains and there is an awful lot more to do.

During 1977 when I first came to find out more about Leukaemia, it was just a case of me handing over £50 for a party for those children suffering from the disease whom I had encountered during my visit to the Musgrove Park Hospital. Then, as time progressed, I started to think about how I could exploit my position in the public eye to raise real money for the fight against the disease. Whenever possible I carried on making visits to various hospitals, but I felt there had to be more I could do. I wanted to come up with an idea that would help create large enough funds to attack the causes of leukaemia itself, not just to help a few sufferers cope with its effects.

One Easter in the Lake District, Kath and I were agonizing over the next move when it hit me: 'I know – a sponsored walk,' I said.

'Good idea,' she replied, probably envisaging a gentle 20-mile stroll.

'Yes, a sponsored walk from John O'Groats to Land's End,' I said.

Kath looked at me in disbelief. 'I thought you would come up with something sensible.'

The bit was between my teeth and whatever the difficulties involved I was going to do it. I only had to think of those children, who looked so well but were actually dying. If ever anyone needed a spur, that was it. And from the first step all those years ago, right up to the last in November 1999, whenever I was in need of an extra bit of motivation to help me get through the pain of the walks, all I had to do is conjure up an image of the smile on the face of one of those brave kids.

Bearing in mind the fact that each walk now takes from a year to eighteen months to organize (or should I say for Kath to organize), it is amazing to think that our first effort was more or less made up as we went along.

Looking back on it now the extent of our naivety was quite ridiculous. It really was like walking into the unknown. The first problem we had to confront was the cynicism of those who suggested that I had only come up with the idea in the first place as a way of getting back into people's good books after my conviction for possessing drugs at the start of the year. If that was all I wanted to do, I could have found plenty of other infinitely more comfortable ways of doing it. In any case, I felt no compulsion to put on the sack cloth and ashes. This idea was up and in progress well before the court case. Furthermore, Tim Hudson had made it quite clear to me that I would be hitting myself in the pocket by spending so much time committing myself to this rather than to chasing any of the rainbows he was busy painting in his own mind.

What was absolutely vital to the success of the first venture was publicity. In this respect, I was lucky that Chris Lander was one of the three other guys who walked every step of the way with me (the other two being John Border, the brother of Allan, and Phil Rance, a Manchester businessman whose father had died of leukaemia). Crash was working for the *Daily Mirror* and had done a piece with Jimmy Savile about the torture ahead, and had followed up the story by driving to John O'Groats for the first day. He had no intention of staying for the trip but Alisdair Ross, the *Sun* reporter, had a £1000 bet with me that he (Ross) would still be standing by the fourth day. Pitching the *Daily Mirror* against the *Sun* seemed to work a treat because now both papers were determined to outlast the other. Crash tried to get out of it a few times and early on he came to me, said he had his story, had walked further than he had ever done before in his life – which was something like eight miles – and could he go home now, please? I just told him that if Ross could do it, then so could he. When Ross finally bit the dust Crash tried once more to wriggle free, but I hooked him with the following challenge: 'You've got to stick with it. You're the only national newspaper man left on his feet'. Crash had originally left his car at John O'Groats for an overnight stay: it was 36 days before he returned to collect it!

I realized Crash was struggling and whinging during the early stages so when we hit the 100-mile barrier I left a bottle of scotch by the side of the road with a note. It read: 'Only 800 miles to go. Man or mouse?' That did the job: he never uttered another squeak.

Our other stroke of good fortune in terms of generating public awareness was the response of the BBC. Initially, they had planned to dip in and out of the walk with occasional broadcasts on their Breakfast Time programme introduced by Frank Bough and Selina Scott. But when they received so much positive feedback from the first of these transmissions, they decided to stick with the walk until the bitter end.

When I drove up to John O'Groats with Kath on Friday 25 October 1985 in preparation for starting the walk the following day, I really did not know what to expect, as I had no formal training in road walking. My attitude was simply: 'There's the road, walk on it until you get to the other end'. And I have to admit that those last few miles of the drive to the top of the British Isles were pretty sobering. It was then that it dawned on me as I sped along in the car that the next time I crossed these long, lonely roads, it would be on foot.

The other thing that struck me was how flat the area

around John O'Groats actually was. For someone like me who had never been to the place in my life before, the impression is that the north of Scotland is one big mountain range full of bagpipers and caber-tossers. It was a bit odd to see that there were no hills in sight.

The first thing I did on the opening day of the walk was to stroll down to the harbour and dip my toes into the water. It was the coldest thing I had ever experienced.

Before I set off, some of my England team-mates thought I was completely barking. I must admit that I was apprehensive at first. I had no idea about such technicalities as pacing myself, but I quickly learnt about running up hills and walking down them, sometimes backwards. It was crucial that once I had set my pace I did not stop, slow down or slacken off. You simply cannot change your stride pattern by dropping back to help someone else because you would both suffer. I had to drag my colleagues through it by any means, fair or foul, bullying and cajoling all the time. The hardest part is dealing with and going through the pain barrier. It took some time for me to realize that no matter how much pain I was suffering, somehow the body would always manage to look after itself and the pain would eventually subside. It was simply a matter of trial and error. I knew that there would be a bit of physical hardship but I never really understood what it would be like. After a while I had no say in the matter. Physically, mentally and emotionally, I and my colleagues became 'Prisoners of the Walk'.

The first day was a bit of a breeze. But on Day Two I nearly did myself so much damage that the walk might have finished there and then. Rather stupidly, I ran the 36-mile stage in bursts and by the end of the day I was in desperate agony with sore shins. The pain was almost unbearable, as if a dozen guys in hob-nail boots had been kicking my shins for a week. I learnt that this is a common complaint among serious walkers: the only remedies are massage and sleeping with your feet propped up on pillows, but in truth that particular pain never really leaves you, its just something you have to put up with. From then on I tried to make sure I stuck to an optimum walking pace.

Although the north of Scotland was bleak and the roads seemed to run for ever this was a crucial stage in the proceedings. The TV cameras and the press were there and we had to capitalize on their presence because at that time there was no telling how long they would stay with the story.

We had a tight schedule to follow so there was never a chance of reaching the end of one day and saying 'OK, let's soak our feet and take some time off'. It was a case of patching up the wounds and making sure the alarm clocks were set, then, at the crack of dawn, getting on the road again and putting up with the pain.

The first week in particular was extremely testing because travelling south on the A9, there was nothing at all bar miles and miles of lonely road. There could be 50 miles between towns at some stages and although the scenery was fantastic, the sense of isolation was sometimes difficult to cope with. What did help drive us on was the amazing public response.

The lorry drivers, for example, were the first who made us realize that the word was spreading. They would toot their horns as they passed us. For all knew that was the last we were going to see of them, then, a week later, as they completed their return journey, the same guys would stop and hand over bags stuffed full of the money they had collected from their depots. One guy gave us a bundle wrapped up in a plastic carrier bag and when we opened it and counted up, it came to £60 in change. That sort of gesture lifted us more than words could say, and I began to realize how we were capturing the public's imagination.

In the days ahead that support helped enormously, because as we neared the English border we walked into some really bad weather for the first time.

The Gretna leg was very tough, probably the worst of the lot. It was the longest section in terms of distance, over 38 miles, and it rained cats and dogs all day long.

Of all the days of all the walks, that is the one that still sticks out as the most wearing of the lot. We started at first light and by the time we had reached the end of the stage we had been on the road for thirteen hours. The weather had slowed the pace to around two and a half miles an hour. The last two hours were walked in darkness because by 4 p.m. the sun had set. We were hemmed in on the road with cars zooming past and heading straight into driving rain and hail, and even though the road twisted and turned all the time we always seemed to be walking straight into the face of the storm. We pulled our hats down over our faces for protection but at the end of it all, we looked as though someone had spent the day throwing wet sponges at us.

Brian Close walked that stage and arrived in totally the wrong shoes, but Closey being Closey, he would not be told, nor put off for that matter. As we walked along and came to the milestone indicating that Gretna was 12 miles away he would turn round and say 'I know this bit of road, it's nothing like that far'. But of course it was, and by the time we reached the end he was in agony – I don't think he walked properly for weeks after that. Shortening the distances in his mind was his way of keeping going.

Just how successful the venture had been thus far was demonstrated soon afterwards. The Leukaemia Research people thought if they made £100,000 from the whole walk they would be doing well, but the Scots proved their generosity beyond any doubt and by the time we had crossed the border there was already £100,000 in the bank and we were only a third of the way along. That shows how infectious interest in the walk had become, and it just spread and spread as we went on. I was amazed because the Scots are not exactly renowned for their love of cricket. Yet the cause touched them and they responded superbly. On one occasion, for instance, there we were, marching through the Highlands when two little old ladies came tottering down the path from their bungalow and handed over £40. It was like this all the way through

Becky was born on the first walk – we never did things by halves. Kath had wanted to join me and had been buzzing around the place setting things up before heading to the Doncaster Royal Infirmary to give birth. I could not break from the walk but I received constant updates on how things were going and we were just north of Manchester when news came that Becky's birth was imminent – two days early. A guy called Bob Whittaker, who was walking with us, arranged a vintage white Daimler on behalf of the BBC to whisk me up to Doncaster. It was a case of walking straight off the road into a bath, jumping out, throwing on some clothes and heading north to the hospital. I managed to have a couple of hours with Kath, and Becky, and Liam and Sarah were also at the hospital so there was something of a family reunion. Exhausted, I lay on the bed next to Kath, asked how she was and promptly fell asleep!

I returned to Manchester where Crash, the lads and I had a few drinks to celebrate. I think I must have overdone things because the next day I set off much too fast and really suffered for it. During the regular Breakfast Time television slot on the morning after Becky was born, Selina Scott was asking me about the new baby and whether we had a name for her yet. When I said 'no' and perhaps we should call her 'Selina', the amount of cash being pledged over the phone surged. Douglas Osborne, who went on to become the director of Leukaemia Research, said that they received so many calls that the telephone system at Great Ormond Street blew up. In the end they raised £250,000 in telephone credit-card pledges alone.

Kath was to spring another surprise on me later. She had been released from hospital the day after Becky's birth and went to stay with her sister, Lindsay and her husband Paul at their home near Ombersley, in Worcestershire. As we covered the stretch of walk from Kidderminster which took us through the village, Kath suddenly appeared from the crowd, new babe in arms, and joined me for a few yards. It caught everyone by surprise and one of the photographers on the walk who hadn't worked out the identity of this mystery woman was convinced he had got a real scoop.

Part of our success was that we went out of our way, getting the public on our side. We were going to the people, they did not have to come to us. We were literally walking past people's doorsteps. Manual labourers, like farmers, for instance, could not give up a day's work to

CONTROVERSY

FLASHPOINTS ... passing the time of day with that nice man Salim Yousuf (right) at Headingley in 1987; he claimed he had caught me after the ball clearly bounced. David Gower tries to restore calm (below) after I've had words with umpire Alan Whitehead against Australia in 1985. Greg Ritchie looks on.

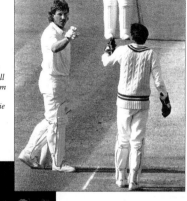

RAMBOTHAM ... and you thought Michael Holding was lethal!

I STILL LIKE THE CLOTHES ... but not the man. With my one-time agent Tim Hudson.

ON THE STREETS ... for
*Leukaemia Research. The
family (right) join me during
the 1987 walk through
Belfast. Liam leads, while
Kathy has her arm around
Sarah. At least this lot (below)
don't answer back. Me with
two of the elephants used on
the 1988 Hannibal Walk over
the Alps.*

THE LONGEST PUB
CRAWL IN HISTORY ... at
*least that's how Jimmy
Greaves described our march
from John O'Groats to Land's
End on the first Leukaemia
Research Fund charity walk in
November 1985.*

CHARITY WALKS

BRAZIL 3783
FALKLAND IS. 6658

VANCOUVER 4027
HAWAII 6268

ISLES OF SCILLY 28
NEW YORK 2827
LONGSHIPS LIGHTHOUSE 1½
TRINIDAD 3607 PANAMA 4360

CAIRO 2475
PEKING 5601

JOHN O'GROATS 874
BERLIN 730 MOSCOW 1586

WELL DONE IAN BOTHAM
29 NOVEMBER 1985

END OF THE ROAD ... a handshake from fellow walker John Border (Allan's brother) signals the end of the first Leukaemia Walk at Land's End. If I could have walked on water I might have kept on straight ahead.

WHAT IT'S ALL ABOUT ... two very good reasons for continuing with the Leukaemia Research walks.

NOT JUST A CRICKETER

IF I HADN'T BEEN A CRICKETER
… playing baseball at The Oval
(above left) and golf with Nigel
Mansell ('his driving is all right but
I'm not so sure about the putting') in a
Nick Faldo challenge match.

NOT ME, REF … discussing the
state of the nation with a referee
while playing football for
Scunthorpe United.

come and find us, so we went out to them. I always remember one incident on the A9 where we walked past farm after farm and came to a group of farmers who had gathered on their tractors to watch us go by. There were four of them and they had collected money from all around the district. On seeing us approaching they hopped over the fence to give us the donation before returning to the fields to cheer us on.

That sort of experience picked us up when we hurt the most. There's nothing better than the sight and sound of a few thousand people jumping up and down wishing you well to get you going again.

What some people do for you is enough to bring tears to your eyes. At one point we were walking along a dual carriageway when on the opposite side of the road, a car suddenly screamed to a halt. A very elegant middle-aged woman leapt out and ran back down the road after us, climbing over the barrier. She said she had been phoning the police all morning to find out where we were and started saying what a great effort she thought we were putting in. I thanked her and asked what her why she was so interested in Leukaemia Research and she said that her husband had died of the disease only six weeks ago. I went to put my arms round her and she said 'No, I had 25 years of wonderful marriage and I want to give you something – my car's up there, so take this'. She pulled off her wedding ring, pressed it into my hand and despite my protests that we couldn't take it, insisted. She then ran up the road back to her car and was gone. The ring was auctioned and raised more than £1000.

If we thought the media interest was going to flag by the time we reached Somerset, we could not have been more wrong. Walking into Taunton was unbelievable. All my old mates were there stopping the traffic on the A38 and charging drivers a Leukaemia toll, while there were dozens of jugs of cider and a banner reading 'You're home Beefy, welcome back.' It was market day in Taunton and the place was chaos; the police lost control of the situation but it hardly mattered because the street collection raised an incredible £26,000. From there it was on to Bristol with David Graveney, himself a former Gloucestershire, Somerset and Durham player, who was slightly worried about the response we would get. 'The people of Bristol are so fickle and they hate Somerset cricketers,' he warned. We needn't have worried as we walked into this huge ticker-tape welcome with jazz bands playing and thousands of people lining the streets. It took my breath away and I'll never forget the scene. In the buckets that day we collected over £40,000.

On heading west towards Devon, there was a surprise awaiting me in Okehampton, the small market town almost on the Devon/Cornwall border. Trudging through the town early in the morning, I was flagged down by a chap who had I seen jump out of a Rolls-Royce in a side street, and on catching up with me he thrust a huge cheque in my hand before disappearing as swiftly as he had appeared. It turned out to be Elton John. Another guy to pop up on a street corner was former England wicket-keeper Bob Taylor, who was waiting in his tracksuit as we went through Stone, in Derbyshire and promptly joined in the march.

Of course there were still people trying to snipe at me and it was horrifying how low some people could stoop. There was an especially hideous character called Simon

Worthington, a shortish, fresh-faced freelance reporter in his mid-twenties, who turned up and told us he was doing a piece for a fitness magazine. I had my doubts about him from the start, but he stuck with us for two or three days through the West Country and turned up at the various functions along the route. When we reached Cornwall, Worthington mysteriously disappeared. Later we learnt why. He had gone to the police claiming we were smoking dope during the walk. Of course, the tabloids were quick to spot an opportunity.

CHARITY WALK SHOCK: DRUGS INQUIRY BY POLICE INTO IAN'S MARATHON

The Devon and Cornwall police were compelled to investigate his allegation and interviewed all the principal walkers. Of course, they found not one ounce of truth in the accusations. We had a police motorbike escort with us all the way and were walking past thousands of people; how could we have been smoking joints so publicly?

In fact, what we had used to keep us going was a drink we invented during the walk and which became known as 'Rocket Fuel'. We had tried lots of experimenting with various drinks, as you can imagine. A pint of beer was never any good because you are always having to dash off into the bushes; rum would have been all right except that one day Crash, who had offered to act as guinea pig, over-imbibed and subsequently found his navigational skills had deserted him; scotch and water was pretty effective but eventually we ran out of supplies. I hit upon the perfect mixture – tequila and orange fanta, a concoction I remembered for the New Zealand tour of 1983/84. It is absolute dynamite and the great thing is that no one need know you are actually drinking booze to keep you going. Many is the time I've walked along swigging from the fanta bottle and heard kids in the crowd shout 'Hey mum, can I have some of that! It's good for you, full of vitamin C!' If only they knew. Sometimes, however, it was the only thing that worked to combat the pain.

After the Worthington incident came another spot of bother, namely a fracas with a policeman on Bodmin Moor. Phil Rance was hurting and having a very bad day. He had broken the back of the walk but was now in so much trouble that it was taking every ounce of his energy to pull through. Our march across the moors attracted the attention of a quite high-ranking police officer. We thought he had come to say 'well done, lads' but what he actually said was that if Phil, who was about a mile and a half behind at this stage, didn't catch up he would have him off the walk. I said to the escort riders that this was unfair – and these guys had been great to us all along – but one of them, whether pressurised by the appearance of a senior officer or for some other reason, came over and started giving me a real lecture. In my anger, I turned to face him and took a swing. I was at breaking point. Phil was struggling and I was in a lot of pain because of my back trouble; in fact the discomfort was so intense that I was on painkillers. I just didn't need this aggro on top of all that. Phil was going through bloody murder down there, he had completed 750 miles and had less than 100 or so to go, and this police officer was saying because he was a mile back down the road he was about to be thrown off the walk.

My wild punch caught the officer on the side of his crash helmet (I actually broke a bone in my knuckle without doing him any harm). It was one of those things I regretted the second it happened. Then, later that evening when we were in Redruth, the story broke on the local radio station. Just 24 hours before the end of the walk the last thing we needed was more bad publicity. In the end, even the officer I hit realized it had all been a storm in a tea cup and he came up to me the next day to apologize for being so officious. I told him I was very sorry for what had happened and admitted I shouldn't have snapped. We laughed about it and had a drink afterwards, and later he even gave up three days of leave to help us out. That was a magnificent gesture on his part.

I wanted to end that memorable first walk with a flourish. I had dipped my big toe in the sea at John O'Groats; at Land's End I wanted to dive in. Unfortunately, a steep cliff makes that pretty well impossible, so instead, when we got to within a mile of the end, we popped into a pub, changed into top hats and tails, then completed the last mile before going down to the sea – and hurling Crash through the breakers! It was a freezing cold December day, but by that time he didn't care.

We had done what we set out to do and raised over £1 million in the process. The Leukaemia Research fund had committed themselves to some big research projects, so the timing of the walk could not have been better. They also gained from the raising of the profile of the charity for now, through our efforts, people all over the country who previously hadn't had a clue about leukaemia now knew more about the disease.

The walk had been a fantastic experience. It had created

new friendships and bonded existing ones. What's more, we had had a lot of fun. Early on we had set up a kangaroo court in order to try regular walkers on trumped-up charges. Once I was done for singing, but got off on a technicality – I can't sing. Graham Morris, the sports photographer, almost felt the full force of the law for losing the top of a mobile home which he had attempted to drive under a low bridge in Aviemore. His plea in mitigation, which was somehow accepted by the jury, was that he had come from a 'broken' mobile home.

There was a strange void when the walk came to an end. We had all been through a lot together – the pain and the hardship, the deflation and the elation – and suddenly the party was over. As with all future walks, euphoria quickly gave way to emptiness.

Kath, in particular, suffered initially from my post-walk blues. I found it very difficult to return to normality after such an extraordinary experience and this created a problems of communication between us.

Over the years she has learnt to cope better for the simple reason that she is now as much a part of the walks as I am. She throws herself into the organizing and even into the walking, so we have been able to share the highs and lows together.

Kath has been totally behind me and her involvement since the beginning has grown enormously to the point where she understands that empty feeling when it is all over. She is so involved in the projects now that, in the weeks leading up to the next walk, nothing else is talked about in our house.

We capped the first walk with a march round London which added another £30,000 from a street collection and that was the icing on the cake. I would never have imagined the response we received in my wildest dreams. When, on that lap of honour, we arrived at Great Ormond Street Hospital we walked into complete chaos. The Leukaemia Research Fund operate from a small office and there were people hanging from the every window, not to mention so many press and television people that you could hardly breathe. But more important than this, it was the children that mattered and the moment I remember most vividly was a young girl in a car outside the building. She was paralysed by the disease and could not get out of the vehicle to present me with a cheque, so I wormed my way through the cameras, microphones and flashlights to spend a few moments with her. Accepting that donation meant more than all the razzmatazz going on around me. This young girl represented one of the reasons why we had done the walk.

Over the years we have raised more and more money for the Leukaemia Research fund, a fact which was acknowledged when they honoured me by naming the Leukaemia Research laboratories in Glasgow after me. That was a very touching gesture. One thing is for sure, the work will go on until the disease is beaten.

After that triumphant first walk the question was – what do we do now? There have been walks around the Channel Islands, Belfast and the East Coast and more are planned. But I had to do something to keep the message high-profile. I had played with the idea of following Napoleon's retreat from Moscow but instead came up with the Hannibal Alps Walk, complete with elephants, which took place in 1988.

It was a good idea that didn't quite come up to

expectations. Perhaps it was a bad omen to fly into Perpignan only to find that Queensland had sacked me. The media circus was running riot with the news and I was blissfully unaware of what was going on until I returned to my hotel later that night having been out for a family meal. How ironic that my Australian team should sack me for 'boorish behaviour' when there, pinned to the notice board of the Novotel Perpignan, was a letter from the Duke of Kent thanking me for my efforts for Leukaemia Research and wishing me the best on this latest adventure!

They say never work with animals and children and certainly there were dangers taking on the elephants even if their part was purely cosmetic. At this time my critics were lining up to have a pot at me again and even the precaution of having with us David Taylor, probably the best veterinary surgeon in the country, could not stop some people having a go. The animals had come from a circus and we wanted them for the publicity. They needed to be in tip-top condition at the start and end of each day of the walk and David was there to keep an eye on them. To expect them to follow us was asking too much. Each morning we would come to the start, the elephants would walk the mile and a half out of town and then be loaded into huge transporters and driven to the day's destination for a roll around in a field and some food. Most of the French were delighted by them and were pampering them until it was time for the elephants to meet us and walk over the finishing line. Those elephants probably had the best time of their lives.

Then another paper roped in that queen of French animal rights, Brigitte Bardot. She made some comments based on hearsay and I challenged her to come and look at the elephants for herself if she really was that interested. That wasn't the end of it either. Another paper flew out Bill Travers, the actor who played George Adamson in the film *Born Free* and who now represented Zoo Check, an organization that champions the rights of wild animals kept in captivity, in the hope that he would claim the animals were being maltreated.

That particular situation fizzled out, while a visit from the French Animal Liberation Front ended with them being so impressed that they gave us a sizeable donation!

Even so, I think these stories affected the success of the walk, especially the donations in England. We only made £300,000, which, considering the work and effort that went into it, was a ridiculously small amount. For instance, Alan Dyer, my pilot friend, had to go through hell to make the walk in the first place. Having suffered a horrific car accident on the Boxing Day which left him with five broken ribs, collapsed lung, broken pelvis and pneumonia, he was desperate to make the walk. Very few of us gave him much chance but in the days building up to it he forced himself back to fitness by walking around his home with the aid of a walking stick. First a hundred yards, then a bit more and so on. He flew out with the target of doing one day, and ended up doing the whole trip. It was a great performance and he was quickly back in to the spirit of things – the swine even poured a jug of water over me in a restaurant. Yet that kind of effort was undermined by the media snipers.

We had the same kind of problem when, during the two months ban after the *Mail on Sunday* drugs case, Benson and Hedges did a Hamlet cigar advert using my picture and donated the fee to Leukaemia Research. That particular gesture raised a storm along the lines of what was a cancer charity doing taking the money from the tobacco industry? Of course, if the money had gone in my back pocket nobody would have said a word. As it is, thousands of people who have handed cash over to the charity must be smokers and nobody expected me to say I couldn't take their money because of their habits.

If the elephants were having a good time in the Alps, some of the walkers were not. My Queensland team-mate Greg Ritchie joined this trek and it came as a bit of a shock to him. During the three-week walk he lost a stone and a half; he was in a pretty bad way for the first week, retiring to bed the minute we reached each base camp and staying there until the next morning, feet propped up in the air. He suffered so badly that he couldn't get out of bed to use the toilet and had to resort to a bed pan and bottle!

Apart from the negative reaction back home, the main problems on the Hannibal trip stemmed from the fact that, apart from the elephant lovers, the French public were also strangely apathetic to it all. They thought we were crazy and didn't really comprehend the purpose or cause. A further complication were the laws in France which forbid street collections, and despite having printed up some leaflets – in French – explaining what we were doing, it all seemed to fall on deaf ears. There were loads of blank faces as we plodded on and that only changed when we crossed the Alps and reached Italy, where in fact most of the money was collected. The Italians were magnificent: they like their cricket over there and the Italian Cricket Association threw themselves behind us. The Mayor of Turin even held a reception in our honour.

If the Hannibal walk was financially the least rewarding

walk, the East Coast walk was the most painful of the lot. I remember we were nearing Ipswich when we encountered a group of children riding around on mountain bikes. One of them ran over my blistered heel on his bike, and the thick hard-tread tyre caught me in just the wrong place, ripping the skin from my heel. The pain was excruciating and the wound became infected. Luckily it was raining so I pulled down my hood, gritted my teeth and marched on. It was four hours of searing agony.

That was the time I was most grateful for the efforts of Dave 'Rooster' Roberts, the England physio who I first met when he was doing the job at Worcestershire shortly after I moved there from Somerset and whose help I enlisted on every walk after that. Rooster is a great bloke, not only is he good at his job but he shares my sense of humour, and the most important aspect of his contribution was the fact that he, like me, will never admit to being beaten. The wound, in this case, was so badly infected that Rooster had no alternative but to cut out chunks of the flesh around the heel. For weeks afterwards it was bloody sore, but Rooster and I both knew that nothing short of a broken leg was going to stop me. It is possible other medical men might have urged me, or even tried to force me to quit there and then, but Rooster and I were on the same wavelength. It was a case of get there or die trying.

The funniest moment? Jimmy Greaves' line when he came to do a piece for Central TV on the first walk: 'Christ, Beef. This is going to be the longest pub crawl of all time'. And the most irritating? It had to be on the South Coast walk in September 1992, when a guy seriously threatened to run us down because he objected to being held up.

Inevitably the walks have led to spin-off fund raising events. I try to make myself available whenever possible for Leukaemia Research but there was one moment when I wish I hadn't, following a Christmas Carol service at the Albert Hall in 1988. I was the guest of honour and the whole thing went really well. Afterwards, we sauntered off to party at the Sheraton Towers Hotel being hosted by the *TV Times* and when that was over we headed for the hotel forecourt to wait for a taxi. We had hung about for twenty minutes and twice I asked the porter if he could get a cab. By this time there was quite a queue of people waiting.

Eventually someone else in our party went round the corner and successfully flagged down a taxi, so we piled in for the short journey back to the Tara Hotel where we were staying. As we were going along I was aware of a police car, with lights flashing, following us, and as we turned into the hotel forecourt a dozen or so police officers leapt out of several vehicles and stormed our taxi.

It was unreal, almost like a scene from *The Sweeney*. You would have thought by their reaction that I was the world's most wanted man. I was dragged out of the cab and hurled in the back of a police car, arms pinned behind my back. Despite having had a back operation six months earlier, and despite me pointing this out, I was given some pretty rough treatment with one constable in particular, who delighted in baiting me and roughing me up with a couple of rib-ticklers.

At this stage I had no idea what was going on and I really wanted to get at this big brave officer who was giving me hell, safe in the knowledge that he had his mates with him to provide back-up. Eventually I was taken into a room at the back of Chelsea police station and was told the police doctor was seeing the other man. I asked them: 'What other man?'

Then the story came out. The hotel porter at the Sheraton, Kevin Batten, had accused me of head-butting him. However, when the doctor examined Batten he could not find a mark on him, and then the mood began to change. All of a sudden the attitude of the police became all sweetness and light. Nothing was too much trouble for them. Could they run me back to my hotel? Could they do this, and that? In fact when they realized from the doctor that there was no evidence that anyone had laid a finger on Batten, a senior officer appeared from nowhere and started to apologize profusely for the inconvenience. And when I told him what had happened in the police car and that I was far from happy he drove me back to the hotel. I was livid at my disgraceful treatment at the hands of the police. A hardened criminal didn't deserve to go through what I had just suffered. What's more, the incident outside the Sheraton had taken place in front of my family, including my nine-year-old daughter Sarah, who was beside herself. By the time I got back to the hotel at around 2 a.m. they were all wondering what the hell was going on.

The *Sun* splashed Batten's allegations on their front page the following morning.

BOOZED BOTHAM NUTTED HOTEL'S GUARD

However, when the police refused to press charges, the press started to look as if they were on dodgy ground. Then, Batten started a private prosecution which he

Summons (M.C. Act 1952, S.1: M.C. Rules 1968, r.81)

......Horseferry Road.................. Magistrates' Court (Code 2660)

Mr Ian Botham
Park House
Ravensworth
Near Richmond
North Yorkshire

You are hereby summoned to appear on 20.3.89 at 10 am. before the

Magistrates' Court at 70, Horseferry Road, London, SW1P 2AX in Court No.1
to answer to the following information laid to-day 7.2.89 that you on

14th December 1988 at the Sheraton Park Tower Hotel, 101
Alleged Knightsbridge, London, SW1.
offence did unlawfully assault and beat Kevin James BATTEN.

...... etc.

Contrary to Common Law and triable pursuant to Section 39 of the Criminal Justice Act, 1988.
Informant Kevin BATTEN

Address 6 Betjeman Walk, Yateley, Near Camberley, Surrey.

Date 7 February 1989

M.C.A.2—
B.27
—
SUMMONS
Common
Assault

Metropolitan Stipendiary Magistrate.

The receipt of this summons should be acknowledged to the Clerk of the Court forthwith on the tear-off slip below. Please sign and return this slip. The correct postage must be paid.

ACKNOWLEDGEMENT OF SUMMONS

M.C.A.2—
B.27
—
SUMMONS
Common
Assault

Name of Defendant... Ian Botham......

Date of hearing......20.3.89.............19.... (time)...10am.....

Court ......1. Horseferry Road.............Magistrates' Court.

I hereby acknowledge the receipt of a summons to appear at the time and place shown above.

(The Defendant should sign

and date this form here)...... 13ᵗʰ Feb 1989.

subsequently dropped by applying to the magistrate to withdraw, having offered the court no evidence. (His solic-itor told the court that Batten was 'under considerable pressure in his private life'.) In the end there was an out-of-court settlement from the *Sun*, but it had been an horrific experience.

Once again the headlines had been hijacked by that small minority of bad out there on the streets. It had been a lovely evening ruined by a ridiculous allegation. I was angry, and more so because so much good that has come out of the Leukaemia Research efforts has, from time to time, been overshadowed by this kind of incident. It only takes one mad man, or the kind of crazy allegations like those about drugs that Simon Worthington came up with on the first Leukaemia Walk, to make people think twice before making a donation.

That doesn't hurt me, it hurts the kids we are trying to help.

Of course, apart from the research fund and the kids, the main beneficiary of the walk has been myself. When I started it all off all those years ago, raising money in this way was something I wanted to do for its own sake, but you can't put a value on the experiences I have had since then.

There are times when you feel you simply can't go on. The last five miles of every stage are awful. Terrible. That is the point where you are like a human cabbage: you can see the destination but it just won't come any closer. It is then that I pinch myself and remind myself just what I am doing, why I am on this road. I think of the children I saw in the Leukaemia Research unit – I especially remember those boys sitting around a table playing Monopoly and thinking to myself how normal they looked, perfect kids. Then the shattering experience of being told that none of them were going to be around for much longer.

In the autumn of 1999 I set off on what was positively, absolutely and definitely the last of my charity walks in aid of Leukaemia Research. I intend to continue doing what I can to further the cause, but, as I found between 10 a.m. on Monday 11th October and approximately 3.30p.m. on Saturday 13th November, 34 days later, the body is the sole judge of these matters. And, at the age of 45, fourteen years after it walked the 886 miles from John O'Groats to Lands End the first time, the body said twice is enough in any lifetime.

I could not think of a better way of signing off from my charity walking than by repeating the first of all the walks and certainly the toughest one last time. And the response from the public was, as always magnificent.

I must admit my final preparation was not exactly by the book as, on the eve of the first leg from John O'Groats to Occumster, I did the professional thing and got completely banjaxed with a few of the usual suspects. Mark McNulty and Nick Price decided I would need some last-minute motivation and, on their way to the Dunhill Masters, they popped in at our base camp at the Ackergill Tower Castle for an impromptu Burns Night.

I cannot recall too much of the specifics of what went on that night, but as I drove myself cartoon-style into gale-force winds the next day, flashes of it came gruesomely back into focus.

The weather on that first day was shocking, perhaps the worst I can recall from any of the walks. And I certainly appreciated the cheery waves of Price and McNulty as they sped southwards in their warm limousines. By the time day one was over I was in bits, seriously questioning whether there would actually be a day two.

There was, of course and thanks to the normal supplies of Rocket Fuel, the care and attention of Dave Roberts, the teamwork and cameraderie provided by my fellow every-step sufferers, Dave 'the bet' Chisnell, David Parker from the British Diabetic Association and Stuart Watson, the back-up and support from the unsteady crew including Duncan March a former Royal Marine who operated under the ludicrously overblown title of 'walk organizer' and the wonderful inspirational generosity of the public, there was a day 34 as well.

Perhaps the most gratifying milestones of this particular jaunt were reached when we entered the Midlands town of Bridgnorth. As we breasted the invisible tape there, the clock ticked around to 4,000 miles walked for Leukaemia Research and simultaneously the cash register hit the figure of £4m. There were big crowds at Worcester and in Penzance around 4,000 people turned out. And then came the euphoria of reaching the target once again . . . and of knowing that these battered old plates would never have to tramp the long road again! There might be easier ways of dropping a couple of stones, but certainly none as satisfying.

When I look back now at everything we have achieved it fills me with tremendous pride, but from a personal point of view as well I have the satisfaction of knowing that if I can get through one of these walks, and get through the pain, I can get through anything.

16
THE LAST DANCE

Ever since that cold day in April 1980 when I first felt a twinge in my back, I knew my career was one bad injury away from crisis.

I played on throughout the decade in varying degrees of discomfort, but the critical point arrived just after the start of the 1988 season during a three-day match against, of all teams, Somerset. On the second day, I had just taken my first championship wicket of the summer, when I dived to try and stop a ball in the slips and fell awkwardly. Soon afterwards we left the field because of rain, and as we hung about in the dressing room I realized that this was more than just the normal early season stiffness. When the umpires told us it was time to get back on the pitch, I tried to stand up but I simply couldn't move. I was virtually paralysed and had to be helped to my feet.

Almost immediately it was decided that the operation I had put off for so long was no longer an option. It had become a necessity.

The surgeon, John Davies, gave me an 80 per cent chance of making a full recovery but only a 50 per cent chance of playing top-class cricket again. After the X-ray he put me in plaster from neck to waist to minimize movement of the spine and five days later I was in the operating theatre.

One further complication for John and his brilliant team was that the Leukaemia walks had strengthened the muscles in my back and stomach to such an extent that by the time they had cut through them to get at my spine, the operation had taken two hours longer than expected.

The recovery period was a time for reflection and decision. Initially, there was little I could do but lie there and wait. I spent two weeks being turned like a chicken on a spit. After that I was allowed to make a few tentative steps around the grounds of the hospital, which were like wading through treacle, then, three-and-a-half weeks later I was finally allowed home.

For the next six months I could still hardly move and consequently my weight ballooned. It was a pretty depressing time, particularly for someone like me who had been so active throughout my life. Realistically, I thought I had a 50–50 chance of playing cricket again, but I didn't want people worrying and fretting so I told everyone that it was simply a matter of time. Quite frankly, the prospect of being on the scrapheap at the age of thirty-two scared me to death. I always felt that there were other things in life I could have done, but there was nothing I wanted to do more than play cricket. I still had an awful lot to prove to myself and to everyone else; but I had to confront the fact that this could have been the end and I took myself off to the moors near our home in north Yorkshire to consider the possibility. I would get up first thing in the morning, bundle our boxer dog Tigger into the car, drive up to the nearby army range and wander alone with my thoughts.

At first I could only walk 50 yards at a time. Gradually that became 100 yards, then 500, then a mile and then, eventually, as far as I wanted. I would get so wrapped up by what the future might hold that on occasions I was totally unaware of anything else. Once, while I was in this mental cocoon, I even wandered directly into the path of a Chieftan tank that had just emerged from over the brow of a hill. It was very nearly on top of me before I noticed its presence and I just managed to scramble out of the way in time. I've heard of some funny ways to go but that would have really been something special. You could imagine the headlines – 'Beefy – tanks for the memories'.

When finally I was fit enough to start very light training I found a fantastic ally in Dave Roberts, the Worcestershire physio. Over the months that followed he encouraged me, cajoled me, and bullied me, and took a lot of flak in the process. The most important thing he did was persuade me to think positively, and I owe him a lot for that.

Even so, I discovered during countless games of racquetball with my team-mate Gordon Lord that although I would be able to play again, I would never regain the flexibility I once had.

Kath was brilliant during this difficult period. She never put any pressure on me but said simply, 'You know what's best for you. Whatever you decide I will do all I can to help'.

But what had sustained me more than anything else during my rehabilitation was ambition, pure and simple. During that period, I took a long look at myself and my career, and came to an important decision. There was no point in going through all this simply to make up the numbers: if I was going to get back into cricket it had to be at the top. I knew I wasn't going to be able to bowl fast ever again, but I was determined not simply to fade away.

So when the 1989 season started I was determined to show that no matter what had happened I was still worth a place in the England side to play against the auld enemy, Allan Border's Australians. I was helped, of course, by the fact that under Ted Dexter, the new chairman of selectors, and David Gower, the new captain appointed following the shambles against the West Indies the previous summer, the regime was apparently ready to make changes.

Although Geoff Boycott had more or less written me off in a particularly nasty newspaper article in which he wrote that I was finished as a Test bowler, by the time the selectors had met to decide the side for the third Test at Edgbaston, the all-rounder spot was still vacant and I was more than ready to give it a go.

David had intended that I should be brought back at the start of the summer. Unfortunately, as a result of suffering a fractured cheekbone when mis-hooking Glamorgan's Steve Barwick during a county match, that plan had been put on hold. Finally, prior to the Edgbaston Test, David asked me if I felt I was ready and if I felt I could do the job. Needless to say, I had no hesitation in saying 'yes' to both questions.

I had to wait slightly longer than usual to make my mark but finally, after 23 months' absence, I trapped opener Geoff Marsh lbw in my thirteenth over. When I walked out to the crease to bat for the first time, I was faced with an uncomfortably familiar situation. In reply to Australia's 422, we were 75 for four, then 75 for five when Kim Barnett was dismissed almost immediately. The situation called for another Beefy rescue act, and I had batted for two-and-a-half hours for 46 before my patience finally snapped. Nevertheless, with help from the weather, the partnership I put on with Jack Russell of nearly a hundred was enough to make the game safe and to encourage Micky Stewart on behalf of the England management to try and persuade me to turn my back on the offer to join the South African rebels and make myself available for the winter trip to the West Indies.

In many ways the disappointment of being subsequently left out of the squad was all the more intense because of what I had to go through to get back in the first place. And the realization that unless the situation altered dramatically the likelihood was that I would never be selected for England again, meant that it had all been more or less for nought.

So, by the time I actually did return two years later for the final Test against the West Indies in 1991, all candidates for my all-rounder spot having tried and failed to fill my place, I was doubly determined to show the selectors what they had been missing.

Of course, in my absence I had heard all the stories about how the new regime of Graham Gooch and Micky Stewart had been working. I knew about Ted's eccentricities from first-hand experience, and I will never forget the song-sheet episode that had greeted me on my comeback in 1989.

All the other tales concerning the new work ethic that was the order of the day in the England camp had made my hair stand on end. Furthermore, I was as incensed as everyone else had been about the treatment of David Gower, whose reluctance to go against his own nature and toe the line probably cost him two years' worth of international cricket.

But it was only after I had been selected for the trip to New Zealand at the end of 1991, followed by the World Cup in Australia and New Zealand, that I came face to face with the realities of what the players had been forced to put up with.

I should have guessed that there were going to be problems following an incident prior to my late departure for the trip. At the end of the series against the West Indies, Graham Gooch was one of the guests on Question of Sport. Before the programme was filmed we were enjoying the usual hospitality when Goochie called me to one side and asked me what I was doing about my training. There is a time and a place for these things and I regarded it as rather an impertinent question anyway. I told him I was a professional; I had been playing as long, in fact longer, than he had at international level and I wasn't going to let him, England or myself down. This little conversation annoyed me intensely. By way of a joke I also said something to the effect 'It's too late to worry about that now, Goochie. I'm on the plane, mate'.

I was staggered by his reply. 'We can soon see about that,' he said.

Goochie's addiction to physical fitness stemmed from the time that he himself realized he would struggle to get anywhere in the game until he lost the extra weight he was carrying with him during the early part of his career. If you look at film of his Test debut, when he got a pair against Australia at Edgbaston in 1975, you'll see what I mean: he was positively portly. Clearly his devotion to training enabled him to make the most of his talents and he was still going strong as a Test player beyond the age when most people have given the game away. He actually got better as a batsman as time wore on. There's no doubt that the physical preparation of the players on his first tour to the West Indies in 1989/90 had a positive bearing on their performance. As far as I'm concerned, the problems arose when his team started to do badly, particularly on the following winter's tour to Australia when the only response to players struggling for form was to increase the physical work load.

I have tremendous admiration for Goochie's determination and single-mindedness, but what he could never come to terms with was the fact that what worked for him was not necessarily the answer for everyone else. It's all very well for Goochie to punish himself by spending hours bending, stretching, pumping weights and running around the outfield, but there is absolutely no point whatsoever in asking David Gower or myself to do exactly the same. With Micky Stewart as his workaholic ally, Gooch instilled the principle that if he was going to do these things everyone had to do them. In his eyes he might have been applying a principle of all for one and one for all designed to bring the players closer together. But the policy meant that there was no room for flexibility. Micky, instead of concentrating on helping players deal with specific technical flaws, wrapped himself up in a sergeant major's role, barking out orders as though he was on the parade ground rather than the cricket ground.

The whole thing was utterly ridiculous, and there were other signs that this generation of a sense of collective purpose through hardship and adversity, a sort of masochistic ritualization of the things that make up team spirit, was beginning to go way over the top. For a period of time, some really weird things started to creep in on and off the field which bordered on Freemasonry for Beginners. For instance, Goochie brought in some exercises in bonding which would have given Sigmund Freud enough material for a book or two.

The first one was known as the thumb press. Whenever a bowler took a wicket or a fielder took a catch, his team-mates would run up to him brandishing the thumb of their right hand, at which point the guy in question would flour-ish his own thumb and they would all come together in a thumb-to-thumb orgy. I found it quite bizarre – but not as peculiar as one of the other things they did. This was called 'chest bumping' and it went like this: bowler takes wicket, fielder rushes up and the two of them leap into the air thrusting their chests at each other. If they had carried on like this it wouldn't have been long before Goochie would have insisted on all-in snogging on the pitch! To me, they all looked like a bunch of prancing poofters. If anyone had run up to me brandishing his thumb, chest or any other part of his anatomy, I would have punched his lights out. Whatever happened to the handshake or the pat on the back?

It was about this time that another strange character emerged. His name was Colin Tomlin, a fitness expert who had devised some punishing physical work load for Kent which, apparently, was supposed to make them battle-hardened. He would take the players out for long runs and push them to the point of being physically sick to make 'men' out of them. Some of the stories I heard from the players were quite alarming; needless to say, Tomlin was not on the top of David Gower's Christmas-card list. The autumn before I joined up with the England team in New Zealand I got a phone call from Tomlin during which he informed me that he was coming to see me to assess my fitness. I was a little bit puzzled because not only had I been cleared by John Brewer, the head of the Football Association's human performance unit at Lilleshall, but as far as I was concerned Tomlin had no official standing within the set-up. I also received a fax from him on headed notepaper which read something like 'Colin Tomlin – interior designer'. I thought to myself, 'Hang on a minute. I'm off to take part in the World Cup, not an international wall-papering contest'.

I was training with Bournemouth Football Club at the time as I was in panto nearby, and I said to Tomlin that I didn't want him to make a wasted journey. I asked him for his medical qualifications and warned him that as I had had major surgery on my back and on my knees I was not prepared to be looked at by anyone other than a specialist. After putting the phone down, I made some other calls to find out exactly who he was. I rang Medha Laud, Micky Stewart's secretary, and found out that he was a mate of Micky and Goochie's. I then told Micky I was not letting the man near me. But this maniac was not out of my life yet: one day after training with Bournemouth, their manager Harry Redknapp called me across and asked me if the name Colin Tomlin meant anything to me. I said yes, told him everything and he laughed. He then explained that Tomlin had called him and insisted that Harry should supervise me in the gym on a special training exercise. He told Harry he wanted me to run around in circles, fully padded up, holding a bat above my head. I nearly wet myself. Fortunately Harry had given him short shrift, told him he had better things to do than invite an England cricketer to make a complete fool of himself and that, finally, brought the matter to an end.

Gooch had found a method that worked brilliantly for him, but all this was just madness. There is no doubt that the biggest casualty of the whole business was Gower. Here was one of the great flair players in modern times being asked to run around in circles – what a farce. I really feel that in the end he just gave up on Gooch. He tried to persuade him that there is more than one way of approaching Test cricket, but Gooch wouldn't have it. His obsession had taken complete hold of him.

Micky Stewart's role in all this needs examining as well. On the other occasion when I went on tour with England under Micky he was as good as gold. He had just come into the job and Mike Gatting, the captain on the 1986/87 tour to Australia, was strong enough to be able to run things the way he wanted, with as little interference from the manager as possible.

By the time Micky teamed up with Gooch, there was a clear opportunity for him to stamp his so-called authority on what went on, and this was the signal for all his soccer-style gibberish to come spouting out. First of all, we had the 'corridor of uncertainty'. This was the area just outside off stump where Micky and Gooch wanted all the bowlers to put the ball time after time. What they didn't seem to realize was that if a bowler runs up and puts the ball in roughly the same place every time, any batsman worth his salt is going to be most appreciative because then he knows exactly where he has to play.

Micky would come prepared with files on opponents and used to bore me to tears with this drivel about 'he hits the ball through here, you've got to bowl to him there, do this, don't do that' etc. It was schoolboy stuff. Most bowlers worth their salt are actually fully aware that it is preferable to avoid bowling half-volleys, long-hops and full tosses to international-class batsmen, although you wouldn't have thought so if you had listened to Micky. The other problem about all this was Gooch and Micky's desire that sixteen or seventeen players should spend virtually all their time together, training, practising, playing and talking about the game all day and all night. The trouble is, on a long overseas tour you see enough of the other players as it is. If you don't get away from them once in a while, you go out of your mind. International cricketers were being treated like kids even to the extent that after a poor performance the players would be brought in after school for 'naughty boy' nets. As a senior pro on that tour listening to the players talk, the recurring theme of their moans was that it was all work, work, work. In my long experience of touring I had never heard comments like those flying around the dressing rooms of New Zealand and Australia that winter – 'Oh no, not bloody nets again' and 'I'm knackered'. It was a relentless, mind-numbing grind and in the end it finally caught up with us.

I believe that this over-emphasis on physical training was directly responsible for our defeat in the 1992 World Cup final.

At least my arrival in New Zealand towards the end of January 1992 took some of the pressure off the other players in terms of media interest. Almost as soon as I stepped off the plane, I was in the headlines again over what I considered to be a total non-story. Of course, I had put on a bit of weight before I came out but it was nothing that couldn't be removed by a couple of weeks of gentle exercise. I asked Micky if he wanted me to get involved straight away and he said that the best thing for me would be an afternoon on the golf course to get myself acclimatised. One of the photographers happened to take a snap of me which did not show me off in the most flattering light, and after a story went round that I had skipped nets without permission, the *Sun* and the *Daily Star* put the photograph and some words together to point out that, in their eyes, my absence from the ground indicated a lack of professionalism.

BOTHAM PUTS HIS GUTS INTO PUTTS

TUBBY IAN IGNORES UPROAR OVER HIS WEIGHTING GAME

It was untrue, of course, and I made them pay for it later in an out-of-court settlement.

It wasn't originally intended that I should take part in any of the actual matches in New Zealand but injuries to Chris Lewis and Derek Pringle meant I was called into the side for the third Test at Wellington where I collected my 100th cap. It was a memorable game, but for all the wrong reasons. After Jack Russell and Allan Lamb had made the game a contest with a century stand, we were going through the motions as the match drew to a close. Then, an incident happened which made all our rigid training look daft. David 'Syd' Lawrence was charging in to bowl like a bull elephant, rose up in the delivery stride, then landed in a howling heap on the ground. You could tell he was in big trouble because the crack of bone rang out like a rifle shot. As his team-mate Jack Russell, who was on the pitch at the time, was fond of recalling, Syd never made a fuss about anything in his life. Yet here he was, a strong and courageous lad screaming in agony. We got him on a stretcher as quickly as possible and although we realized it was serious, neither he nor we could possibly know that was virtually the last ball he would ever bowl in his career. As we took him off the pitch on the stretcher, a New Zealand TV camera crew became a little too intrusive for Jack's liking, and he ended up chasing one fellow away. Then Micky got involved in some pushing and shoving with a female member of the crew. You could understand his reaction as we were all tremendously upset. Injuries like that you simply cannot legislate for and when people turn round and say top sportsmen are overpaid, I simply point to Syd's example.

The next casualty of the trip was rather less severe for the victim but highly significant nonetheless. Allan Lamb's dodgy hamstring, which went in the final one-day international at Christchurch, ruled him out of all our World Cup matches until the last two qualifying games.

At this stage, our success in New Zealand had put us in high spirits for the World Cup ahead but as it transpired, it had also taken a lot out of us. What we should have done, in hindsight, was organize the tour so we could have some time off there and then to recharge the batteries. But it was on with the Micky and Goochie show. Instead of flying to somewhere like the Barrier Reef to relax and go swimming, snorkelling or anything to get away from the cricket and let the niggling pains settle down, we flew straight into Sydney and started playing pointless practise games against ourselves without a respite. When I tried to suggest to Goochie that it was all too intense, he simply wouldn't have it. I remember one incident when I turned up at a game with a massive water pistol and spent the afternoon spraying everyone in sight, including a few of the press. Afterwards, it was made quite clear to me that my behaviour had not been welcomed by the management. I was banging my head against a wall. Players needed time off and they needed to get away from the pressure. I talked to Gooch about it until I was blue in the face but it was all falling on deaf ears. In the end, I gave up because I just wasn't getting through. The thing I kept hearing was that we had to be seen to be doing the 'right thing', and the results of that were to become obvious later.

The next month or so was highly successful on the field but murder off it, what with the constant travelling between games and the insistence of Gooch and Stewart in pushing ourselves to the limit on the training ground. We began in Perth against India where we won a tight game in the last over. They had needed 11 to win from the last six balls but when Phil DeFreitas ran out Ravi Shastri we were home and dry.

From there we travelled to Melbourne where we beat the West Indies easily. The plan for myself to open with Goochie to try and take advantage of the rules on fielding restrictions in the first fifteen overs worked well, as we built a first wicket stand of 50 that helped us to win the game with ten overs to spare. Then came the match which turned out to be crucial. The weather at the Adelaide Oval that day was overcast and muggy and there was a bit of life in the pitch for the bowlers. We were inspired in the field, we bowled well and every catch stuck as we rolled Pakistan over for 74 – their lowest-ever one-day total and the lowest one-day score by a Test side in the World Cup. Had we been able to complete the formality of a victory there is no doubt that Pakistan would have been out of the competition and even Imran Khan's dramatic speech to his players, in which he urged them to 'Be as a cornered tiger, come out and fight', would have been irrelevant. We were well on our way to victory when the rain began falling persistently and the match was declared void. It was very disappointing in the light of what happened in the final, but it was also proof that we were the best side in the competition, a fact we underlined in the next match against the Aussies in Sydney. That was a great night under the floodlights as I ended up with four for 31, which included a spell of four wickets for no runs in seven balls, including that of Allan Border. Australia made only 171, before I opened the innings with Goochie again and I scored my first ever half century in the World Cup. We strolled to victory by eight wickets, then took another step towards the final when we went up-country to Ballarat and thrashed Sri Lanka.

After that we returned to Melbourne to play South Africa for the first time in international cricket since 1965, and here it became clear that the heavy workload was beginning to take its toll. Gooch had pulled a hamstring in Ballarat as he chased a ball through the covers and was unfit for the game with the Springboks. DeFreitas did play but was limping heavily and had to go off at the end of his ten overs, while Dermot Reeve failed to complete his third over after falling and bruising his back. In fact, we were lucky to get out of that game in one piece. South Africa made 151 for the first wicket but after that we managed to peg them back to 236. However, we were soon struggling at 166 for five chasing a rain-reduced target. Fortunately, Neil Fairbrother played a terrific innings of 75 not out, probably his best knock for England, and he and Daffy got us home with a ball to spare.

The casualty list was growing and the constant travelling was also taking a heavy toll. It was lucky that we had already qualified for the semi-final stages of the competition because the wheels were just about to fall off in a big way. We flew to Wellington to play New Zealand in the seventh qualifying match and the next man to fall was Derek Pringle who broke down in mid-over with a rib injury. Lamby came in for his first game but we made only 200, a total the Kiwis easily outstripped to send us to our first defeat of the competition.

Just how exhausted we were by this stage was proved when we collapsed to a humiliating defeat in our last qualifying match against Zimbabwe. Our opponents had lost 18 successive one-day matches before we met at Albury that day and were yet to score a single point in the tournament. We were clear favourites to lift the cup at this stage but having bowled them out for 134 we simply ran out of steam in our reply when we fell foul of a chicken farmer named Eddo Brandes, who took four for 21 as we were rolled over for 125.

Under the circumstances we were grateful for the rain and the tournament's rain-rules in the semi-final. A crowd of 35,000 had turned up in Sydney to watch the game with South Africa. Kepler Wessels intentionally slowed things down so that the South Africans only bowled 45 overs in the allotted time, during which we made 252 for six, thanks largely to Graeme Hick's excellent 83. Then when rain intervened near the end of the South Africa innings, when they needed 22 from 13 balls, the rule which was supposed to create exciting finishes produced a nonsensical one. The target was revised to 22 runs from seven balls and then, in front of an increasingly confused and aggravated crowd, 21 from one ball. It was embarrassing. Neither team would have wanted to win in that way. What's more, as the match was being played under floodlights anyway, there was nothing to stop us bowling the full 45 overs. The South Africans took the blow as well as could be expected, while our feelings were definitely mixed. Ludicrous rule or not, however, we were in the final and that was all that mattered.

Then, what should have been a magnificent occasion and one of the jewels in the crown of my international career, had the gloss knocked off it before the very start.

The night before the final in Melbourne we had to attend a banquet, although it was the last thing we wanted to do. It began pleasantly enough. The mood was good, we had a few glasses of wine and enjoyed ourselves. When the meal finished we all sat back ready for the cabaret. Then, to our horror and in front of the other teams and all the other guests we were treated to a stream of insults and abuse in the name of entertainment. Some grotesque drag artist took to the stage and started to take the mickey out of the Queen. It was not subtle and it was not funny. Not only that, it was coarse, crude and totally unnecessary. If they had put a turban on the man's head, blackened his face and let him tell gags about the Indians or Pakistanis, he would have been lynched. Yet for some reason, the monarchy was fair game.

For ten minutes I sat there thinking this could not possibly go on much longer. But it did; in fact, it got worse and worse. Then I snapped. I pushed back my chair, fixed my eyes on the exit sign above the door and headed straight for it. On the way out I was joined by Goochie, and Micky Stewart very nearly came too. I was not going to sit around and listen to this rubbish and I made my protest in the only way I know how. We went back to Gooch's room, ordered a bottle of wine, put on one of his Van Morrison tapes and gradually calmed down, but there is no doubt that the whole episode had soured the build up to the great occasion. Can you imagine the TCCB hosting a pre-final banquet at Lord's, inviting Australia as the finalists then putting on a cabaret in which they made fools out of their guests.

Of course, I knew there would be fireworks the following day and, sure enough, the hotel was besieged by the press and television. Bearing in mind the comments of Paul Keating, the Australian Prime Minister, who, when told I had left the banquet described me as 'precious', I decided to have a go myself. The press boys were falling over themselves to get a quote so I gave them one. I said, 'I'm very, very proud of my heritage – and, unlike Mr Keating I have one'.

This was my second appearance in the final, after a gap of 13 years. Back in 1979 I had played against the West Indies and been on the receiving end of one of Viv Richards' greatest innings. We lost by 92 runs and, disappointing though it was, I was a young player with the whole of my career in front of me and I knew there was plenty of time for another chance. I missed the next occasion England got to the final in 1987 and I knew this was the last chance for me. The purists criticize one-day cricket as nothing more than a pyjama game which bears no resemblance to the real thing, and in some ways of course they are right. But I can tell you that anyone who has ever played in a World Cup competition considers it to be a highlight, if not the highlight of their career. Victory in one of these tournaments means you are the best side in the world. Moreover, bearing in mind the ups and downs of my career and the fightback from the injury that nearly ended it, I saw this as the one prize I was determined not to let slip from my grasp.

I really do believe if the game had been played ten days earlier when we were fitter, we would have run out easy winners. As it was, our resilience was low. We were vulnerable and I could see that if things did not go our way we might be exposed. How Goochie and I would like to have crowned the twilight years of our international cricketing careers by getting our hands on that trophy.

There were three days between the semi-final victory and the final and what astonished me was the hostility towards England in the build up. Everyone, bar the Brits who lived out there or had flown over was rooting for Pakistan. And it was not good-humoured banter, it was barely disguised hate. The England fans in the crowd of over 87,000 suffered some terrible abuse and it was coming from all parts of the ground. I should think that some 80,000 of these were cheering for Pakistan. Kath was in the stand with some friends and she said the language was shocking and not restricted to the few who had downed too many beers – even children as young as eight were coming out with some foul words. If my kids had said some of the things that were reported back to me, they would have received a clip round the ear.

We started off well enough after Imran won the toss and decided to bat. They were 24 for two and Javed Miandad had made just two, when Derek Pringle was convinced he had him plumb leg before only for the decision to go against us. Imran had promoted himself up the order but Pakistan were still going nowhere fast. In fact he had made just nine from 16 overs when he misjudged an attempted drive and skyed the ball towards mid-wicket. Goochie had to run sideways and backwards to get into position for the catch but having made good ground he then spilled it. It was one of those he would have taken nine times out of ten, but this time he failed and it proved crucial. Imran went on to make 72 in a stand of nearly 140 with Javed and then Inzamam-ul-Haq hit 42 from 35 balls and Wasim Akram 33 from 18 to add a vital 52 in the last six overs. In the last 20 overs, Pakistan made 153 and their total of 249, although by no means out of reach, was a stiff one.

Then came crushing disappointment as I opened the England innings. Wasim Akram and Aqib Javed started well and were moving the ball about considerably. One ball from Wasim moved so much that it deceived me completely as I played and missed outside the off stump. Unfortunately for me the umpire, Brian Aldridge of New Zealand, decided I had played and hit. This was one of those sickening moments when although I knew I hadn't hit the ball I also knew the distance it had travelled off the straight meant that it would have been easy for any umpire to make a mistake. As anyone who saw the replay of my reaction will know, the ball was nowhere near my bat or hands but caught the upper part of my sleeve. Those observers will also know how I felt about the decision and it was at that point that one of the Pakistan fielders, Aamir Sohail, decided to rub it in. Harking back to my comments of nearly a decade before, he goaded me with the words, 'Why don't you send out your mother-in-law now? She couldn't do any worse'. In one respect, he was right because whatever I felt about the injustice of the decision the scoreboard spelled out the truth of the matter – I.T. Botham c Moin Khan b Wasim Akram 0, England 6 for one.

What could I do? To have come this far and to have achieved so little left me feeling angry and powerless. I was out of the game and nothing I could do from that point on would influence the outcome. My mood on the walk back to the pavilion was not improved by the sight of a couple of highly educated Aussie fans giving me the two-fingered salute.

When I pushed through the dressing room door the other players could see I was not a happy man, and they made themselves scarce. Someone made the mistake of saying 'bad luck' and I flipped. I picked up the bat, took it behind the pavilion and smashed it into little pieces. I had to relieve the tension and frustration and this was the only way I could think of doing it without causing myself or someone else serious harm. Still, the full impact of my dismissal had not sunk in. I stomped around for another ten minutes or so, had a shower then went to join the rest of the players on the balcony. After we slumped to 69 for four we knew it was going to be uphill all the way, yet our hopes started to rise again when Lamby and Neil

Fairbrother put on 72 in 14 overs. If they had carried on as they were going victory was not out of the question. Then came the moment when all prospects of winning disappeared.

Bearing in mind the enormous controversy about to erupt over certain underhand practices relating to ball tampering, the two deliveries Wasim Akram produced to dismiss Lamby and Chris Lewis, first ball, became more significant as the months rolled on. Let me put it this way: I've never seen a ball behave like those two did. They were two of the most extraordinary deliveries I have ever seen bowled and you will read my full thoughts on them a little later. For the moment, suffice to say, they meant the end of our World Cup dreams.

As I watched the match unfold I realized there would never be another chance for me. The prize had been right in front of my nose and it had been snatched away. Looking around the dressing room at the end of the match, I witnessed a scene of utter dejection. Perhaps the hardest hit was a player who hadn't even made it on the field at all. Robin Smith, who had been left out on the morning of the match in favour of Lamby, was absolutely distraught but to be honest none of us were in much better shape. We were then treated to one of the most bizarre moments I can remember on a cricket field. On returning to the pitch for the presentation ceremony we were totally amazed (and were not the only ones judging from the looks on the faces of the Pakistan players) by the contents of Imran Khan's acceptance speech. It was all along the lines of this being the greatest moment of his career, how delighted he was, and how he was going to dedicate it to the charity work he was doing in aid of the cancer hospital he was building. The Pakistan captain talked as though no one else had been involved in the match, neglected to mention any of his team and ignored the normal protocol of thanking the sponsors. However, he did thank someone. He thanked the England team for helping to give him one of the proudest moments of his life. Thanks very much, Imran.

Goochie, for whom this defeat meant he was a three-time loser in the World Cup final, was in a state of shock. He and I decided to drink ourselves into oblivion but even that could not remove the pain of what we had been through. I reflected back to all the times when I had tried to get him to ease up on the players during the tour, and when we would have benefited far more from a day off rather than another day in the nets. But all those thoughts disappeared when I saw how much it meant to him to have got to the very brink of the greatest achievement in his career, only to be denied at the last hurdle.

At that moment I would have been quite happy if I had never played against another Pakistan cricketer but, as time progressed and we prepared for the summer's action against them, that mood was replaced by a desire for revenge.

As it turned out, my appearances in all five Texaco Trophy matches and the first two Tests in 1992 were to be my last in international cricket. Even then, although I did not go out in a blaze of glory, events conspired to make sure that I did not go quietly. The fourth of those one-day internationals, at Lord's, was the scene for the start of a controversy that raged unabated for the remainder of the decade.

17
BALL TAMPERING

By his own admission, Imran Khan, the former Pakistan captain and one of the most successful all-rounders in the modern game, tampered with cricket balls. Yet, according to Imran, ball tampering is not cheating.

Well, according to me and to many others, it is.

For the sake of the game, it is time that the ICC decided who is right and who is wrong.

In Ivo Tennant's authorized biography, Imran stated: 'I occasionally scratched the side (of the ball) and lifted the seam . . . Only once did I use an object. When Sussex were playing Hampshire in 1981 the ball was not deviating at all. I got the 12th man to bring on a bottle top and it started to move around a lot . . .'*

One week after his admission appeared in the *Mail on Sunday*, Imran quit as Pakistan's representative on the International Cricket Council, an action their chief executive David Richards described as 'entirely appropriate'.

All clear, so far? It is what happened after Imran made his confession that you may find puzzling. It certainly

---

*An extract from *Imran Khan* by Ivo Tennant, Headline, 1994

baffled me. Firstly he confirmed that he had used a bottle-top to gouge the surface of the ball, and to make sure as many people as possible got the message he appeared on ITV's *Sport in Question* chat-show programme to demonstrate to millions of British television viewers exactly how he did it.

Imran spelled out his point of view in some detail. His position was that tampering with the ball by scratching the side and lifting the seam were an accepted part of the game and did not amount to cheating. Correct me if I'm wrong but haven't I read somewhere that they *do*? The Laws of Cricket 42.4 and 42.5 governing unfair play, for example:

LAW 42.4 Lifting the seam: A player shall not lift the seam of the ball for any reason. Should this be done, the umpire shall change the ball for one of similar condition to that in use prior to the contravention.

LAW 42.5 Changing the condition of the ball: Any member of the fielding side may polish the ball providing that such polishing wastes no time and that no artificial substance is used. No one shall rub the ball on the ground or use any artificial substance or take any other action to alter the condition of the ball. In the event of a contravention of this law, the umpires, after consultation, shall change the ball for one of similar condition to that in use prior to the contravention. The Law does not prevent a member of the fielding side from drying a wet ball, or removing mud from the ball.

Almost Imran's last words on the subject were 'I don't blame anyone for cheating'. Well, he wouldn't, would he?

In Tennant's book, Imran claimed that at one time or another 'almost every seamer' has been guilty of ball tampering. Later, in an article in the *Daily Telegraph* he stated 'no one will accuse the likes of John Snow, Dennis Lillee, Malcolm Marshall, Clive Rice, Michael Holding, Andy Roberts and Sir Richard Hadlee of cheating'. But he added 'yet they are not likely to deny that occasionally they too lifted the seam'. Then, in an interview published with the *Sun* he implied that the late Jim Laker, England's greatest off-spinner – who among his other claims to fame once took 19 wickets in a Test match against Australia including all 10 in the second innings – had fiddled with the ball. And in the same piece he declared that 'the biggest names in English cricket have all done it'.

Well, Imran, that is news to me.

With hand on heart I can categorically state that never once have I done anything illegal with a cricket ball. Unlike Imran Khan, I have never lifted the seam. I have never scratched the surface of the ball, and I have never gouged one with a bottletop.

Unfortunately, ball tampering was not the only accusation indirectly levelled against me. Following the row that erupted in the English newspapers after his admission and his later allegations, Imran gave an extensive interview to *India Today* magazine in which, in my opinion, he implied that I am a racist.

'It's the English media and a section of cricketers', he stated, 'who have blown it [the ball-tampering row] out of all proportion.'

When asked what the motive for such actions might be, he replied: 'There is a lot of racism here. When Bob Willis or Freddie Trueman were tearing the heart out of India or

Pakistan we never heard an outcry about short-pitched bowling. How come the noise started when the West Indies and Pakistan began winning matches with their fast bowlers? How come we never heard about slow over-rates until the West Indies fast bowlers came along? Australians can get away with anything because they are white. There is a lot of racism in this society. Look at people such as Lamb and Botham making statements like: "Oh, I never thought much of him anyway and now it's been proven he's a cheat." Where is this hatred coming from?'

Finally he brought what he called 'class' into it.

He claimed that those who had taken the rational side in the argument (i.e. his) were men such as journalist and BBC commentator Christopher Martin-Jenkins and former England internationals Tony Lewis and Derek Pringle who, according to Imran 'are all educated, Oxbridge-types'. His detractors, on the other hand, were below-stairs types. He said: 'Look at the others: Lamb, Botham, Trueman. The difference in class and upbringing makes a difference.'

I notice that, in this context, Imran referred to us by our surnames. I notice also that Imran went to Oxford. If an Oxford education tells you it's all right to cheat, and it's all right to accuse a dead man of cheating as well, then give me Buckler's Mead Secondary Modern School any-time.

Imran wrote to me completely out of the blue on 6 June 1994. His letter started by saying he considered me a 'worthy opponent and an outstanding sportsman' and that he wanted to 'put the record straight'. He then said that he had 'never called anyone lower class or under class' since he 'didn't believe in the class system'.

The letter continued with Imran saying that the proof was clearly in the books he had written, as well as the Ivo Tennant book. He said that using terms like 'Paki cheats' about ball tampering is an uneducated approach and that an educated approach has nothing to do with degrees. He added that he had 'never wanted this issue to get personal' between himself and 'any players'; he simply wanted the ICC to 'define what were acceptable limits of ball tampering'. According to Imran, 'clearly ball tampering has gone on ever since the game has been played' and he was 'not the only cricketer who thinks so'. He went on to say the time has come to 'pass legislation and end the crises (sic) as it happened in baseball'.

He finished by stating he was 'sad that this issue has brought so much unpleasantness between the two cricketing nations' and between players like himself and me.

That was all very well, but did Imran seriously expect me to be satisfied with a private letter when he himself had made his comments so publicly in the *Sun* and *India Today*?

I had no choice but to instruct my solicitor Alan Herd to demand a public retraction of his comments and a public apology. That was the only way to clear the air, as far as I was concerned.

On my behalf Alan wrote to Imran. Here are excerpts from his letter dated 9 June 1994:

It is totally unjustifiable to allege publicly that Ian Botham is a racist motivated by 'hatred' – when you know perfectly well that he is not. It is just as serious to attribute to him (and indeed to Allan Lamb) a statement like 'Oh, I never thought much of him anyway and now it's been proven he's a cheat' when Ian has neither said nor written any such thing.

You state in your letter of 6 June that 'I have never called anyone lower class or under class since I don't believe in the class system'. That is in complete contradiction of your remarks published in *India Today* referring to 'Lamb, Botham and Trueman', remarks which received massive media coverage in this country. Your comments on Ian's class, education and upbringing are grossly insulting, not only to Ian but to his parents and family.

Your comments published in the *Sun* on 21 May with reference to ball tampering were that 'the biggest names of English cricket have all done it. And, when I say big names, I mean as big as you can get'. Ian Botham is of course one of the 'biggest names'.

Regrettably you have seriously libelled Ian. He has no wish to sue you, which would be an unseemly and distasteful matter between two great cricketers between whom, so far as Ian is concerned, there has not been any personal animosity in the past.

Ian is therefore prepared to let the matter rest if you publicly acknowledge the following:–

(a)   that he has never accused you of cheating;

(b)   that he is not a racist; and

(c)   that he has never treated a cricket ball in a manner which contravenes the laws of cricket.

He also requires a public apology for your unfounded allegations and your undertaking not to repeat them again. If you are prepared to meet Ian's terms, then he will take the matter no further, and you and I can discuss how the public acknowledgement and apology is to be made.

In the meantime Ian's rights to sue for an apology in Open Court and for damages and costs are reserved.

As no satisfactory reply was forthcoming, on the 21 July I instructed Alan Herd to issue a writ for libel to Imran, and the next day Allan Lamb followed suit.

Almost until the moment the court case began more than two years later, on Monday July 15, 1996, I never really expected the matter to reach the ears of m'learned friends. So clear and strong were the indications from our legal advisers that it was open and shut that the nearer we came to the date of the case the more convinced I was that Imran would finally hold his hands up and apologise.

It was reported in some quarters that Allan and I saw this as an opportunity to settle old scores for our defeat at the hands of Pakistan in the 1992 World Cup and the subsequent Test series. It was also suggested that we saw a chance to make a few bob for ourselves. And our action was certainly presented by some observers as a case of me and Lamb ganging up to put Imran Khan in his place. All of which interpretations of events were, of course, nonsense.

I always respected Imran as one of the greatest cricketers I played against. All I ever wanted from him was a clear, unequivocal and public apology for his comments that my views over ball tampering stemmed from the fact that I was racist and lacked class and upbringing, and an apology for his clear accusation that I myself had tampered with the ball.

Imran claimed that the reason I rejected his offers to

apologise was that I wanted to humiliate him. The reason I rejected his offers to apologise was that they were nothing of the kind.

To me, his excuse for an 'apology' – and we saw a draft of a letter he was proposing to write to *The Times* – was all about the old chestnuts of his words being misinterpreted and him being misquoted. I'm sorry, that simply wasn't good enough. You only had to read what he had written and said in those articles and in the biography written by Ivo Tennant to see what he really thought. And if Imran wanted to prove he had been misquoted why didn't he call Tennant to the witness stand? Why didn't he call the man who wrote the article in *India Today*? Why didn't he call the reporter who interviewed him for the *Sun*?

Just before the case was to be heard Imran changed his tune and his tactics over his allegation that I was a cheat. In this matter he was going to defend himself on the grounds that the allegation was true.

And so, with no apology forthcoming and Imran determined to insist that I was as guilty of ball tampering as he himself had admitted to being, we arrived in court 13 of the High Court in the Strand on Monday July 15th to settle the matter once and for all.

Thirteen days later, on Wednesday 31 July, 1996, the courtroom was packed for the climax of the case. The moment the foreman of the jury delivered his verdict will live with me forever. And to the day I go to my grave I will never understand how they reached it.

As we waited the four and a half hours for the jury to come to their decision, neither Allan nor myself paid any attention to the fact that there seemed to be rather too many 'thirteens' for comfort involved in the equation. Not once, neither then nor in the months prior to the trial did Allan or I have the slightest doubt that our case would be proven. Kath was similarly convinced and while Lindsay Lamb said she was slightly concerned at the length of time the jury was taking, we all reassured her that Imran and his party were looking every inch a beaten team. Our barrister, Charles Gray QC had done a good job in presenting our case and he was similarly confident that he had beaten his old sparring partner, George Carman QC.

So when the foreman of the jury stood up and announced that they had found for 'the defence' on both counts, none of us could believe what we were hearing. We were stunned. And the feeling stayed with me for an awfully long time.

It was clear that Imran's side believed they had lost the case. We had heard that they had been told to prepare for the worst. And in the instant of the foreman's announcement the immediate reaction of Imran and his young wife, Jemima, daughter of the billionaire Sir James Goldsmith, said it all. 'Oh God, we've done it!' she exclaimed, as much in shock as in celebration.

The reaction of the judge, Mr. Justice French, was also illuminating. During his summing up he seemed to us at least to be directing the jury our way. Immediately after he had finished however, at around 10.20 on that final morning and just as the jury were about to retire to consider their verdict, Carman jumped in and advised the judge that he wished to raise several points.

The jury was allowed to retire but instructed not to start deliberating until they were told to. Then, for the next hour and a half, Carman launched a violent attack on the judge's summing up, accusing him of not summarising some of the witnesses' evidence and other matters, even raising the implied threat of a re-trial.

By the time the judge recalled the jury and made several amendments to his summing-up their heads must have been spinning. Yet whatever the changes in detail his message was substantially the same as it had been before Mr. Carman intervened.

So when, after first asking the judge to accept a majority verdict, they found as they did, Mr Justice French's response showed exactly what he thought of the outcome. He stood up, bowed to the jury in the most perfunctory fashion, then walked out of court without thanking them, as is usually the case, indeed without uttering a word to them.

As the full impact of what had happened started to sink in, I looked across at the faces of the jurors, searching for clues. One young girl said quite clearly: 'I'm sorry.' Then she burst into tears.

In the intervening years, the sense of shock has diminished, but it has never quite disappeared. As we considered whether to appeal the same simple question kept going around and round in my head: How did we lose? And I still have no clear answers.

As far as I was concerned I had no choice but to sue Imran for libel. To my mind he had slandered me on two counts. First Imran had implied that the only reason I was calling into question certain practices by Pakistan bowlers was that I was a racist. That, I am afraid simply would not do. Imran knew me well enough to know it was not true. In my opinion he had also implied that I myself had cheated at cricket by tampering with the ball. Then he sought to justify the allegations on the grounds that it was true. It was not.

My comments were based on a desire for the absolute truth of the practice of ball tampering to be brought out into the open once and for all.

From the outset I made my position clear. I had come to court to defend myself against these allegations because, to my mind, to be called racist and a cheat are among the worst things that you could possibly be accused of. By accusing me of ball tampering he was implying that I had used illegal methods to succeed at cricket. In short, he was saying that I only achieved what I did in the game because I cheated. By doing so he was calling into question every Test wicket I had taken. Whatever other people may have felt about that, I believed my reputation was at stake.

Imran's supporters made great play of the fact that both Allan Lamb and I refused to settle when a businessman named Jim Slater, a good friend of Goldsmith, offered to meet most of the costs already incurred if we would all shake hands on the steps of the court and call it quits. We would have been happy to do so had Imran apologised, but he refused to do so. If I had walked away then without an apology there would have been a shadow over my career for the rest of my days. This wasn't about a 'pub brawl' or a 'mystery blonde'. I don't care about those sorts of allegations. This was about my professional career; it was about my integrity as a sportsman and a man.

How could I be expected to take such slurs against my character from a man who himself had freely admitted to ball tampering and not defend myself to the hilt?

To me, his admission that he had used a bottle-top to

tamper with a ball represented the beginning of the story, not the end.

Yet when I indicated as such in my articles, all Imran could think of was to try and justify his own illegal action by claiming that some of the biggest names in English cricket had adopted similar practices, by which, all observers were agreed and he later confirmed, he meant me.

I say it again and I will say it until I am blue in the face. I have never ever picked the seam of a cricket ball during a match, I have never tried to scratch the surface or gouge a ball. And I have never sought to obtain unfair advantage by tampering with a cricket ball in any way. Unlike Imran, I never felt it necessary to do so.

As for the tactics emplyed by Imran's side to present me as an untrustworthy character, I considered them cowardly and utterly beneath contempt. I fully understand that Imran needed to come out fighting. But what I will never forgive him for is that he and his side decided that the best form of defence was to attack me in the most vicious, personal and spiteful ways imaginable.

For three long and boring days, Carman raked up the past, throwing any mud he could lay his hands on in the hope that some of it stuck. He went through the whole menu, Miss Barbados, sex, drugs, rock and roll, all the stuff that had been gathering dust on the newspaper library shelves for more than a decade. Carman's performance was a tour de force. Snarling, sarcastic and bullying, it was obvious he was trying to provoke me into losing my temper. But I refused to let him. No matter how hostile or cheap his attempts to drag my name through the dirt became I was determined not to lose my cool. And the more I rode the punches the more irritated I believe Mr. Carman became.

But while I was perfectly capable of handling any question Carman wanted to ask, I felt it totally unfair that Kath should have to go through all that crap over and over again. It must have been torture for her to have to listen to all the old unproven and downright ludicrous allegations about me that had made her life a misery and stretched our marriage near to breaking point during the dark days.

Commenting on Imran's review of the first publication of my autobiography, in which he wrote that Kath was the 'real hero' of the book and saying: 'I wish her all the luck in the remainder of her marriage'. I looked Imran straight in the eye and said : 'I thought it was an extremely arrogant remark and I would like to inform Imran that my wife and I have a very successful marriage, thank you.'

Early in the whole process of devising our strategy, Allan and I were warned that Imran's side would probably try such tactics to try and discredit me in the eyes of the jury. And we were given the opportunity of employing similar tactics to undermine Imran. We chose not to go down that road. Kath, who had been through so much herself and knew what it was like to hear her husband vilified was concerned of the effect that some of the accusations might have on the pregnant Jemima. Bearing in mind it was as much her decision as mine and Allan's not to ditch the considerable amount of dirt available to us, Kath found Jemima's gloating attitude after our defeat particularly hard to take. And while Imran's side talked at length of all the work he had been doing to raise money for his cancer hospital in Pakistan (and good on him, incidentally, for that), we hardly mentioned my walks for Leukaemia

Research or Allan's efforts on behalf of those seeking to find a cure for Cystic Fibrosis.

It did not take a genius to work out why Imran chose to employ such grubby tactics. Not for a moment am I suggesting that it had anything to do with him lacking class or upbringing, you understand. It was simply that Imran had nothing but muck with which to defend himself.

After we had been through that terrible ordeal, having to defend myself against Imran's proposition that I had been a ball-tampering cheat seemed like a walk in the park.

Most of this part of the case was taken up with Imran's side calling a succession of witnesses to say that picking the seam of the ball was accepted practice in all forms of cricket. I never said it wasn't. What I was adamant about was that not only did I never do it myself, but I considered it to be unacceptable practice.

Then Imran tried to prove that I had tampered with the ball by submitting two pieces of film showing incidents that had happened fourteen years previously.

Of all the hundreds of hours of television footage of my playing career for England, Somerset, Worcestershire and Durham, the best Imran could come up with was this: the first clip showed an incident during the Test match between England and India at The Oval when I threw a new ball at our wicket-keeper Bob Taylor for him to dry it with his gloves.

The second clip showed me trying to push a ball back into shape with my fingers during a Test against Pakistan in the same year, not surreptitiously, but in plain view while walking back to my bowling mark.

No wonder that on the ninth day of the case, having

spent all that time and all that money trying to prove an unprovable accusation, calling witnesses like David Lloyd and Mike Atherton who were trying to prepare for a Lord's Test match, and giving Geoffrey Boycott the limelight for his fifteen seconds of childish posturing, more of which anon, and forcing me to bring into court guys like David Gower and Robin Smith and others to refute the claims, Imran announced he was withdrawing his defence that his allegations of ball-tampering against me were justified.

On Thursday, July 26, that part of the case was concluded like this.............

Charles Gray to Imran Khan: 'You accused him of illegally tampering with the ball by using his thumbnails to pick the seam and scratching it, and by throwing the ball so it could be scuffed. Do you realise Mr. Botham regards these allegations as extremely serious?'

Imran Khan: 'Cheating is serious, yes, sir.'

Gray: 'Now you have heard the explanation are you prepared to apologise for the fact that the allegation was made in court and persisted with for nine days?'

Imran: 'Yes, sir. If Mr. Botham says he was squeezing the ball, I will accept it.'

Gray: 'The allegations of cheating have received the widest publicity and yet are only being withdrawn now.'

At least Imran had to pay a proportionate amount of costs for the wasted time. But, in hindsight, the damage caused by the mud-slinging Carman had employed earlier may already have been done. For although the judge told the jury to disregard it, no one can unsay the words that have been spoken or undo the effect those words may have had.

At the time, however, I really did believe that this was the moment when we won the case.

As I have said, when the jury finally reached their verdict on that fateful day, none of us could quite believe what we were hearing, neither on our side or Imran's. In the end I have to believe that the jury simply did not understand the case, that they were bamboozled by Carman's tactics and that they simply could not get their heads around the complexities of ball tampering, nor the evidence of a constant stream of witnesses who were experts on the subject. I was bored listening to them and I knew what they were talking about. How would the jury have felt? I have no other explanation for the fact that the only people in Court 13 that day who thought the case should be settled in favour of Imran Khan were the twelve men and women of the jury.

As we left the courtroom to face the waiting media I tried to put into words what Kath and I had thought of Imran's decision to attempt to assassinate my character. I told the press: 'I don't understand why Khan wanted to drag all that up. We could have attacked him over his private life, but his wife is just 22 years old and six months pregnant and we would never have put her through what George Carman put Kathy through. I wouldn't want it to happen to my worst enemy.'

It may have been Carman's decision to rake up the past. But in the end it was Imran who was instructing him. I wouldn't employ Mr. Carman. I don't like his tactics. They are dirty rats'. I meant every word.

Time heals most wounds, but every so often Kath and I think back to the case and we both get depressed by the memories.

As for Boycott's attempt to derail the entire proceedings, his performance only deepened my contempt for the man.

He had been called by Imran's side to repeat in court what he had said in the newspapers and on television: namely that fiddling with the ball had been common practice in the English game. But his appearance just made a mockery of a very serious business.

The previous day Brian Close had refuted Boycott's suggestions. He told the court that while sweat had been used on the ball by 'just about everyone in the history of cricket' using artificial substances and picking the seam was breaking the laws. Asked if he was surprised that Boycott had said such tampering was common practice he replied: 'No, I'm not surprised, knowing his personality. He is trying to be full of bravado or whatever. I think he is making assumptions that are wrong.'

Carman asked him: 'You'd say he is an honest man, though?'

Close replied: 'I wouldn't like to answer that.'

Boycott appeared wearing a white shirt with a Wills cigarette logo on the left breast and clutching a cricket boot in his hand and after telling the court that he believed ball tampering was like speeding on the motorway, he seemed intent on defending himself against what Close had said, even though it was entirely irrelevant to the case. In fact, the judge got so irritated by his attempts to do so that he ordered him to be quiet.

As for what he was wearing, his sponsored shirt was beyond a joke. One thing on which Geoffrey has always prided himself is trying to look smart in public. For him to claim that he had forgotten his jacket because he had had to leave the Lord's Test in a hurry and then just to happen to be wearing a shirt bearing a sponsor's logo struck many people as more than odd.

It couldn't have had anything to do with the fact that the case had attracted massive publicity in India and Pakistan, where Wills apparently sell an awful lot of fags. Could it?

Incidentally, I was very sad to see Boycott in court himself a year or so later accused of beating up his girlfriend. Strange that I wasn't called as a character witness, though.

Of course, the entire controversy over ball tampering stems from events that took place in the matches between England and Pakistan during 1992.

The first occurred in front of 87,000 people in the World Cup Final at the Melbourne Cricket Ground. Approximately halfway through our reply to Pakistan's 250, following the early losses of myself, Alec Stewart, Graeme Hick and Graham Gooch, the middle-order batsmen Allan Lamb and Neil Fairbrother had got us back on course. If they had stayed together until the end of the innings, I believe we would almost certainly have lifted the trophy. Then, in the space of two of the most extraordinary deliveries I have ever seen, our hopes were crushed.

First Wasim Akram, bowling around the wicket, sent down a ball to Lamb that I consider was quite unplayable; what's more it came totally out of the blue. The ball started off heading wide down the leg side, then two-thirds of the way down the wicket it started swinging towards off stump. The next thing Lamby knew, his off bail had been removed. The look of absolute astonishment on his face said it all.

The next delivery, to Chris Lewis, started wide of off stump, and suddenly swung in like a banana and smashed into the timbers.

We have all swung the ball in our time, but I have never witnessed anything like that.

The next incident happened during the fourth Texaco Trophy match against Pakistan at Lord's that summer. I was filling in for the injured Graham Gooch as opener, and for a while I was partnered by Lamby. A short time after I was out, and just before the lunch break, I saw him pick up the ball, take it across to umpire Ken Palmer and say something to the effect of 'What the hell's going on here?' I had noticed the state of the ball myself while I was out there during my innings. On one side it was so badly chewed up that it looked about 300 overs old. The other side was perfectly normal.

The umpires John Hampshire and Ken Palmer took one look at the ball and in no time at all came to the conclusion that it had been tampered with. During that interval the ball was changed and we were told not to discuss with anybody what had gone on. But of course the story got out – and why not? Why should I be party to a cover-up when cheating is going on? To keep my mouth shut would have been to condone it, so I spilt the beans to the reporter Chris Lander in the hope that he would run the story in his paper, because I felt strongly the public should know what was happening.

The England team was getting a beating on the field and we certainly didn't appreciate being accused of being useless when we were losing to a Pakistan side that we all knew was using underhand methods. We were expected to stomach terrible rubbishings in the press for our performances and not whisper a word of complaint.

The Pakistani management and the TCCB (under pressure from a variety of sources) did all they could to keep the thing under wraps. I also think the match referee Deryck Murray has a lot to answer for. He should have shown the ball to the world, not run for cover within Lord's and so become a part of the conspiracy of silence.

The matter came to court after Sarfraz Nawaz, the former Pakistan Test bowler, sued Lamby over his allegations that Sarfraz had shown him the methods used to tamper with the ball while they were team-mates at Northamptonshire, the ball used at Lord's that day was a crucial exhibit in Lamb's defence. Yet the TCCB refused to release the main pieces of evidence: the ball and the umpires' reports.

I never made the witness box when Lamb was being sued for libel by Sarfraz Nawaz because Sarfraz dropped the case just as I was about to step up. But let there be no doubts – what Lamby said was spot on. Over the years I have seen Pakistan players fiddle with the ball illegally, and they were at it again when I faced them in all five one-day internationals and appeared in the first two Tests, at Edgbaston and Lord's in 1992. What happened to the ball was a clear and deliberate breach of Laws 42.4 and 42.5 of the game of cricket.

The issue was raised with the captain Graham Gooch and manager Micky Stewart. At each team meeting before the first two Tests the subject of ball tampering came up, and there is no doubt Micky was livid that it was going on and the Pakistanis were getting away with it. I kept pleading 'What are we going to do about this bloody ball-tampering?' but as usual there was no response or reaction beyond the dressing room door.

The methods used in ball tampering are very sly. I have sat in the dressing room and watched Wasim Akram,

Waqar Younis and Aqib Javed at work out on the field. They wait for the ball to get smacked into the boundary boards a couple of times so that the leather starts to crack; then they work thumb and fingernails around the cracks and basically rough it up while keeping one side as shiny as possible.

There were a number of times when I saw Wasim, Waqar and Aqib clearly fiddling with the ball, and it was even more obvious when I was at the non-striker's end. Eventually after some 40 overs the effect was to produce reverse swing. The ball, as well as the bowler, had become an awesome weapon. Although I regarded Aqib as an ordinary bowler, what saddened me was that Wasim and Waqar were extremely good ones, good enough not to have had to resort to those measures and to tamper with the ball. They both should have been above all that.

Ball tampering is one of those issues where the more you look back and think about it, the more you come across times when you have reasonable grounds for suspicion.

As I see it Imran has admitted one offence, but I am left wondering just how many others need to be taken into consideration. I know for a fact, for instance, that Imran once told Lamby and Robin Smith that he was worried that Aqib Javed was too blatant when he doctored the ball!

As far back as 1982 I had a run-in with Imran during the Lord's Test against Pakistan. Lamby was hit on the head by Imran and we could clearly see that the quarter-seam was coming up and had been picked at. I took the ball to umpires Dickie Bird and David Constant and asked them to have a look at it, and they were clearly concerned by the state it was in. At the end of the over I had a word with Imran about it and he said, rather ambiguously, that the English bowlers might get it to swing a bit more if they 'looked after it a bit better'.

We made a complaint to the TCCB and the ball was taken away, but nothing happened. Then when I was playing for Worcestershire against Surrey in a Sunday League game some years later, Waqar Younis started to finger the ball and minutes later was bowling some of the most outrageously swinging deliveries I've ever seen. Up until that point, the ball had been behaving perfectly normally, and it was only later that the significance of what he was doing sunk in.

It wasn't just the players who had tales to tell during that summer of 1992: the BBC film evidence was also very damning. By and large, the methods for doctoring the ball are very subtle, with the players polishing one side while lifting the seam and scratching and gouging the other half to create exaggerated swing. But if a commentator as experienced as Richie Benaud suddenly says 'Cor, steady on' as he watches Aqib Javed with the ball in his hand, then you know that something sinister is happening.

When the court case started it was amazing how many top-class umpires were out of the country, unavailable to stand as witnesses. The one who did, the one who had the guts to stand up and say 'Yes, they did tamper with the ball' was Don Oslear, who as the third umpire during that Texaco match at Lord's, had seen exactly what went on. And what happened to him? He was struck off the umpiring list. I know he was approaching retirement, but he still earned good marks that year. You have to wonder whether in the circumstances he would have been treated so shabbily if he had not been involved in the controversy and if he hadn't had the courage to stand up and tell the truth.

Oslear's sacking was not what you might call a brilliant piece of public relations on behalf of the TCCB. The man in the street heard that he had gone and put two and two together.

The Lamb case and Imran's confession have given the cricketing authorities the chance to act positively on the issue, but it is infuriating that they have not seized the chance, not only for the sake and spirit of the game but also to vindicate Lamby for having the guts to stand up and be counted. Yet again, they seemed happy to let everything be swept under the carpet, and it just made me feel all the more justified in saying that those sitting at Lord's who were set on not rocking the boat were not fit to run the game because they clearly did not have the spirit of cricket at heart. If they had done they would have acted immediately to sort out the row.

Lamby suffered for his courage in making that stand and nobody in cricket's hierarchy seemed to want to know him. Surely it was no coincidence that after he spoke out he never again played for England. He said what others have been frightened to admit, and I wanted to see him exonerated for raising the issue, not blamed for causing an international incident. The guy scored runs consistently over the years for club and country, but it was obvious to me that however well he performed after the ball tampering allegations, he never had a chance of more international honours because he was blacklisted.

Sadly the problems with Pakistan don't end at ball tampering. At Headingley in 1987 Salim Yousuf dived and blatantly claimed a catch off at least the second bounce from my edge. I was livid and called him a cheating little bastard, warning him if he ever tried that stunt again I would knock his head off. Kenny Palmer was the umpire and told Salim he was not happy about the appeal. He then ordered him to go back to his position. At the end of the over, Imran came across and I asked him what he was going to do about it. He told me that if I hadn't sworn at Salim Yousuf he would have instructed him to apologise. What was I meant to say to Salim Yousuf? 'We'll laugh about this in years to come, old boy.'

Frankly, the recent allegations made by Australian Test stars Shane Warne, Tim May and Mark Waugh over bribery and match-fixing did not surprise me in the slightest. According to a story that first appeared in the *Sydney Morning Herald* at the end of England's 1994/95 winter tour Down Under, the players were approached prior to the start of the first Test on their 1994 tour to Pakistan in Karachi by the home captain Salim Malik, who then proceeded to offer them a bribe to throw the match.

The Australian Cricket Board confirmed the tale and revealed that their dossier on the incidents contained the following allegations: that Salim Malik had offered Warne and May the equivalent of £33,000 each to throw the Test and that Mark Waugh alleged he was offered £65,000 if he deliberately lost his wicket in the same Test.

Salim Malik immediately issued a public denial, calling the allegations 'malicious and baseless'. But, as with the ball-tampering furore, once the can of worms was opened, other stories soon came tumbling out. Allan Border, the former Aussie captain, recounted an incident during the Australian tour to England in 1993 when, according to him, a former Pakistan all-rounder offered him £500,000 to lose the Edgbaston Test. Mushtaq Mohammed soon admitted that he was the player involved but made it clear that the 'offer' had been meant as a joke. AB didn't see the funny side. Soon afterwards another Aussie Test player, my former Durham team-mate Dean Jones who I would trust if he told me day was night, revealed that, while competing in a one-day tournament in Sri Lanka, he had been offered £30,000 to act as a bookmaker's informant, the money to be left in a biscuit tin! Finally, Sarfraz Nawaz alleged that some Pakistan players, whose names he didn't reveal, had been bribed to lose the 1992 one-day international at Trent Bridge, which England won by 198 runs.

It is an open and not very well-guarded secret that gambling on the outcome of cricket matches has long been a highly productive black-market industry in India and Pakistan. Apart from horseracing, gambling is illegal in India and absolutely outlawed in the Islamic state of Pakistan. Of course, this hasn't deterred scores of bookmakers operating by word of mouth. The centre of the business, by all accounts, is the Bombay Stock Exchange, through which vast sums have been wagered, won and lost over the years. The bookies' agents, some masquerading as journalists, set themselves up in cricket press boxes at nearly every Test series supplying instant information on weather conditions, the state of the pitch and the total number of runs each team is likely to manage, on which they then base the odds.

It did not take certain wealthy punters long to figure out that if they could guarantee 'freak' results by getting at the players, the killings could be massive.

Throughout 1994 rumours began to circulate over Pakistan's results. In October, after they had beaten Sri Lanka 2–0 in their Test series and then 4–1 in a one-day series, they suddenly experienced a lull in form which led to defeats by the same team in a one-day tournament. Even at this early stage, the Federal Intelligence Agency in Pakistan was advised by the National Sports Board to look into the matter. Then, when Pakistan were heavily beaten by South Africa and later by Zimbabwe certain observers drew their own conclusions. It was obvious that even those within the set-up were concerned with what was going on. Why else would manager Intikhab Alam insist that all players swear on the *Koran* not to take bribes or perform poorly on purpose?

Against this background, more allegations concerning Pakistan players hardly came as a bolt from the blue, although I must confess the identity of the man allegedly involved in the latest of them, Pakistan captain Salim Malik, was a shock to me. Malik, known by his former county colleagues at Essex as 'Honest Sal', has always been regarded as a top professional.

And there was more to come. During England's tour of Australia in the winter of 1998-99 the Australian Cricket Board revealed that Shane Warne and Mark Waugh had been paid by bookmakers to supply information on weather conditions and the like, thus confirming the existence of these powerful dark forces in the game. For a while the backlash against the Aussie players even threatened their future in the game. Almost immediately afterwards, Adam Hollioake, the captain of the England one-day side that won the Champions Cup in Sharjah in 1997, revealed to the *Mail on Sunday* how he had been approached by individuals offering him huge sums to fix matches. And in 1999 Chris Lewis claimed he had been approached by a 'Mr. Patel' who had tried to persuade him to enlist the services of Alan Mullally and Alec Stewart in a £1m plan to nobble England against New Zealand.

After more than a year investigating claims of match-fixing and bribery, the judicial enquiry set up in Pakistan, although reported to have identified several prominent players as being guilty, were still no nearer producing an official finding.

Perhaps the biggest scandal of all is that despite all the evidence that shady practices are commonplace in the world game, the ICC, the governing body of the world game continues to deny that a real problem exists. What cricket needs is a full open investigation into match-fixing, betting and bribery on a worldwide scale. Until that happens and until steps are taken to deal with the real issues, the possibility exists that the cheats will continue to prosper. The world game needs people to believe it is honest and straight. If not, what is the point of having it?

18
OFF THE FIELD

Success on the cricket pitch has opened doors that would otherwise have been closed. Even so, you still have to want to go through them. I may be approaching my 40th birthday, but off the field as well as on it, I have had a life so full it would take ten men to live it. Of course, there are things I would have changed, but by and large my attitude has been straightforward: I believe in going for it, then going for more. So the range of my off-field activities has been extensive.

Away from the cricket pitches of the world it has been Beefy the Pilot, Beefy the Actor, Beefy the Golfer, Beefy the Quiz Show Captain and so on.

The most high profile of all these extra-curricular activities was the BBC's *Question of Sport* which seemed to get more and more popular as time marched on.

I have known Bill Beaumont since 1980, when he was leading England to rugby's Five Nations Grand Slam. I was up at Murrayfield for the last match of the season with Tony Bond, who had played his full part in England's success but was on crutches after breaking his leg playing against Ireland. I had met most of the team before, and when they invited us along for a drink after the official function we were delighted to accept.

When we arrived at the hotel, we made our way through to the bar adjoining the function room. When we got there an obnoxious official from the Scottish Rugby Football Union told us in no uncertain terms that we were not welcome. He said that it was an official SRFU party and even though we pointed out that we had an invitation, he was having none of it. The SRFU were paying for it, he told us, and they were not having any gatecrashers. I saw red and told him that as the gin and tonic I was cradling in my hand so obviously belonged to him, he could have it back, and I promptly poured it over his head.

I was then frog-marched from the room along with poor old Tony who was still hobbling on crutches. Bill and David Brooks, then president of the RFU, saw what had happened and decided to leave the party with us. They bought bottles of gin and scotch from over the bar and we went up to Brooks's room and had a party. Their attitude was that if their guests weren't good enough for the SRFU then they didn't want to stay. This was typical of Bill, and over the years our friendship has grown stronger and stronger.

Our relationship made sure that during the years when *A Question Of Sport* was among the top-rated programmes on BBC 1, friendly rivalry never got out of hand. The show's popularity was down to two elements. First and foremost, the contests were for real. How could they have been otherwise with such natural-born competitors as Bill and myself as team captains? Secondly, great stars like Nigel Mansell, Nick Faldo, Steve Davis, Linford Christie and Bryan Robson were encouraged to let their hair down.

For those who watched these dedicated performers push themselves to the limit in their chosen sport, it was a pleasant change to see them relax and have fun. I cannot think of one guest who did not enter fully into the spirit and the public responded.

Since Bill and I ended our involvement with the programme, I have been fortunate to be part of Sky TV's commentary team under the strict guidance of producer John Gayleard and others, covering England cricket at Test, one-day international and domestic level. I'm not just saying this because I work for them, but I really do believe that Sky's innovations such as super slo-mo cameras, the magic carpet and the like have revolutionised the televising of the game worldwide. And we are really only standing at the starting line of the race to embrace new technology.

Surely the next step will be for TV umpires to rule on more and more decisions. Whatever the purists may say about human error adding to the glorious uncertainty of sport, the fact is that livelihoods are now at stake. How would you like it if your career was adversely affected, or even damaged beyond repair by a decision you knew to be wrong, yet were powerless to overturn or even appeal against? When the technology exists to make absolutely certain whether a batsman is out or not, to put a player's job at risk for the sake of some nebulous notion about taking the rough with the smooth is merely perverse. In the end, the principle that the batsman will always receive the benefit of the doubt will still remain intact, yet umpires will be allowed to get on with their main job of making sure the game runs smoothly without the intolerable pressure of being proved wrong by the cameras.

From television to motion pictures, the nearest I came to shining on the silver screen was during that ridiculous trip to Hollywood with Tim Hudson in the mid-1980s, but over the years Shredded Wheat, Heinz baked beans and Minties mints are just some of the products which I have advertised on your TV screens.

I have been on stage, of course, both in panto and on the speaking tours I've done over the years with Viv Richards, Allan Lamb, Jeremy Atkinson and David English, the creator of *Bunbury Tales*.

English, or 'Loon' as I call him, is a complete psycho and over the years he has played a big part in cheering me up whenever I have needed it. He was not a bad club cricketer, but as an actor he made a pretty good dustman. The first time I saw him was on TV when he starred in a bizarre advert for Head and Shoulders shampoo. The film showed him walking off the cricket pitch at the end of play, removing his cap and shaking out a snowstorm. That was before he started using Head and Shoulders, of course.

He claims his film credits include a role in Sir Richard Attenborough's war-time epic *A Bridge Too Far* in which he played a dead German soldier. I didn't actually notice his name alongside those of Olivier, Caine, Redford and Peck but he insists he did actually say something. It was probably 'Achtung! I've been shot'.

I first came into contact with Loon around the time I gave up the England captaincy in 1981. The night before I was due to visit a Saab showroom in London to do some promotional work I had been out drinking with him. I didn't know it then, but he does not have a great capacity for drink. It wasn't long before I found out, however.

We arranged to meet in the Saab showroom at 10

o'clock the following morning from where we were due to travel later to the Motor Show. Loon arrived early, somewhat the worse for wear. The salesman told him that I would be along shortly and suggested showing him some of the top models like the GLS and the Turbo. Loon sat in the car with this salesman who was giving him the whole spiel about electric windows and reclining seats when, suddenly, he leapt out of the car, bent over and threw up all over the shiny new bonnet. It was at this very moment that Kath and I walked in. I took one look at him and said, 'Say nothing. Do nothing. I'll look after you'.

So we all piled into a taxi to go to the Motor Show. In an attempt to get Loon back in gear I said, 'Tell us the one about the submarine, the one you told me last night'. It was a bad mistake. The moment he opened his mouth to try and tell the joke he was sick again all over the floor of the cab.

That night Loon appeared in the theatre at Cheltenham and the following morning his landlady woke him up to say, 'There's a man here to see you'. He walked down the stairs to be met by a man from Saab. I had organized a test drive for him. The problem was that Loon's idea of a test drive was to test the car for two years. At the end of that period he received a letter from Ian Williamson, the managing director of the Saab main dealer involved.

Dear Dave English
The sky is blue, rivers are deep, we like you, can we have our f---ing car back?
Ian Williamson, Managing Director

That wasn't my only dealing with Saab. A year later when I went racing at Thruxton for them, I managed to write off two of their machines in the same day at a cost of around £24,000. I had fancied giving it a real blast; here was a chance to pin back my ears and go as fast as I could. I went out there with a rally driver who talked me through the course and all was going well until we approached what looked like a reasonably comfortable corner. At the apex there was a hump but the technique for getting round was simple, or so I thought. What I was supposed to do was put my foot down and just drive through it. We had built our speed up nicely, I did as I had been told and came through the corner flat out. The problem was that once we were past the hump I overcompensated, with the result that we slid on to the grass and through the barrier of bales and straw, totally out of control.

It was amazing that no one was hurt because the impact shunted the chassis to such an extent that the car was wrecked. The only damage (at least to myself) had been to my pride and I was determined to get back out there as soon as possible. Within an hour, Saab had fitted me up with another car and this time we put in three or four good laps, and managed to clock up some impressive times.

On the fifth circuit I felt I had the speed just right, around 110 mph, when the wheels slid and caught the drainage ditch on the far side of the same corner. The car slipped up in the air, the nearside wheels snapped off and we found ourselves rolling down the hill. The car went over four or five times and it felt like being on the inside of a spin-dryer. I was dead lucky again to walk off unscathed although my co-driver Mike Bennion cut his head on the driver's mirror. As for the car, this time there was no doubt whatsoever that it was a complete write-off. Apart from the missing wheels, the bonnet, boot and roof had caved in. The only things that worked were the doors. At least I proved that Saab's cars did the job when it came to safety. I showed the world that you can crash Saabs at over 100 mph and still walk away smiling! Saab were not slow at spotting the opportunity and proceeded to tour the car around for the next six months letting people know just that.

Loon and I got into various other scrapes together over the years, particularly on the speaking tours, where he did a great job as compère. The seeds for these talk shows were sown during my benefit year at Somerset in 1984, when Loon had appeared in a few of my celebrity matches. He had contacts in the music business and his 'Bunbury' cricket XI, who play matches for charity all over the country, has included stars like Roger Daltry, Bill Wyman, Eric Clapton and many others with whom I have shared many good times.

The idea came to fruition when I was having my spell with Queensland in 1988. With a few spare days in the middle of the itinerary, I accepted an invitation to talk in the small town of Bury, South Australia. We ended up making the journey in a small light aircraft but had neglected to find out if anyone actually knew the way. Somehow, we managed to persuade the pilot to let me take the controls and I decided to fly low enough so that we could read the road signs as we went along. Loon gave a little preamble then I did my bit, taking questions from the floor, telling a few stories and then signing a few autographs. We decided there and then to repeat the exercise in England.

The tour was set up but this time we approached it rather more professionally. We got hold of a promoter called Nick Leigh at Kennedy Street Enterprises and made a 35-minute film featuring various cricketing highlights to start the whole thing off. By now I was with Worcestershire, and we opened in Stourbridge. Loon did his introductions, the film ran and then it was down to the questions and answers. Loon pulled the first question out of the box at random and, before he could stop himself, read it out in full to an audience that happened to include Kath. It said: 'My name is Kate. I live just above the chip shop in the High Street. Is it true you are hung like a rhino?'

Of course, from time to time we have had problems with hecklers but they are easily dealt with and I have a stock of answers with which to take the sting out of most situations. We have now done over 150 shows around the world; we are constantly on the move otherwise it can get a bit stale. Viv and I had a marvellous relationship, of course, but being in each other's company without a break can obviously cause a bit of friction and the Loon has been great in defusing those situations.

He was also responsible for me making my recording debut with Eric Clapton.

Eric had been fishing with me on a couple of occasions as well as playing in the Bunbury XI but his cricket career came to an end when he suffered a couple of career-threatening knocks at a charity match in Buckinghamshire in which his manager, Roger Forrester, was also playing. The batsman slashed at the first ball which whistled off the outside edge straight towards Eric in the gully. He stuck a hand out and the ball smacked into it, leaving the world's greatest rock guitarist with a dislocated finger. Roger went various shades of puce before telling his man to leave the pitch, but as Eric walked off, wringing his sore hand, a bee landed on the other one and stung him. That left Eric sitting on the pavilion balcony with both hands immersed in buckets of ice just a few days before flying out on a lucrative tour to Japan.

As a result of the friendship that had grown over the years I was invited to do some Telly Savalas style talkovers when Eric headed a roll call of rock stars who were recording a track for the Bunburys called 'Fight'.

I got on well with Eric as I have done with a number of rock stars. In a way our lives are similar, we are both on a big stage where everyone is looking at you and we both find privacy, at times, hard to come by. Eric was a regular visitor to Worcester and one memorable day in particular he issued the following challenge: 'Score a hundred and I'll play in the pub tonight'. He had already cleaned out the dressing room poker school and was on a bit of a winning streak. I kept my side of the deal, cracking 125 in a Sunday league match against Essex and Eric disappeared into Worcester to find an amplifier. He managed to come across a music shop that was open, picked a suitable amplifier and handed the assistant his credit-card but the man behind the counter thought he was having his leg pulled. It took several calls to the credit card company before Eric could walk out with the goods.

What followed was a brilliant night. Deep in the Worcestershire countryside we descended on this pub. When we arrived people were sitting around sipping pints or playing dominoes and darts while a dog was yawning by the fireplace. Suddenly, in walked the world's greatest guitarist asking the landlord if he could plug in his amp and play a few songs. The players from both teams had been alerted and we all turned up to hear Eric play for about two hours. Later, as word spread, we were joined by the bride, groom and most of the guests at their wedding reception taking place up the road. At the end of that evening I gave Eric the bat I had used on the 1986/87 tour to Australia and he presented me with a Fender Stratocaster inscribed with the words: 'To brother Beefy'.

As a 'performing artist' I have seldom had to confront the huge crowds that Eric has but the first time I appeared in panto, I felt as if the eyes of the world were on me.

I persuaded Max Boyce, who I had known for a long time, to let me appear in his show *Jack and the Beanstalk* and we did so successfully for three years. Max was hardly keen at first because, I suspect, he thought I wasn't being serious. Anyone who visited my dressing room during that first show at the Bradford Alhambra might have got a similar impression because there on my make-up table was a huge pile of condoms. I should point out that they were there for an entirely innocent purpose, however. It had become crystal clear that there was no point in me joining in the singing for the performance. But the producer was dead against me miming because he knew that would be obvious to the audience. So he hit on an ingenious idea: I would stick a couple of these condoms over the radio microphone clipped to my costume. So when the time came, I could belt out the songs without anyone realizing that they were actually hearing the rest of the cast, bar me. Although the reviews were not exactly ecstatic – one critic said 'The only thing more wooden than the beanstalk was Ian Botham' – the kids loved it. We moved on to

Bournemouth the next year, then on to Stockport in 1992 at which point I decided it was time to strike out on my own.

The following year I appeared with Robin Askwith, my long-time friend, in *Dick Whittington* at the Theatre Royal, Bath with among others, June Brown, the actress who played Dot Cotton in *EastEnders*.

Performing in these shows has been one of the most satisfying things I have ever done professionally, and also one of the most stimulating. But probably the most dramatic of all my exploits has taken place up in the sky.

I first dabbled with flying back in 1981 when I called in at the Bristol and Wessex Club for lessons. In the back of my mind, I harboured the idea of doing a round-the-world trip for charity. It was more than just fanciful dreaming and enough of a genuine prospect for my agent at the time, Reg Hayter, to find an experienced pilot to help do some groundwork on the scheme. As a result I was introduced to Alan Dyer, a pilot who had done the trip before. A great friendship developed and Alan now is godfather to Becky, my youngest daughter.

My appetite for the high life had also been whetted by an invitation from John Blackwell to go flying with the Red Arrows. John was the leader of the team at the time and it was an offer I just could not refuse. I went up to RAF Kemble, the team's base, where there was a practice session to see whether I was up to the strains of a flat-out run. I donned the G-force suit and up we went. It was an amazing experience – and this was only the warm up. But when we landed I felt less than well; in fact I turned green and it was only then that we found out my suit had not been functioning properly. As usual, I was determined to carry on and, fitted out properly in a new suit, enjoyed the most exhilarating experiences of my life.

I got on well with the lads, so well in fact that when I had my benefit in 1984, the Red Arrows paid me an extraordinary tribute. At the close of play at the end of a game at Taunton in mid-summer we were all in the bar having a drink when I told the players I had to go out on the pitch because the Red Arrows were going to fly by and give me a salute. There were a number of cynical snorts from the doubting Thomases, but I wandered out anyway to the middle of the square and stood looking up at the sky. This behaviour prompted a few disbelieving looks but, right on time, the planes suddenly appeared in formation on the horizon and they roared in, sweeping low over the ground and caused a few spilled pints in the bar. It was a great gesture and meant a lot to me. I later found out that the team were given a ticking off for their slight detour; in fact the Ministry of Defence went berserk.

Alan Dyer meanwhile was drawing up plans for the round-the-world trip, a journey he had made and just survived in 1974. We met to discuss the project at the Westmoreland Hotel near Lord's in March 1982. AD came into the bar and laid out a huge map of the Pacific Ocean. I noticed to my consternation that there was an awful lot of blue sea. He then explained that the hard part was navigation. It's just possible he was trying to put me off the trip. He failed and I think it would have been a fabulous adventure. Sadly it came to nought because of time commitments, but that was not the end of my flying partnership with Alan Dyer. Together we took part in the King's Cup Air Race at Finningly in Yorkshire in 1982. My job was to keep an eye out for other planes!

A few years later we made our way together to the Paris Air Show, although how we got back I'll never know. Alan had some business out there and I fancied going, not just for the air show but because the Rolling Stones were recording in a studio in Paris. I had met Mick Jagger, a cricket enthusiast, a few times and there was an invite to drop in and listen to the band at work. We took off from Elstree in north London and flew out across the Channel. As we approached the French coast Alan asked if I fancied some low-flying. It seemed a good idea and Alan asked me to look out for pylons. The plane was whizzing along at about 200 mph over these villages and farms and I was sitting in the co-pilot seat staring up at the wide blue yonder.

'What the bloody hell are you doing?' yelled Alan.

'I'm keeping an eye out for pilots,' I replied.

'I said pylons, not pilots!'

It was a great weekend. Alan was overwhelmed by the welcome we received from Jagger and really enjoyed watching the world's greatest rock band at work. His pleasure was somewhat heightened when he helped himself to the Stones' obligatory case of Jack Daniels and when we wandered out at 5.30 a.m. he was a little unsteady on his pins. In fact, he rated the experience of the next morning as one of the six great hangovers of his life. Despite the necessary eight hours sleep and several gallons of black coffee, he was still a little peeky when, as we were waiting to take off for home, a group of businessmen strolled across for a chat and an autograph. One of them asked how I was getting back to England. I pointed out the plane to them and he nodded his approval. Then he asked me who was flying. I pointed to Alan and he nearly fainted.

I wouldn't want you all to think I'm going soft in my

old age but one of my great passions now is golf. I sometimes wonder what might have happened if someone had come along and put a seven iron in my hand when I was a youngster. The way I feel about the game now it is quite possible that I might have changed course completely and spent my time on the golf courses rather than the cricket pitches of the world. I've always been able to hit the ball a long way off the tee, as I proved during a game with Allan Border at The Belfry when we were playing against the Australians in the summer of 1985. I was having a wretched round, so by the time we got to the tenth hole I just thought: 'What the hell, I'll go for it'. It is quite a tricky hole, a slight dog-leg to the right over water with trees guarding the green. It is 301 yards to the pin and, until that point, only two other golfers had managed to drive the green – Greg Norman and Seve Ballesteros. When I announced I intended to be the third Allan freaked out. We were playing against Greg Ritchie and Craig McDermott and the game was evenly poised despite my poor display. I said, 'All right. You go first and just lay up'. Which he did. 'But I'm still going for it,' I said. I proceeded to unleash a drive that just happened to fade at the right time and ended up on the putting surface. Not a lot of people know that the real story was just about to start. I managed to three-putt while Allan got up and down in two more for a birdie. He won the hole but the commemorative plaque by the side of the tee bears my name, not his.

I have enjoyed all these off-field activities for the sheer fun of them but the most humbling experiences I have had away from the cricket field have been when coming into contact with the huge variety of wildlife it has been my privilege to have seen all over the world.

I'm not too keen on snakes, sharks and crocodiles but, otherwise, put me in the great outdoors and I have a great time. On safari in Africa with Kath in the autumn of 1993 we experienced sights and sounds that I will take with me to the grave. True to form, I even managed to get charged by a cow elephant, a lioness and a crocodile all on the same day.

The cow elephant had just given birth and took exception to us being so near to her offspring. She responded according to her nature and chased after us. After making a huge detour to get out of her way we reached a river where we came across the tracks of two lionesses. As we rounded a bend in the river, we suddenly came face to face with one of them who charged straight for us, stopping only some 40 yards away. Unfortunately, two middle-aged Germans who were travelling with us panicked, which is just about the worst thing you can do, and the lioness started her charge again. This time she got to within ten feet before finally backing away. The game warden I was with later told me that if she had come any closer, he would have had to pull the trigger.

From there, we went to a commercial crocodile farm where we met a man doing some environmental research. He said he was going into one of the pens to take a closer look at some eggs and asked me if I wanted to join him. There were two of these researchers studying the eggs and another three standing guard at the edge of the pond, armed with sticks. Suddenly this crocodile sprang out of the water and there I was, gone. I had cleared the wall of the pen by about three feet. Colin Jackson wouldn't have got anywhere near me.

So life away from cricket has been rich and varied and

I've enjoyed every minute of it. It sounds like a cliché and, of course, in some ways it is but I have always been a man of action first and foremost. I fully sympathize with the mountain climbers, round-the-world yachtsmen, cave divers or dangerous sportsmen of the world. My attitude is very much the same as theirs – if it is there to do, then I do it.

Bearing in mind my upbringing and the character and personality of my Mum and Dad, there was never any danger of me becoming a librarian. That's not to say that I consider myself to be thick, although many observers clearly think I am. The point is, I really do believe that I am one of those who has simply been blessed with the ability to turn my hand to anything I chose. And I chose to try and learn about life by doing it rather than reading about it. It has been one hell of an education and, God willing, there's an awful lot more to go.

I suppose what it all comes down to is an inquisitive nature. The thing that has made me want to try and squeeze the last drop of experience out of every situation is the desire to discover just what kind of man I am and what I am capable of. That's what my life has all been about and nothing will alter me now.

19

THE WORST TEAM
IN THE WORLD

One forty-nine p.m., Sunday 22 August, 1999, The Oval.

Supporters of English cricket should mark the time, date and place and never forget. For this was the time, the date and the place that the event some of us had been dreading and predicting for so long finally came to pass.

At 1.49 p.m. on Sunday, 22 August, 1999, England's final Test of the summer series against New Zealand at The Oval came to a premature end. And in the moment a ball from Chris Cairns launched high into the murky South London sky by Leicestershire's Alan Mullally finally came to rest in the hands of Roger Twose, England were confirmed as the worst Test team in the world.

By slithering to inglorious defeat in the four-match series against the Kiwis, England replaced their opponents at the foot of *Wisden* magazine's unofficial world championship of Test cricket, while those who still sought to prove that things were not as bad as they looked by pointing out supposed deficiencies in the formulation of the table – ECB chief executive Tim Lamb called the table 'whimsical' and 'arbitrary'. Well, he would say that, wouldn't he? – those who chose instead to believe the evidence provided by their own eyes and ears knew the truth.

The unofficial conclusion arrived at by *Wisden* was, in fact, indisputable. At the end of a twelve-month period during which England had also failed to win back the Ashes for the sixth time in succession, they had achieved the status they truly deserved – rock bottom, ninth out of nine, lowest of the low, crap at Test cricket.

And that was only half of the story. For, in conceding defeat by two Tests to one after actually winning the first at Edgbaston, England completed an extraordinary lose-double. Before the Test series had even begun, as the spring of 1999 gave way to the final English summer of the Millennium, England's embarrassing elimination from the World Cup at the qualifying stage had already confirmed that we were crap at one-day cricket too.

Observing these events unfold in my capacity as commentator for Sky television and columnist for the *Mirror*, on more than one occasion I had reason to question whether I was not in the throes of some terrible nightmare from which I simply could not awake.

The fact is that had New Zealand batted anything like properly in the first Test and had the weather not intervened to help England to safety in the third at Old Trafford, the Kiwis could have won the series 4-0 and they would have deserved to do so.

Bearing in mind this was only the second time in 68 years that England lost a home series to New Zealand, and with all due respect to Stephen Fleming and his men (I thought several of them, including Cairns, Dion Nash, Daniel Vettori and the highly-underrated Matthew Horne whose hundred at Lord's was the only century of the entire series by either side, played out of their skins by the way) for England supporters, such a result would have been nothing less than a catastrophy. 2-1 was bad enough.

Apologists for England's dreadful displays will point out that Darren Gough, their main strike bowler, missed the series through injury; that Alex Tudor, the young Surrey paceman whose brilliant 99 on his home Test debut in Birmingham had done much to paper over the cracks that had already started to appear, was curiously absent thereafter; and that the new England captain Nasser Hussain was forced to miss a Test and a half after breaking his finger misfielding at Headquarters. But they should also be asking themselves why England seem to finish every series with a list of excuses that could stretch from one end of the Long Room to the other.

In any case, New Zealand were also seriously hampered by injury and ill-fortune. After the opening match in Birmingham Simon Doull and Geoff Allott, their first-choice new-ball pair, never bowled again together in the series, the left-armer Allott missing the next three Tests and Doull the last two.

Reacting to England's spineless capitulation in the second Test at Lord's, I was moved to comment that I felt ashamed to be English. Unfortunately, the feeling stayed with me for the rest of the series and by the time the white flag was finally raised at The Oval, I was in a state of utter despair.

I was not the only one. As Hussain attempted to find something positive to say to the nation in an interview with Channel Four's Dermot Reeve, he had to fight to make himself heard above the chorus of boos and jeers rising from the England supporters covering the outfield below. 'What a load of rubbish' they chanted and 'We're s***, and we know we are'. They were perfectly entitled to their opinion and perfectly entitled to express it. They had been short-changed once too often. The sounds and sights must have been ghastly for Hussain to experience. No wonder there were tears in his eyes.

Later, he tried to back his players, publicly at least, claiming: 'I'm very proud of the way my team fought. If they play like that in the future they won't go far wrong. All the things that I've asked for, all the things the public have asked for, about body language and attitude and determination were there. Every time I asked them to come back at the New Zealanders they did.' And from the perspective of loyalty, he was right to do so.

But since the fight Hussain described manifested itself in yet another batting collapse costing England their last eight wickets for 39 runs in 77 minutes, it was hardly surprising that, for his trouble, the skipper was described in more than one paper as Nasser Insane.

Inevitably and understandably, mirroring the mood of the public the media piled in. The front cover of the *Sun*, for instance, was devoted entirely to their version of the New Ashes. While the centre of the page was taken up by a photograph of burning bails on top of a set of stumps, the words surrounding it read 'Official: The death of our national game. English Cricket 1744-1999. In affectionate remembrance of English cricket which died at The Oval, 22nd August, 1999. Deeply lamented by a large circle of sorrowing friends and acquaintances, R.I.P.. N.B. The body will be cremated and the Ashes taken to New Zealand.'

In the news pages of various papers some players were castigated for drowning their sorrows in a pub.

Although the tone of much of the tabloid coverage was mickey-taking it was hard to argue with the sentiments behind it and the sense of shock and bewilderment that our national team had been allowed to slip into the gutter of world cricket. According to *The Guardian*: 'There can be no more hiding, no more prevaricating, no more refusal to accept the truth. England are now confirmed as the worst Test side in the world. Only if despair spreads far and wide might any lasting recovery begin.'

More than anything else, the mood was one of incredulity. The questions were: How on earth had this happened? and How on earth had this been allowed to happen? And pretty soon everyone was coming up with their own answers.

In the short term, clearly a large amount of blame must be placed at the door of the England players themselves. Some of those I watched all summer lurching from one crisis to another put in gutless, brainless and purposeless performances. Looking at them closely I watched a group of cricketers gradually lose the will to compete. As the series developed and they realised they had a real fight on their hands, they seemed scared of failure, dwarfed by pressure and simply unable to cope with the competitive aggression of their highly-motivated opponents. I've seen braver characters caught in car headlights than some of the players masquerading as England cricketers and it made my blood boil.

In many respects you could forgive them if, on that final fateful day, their heads were spinning. At the end of a summer filled with plot changes so bewildering that the scriptwriters of *Eastenders* would have dismissed them as too far-fetched, I know how they felt.

In fact, as a snapshot of the kind of muddled thinking and acting among management and administrators that had done so much to cripple England efforts over the past decade, the year that followed their first victory in a five-Test series for twelve years, their 2-1 win over South Africa in August 1998, could hardly be bettered.

In the next twelve months not only did England lose series to Sri Lanka, Australia and New Zealand and suffer elimination from a World Cup on home soil that should have been their chance to grip the attention of the sporting public, they also lost their coach David Lloyd, who resigned prior to the competition after the ECB made it clear they would not re-employ him when his contract expired at the end of the summer; captain Alec Stewart, the man who had led them to victory over South Africa was sacked at the end of the World Cup and replaced by Hussain and two selectors, Graham Gooch and Mike Gatting, who were both subsequently shown the door prior to the final Test at The Oval against the Kiwis. In terms of selection policy and management almost everyone concerned with running the England team seemed to completely lose the plot.

Whatever the official explanation for Stewart's dismissal – and I don't recall ever hearing one given – I suspect the real reasons will never be publicly admitted. Near the end of a long and exhausting schedule in Australia, Alec had allowed himself to get involved in the unseemly events at Adelaide that completely dominated what should have been a routine one-day match in the Tri-nation series between England and Sri Lanka. In fact, I suspect his removal following the World Cup can be traced back to that fatal day.

For the ill-feeling that boiled over into blatant on-field animosity, I place most of the responsibility squarely on the shoulders of the Australian umpire Ross Emerson. As far as I could tell he got almost every major decision wrong that day, and quite what point he was trying to prove by no-balling Sri Lankan off-spinner Muttiah Muralitharan for chucking after an ICC panel of experts had officially cleared his action is beyond me.

In any case, having lit the blue touch-paper he proceeded to blow on it with a series of terrible judgements so that, by the climax of the match, both teams were filled with and fuelled by strong feelings of injustice. When Gough was barged out of his stride by Roshan Mahanama in the action of attempting to run him out, Emerson wrongly turned down England's appeals for obstructing the field and Gough and Stewart, briefly, lost it. Gough feigned a head-butt on Mahanama, then as the players crossed to begin the next over, Stewart quite clearly barged him.

Let me say here and now that Stewart should not have acted as he did. Mahanama was obviously out of order, should have been given out and should have been charged with bringing the game into disrepute, but so should Stewart have been. There is no place on the cricket field for actions like his or Gough's. Stewart himself described his actions as a brush of shoulders. It wasn't. It was a shove and to me the next thing that comes after a shove is a push, then a punch, then, on the cricket field at least, anarchy. No matter how wronged Stewart himself felt by what had happened, if players cannot keep their emotions in check in high-pressure situations they deserve everything that comes their way.

But Stewart's superiors compounded the felony by doing precisely nothing in response. Instead of leaving the match referee to sort out the whole unholy mess, the ECB officials concerned should have stepped in straight away and taken matters into their own hands, either by fining the players involved or at the very least instructing Stewart and Gough to make a formal apology. The man on the ground was chairman of selectors David Graveney, present in his capacity as manager of the one-day squad. He should have acted immediately and strongly. Had he done so the situation would have been quickly resolved. Because he didn't he allowed clouds of uncertainty and dissent to brew up over Stewart's head. What were the ECB afraid of? Why didn't they act? Surely the reason could not have been that Alec had recently been awarded the MBE and taking action against him would have caused them too much embarrassment.

When Stewart then allowed himself to be presented as the players' negotiator in the pay dispute with the ECB over World Cup fees that even Graveney admitted was a distraction to their warm-up preparations in Sharjah, the cloud over the captain's head darkened and filled up. With only weeks to go before the World Cup warm-up matches against the counties, it was by now too late to junk Stewart even if certain Board members had wanted to. But as soon as India brought England's World Cup to an end at Edgbaston, Stewart was dumped.

To me what happened to Stewart was an uncomfortable reminder of how the TCCB got rid of Mike Gatting as captain more than a decade before. The event for which they eventually nailed Gatt was his supposed misdemeanour with a barmaid during England's first Test against West

Indies in June 1988, but no one was in any doubt that the real reason he lost the job was his stand-up row with Pakistan umpire Shakoor Rana back in December 1987, six months before.

The saga featuring the next major casualty, the coach David Lloyd, was just as convoluted.

After having replaced Ray Illingworth at the end of England's disastrous 1996 World Cup campaign, the Lancastrian super-enthusiast developed an unfortunate knack of rubbing some people up the wrong way.

His infamous 'we murdered 'em' outburst in Bulawayo after England had drawn Zimbabwe to death in their first ever meeting at Test level earned him an early rebuke from ECB officials. And although they made sure he was taken out of the media firing line by appointing Gooch as tour manager for the 1998-99 Ashes series, when Lloyd began asking them what the future held, the silences began to get longer and more deafening. When he pushed them for a final answer just before the World Cup began, they said thanks but no thanks.

What happened next was a joke.

The Board should have taken all necessary steps to replace Lloyd with a new coach immediately, at the latest in time for the start of the summer series against New Zealand. Instead they announced that they weren't going to bother; that chairman of selectors David Graveney would manage the side, joined eventually by new captain Hussain, and that with specialist coaches Gooch and Bob Cottam around they were more than adequately covered. 'After all, it is only New Zealand', you could almost hear them saying. How they paid for their arrogance and incompetence.

Most people believed that the ECB adopted this stance to cover for the fact that their preferred choice, the former England Test player and current South African coach Bob Woolmer would not be available until the end of the season at the very earliest. Woolmer, they reasoned, would be well worth the wait. But once it became clear that Woolmer was not going to be available at all on their terms, they simply had to move to appoint immediately the next on their list, Duncan Fletcher, the Zimbabwean coach of Glamorgan.

They didn't and the resulting farce did much to damage England's summer campaigns. The Board did announce that Fletcher was indeed to take on the job. But in the same breath they admitted that he would not be doing so until October, the best part of two months after the series against New Zealand was history. Work that one out.

Would Glamorgan have released Fletcher to begin work straightaway? Did anyone ask them? Or, after having had to pay Lloyd to the end of his contract (August 1999) were the ECB, cash-strapped after revenues for the World Cup had failed to meet projections, so concerned with saving money that they baulked at the idea of having to pay Glamorgan compensation for losing Fletcher as well ?

Thus, instead of starting afresh with Hussain and Fletcher, allowed to give free rein to their new ideas, England bumbled on with the mish-mash of old and new and the selectors, Graveney, Gooch and Gatting plus Hussain, seemingly unsure whether to start the process of rebuilding by investing in youth or whether to get the series against New Zealand over with before beginning any long-term planning they might not be given the chance to continue themselves. The results were inevitable.

At first England got lucky, thanks to Tudor. By selecting a new wicket-keeper Chris Read and a new front-line batsman Aftab Habib and by giving Tudor his head, they showed their intention to take risks. By bringing back Andy Caddick and Phil Tufnell after both had been ludicrously omitted from the Ashes tour party they also showed they were not afraid of admitting past mistakes. But the fact was that until New Zealand threw away their advantage with their second innings batting and then nightwatchman Tudor intervened with his wonderfully improbable 99 not out to win the match, the Kiwis appeared the more likely winners.

After that, slowly but surely things just fell apart. True, England were not helped when Hussain injured himself at Lord's, but when the selectors reacted to that and to their dismal defeat by appointing Mark Butcher as stand-in captain and recalling Graeme Hick and Peter Such out of nowhere, the lacklustre performance in Manchester persuaded certain influential figures that the time had come for action.

In a former life Brian Bolus had been one of Ray Illingworth's England selectors. Notable chiefly for his utter conviction that everything his chairman said was undeniably correct and anything the young captain Michael Atherton dared to suggest was utter poppycock, Bolus had been busy during his years out of the spotlight.

By the autumn of 1998 he had somehow managed to manoeuvre himself into the position of chairman of the England Management Advisory Committee. Some of the smaller and less influential counties, scared at the rate of progress desired and demanded by ECB chairman Lord MacLaurin, saw Bolus as the man to put across their point of view in the corridors of power. And many saw his fingerprints on the implements that removed Lloyd and Stewart from the England scene.

Now, as far as Gooch and Gatting were concerned, it was Mr. Bolus with the dagger in the dining room. At a meeting over dinner at the England hotel in Worsley, attended by Hussain, Fletcher, Graveney, ECB chairman Lord MacLaurin and the International Teams Director Simon Pack, ridiculously described by MacLaurin as 'just a drink among friends', Bolus pushed for the removal of Gatting and Gooch and won the day. I am sure they were as puzzled as many observers when, in the spring of 2000, Hick was one of twelve players offered central contracts by the ECB.

Graham Thorpe announced halfway through the final Test at The Oval that he, for one, would rather stay home with the wife and kids than spend the winter touring with England in South Africa. After all the goings-on of the previous year, a fittingly fun-filled end to a decade of confusion and despair, who could blame him?

But, quite apart from all the off-field nonsense affecting England's performance against New Zealand, the bottom line was that in that final home Test of the century against a team unofficially rated as the weakest in the world, when England cricketers were called upon to dig down to the depths of themselves to show the kind of commitment their leaders and their supporters had every right to demand as the very minimum contribution, once again too many were found wanting. In fact too many were nowhere to be found at all.

And no one who monitored the fortunes of English cricket during the 1990s should have been the slightest bit surprised. As some of us went blue in the face trying to point out, the complacency, self-interest and indolence of some of the men running English cricket in the past decade meant that such an outcome was merely a matter of time.

For the plain fact is that the players representing England on the day they completed their journey to the bottom of the earth: Nasser Hussain (Essex), Mike Atherton (Lancashire), Darren Maddy (Leicestershire), Graham Thorpe (Surrey), Alec Stewart (Surrey), Mark Ramprakash (Middlesex), Ronnie Irani (Essex), Andrew Caddick (Somerset), Alan Mullally (Leicestershire), Phil Tufnell (Middlesex) and Ed Giddins (Warwickshire) were merely the end product of the flawed process known as English domestic cricket.

And if you want to know why goods are faulty, you have to examine first the machinery that made them.

Of course, you could look back over the decade that ended with England in their lowest ever position and apportion blame to certain individuals over selection and management. I did.

I blamed 'Screaming Lord' Ted Dexter for being totally out of touch, Micky Stewart and Graham Gooch for being too regimented in their thinking, Keith Fletcher for his tendency to be too negative and Raymond Illingworth for tearing up the one credible selection policy England tried to adopt in ten years, that of allowing Mike Atherton to bring together and develop a young side, and for then spending most of his tenure attempting to prove to his captain who was boss.

And I stand by all of those criticisms, most particularly concerning Illingworth.

When Illy was given the job of supremo in charge of the

FRIENDS

FRIENDS IN HIGH PLACES ... Jeff Lynne, George Harrison, Eric Clapton and Elton John join me and the Worcestershire kit man, Jack Turner, on the players' balcony at New Road.

BEST OF MATES ... on the beach with Viv.

TAKING A BREAK ... David Gower and I (below left) relaxing before a boat trip round St Vincent in 1986 while the rest of the lads were busy being bowled out for 94 by the Windward Islands. The fishing trip with Allan Lamb (below) ended pretty successfully.

FAMILY

TYING THE KNOT ... Kath and I cut the cake on that famous day, 31 January 1976.

HOME ALONE ... but not quite as the family help me cut the cake to mark my 35th birthday (above) and Kath visits me in hospital (right) after a shoulder operation in 1993.

I'VE GOT YOU BABE ... *even Kath isn't spared a dunking when I'm around.*

THE TRIBE ... *I'm holding Becky alongside Sarah, Liam and Kath for this family portrait (right). Liam is following in my footsteps and joins me in an autograph signing session at Hove (below) after a charity match.*

ON STAGE AND SCREEN

STAGE FRIGHT ... in panto as the king in 'Jack and the Beanstalk' (right) and being handed the famous Red Book by Eamonn Andrews (below) on 'This Is Your Life', under the watchful eye of Sir Garfield Sobers.

SPARRING PARTNERS ... with David Coleman and Bill Beaumont on the 'Question of Sport' show. It's just worrying Bill knows more about cricket than I do!

HAPPINESS IS ... a cigar called Hamlet. It would probably be something else if the tabloids had their way.

selection and running of the Test side, I applauded the decision. The principle of having one man at the top must be correct because it removes any doubt over who is responsible for England's performances. This way everyone knows exactly who to point the finger at if things go wrong, and who to pat on the back if things go right. The principle is one thing. Whether Illingworth was the right man for the job is another matter entirely. In my opinion the answer is – absolutely not.

Illingworth might have been a fine player and, according to many judges, he was one of the shrewdest cricket thinkers of his time. The problem is that his time is long gone. Ten or fifteen years previously Illingworth might well have been the right man. But we were talking about 1995, not 1975.

In my view Illingworth was totally out of touch with the modern game and unsympathetic as to what the players of the modern era have to deal with on and off the field. Here was a man aged 61 whose only contact with players under 50 years old was from his seat in the press box or the television commentary position, where he had managed to spend the best part of the previous ten years contradicting himself by criticizing their efforts one minute, then praising them the next.

If those players were confused over some of the things he said who could blame them? Shortly after he was appointed I was quoted in an article in the *News of the World* which highlighted examples of Illy's ability to talk in circles in his newspaper columns for the *Daily Express*. In the middle of the 1992 series against Pakistan, for instance, he announced, 'Graeme Hick should bat at number 7'. Eleven days later, on the other hand, he insisted

'Forget all this pussyfooting, dropping Hick down to number 7. Hick is scoring for his county at number 3 and that is where I would play him for England'.

Just look at what he said about Mike Gatting during the summer of 1993. First, after the second Test against Australia at Lord's he said, 'Mike Gatting must be ditched immediately'. Then, a month later he did a complete about-turn . . . in the space of two days! After Gooch had stepped down as England's leader, Illy announced, 'It's time to rebuild with a new young captain'. Forty-eight hours later he said: 'Mike Gatting wants the job. I think he should get it. It is vital we have an experienced captain'.

I wonder what the players who gave their all on the 1994 West Indies tour, bouncing back from being 3–0 down by winning the Barbados Test then drawing in Antigua, thought when they read what Illingworth had to say in *The Cricketer* magazine about their efforts? In a questionnaire Illy was asked which current players he admired.

His answer was summed up in one word: 'None'.

When Illy met the manager Keith Fletcher at Lord's to open discussions over the new selection process he had to spend the first couple of minutes apologizing for the way some of his comments had been misinterpreted by the press. His early dealings with the new captain Mike Atherton did not fill me with confidence either. As skipper 'Athers' was his own man: he knew what he wanted, and the type of player he needed. The first thing Illy did when England returned from the West Indies was announce at a press conference that most of Atherton's selections for that trip were not up to the task and that *he* was in overall charge of selection from now on, and not the captain.

Next, up cropped two of his old mates, Fred Titmus and Brian Bolus, as co-selectors. Just think, you could put together the combined ages of the England cricket selectors and come up with a figure not far from the number of runs Brian Lara scored in Antigua.

Why was it the case in cricket that, until recently, you had to be pushing sixty before you were even considered for a position of power and authority in the game?

What did the 'Sanatogen Set' really know about players forty years younger than them? How could they understand what made them tick, what motivated them, and what they were physically, mentally and temperamentally capable of? What possible common ground could there have been?

There were plenty of people around who I would have backed to do the job of chairman of selectors ahead of Illy because their experience of the current players is far more up to date. I would have given the job to my old sparring partner Bob Willis but, unfortunately, Bob was never in the running because he had not yet qualified for his bus pass.

Let me refer to some of the selections and policy decisions for which Illingworth was responsible after initially taking over the job of chairman of selectors in April 1994.

Employing five specialist batsmen and picking an all-rounder at number six to increase your bowling options may be an attractive idea. But if you don't have the personnel to put the theory into practice at Test level, it's nothing more than fantasy cricket. Illingworth thought Yorkshire's Craig White was the answer. I was not alone in thinking that anyone who based that judgement on the evidence of 120 overs of seam bowling in White's entire first-class career was being somewhat optimistic. I have nothing against White and I think he has the potential to become a very exciting cricketer, but his selection for the tour to Australia did strike me as somewhat bizarre bearing in mind the fact that he missed more than half of the 1994 season through injury.

Indeed, it was not until the second Test of the 1995 series against West Indies at Lord's that Dominic Cork, the one all-rounder most good judges believed might be capable of reproducing his county form at the highest level, was belatedly given his chance to prove it. His matchwinning analysis of seven for 43 were the best figures produced by a bowler in his first match for England and suggested what they might have been missing while Illingworth insisted on persevering with White.

And what about some other selection decisions? After the improvement Graham Thorpe achieved against the West Indies during the winter tour of 1994, he would not have been the only one scratching his head over his absence from the side until the fifth Test of the following summer. And just how Paul Taylor, the Northamptonshire left-armer, was preferred to Devon Malcolm for the second Test of the series against New Zealand at Lord's remains a mystery.

Then, of course, we had the case of Angus Fraser. Everyone is now fully aware that it was Illingworth's finger on the trigger of the gun that blew the Middlesex paceman out of the winter tour party. However, not many appreciated the extent to which I believe he managed to undermine Fraser's confidence from the word go. The process started even before Fraser returned from the West Indies, when Illingworth exhibited the first symptoms of the foot-in-mouth disease that has afflicted him ever since he took the job. Fraser was only one of several England players subjected to Illingworth's criticisms from the other side of the Atlantic, but this tireless trier, whose eight for 75 in the fourth Test in Barbados helped set up England's first win against the West Indies at the Kensington Oval for 59 years, took these less-than-flattering comments to heart. Just when he should have been congratulated for his efforts in breathing some life into the England corpse after Trinidad, the message he received instead was that, as far as the new chairman was concerned, his place was on the line.

When Fraser did not immediately fill his boots with Kiwi wickets, what he needed was the psychological boost of knowing that his talent and ability would be backed all the way. What he heard instead were suggestions from Illingworth, in public as well as in private, that Fraser needed to find something extra. 'We've got to get Gus to swing the ball,' was Illy's considered opinion and his two co-selectors Bolus and Titmus, not exactly renowned for their violent disagreements with the chairman, nodded sagely in response.

No wonder Fraser struggled that season. Instead of concentrating on the kind of bowling that had brought him success, and with which he had fought back from injuries that would have broken the spirit of a lesser player, he was tying himself up in knots in an attempt to satisfy Illingworth's requirements.

At that time Angus Fraser was one of the best seam bowlers in the country. He put pressure on batsmen by keeping things tight and he's done it all over the world. So why try and change him? If Illy wanted a swing bowler why didn't he pick a swing bowler, instead of undermining a seam bowler's confidence by attempting to convert him into something he isn't? Barmy, if you ask me.

As if leaving Fraser out of the squad to tour Australia last winter in favour of Martin McCague was not bad enough, the events of the 72 hours immediately following the announcement of the party defied belief.

First an article appeared in the *News of the World* in which the Middlesex paceman revealed that he had only found out about his surprise omission when he saw Illingworth announce the squad on television. He also suggested that he might have been entitled to a phone call from someone to let him know in person.

In itself the piece was fairly harmless. The problem was that the headline over the article read 'YOU'RE GUTLESS'. Nowhere in the article is Fraser quoted as describing Illingworth, Mike Atherton or any of the selectors as such, yet Illingworth was so incensed by this that not only did he insist that Fraser be fined £2,000 but that he should also be removed from the list of players put on stand-by in case of injuries. How petty can you get?

Even if Fraser had said what Illingworth thought he had, the chairman should have been big enough to let it pass. Instead he let his pride affect his judgement and never even bothered to check the full facts of the case.

Furthermore the selection of Kent's Martin McCague ahead of Fraser underlined the extent to which Illingworth had lost touch with the modern game. According to Illingworth's master plan, McCague's extra pace would prove hugely effective on the hard, fast and bouncy pitches Down Under. Nice theory. But for the best part of the last twenty years Australian pitches have been about as hard, fast and bouncy as treacle pudding. Moreover, it was common knowledge that McCague was injury prone. So much so that no one batted an eyelid when, after bowling poorly in the first innings of the first Test in Brisbane he broke down and had to be sent home.

Fraser was eventually brought into the action after Martin McCague had disappeared and proceeded to show what a mistake his initial omission had been when he very nearly won the Sydney Test match for England. Even after that, Illingworth still managed to leave him out of the first Test against the West Indies at Headingley in the summer of 1995 . . . with disastrous results. Fraser underlined the folly of that decision with his performance in the Lord's Test but by then must have been wondering just how many times he had to prove himself to the chairman.

Perhaps the worst aspect of Illingworth's performance was his treatment of Michael Atherton. As far as I'm concerned, there's only one word for it – diabolical.

To keep Atherton dangling on a rope for the best part of two months before he finally confirmed his appointment as captain against the West Indies was just pathetic. Everyone knew what Illy was up to. After having his feathers ruffled by remarks attributed to Atherton over the selection of the party for the Ashes trip, notably the omission of Fraser, and his plea for younger players and younger selectors in touch with the dynamics of the modern game at his final tour press conference in Perth, Illingworth had decided to let the young pup know who was in charge. In effect he treated the England captain like a naughty schoolboy.

Illingworth claimed that Atherton's remarks had betrayed disloyalty and undermined the confidence of the tour party. That's rich, coming from the man who, three days before the first Ashes Test in Brisbane had entertained a group of journalists at a Sportwriters Association lunch in London with a performance that several of those present considered quite embarrassing.

First he lambasted Atherton for not telephoning him to discuss various selection issues and came up with the priceless statement: 'I saved his neck last year when I fined him £2,000 for the alleged ball-tampering incident at Lord's and this is how he repays me.'

He went on: 'If I hadn't fined him he would have been banned for two matches and he wouldn't be England captain now. The least I expected was a phone call to let me know how things were going. He had all my numbers in Spain and elsewhere and he has chosen not to use them.'

I can only suppose Illingworth had mislaid his copy of the tour itinerary – in which was published the names of all the team hotels, their addresses, telephone numbers and fax numbers.

Then he piled into Athers over his suggestion that Fraser, who was out in Australia playing grade cricket for Western Suburbs in Sydney, might be brought into the squad in place of Devon Malcolm who had gone down with chicken-pox.

'Fraser did bugger all last summer,' he insisted. 'I can't believe there is serious talk from the captain about drafting him in as a replacement. If he is suggesting that Fraser plays in the first Test I will be on the phone to him like a rocket.

'We agreed before the party left that Fraser never looked up to it. He struggled in the West Indies and, although Atherton wanted him to go, he just wasn't the man for the job.'

He went on: 'I don't know what is going on and let's just say I would have had a few recommendations to make if he had bothered to give me a call. I can't understand why he played Steve Rhodes as an opener on a couple of occasions and not Craig White. Everyone says Craig can't yet bat at No. 6 in Tests because he is not making hundreds, but I would have thought that putting him in first would have given him an ideal opportunity to do just that.'

Illingworth's next target was Keith Fletcher. When asked about Fletcher's exact role, he turned to the person next to him and said: 'He's team manager, isn't he? He nicks a few catches in practice.' A joke, maybe ... but I wonder whether Atherton, Fletcher or Fraser, for that matter, saw the funny side of things.

In my opinion, it was quite obvious from the start of Illy's reign that he would never be satisfied until he had absolute power over the selection and running of the team. It's easy to say in hindsight, but it was also pretty obvious from the moment Illy was appointed that Fletcher was living on borrowed time.

As I've said, I happen to agree with the principle that one man should have overall responsibility and be judged accordingly, but surely Illingworth should have had the courage of his convictions and insisted on Fletcher's immediate removal the moment Illy was given the job back in April 1994. Instead, Fletcher suffered a slow lingering death, unsure of his own authority and undermined by the public pronouncements of his chairman of selectors.

If all of the above are supposed to be examples of the motivational skill for which Illy is so famous, all I can say is he couldn't man-manage his way out of a paper-bag! You don't have to take my word for it either; ask Patrick

Whittingdale, head of the City fund management company who backed English cricket to the tune of £3 million during a four-year sponsorship of the preparation and training of England touring teams. It was a sponsorship that Micky Stewart, the former coach, described as not just necessary but essential. And Illingworth contributed to it disappearing down the plughole.

When Whittingdale announced he was not going to renew the relationship at the end of the season he spelled out the reasons for his decision in great detail. In an article in the *Daily Telegraph* he was quoted as follows:

'Mike Atherton has been appallingly treated in the last two months. He has been made to grovel to retain the England captaincy. He was given a very difficult job, one of the hardest in all sport, and he needs and deserves to get support, not criticism.

'I feel the criticism through the media of players from a distance such as there was in the winter is very bad manmanagement. It does not get the best out of them. Nor has the treatment of Angus Fraser been acceptable.

'I've been very close to Angus and saw him make a grand effort to get back from his injury. His reward when he worked his way back into the side was to be told that he was overweight. They've no idea how to treat people.

'Ray Illingworth said when he became manager that his job was to instill confidence and make the best of the limited talent at his disposal. I don't subscribe to the view that talent is limited. But we are not getting the best out of the talent.

'I'm not pretending to be a cricket expert but in any walk of life you will not get a highly motivated side or a winning team led by a captain who is being undermined and is made to grovel.'

Illingworth's response was a masterpiece of diplomacy. It probably had the marketing people at the TCCB cringing. He said, 'A lot of good sponsors who are still with us don't try to run the game. Of course any sponsorship is welcome, but not at any price. What I find most irritating is that we are getting all this criticism and we haven't even started playing yet.'

I wonder why. Perhaps Matthew Engel, editor of the cricketing bible, *Wisden*, summed up the situation best of all. In his notes in the 1995 edition he wrote:

'Everyone respects Illingworth's feel for the game; but he sometimes seemed to forget that one of the beauties of this most complex pastime is that no one has ever had a monopoly of cricketing wisdom. One began to feel that the right adjective was the one that was never attached to him in his playing days: amateurish.'

Sadly, things got worse. By the time England set off for the 1995-96 winter tour to South Africa to be followed by the World Cup, Illingworth had firmly established himself as manager, coach and chairman of selectors. By the time they returned, beaten by Hansie Cronje's team and humiliated in the World Cup, Illy's reign was effectively at an end. Between arrival and departure Illingworth had used all his famed powers of motivation to so heartily hack off not just Atherton, but the vast majority of the players on tour that, when he finally left the stage at the end of the following summer, they were glad to see the back of him.

Atherton was given a taste of what was to come when, while in mid-air en route to South Africa he was handed a copy of the *Sun*. Inside was the first of a three-part series of articles in which Illingworth openly criticised the captain and called into question his character and temperament. The headline over the first of these pieces read: 'Atherton is so stubborn, inflexible and narrow-minded.'

The next day's offering described how Atherton had been 'daft' to axe Phil DeFreitas from his plans and indicated that he had only done so because he disliked him. And the final piece ran under the title: 'Tufnell? he's simply too much trouble for Atherton' and revealed what Illingworth believed to be the real reason for the left-arm spinner's omission.

I saw all the above as blatant undermining of the captain's position and even more digraceful when you consider not only that Illingworth was paid for his contribution to those articles, but also that shortly before departure the England players had received a letter from the Board telling them that : 'Ray (Illingworth) has stipulated that no player will be permitted to write any national or local newspaper articles of any sort, including any diary piece either prior to or during the tour.' In other words, he could write what he liked about them but they could not answer back without risking the wrath of Raymond.

As if all that was not bad enough, Illingworth's subsequent treatment of Devon Malcolm was simply appalling.

Malcolm's destruction of the South African batsmen during the final Test of the 1994 summer meant that when England arrived there both sides understood that he was their main weapon. Yet Illingworth and his specialist bowling coach Peter Lever succeeded in disarming him utterly. Malcolm began the tour gingerly, trying to ease his way back to full fitness following surgery. Yet from the very start Illingworth and Lever badgered him about trying to change his bowling action. When Malcolm resisted Illingworth and Lever made sure the accompanying press corps knew of the problem and who was to blame.

Lever's assessment of Malcolm's value to the side was particularly damaging. He told the reporters: 'He has just one asset – pace. That apart he is a nonentity in cricketing terms' and with that the management washed their hands of him, until the final Test match, when after Malcolm had failed to remove tail-ender Paul Adams, Illingworth spoke to him in a dressing room outburst that included the following cracking pick-you-up: 'You cost us the Test match'.

The reaction of one senior batsman said it all. 'The sooner we get rid of that ****, the better,' he commented.

But, valid and important though I believe those observations over the arrogance, ineptitude or just plain lunacy of several senior figures, the problems have always run much deeper than individual incompetence in captaincy, selection and management.

The simple fact is that for too long, far too much of English domestic cricket has been far too soft and uncompetitive producing soft and uncompetitive cricketers, and the real villains of the piece are the county chairmen who stood in the path of meaningful change for so long.

Throughout the nineties and, to be honest, going back many years before that, the county chairman, the men who actually ran the game in England, believed everything in the garden was rosy, just so long as no one disturbed the peaceful slumberings of the members.

Alright, we normally got slaughtered abroad and, because for a time no one could live with West Indies' ferocious pace battery we were excused repeated thrashings by them. But, from time to time England would win a Test series against Australia, India, Pakistan or New Zealand to keep the dissenters quiet, and even if we didn't, the chairmen could mutter knowingly to each other that fortunes in cricket were cyclical and things would come right again eventually of their own accord.

In the meantime county cricket was allowed to drift quietly along with the occasional fair-to-middling player in the national side replaced by another fair-to-middling player.

But what upset this cosy suicide was the fact that, by the mid-nineties, England had begun losing international matches to countries that weren't even playing Test cricket a decade before. As they did so certain people in the game realised the lack of success of the England team on the field and the lack of any clear leadership for English cricket off it meant that cricket was dying on its feet.

When England performed quite abysmally in the 1996 World Cup in India, Pakistan and Sri Lanka, beating only Holland and the United Arab Emirates, *Wisden* editor Matthew Engel wrote: 'The 1996 cricket season was in some respects the most depressing in memory. The consistent failure of the England team is the biggest single cause of the crisis, but it is not the crisis itself. The blunt fact is that cricket in the UK has become unattractive to the overwhelming majority of the population.'

And when the England team sponsors Tetley admitted that poor performances by the national team were a major factor in their decision to withdraw, certain influential figures started to think about what must be done to shake things up.

Dennis Silk, then the chairman of the old TCCB, had started the ball rolling during the World Cup by publicly describing England as about seventh in the list of Test-playing nations and urging county chairmen to put the needs and aspirations of the national side ahead of their own parochial interest. And although the preparation of a report on the selection, management and coaching of England teams by a working party under Essex chairman David Acfield indicated that Silk had tapped into the mood of dissent, the reactionaries in the county game led, ironically but entirely predictably by Essex, made sure that, for speaking his mind about the state of the English game, Silk's goose was cooked.

Gradually, however, what Silk put in motion gathered momentum.

Enter, through a side door, Sir Ian, later Lord MacLaurin, the outgoing chairman of Tesco. Derided as a jumped-up grocer by those who did not want to hear his message, MacLaurin was soon voted in as the first chairman of the new England and Wales Cricket Board. Although he instantly ruffled a few feathers by announcing in various interviews that he was determined to bring about meaningful change, MacLaurin was given the perfect justification sooner than he might have believed possible.

At the end of 1996 England travelled to the newest Test playing nation, Zimbabwe, confidently expecting to win handsomely. They failed, horribly. They drew both Tests then slumped to an embarrassing 3-0 defeat in the one-day international series. For their efforts on and off the field they received uniformly hostile press coverage and MacLaurin saw his chance to get to work.

Those of us who had campaigned for radical change were enthused by MacLaurin's message and while he set about persuading the county clubs to come aboard, I did some research of my own, in the shape of my book *The Botham Report*, published in August 1997 .

In early 1997 I sent a detailed questionnaire to all county chairmen, coaches, chief executives/club secretaries and captains. I asked questions that those compiling the Acfield Report didn't go near, namely about the state, standard and future direction of domestic cricket. The responses clearly demonstrated that while the majority of players, captains and coaches believed massive changes were vital for the future health of the game, the majority of chairmen and administrators did not.

Try this for instance: In response to my question: 'Do you think the needs of the national side should outweigh the needs of county clubs?', John Higson, the chairman of Gloucestershire replied: 'No. If the counties' needs are subjugated this would detrimentally affect the national side.' On the other hand his captain, Mark Alleyne, had a rather different perspective. 'Yes' he answered. 'The whole point of county cricket is to provide us with a competitive national side.'

On the question of whether an elite group of players should be contracted to England rather than the counties, the response was similarly instructive. Tim Munton, the captain of Warwickshire, said: 'Yes. There has to be an advantage in avoiding burn-out to bowlers, as seen in recent years with Angus Fraser, Dominic Cork and Darren Gough.'

David Acfield disagreed. 'No' he insisted. 'It would affect the standard of the county game and would be difficult to manage if Test players floated in and out. There would be little point in counties developing players only to lose them.' How parochial can you get?

Most relevant of all, in my opinion, were the questions over the structure of the championship.

To my mind the case for a two-division championship with promotion and relegation was irresistible. As representatives of successive England Under-19 teams had shown, young talent had been produced up to and until that level. At the same time as propping up the rest of the world in Test cricket our Under-19s were the reigning world champions. It was what happened to those young players from the point of taking up county cricket full-time that caused the real problems. By the time they had been through the process of playing largely uncompetitive cricket for two or three seasons and entered the comfort zone of sponsored cars, benefit hangers-on and dulled ambition, too often the 19-year-old promising youngster had become the 22-year-old under-achiever.

Stories about youthful arrogance are ten a penny. One England Under-19 player who featured in the 1998 World Cup triumph complained to his county that he didn't like the sponsored car he had been supplied with before he had even made his first-class debut. In Australia during the winter of 1998-99 another young star picked for the one-day series that followed the Test action appeared to be listening intently as Graveney, the chairman of selectors and squad manager urged them to take responsibility for their international future, and with World Cup places still up for grabs, to focus hard on the upcoming tournament and cut out all extra-mural activities.

Then the player approached Graveney at the end of his pep-talk and asked him if he could sort out a hire car for him and his girlfriend to take a trip up the Gold Coast the following day. Was it any wonder that, when called upon to test themselves at the highest level, too many were woefully underprepared for what hit them.

I knew what I believed. But I wanted to find out the mood around the country.

'Are you satisfied with the current format of the county championship?', I asked. The responses were as follows:

Chairmen and chief executives: YES 63%; NO 37%
Captains and coaches: YES 28.5%; NO 71.5%.

And I asked: 'Would you be in favour of a two-division championship?' Again the responses were telling.

Chairmen and chief executives: YES 31%; NO 69%.
Captains and coaches: YES 64%; NO 36%.

According to Higson: 'No. It would condemn certain counties to oblivion'. Acfield said: 'This would simply produce a few top counties and little else.'

Jack Birkenshaw, the coach of Leicestershire, spoke for the rest of us: 'Yes. This would increase the interest in the competition. There is nothing wrong with change.'

Then I put my money where my mouth was by publishing my own ten-point plan for the future of English cricket, as follows:

1. A TWO-DIVISION CHAMPIONSHIP WITH PROMOTION AND RELEGATION.
2. CONTRACT AN ELITE SQUAD OF INTERNATIONAL PLAYERS TO THE CENTRAL BOARD.
3. SCRAP ONE ONE-DAY DOMESTIC COMPETITION; STANDARDISE AT 50 OVERS ONE LEAGUE AND CUP CONTEST; JAZZ UP THE 50-OVER LEAGUE TO ATTRACT CASUAL AND YOUNG SPECTATORS.
4. TRIM PLAYING STAFFS TO MAXIMUM 20 FULL-TIME PROFESSIONALS; REORGANISE 2ND XI CRICKET TO BE YOUTH-ORIENTED.
5. REPLACE THE BENEFIT SYSTEM WITH PENSION FUNDS; GIVE THE PCA FUNDS TO DEVELOP AFTER-CRICKET TRAINING PROGRAMMES.
6. INTRODUCE QUALITY CONTROL IN THE HIRING OF OVERSEAS PLAYERS.
7. ESTABLISH A NATIONAL CRICKET ACADEMY; APPOINT A NATIONAL DIRECTOR OF COACHING.
8. CREATE A LEVEL SCHOOL PLAYING FIELD.
9. REVAMP THE MARKETING OF THE GAME.
10. APPPOINT A CHIEF EXECUTIVE WITH FULL AND UNFETTERED POWER TO MAKE ALL THE ABOVE HAPPEN.

In the immediate aftermath of publication, two things happened. First, persuaded that his desired version of change, two divisions, would not be accepted by the counties, MacLaurin & co. produced a bastardised version. Thankfully the three conference system he came up with was strangled at birth.

And secondly I was contacted by a senior official of the Board.

The gist of his message was that he and some others inside the corridors of power wanted to put my ten-point plan to the county chairmen in its entirety there and then. 'There are a few of us here who agree wholeheartedly with all of your proposals,' I was told. 'We need to change the thinking of some county chairmen who just don't want to know. Coming from you and bearing in mind what you represent, your plan might just change their thinking.'

The Board official urged me to send a copy of the ten-point plan personally to each of the county chairmen, with a note asking them to consider the proposals. He also supplied me with a full list of the home addresses and telephone numbers of every single one of them.

Then he made it clear that although the Board members involved wanted to enlist my help in trying to make some of the chairmen more responsive to change, they themselves did not want to be seen to be supporting the plan.

The deal was that I would be putting myself and my views on the table on behalf of some of the Board members committed to serious change. If placing my plan before them then had the desired effect of getting into the heads of the more reactionary county chairmen, those seeking change would then step up their efforts. If not, they would deny all knowledge of any contact with me.

You might say I was taken aback. Flattered though I was that someone in such a high-ranking position in English cricket should believe my views might have an impact, my second thought was that it all sounded like something from a John le Carré novel. I decided that I would let the Board member and his mates do their own dirty work. In any case, once published, my ten-point plan would speak for itself.

Looking back on those events at the end of the summer of 1999 with England now undisputed world chumps, it is interesting to see how much of my plan has actually been put into operation.

MacLaurin's second attempt to get the counties to agree to two-divisions with promotion and relegation finally succeeded, after his Lordship presented them with financial projections that told their own horror story.

The tumultuous end of the 1999 championship with all but one of the final round of matches having a major bearing on who would start the 2000 season in Division One and Two showed just what level of interest the new system should inspire.

The counties also agreed that an elite group of players should be contracted by ECB rather than their counties from 2000. To my mind bowlers should have been the main beneficiaries of this. If I had my way, between now and the time Darren Gough packs up, he should not play any other cricket except for England – 15 Test matches and 25 one-day internationals in a year should be enough for anyone.

The new CGU national League with its own divisional structure has been the platform for some major innovations, such as floodlit day/night matches. (One one-day domestic competition, the Benson and Hedges Cup, was indeed scrapped, then amazingly reinstated for season 2000.)

At the end of the summer of 1997, during which he helped Glamorgan to their first county championship for 28 years, Hugh Morris was appointed National Technical Director.

And in terms of quality control in the hiring of overseas players, the penny seems finally to have dropped. Try Shane Warne (Hampshire), Glenn McGrath (Worcestershire), Shoaib Akhtar (Nottinghamshire), Jacques Kallis (Glamorgan), Saqlain Mushtaq (Surrey), Muttiah Muralitharan (Lancashire) and Anil Kumble (Leicestershire), all signed up to play county cricket in the summer of 2000, for size.

Indeed, I would go so far as to increase the number of overseas players to two per county.

Looking back to when I played most of my cricket at county level the standard was immeasurably higher for several reasons. The pitches were much better than in the late nineties and this is something that must be addressed by all concerned. But the players who played on them were much better as well. Every county had not one but two world-class overseas stars and they raised the overall standard accordingly.

To survive, let alone prosper against Clive Rice and Richard Hadlee of Nottinghamshire, Imran Khan and Garth le Roux of Sussex, Malcolm Marshall and Gordon Greenidge of Hampshire, Clive Lloyd and Michael Holding of Lancashire, Viv Richards and Joel Garner of Somerset and so on and so on, you had to be able to raise your game.

I firmly believe that the young cricketers who play against Warne, McGrath & co. from season 2000 onwards will improve significantly as a result. And then, when they are ready for selection for Test cricket they will be far better prepared. Logically, two overseas players per county would double the benefits.

It will take time for English cricket to recover from the arrogant complacency and negligence of those who believed they could keep the game in the dark ages for their own personal amusement.

And the need for all of the above to be implemented was underlined first when watching a county championship match between Derbyshire and Surrey towards the end of the previous summer and later, after seeing how some of the new brigade performed as England fell to occasionally plucky but totally predictable defeat in the 1999-2000 tour of South Africa.

Frankly, some of the players in operation for Derbyshire were little better than club standard.

And Mike Atherton felt so deeply about the lowering of standards that, on his return from England's South African tour, he spoke out on BBC Radio 5 live. According to the former England captain, county cricket served no useful purpose and was simply not producing Test cricketers for England. Where Mike and I disagree is over what sort of system should replace it. Mike has little time for two divisions in the county championship and believes the only way forward is with regional cricket. I do not. First things first. Let us try two divisions to start with and add some form of regional competition as we go along. Cricketers and spectators find it hard enough to raise themselves for the county game. Just imagine how they would feel if asked to play for, or support, the East Midlands against London and the Home Counties?

New coach Duncan Fletcher was so unimpressed by the attitude of some of the younger members of the touring party that he was moved to observe: 'a lot of the younger guys have a lack of discipline. It's not that they don't want to succeed, they simply don't understand what is required. We have to develop a work ethic with the modern players, and make them understand that the game is not easy.'

While I accept there will be teething problems with two-divisional cricket, as long as proper pitches are prepared I firmly believe the potential for improvement – tougher, more ruthless and more competitive cricket producing tougher, more ruthless and more competitive cricketers – was worth all the risks involved and more. Frankly, though, did anyone have a choice?

As far as my position is concerned, I have never made any secret of the fact that I would love to be involved with the running of the England team. My ideal job would be manager of the whole shooting match, on a salary commensurate with the responsibilities of picking, training, coaching, preparing and motivating the England side much in the same fashion as the manager of the national football team, and just as accountable for results.

I have, from time to time been used as an unpaid observer and, unofficially at least, as the bowling coach on the tour to Zimbabwe and New Zealand in 1997. But to say that I was involved in the selection of the squad for the South African tour in any other way than to be asked my opinion in an advisory capacity is nonsense. When the issue of selection was raised during the tour and the ECB announced that a fourth selector would be appointed to join chairman David Graveney, Nasser Hussain and Fletcher and a reporter asked me if I was interested in being a candidate, I was only too happy to confirm that I was.

Then the board took the interesting step of appointing my former England colleague Geoff Miller instead.

The road ahead for the English game will be long and the journey arduous. But at least the first steps have finally been taken in the form of a drastic change in the structure of domestic cricket for the first summer of the new millennium. In any case, at 1.49 p.m. on Sunday 22 August, 1999, from our position at rock bottom, the only way was up.

20
THAT'S ALL, FOLKS

> 'It's incredible to me. We expect this chap Botham to
> work cricketing miracles every day and still behave
> like a sombre vegetable – well, you just can't expect
> that, the two things just don't go together.'

These were the words of the late John Arlott as he spoke
on an ITV documentary shortly before I left on England's
1985/86 tour to West Indies, when the tabloid feeding
frenzy was at its most furious.

John and I shared many a happy glass together on the
Channel island of Alderney where he lived until his death
and where I am lucky enough to have a second home.
What always struck me about the man was his generosity
of spirit. That is not to say he never had a bad word to say
about anyone, but those who got it in the neck generally
deserved it and to those fortunate enough to win his
respect he was a fiercely loyal friend. The generosity was
to do with the fact that he treated everyone alike.

When asked to fill out an immigration form on entering
South Africa for the first time he was, rightly, appalled to
be asked to what 'race' he belonged. He wrote 'human'.

He was also one of the few people I have come into contact with over the years to whom a person's essential humanity meant more than status, wealth or fame. Along with Brian Johnston and Reg Hayter, with whom he shared lasting friendships, cricket has lost a magical character in John, and I'd like to imagine that the three of them are busy cracking open a bottle of something somewhere and setting the world to rights.

Whatever other words of wisdom John produced during his wonderful career as writer, broadcaster and member of the human race, and the other countless thousands that have been written about me since I first made an impact on the public consciousness, these made the greatest impression.

For, in a couple of sentences, John managed to put my career and my life into its proper perspective.

I make no apologies for what I've done or the way I am, but I'm certainly not blind to the fact that I have made mistakes. It would be easy to trot out all the usual rubbish along the lines of 'if I knew then what I know now things might have been different etc' but that is the coward's way out. In the end I have no one to answer to but me, Kath and the rest of my family. The bottom line is that I have tried to be true to myself at all times and in all situations and I simply don't think it is realistic to expect anything else. There is no denying however, that, for those around me, and particularly for Kath, there has been a high price to pay.

Kath and I have been together now for the best part of twenty years. That's an awful lot of thick and an awful lot of thin. To most outside observers, especially those who throughout our stickiest period during the mid-1980s were fed a constant diet of rumour, speculation and downright lies about my alleged performances off the field rather than on it, the fact that we are still together at all is considered quite amazing.

How have we managed it? The answer is: it's all down to Kath.

Over the years she has suffered more aggravation and heartache than anyone deserves. I honestly don't know how she has put up with it. Women who marry cricketers know that their life is hardly ever going to be normal. The demands of the profession see to that. I'm sure she was also aware of what a selfish person I can be: well, if she wasn't straightaway, she soon found out, and I think she came to half-accept the fact that in this respect I was probably not much different to any other sportsman utterly determined to reach the top. There are times when you simply have to put on the blinkers and acquire a kind of tunnel vision because you just cannot afford to allow your single-mindedness to be diluted. In the early days she was also the victim of the fact that, as a callow youth, I saw nothing wrong in spending more time with my team-mates in the pub than I did over supper with my young bride. I wasn't intentionally neglecting her, it was more a case of carelessness than malice. But it happened and it upset her greatly.

As things have turned out, of course, a 'normal' life is something that Kath has only ever read about in books.

The most extraordinary period came in the mid-1980s, during the time when my head was full of Hollywood and Hudson. Until now only she and I knew just how close she came to leaving me not once, but twice.

The first occasion was in 1985 when, for a short period,

Kath actually did walk out on me. I will never forget the night she left the party at Birtles Bowl, Hudson's Cheshire estate, with the words: 'Come with me now or we're finished'. I understood the seriousness of the situation. I fully realized that if I stayed put I would be risking our marriage; but I did it all the same. All I can say is that the incident happened in the middle of the kind of experience everyone goes through from time to time; the moments when suddenly, and for no discernible reason, you think to yourself: 'Perhaps I *am* in the wrong plot'.

I wasn't thinking straight. I wasn't thinking about Kath, I wasn't thinking about our wonderful children, Liam and Sarah, and I certainly can't have been thinking about Becky who was still on the way. I was going full throttle on the mad merry-go-round and it was spinning dangerously out of control.

I know that at the time she meant what she said. She had taken a cold look at the marriage and weighed up her options carefully. Life on her own would have meant an end to the newspaper headlines whose cumulative effect had, on occasions, rendered her a nervous, depressed shadow of herself. It would have meant an end to the whispers that subsided the moment she would enter a room; an end to the verbal battles we used to have about where my priorities lay; an end to the sleepless nights she had suffered for years; an end to the terrible feelings of insecurity and loneliness that descended on her whenever I left for an overseas tour; an end to constantly having to defend me and our relationship to the people who never tired of sticking their noses into our business; an end to having to deal with my stubbornness and selfishness, to being excluded from matters that I had convinced myself did not concern her and the long silences when I fell into one of my darker moods.

In the end, I'm sure that she came to her decision to stick with the marriage for the sake of the children. But, although our relationship is now more solid than it has ever been, there was one further period of crisis to go through. Five years later, on Valentine's Day, 1990, things came to a head once again.

I had been in a pretty foul mood all winter. My treatment by the selectors had left me angry, bitter and frustrated. I had worked hard to come back after my operation, they had begged me to make myself available for the winter tour to West Indies by turning down the offer to join Mike Gatting's rebels in South Africa and then they left me out of the tour anyway.

I was on a short fuse. I was also, according to Kath, drinking too much whisky. She has always said that if I get on the scotch then that is the time to run for cover. And this was the time. My temper tantrums had been getting out of hand.

Ironically, we had spent the evening in question in a pretty relaxed mood. We had enjoyed a meal and drinks with Roger Potter, a close fishing friend of mine, and his wife Sue, in the Black Bull pub in Moulton near our home in Ravensworth. As it was Valentine's Day, I had made the usual arrangements. When we arrived at the pub there were 36 red roses hand-tied, delivered and waiting. Ironically, in view of what happened later, it was Roger who got it in the neck from Sue for forgetting to do something along the same lines. I had certainly not been on the whisky that night. Perhaps that is why Kath felt able to take her courage in her hands and do what she was about to do.

There was no warning and no preamble. On the journey back in the car, Kath just turned to me and said: 'I'm sorry, Ian. But I just can't go on living like this. We have got to get things sorted out'.

At first, I was taken aback. Then I tried to trivialize things as I had always done in the past and laugh the moment away. But it soon became clear that it was not going anywhere. Kath was deadly serious; it was obvious that this had been building up for some time. I agreed we needed to talk and we prepared for the event in bizarrely 'civilized' fashion. When we got home, Kath went upstairs to run a bath, as she always does in order to relax before going to bed. I took two glasses of wine up to the bathroom.

She told me that she was at the end of her tether. She was not happy with the way I was behaving and she told me so. She made it quite clear that she was no longer going to put up with my selfishness and my moodiness. And she was damned if she was going to accept the expressions of foul temper I had been guilty of. She told me that I was impossible to live with, that I could never see anyone else's point of view but my own and that constantly having to deal with that had worn her down. She went back over all the problems we had had during the previous fourteen years of marriage, and particularly during that awful period in the mid-1980s when it seemed we could not move for newspaper headlines and she told me that, although she understood my frustration and bitterness at not being involved in the England scene, I had been taking it out on her and the children and she was not going to put up with it any longer. She was not happy with my attitude towards her or the kids and accused me of attempting to use them to get at her, of trying to get them on my side in arguments without any thought of the effect it was having on her or them. She insisted that she couldn't honestly see any way that things were going to improve. She felt that, as a couple, we were 'losing it'. She told me that she was on the very point of throwing in the towel.

It was the first time I had ever heard her talk this way. In fact, I suppose it's fairer to say that it was the first time I had ever given her the chance.

In the past, whenever she had wanted to get things off her chest, my reaction had always been the same. I would fly off the handle telling her that, after getting it in the neck from all and sundry away from home, what I wanted and needed from her when I closed our front door was understanding and support.

This time, I got the message loud and clear. I was being a complete sod to her and the kids and I just couldn't see it. They were not to blame for what had happened but they were the ones getting the blame. They always say that it's the people you love that you hurt most of all, and although I wasn't consciously aware of doing it, this was certainly what had been happening. Kath and the kids were in the firing line because they were closest to me. My obsession with my own problems had blinded me to their needs. I was stroppy and surly and I was taking out my aggression on them. Metaphorically speaking, I was using them as punch bags. Kath had taken a bruising and she was not going to take any more.

She understood the pressures I had been under throughout my career. She was the only one who knew and who really understood the fact that I had never ever taken my place in the England side for granted, that every time I went out to play for my country I felt my place was on the line. She was the only one who knew and really understood how wrapped up in nervous tension I would get before every match I played and that the wall I sometimes put up against the world was a defence mechanism and that I often tried to camouflage my fears with bluff and bravado. But she simply could no longer accept that when I threw up this barrier for self-protection, more often than not, she and the kids were left on the outside looking in.

She told me that she just wasn't happy living with me and she issued an ultimatum. She made it clear to me that unless I changed my ways and paid heed to what she was saying, it would be the end of our relationship. She would leave me and take Liam, Sarah and Becky with her, and the marriage would be over.

For much of the early part of the conversation, I just sat there in silence. But as more and more came flooding out I realized that she was right.

I heard what she was saying. I had been a bloody idiot. I had been selfish to the point of self-obsession. I had been taking everything out on her and the kids and it had worn her down. A lot of the problems had been caused by outside pressures, but some of them had not.

She had always been able to cope with the allegations of sex, drugs and rock 'n' roll. But in her eyes what she was going through now was ten times worse even than what she had had to put up with in the most lurid newspaper article. Take the Lindy Field business, for example. Then it had been a case of my alleged behaviour with someone else. Now it was a case of my actual behaviour with Kath and the children. And whereas she had managed to dismiss the former as someone else's fantasy, this she could not.

This was fact. This was Kath and me, and it was for real.

It was a numbing experience. For possibly the first time I was able to see myself through Kath's eyes. I was able to see what sort of life she had been forced to lead – all the fears, all the uncertainties and all the misery.

I took stock of the situation. No couple could possibly have survived what we had had to go through if the basic bond between them was not strong. We had suffered so much together, and apart, but we had also enjoyed an awful lot of good times. Yet here I was on the point of throwing it all away. Throughout the whole two hours we spent examining the problems and getting them all out in the open, never once did either of us raise our voices. We were calm and relaxed and, for the first time in my life, I think I was able to take not only a subjective look at the marriage but an objective one as well.

On the other occasion when we had almost split up, back in 1985, Kath pulled back from the brink because of the children. This time it was my turn to give. I promised to change, or at least try to. I promised to try to see our life together from her point of view as well as my own and that I would do everything I could to try and make things right between us.

Kath has always said, and still maintains, that I was not designed for living with. Even now she has to take time away from me in order to be able to spend time with me. She relies on the escape to Alderney to recharge her batteries for the exhausting business of being Mrs Ian Botham. But I think we have both come to accept that our life together and with our children is more important to us than anything else.

And I have come to realize just how deeply some of the

things she has been forced to put up with, through no fault of her own, have affected her.

The newspaper headlines have hit her the hardest. Over the years she has worried herself sick over them and, sometimes, literally so. If you believed what you read, I was a boozed-up junkie who had sired half the population of the known world. Even if she didn't believe any of it – and she always maintains that she tried to put it all out of her mind – the cumulative effect was bound to wear her down. No one can withstand the constant drip, drip, drip of the British Newspaper Torture. Apart from anything else, even if Kath was successful at dismissing the reports as rubbish, the fact is that other people read the papers as well; parents of Liam, Sarah and Becky's schoolmates, for instance. The number of times one of them came home with tales of sniggering classmates and being sent to Coventry because of what their Dad was supposed to have done was bound to take its toll.

I really do believe that, as far as the constant media hounding to which I and Kath were subjected is concerned, we were simply in the wrong place at the wrong time – caught in the middle of a tabloid circulation war whose participants fought it out using whatever means, fair or foul, they could lay their hands on. The war was not pretty and there were many innocent casualties. You were either a hero or the meanest villain ever to set foot on the globe. As far as Ian Botham was concerned, nothing in between would do.

Of course, if you swim with the sharks, you are bound to get bitten. In that respect, my decision to enter into various arrangements with the *Sun* and others have left me exposed. But that was not the case in the beginning. In those early days, the deal fixed up for me by Reg Hayter with the *Sun* was straightforward enough. Obviously, they wanted good material and they were not going to be satisfied with bland platitudes. But, by and large, it was all fairly harmless stuff. As time progressed and the mood in Fleet Street changed, the way the material was presented altered accordingly. The impact made by the skilful application of a bloody great headline over a piece is often out of all proportion to its content. Slowly but surely, the stakes were raised. Then, when rival editors decided their papers had to have a piece of that kind of action as well, the sky was no longer the limit.

It got to the stage where, if a rival of the *Sun* couldn't find a good word to say about me, they went looking for bad ones. In turn, the *Sun* would find themselves in a position of having to compete with them! Confused? I was, and some of the great sports stars of the past certainly would have been. Until only quite recently, what happened away from the cricket field for instance, was considered none of anyone's business. How times had changed. Progress? You can keep it.

In the end, newspaper editors stop treating you as fellow human beings, but as targets, pure and simple. It is a thoroughly de-humanizing process. They forget or ignore the effect their stories are having not just on the subject, but also the subject's family and those closest to him as well. What possible justification can there be, for instance, for newspaper reporters badgering Kath's grandmother, as they did when the *Mail on Sunday*'s 'Sex, drugs and rock 'n' roll' allegations were about to be printed. The prevailing mood even went so far as to affect the BBC's news coverage. The day that the Lindy Field story broke in 1986, the BBC actually showed the front page of the *News of the World* to their viewers. Did the BBC really think this was newsworthy, or had they too sunk to the level of the scandal sheets?

The problem for Kath was compounded by my attitude to all these stories. On some occasions, I used to treat them as though they had never been written. My intention was to make it quite clear to Kath that these stories were pure fabrication and that she had nothing whatsoever to worry about. What that actually did was to make her even more upset. Here was a national newspaper saying her husband had slept with another woman and, in Kath's eyes, all I was doing was making a joke of it.

On other occasions, I would go to the opposite extreme. When, after the latest product of the fantasy factory had hit the streets and Kath would want to talk about it, my reaction would actually be aggressive. I would say something along the lines of 'Not you as well. I'm getting all this shit thrown at me from left right and centre and what I need is support, not more aggravation'. I was not and never have been one of those who bottles things up. If something is bothering me I let everyone know about it. Far better to have a ten-minute explosion to clear the air than allow things to eat away at you. A variety of household objects would come off the worse for the experience: coffee tables, cut-glass tumblers, doors, you name it and I've thrown it. Kath, possessing as fiery a temper as me, threw back.

Inevitably these rows had an effect on the kids. Kath told me that Sarah, in particular, would often be left in tears as a result. On more than one occasion she has asked the question all parents dread to hear: 'Are you and Daddy getting divorced?'

Of course, a lot of people reading this will say that the intrusion of the press into our private and personal lives is nothing new and that you simply have to accept this kind of thing if you are in the spotlight and for having the kind of high profile that enables you to earn enough not to have to care.

But I do care, and Kath cares. The kids care and so do our parents and grandparents. How would you feel for instance if some charming soul decided to send human excrement through the post to you? Well, that is exactly what once happened to my mother, Marie. Or if someone sent pubic hair through the post and invited you to 'Smoke this, you bastard'? We all know that fame has its drawbacks, but no one should have to suffer being treated like scum.

I suppose we should have cheerfully accepted the death threats as well. On more than one occasion I have received the usual crank calls. I have had letters from the National Front yobs calling me 'nigger-lover' because of my close friendship with Viv and other black people and threatening to 'do' me.

By and large I have just treated them with the contempt they deserved and ignored them. However, during the summer of 1989, just before the Old Trafford Test against the Australians, I received a series of letters which I had no choice but to take seriously. There was no mistaking the intention of those who sent them. I was a marked man, and they were going to kill me. When I showed the letters to Special Branch they told me I was right to be concerned. They briefed me and my 'minder' Andy Withers on procedure for checking the car for devices and even sent under-cover plain-clothes officers to mingle around me in public places and stand guard from time to time. I never knew who they were or when they would be there, but I'm glad they were. Kath was in Portugal at the time and I decided that there was no point in both of us worrying ourselves silly over it, so I actually didn't tell her about the threats until months later. But it was a traumatic time. I felt vulnerable, especially when one of the letters warned me in black and white that the next time I set foot on a cricket field, they would pull the trigger.

All through these events, on and off the field, Kath has had the courage and the resilience to keep going. It's only now, looking back over all that we have been through together, that I realize how lucky I have been to have her.

In fact, bearing in mind what they have all had to put up with, the greatest tribute I can pay to Kath is the fact that Liam, Sarah and Becky are so self-sufficient and well adjusted. From very early on Liam decided to get on with his own life, and believe me, his success so far on the sports field is wholly down to him and nothing to do with me. Sarah, having understandably become somewhat withdrawn during her early teens, is now well and truly her own young woman and Becky can look after herself in any company. They are all a credit to Kath.

And of course, she and they are not the only things I have to be grateful for. This is not a sob story. Neither of us are looking for sympathy. All things considered, it has been one hell of a life. There have been lows, as you have just read, but there have been fantastic highs as well.

The runs, the wickets, the catches, the walks, the scrapes, the friends. The places I've been to, the wonders I've seen and the sheer fun I have had, all have made everything more than worthwhile.

I'm no saint and I'm not perfect. I never have been and I never will be. What I am is a simple country lad from Yeovil who had the guts to identify what I wanted and grab it with both hands. If I had my time over again, I wouldn't change a letter, a full stop or a comma. My motto has always been the same: Life – be in it.

And where do I go from here?

The straight answer is that I simply have no idea. One thing is certain, however. This may be the end of the book, but I intend to make sure it is not the end of the story.

BEEFY'S
FANTASY CRICKET
SELECTION

BEST OF ENGLAND	BEST OF THE WORLD
Geoffrey Boycott	Sunil Gavaskar
Graham Gooch	Gordon Greenidge
Mike Brearley	Vivian Richards
David Gower	Greg Chappell
Allan Lamb	Javed Miandad
Robin Smith	Allan Border
Ian Botham	Clive Lloyd
Alan Knott	Rodney Marsh
John Emburey	Richard Hadlee
Derek Underwood	Curtly Ambrose
Angus Fraser	Joel Garner
Graham Dilley	Dennis Lillee
Bob Willis	Abdul Qadir

During the course of my career it has been my privilege, my pleasure and sometimes my pain to play with and against some of the greatest cricketers who ever lived.

Although certain observers and commentators may not agree, notably guys like Fred Trueman who rarely had a good word to say about anyone who did not play cricket 'in my day', personally I have no hesitation in saying that the likes of Viv Richards, Dennis Lillee and Geoff Boycott would have shone in any era.

In fact, when selecting players to represent the Best of The World in a match against the Best of England from those with whom I came into contact at Test level, I have had to omit some outstanding talent.

In my World 13 for instance, there is no place for Kapil Dev, Imran Khan, Michael Holding or Malcolm Marshall, while master batsmen like Sachin Tendulkar and Brian Lara miss out because I never actually played against them in Test cricket.

What struck me most when reviewing candidates for my England squad was the lack of genuinely top-notch class pace bowlers available. In fact of those I have chosen, it's probably true that only Bob Willis could be considered world class and even he would struggle to nudge out any of those I have picked to form the World 13's attack.

That is a stinging indictment of the quality of fast bowlers we have produced over the past twenty years. There are many reasons, among them poor coaching, unhelpful pitches, the incredible workload forced on county cricketers and the amount of one-day matches prevalent in domestic cricket but unless we rediscover the art of fast bowling I fear England will never again dominate world cricket.

Perhaps the hardest decisions I have had to make concern captaincy.

My choice of the man to lead the World 13 came down to a toss-up between Allan Border and Clive Lloyd. In the end I went for Lloyd because one of his great strengths as

West Indies captain was his ability to unite players from different Caribbean islands, guys who came to the team with fierce pride in being Jamaicans, Bajans, Antiguans, Trinidadians or Guyanese but, until that point, little notion of allegiance to West Indies as a whole, and got them to play for each other, the team and the flag.

That kind of leadership would be vital when fusing together characters as far apart as Gordon Greenidge and Rod Marsh, or even Lillee and his old 'sparring-partner' Javed Miandad.

Turning to the England captain, my choice had to be Mike Brearley. Brears would be the first to admit that, on merit, as a batsman he would not get anywhere near the side, yet I believe that the right captain in the right place at the right time can mean as much to a team as a century, a five-wicket haul or a couple of stunning catches. In fact I know it can.

Brears was, quite simply, the best captain I ever played for, so it is right and proper that he should lead this, a squad of the best 13 England Test players of my generation:

THE BEST OF ENGLAND

GEOFFREY BOYCOTT
Test debut: 1964 v Australia at Trent Bridge. *Tests:* 108. Runs: 8114. *Highest score:* 246 n.o. *Centuries:* 22. *Average:* 47.72. *Wickets:* 7. *Ave:* 54.52. *BB:* 3 for 47.

The best 'made' batsman I have ever come across. Possessed total dedication to the business of scoring runs and unshakeable belief in his own ability. You knew that once he was 'in' he would never give his wicket away. The other main advantage of having him in my fantasy side is that if he is not out overnight, Allan Lamb and I can stay out late because we know we will not be needed too early the next day. When running with him always make sure you do the calling. That said, Boycs was the first name on my list in more ways than one.

GRAHAM GOOCH

Test debut: 1975 v Australia at Edgbaston. *Tests:* 118. *Runs:* 8900. *HS:* 333. *Centuries:* 20. *Ave:* 42.58. *Wickets:* 23. *Ave:* 46.47. *BB:* 3 for 39.

A very fine player who, like a good red wine, has improved with age. Can destroy an attack single-handedly. The perfect foil for Boycott.

MIKE BREARLEY (capt.)

Test debut: 1976 v West Indies at Trent Bridge. *Tests:* 39. *Runs:* 1442. *HS:* 91. *Ave:* 22.88.

Mike's great ability as captain was that he could get the best out of every player in his team. Unlike Goochie, he understood that we all need to be treated as individuals.

DAVID GOWER

Test debut: 1978 v Pakistan at Edgbaston. *Tests:* 117. *Runs:* 8231. *HS:* 215. *Centuries:* 18. *Ave:* 44.25. *Wickets:* 1. *Ave:* 20.00. *BB:* 1 for 1.

Possibly robbed of the last two years of his Test career by unbending captain and management. A privilege to watch him play. Someone to check the wine list with.

ALLAN LAMB

Test debut: 1982 v India at Lord's. *Tests:* 79. *Runs:* 4656.
HS: 142. *Centuries:* 14. *Ave:* 36.09. *Wickets:* 1. *Ave:*
23.00. *BB:* 1 for 6.

A tenacious and fearless strokeplayer who relished
quick bowling and was underestimated against the spinners. The best 'timer' of shots I've seen. When on song he
could just stand there and punch the ball wherever he
wanted. Someone to make sure that, after a hard day's
play, I stuck to drinking lemonade.

ROBIN SMITH

Test debut: 1988 v West Indies at Headingley. *Tests:* 53.
Runs: 3677. *HS:* 175. *Centuries:* 9. *Ave:* 44.30.

Despite his lean spells, he still averages over 40 in Test
cricket and that is a sure sign of genuine class. A gutsy
player and a tremendous competitor. Might have difficulties against Abdul Qadir, the one slow bowler in my
Best Of The World squad, but I back him to sort out his
problems with spin.

IAN BOTHAM

Test debut: 1977 v Australia at Trent Bridge. *Tests:* 102.
Runs: 5200. *HS:* 208. *Centuries:* 14. *Ave:* 33.54. *Wickets:*
383. *Ave:* 28.40. *BB:* 8 for 34. *Five wickets:* 27. *Ten wickets:* 4.

Reluctant to accept the invitation of the selector (me),
but expertise as social manager invaluable to the well-
being of the side.

ALAN KNOTT (wicket-keeper)
Test debut: 1967 v Pakistan at Trent Bridge. *Tests:* 95.
Runs: 4389. *HS:* 135. *Centuries:* 5. *Ave:* 32.75. *Catches:*
250. *Stumpings:* 19.

A very close thing between Knott and Bob Taylor.
Nothing between them as wicket-keepers. Knotty shades it
on batting.

JOHN EMBUREY
Test debut: 1978 v New Zealand at Lord's. *Tests:* 63.
Runs: 1705. *HS:* 75. *Ave:* 22.73. *Wickets:* 147. *Ave:*
37.85. *BB:* 7 for 78. *Five wickets:* 6.

A shrewd cricketer with a good brain. The best off-
spinner available to England during my time and a handy
performer with the bat with which he was highly unortho-
dox and sometimes just plain bizarre, but very effective on
his day.

DEREK UNDERWOOD
Test debut: 1966 v West Indies at Trent Bridge. *Tests:* 86.
Runs: 937. *HS:* 45 n.o. *Ave:* 11.56. *Wickets:* 297. *Ave:*
25.83. *BB:* 8 for 51. *Five wickets:* 17. *Ten wickets:* 6.

Give him a turning wicket and he was as dangerous as
any bowler there has ever been. His accuracy was phenom-
enal and his pace and turn meant that, on a drying wicket,
he was practically unplayable.

ANGUS FRASER
Test debut: 1989 v Australia at Edgbaston. *Tests:* 24.
Runs: 233. *HS:* 29. *Ave:* 7.76. *Wickets:* 99. *Ave:* 27.86.
BB: 8 for 75. *Five wickets:* 6.

At his absolute peak, before he suffered the hip injury that so badly disrupted his progress, the best of his type during my career. A close choice between him and Mike Hendrick and I wouldn't mind having either in my side, but Gus's ability to hit the bat hard with his 'heavy' ball gives him the edge. The fact that he returned to Test cricket after having been written off by so many experts is a good indication of his never-say-die attitude.

GRAHAM DILLEY
Test debut: 1979 v Australia at Perth. *Tests*: 39. *Runs*: 479. *HS*: 56. *Ave*: 12.94. *Wickets*: 133. *Ave*: 28.48. *BB*: 6 for 38. *Five wickets*: 6.

Prior to his problems with injury he had the ability to swing the ball into as well as away from the bat at genuine pace. Injury-free he could have developed into a real world-class performer. Not the worst tail-end bat either, as he proved at Headingley in 1981.

BOB WILLIS
Test debut: 1971 v Australia at Sydney. *Tests*: 90. *Runs*: 840. *HS*: 28 n.o. *Ave*: 11.50. *Wickets*: 325. *Ave*: 25.50. *BB*: 8 for 43. *Five wickets*: 16.

A tremendous trier. You could throw the ball to him at any time in any match, regardless of the circumstances or how old the ball might be and his response would always be the same – let me at 'em. Shrugged off countless injuries in order to get out there on the field, and at his peak as quick as anyone I've faced. A great team-man and an inspiration.

BEST OF THE WORLD

SUNIL GAVASKAR

Test debut: 1971 v West Indies at Port-of-Spain. *Tests:* 125. *Runs:* 10,122. *HS:* 236 n.o. *Centuries:* 34. *Ave:* 51.12. *Wickets:* 1. *Ave:* 206. *BB:* 1 for 34.

Without doubt the finest opener I ever bowled to. He was the complete player, possessing enormous powers of concentration and every shot in the book. His tremendous record against all countries, including the West Indies, speaks for itself. His wonderful double hundred against England at The Oval in 1979 was one of the greatest innings I ever saw.

GORDON GREENIDGE

Test debut: 1974 v India at Bangalore. *Tests:* 108. *Runs:* 7558. *HS:* 226. *Centuries:* 19. *Ave:* 44.72. *Wickets:* 0. *Ave:* 0. *BB:* 0 for 4.

Wonderful eye. The power of some of his shots left you in awe. A good player when physically sound, devastating when he limped because he was only interested in hitting boundaries. His double-hundred to win the Lord's Test of 1984 was a staggering innings and turned what should have been a difficult task into a stroll.

VIVIAN RICHARDS

Test debut: 1974 v India at Bangalore. *Tests:* 121. *Runs:* 8540. *HS:* 291. *Centuries:* 24. *Ave:* 50.23. *Wickets:* 32. *Ave:* 61.37. *BB:* 2 for 17.

Simply the best of my era and I personally find it hard to believe that there has ever been a better batsman. Whatever the conditions, whatever the match-situation, no matter who the opposition or the type of cricket, he was the man you would back to score runs for your life. An intimidating sight at the crease. His refusal ever to wear a batting helmet sent out a clear message: 'I'm not afraid of anyone and I'm certainly not afraid of you.' Watching him smash me and the rest of the England attack for the fastest century of all time in Antigua in 1986 was one of the most extraordinary experiences of my career. That day I felt I was in the presence of greatness. It was like bowling at God.

GREG CHAPPELL

Test debut: 1970 v England at Perth. *Tests:* 87. *Runs:* 7110. *HS:* 247 n.o. *Centuries:* 24. *Ave:* 53.86. *Wickets:* 47. *Ave:* 40.70. *BB:* 5 for 61. *Five wickets:* 1.

A hard choice between Greg and his brother Ian, but with Viv going in at number three, Greg gets the vote in his specialist position of number four. A stylish craftsman who had the wonderful knack of pacing his innings to perfection. Stubborn in defence and punishing in attack.

JAVED MIANDAD

Test debut: 1976 v New Zealand at Lahore. *Tests:* 121. *Runs:* 8689. *HS:* 280. *Centuries:* 23. *Ave:* 53.30. *Wickets:* 17. *Ave:* 40.11. *BB:* 3 for 74.

He had the qualities of confidence and arrogance all great players possess and they rubbed off on his colleagues. A master improviser, able to conjure runs out of nothing. Pakistan were fortunate to have some great strokeplayers during the period I played against them but he was the best of all.

ALLAN BORDER

Test debut: 1978 v England at Melbourne. *Tests:* 156
Runs: 11,174. *HS:* 205. *Centuries:* 27. *Ave:* 50.56.
Wickets: 39. *Ave:* 38.43. *BB:* 7 for 46. *Five wickets:* 2. *Ten
wickets:* 1.

Tough competitor and an equally uncompromis-
ing team-mate. Never gave up on a situation. It physically
hurt him to lose and he demanded the same level of
commitment from everyone he played with. The ultimate
professional.

CLIVE LLOYD (capt.)

Test debut: 1966 v India at Bombay. *Tests:* 110. *Runs:*
7515. *HS:* 242. *Centuries:* 19. *Ave:* 46.67. *Wickets:* 10.
Ave: 62.20. *BB:* 2 for 13.

His success in uniting players from different islands and
making them the best Test side in the world makes him my
choice as captain ahead of Border. A wonderful languid
strokeplayer who could destroy you when he was in the
mood. Marvellous fielder. Great guy.

RODNEY MARSH (wicket-keeper)

Test debut: 1970 v England at Brisbane. *Tests:* 96. *Runs:*
3633. *HS:* 132. *Centuries:* 3. *Ave:* 26.51. *Catches:* 343.
Stumpings: 12.

The best wicket-keeper in the world standing back, a
dangerous late-order batsman and a magnificent competitor on the field and in the bar.

RICHARD HADLEE

Test debut: 1973 v Pakistan at Wellington. *Tests:* 86.
Runs: 3124. *HS:* 151 n.o. *Centuries:* 2. *Ave:* 27.16.

Wickets: 431. *Ave:* 22.29. *BB:* 9 for 52. *Five wickets:* 36.
Ten wickets: 9.

More control than any other pace bowler I've seen. Capable of generating real pace when necessary, his accuracy and ability to move the ball in the air and off the pitch made him extremely awkward to deal with. No batsman ever felt they were really in command against him.

CURTLY AMBROSE

Test debut: 1988 v Pakistan at Georgetown. *Tests:* 54. *Runs:* 738. *HS:* 53. *Ave:* 11.71. *Wickets:* 237. *Ave:* 21.04. *BB:* 8 for 45. *Five wickets:* 11. *Ten wickets:* 3.

Wonderful destroyer. So difficult to bat against because of the bounce he could extract. Never gave you anything you could remotely describe as a free hit. Lethal when in the mood. Not over-keen on bowling, but even less keen on batsman.

JOEL GARNER

Test debut: 1977 v Pakistan at Bridgetown. *Tests:* 58. *Runs:* 672. *HS:* 60. *Ave:* 12.44. *Wickets:* 259. *Ave:* 20.97. *BB:* 6 for 56. *Five wickets:* 7.

His most deadly delivery was a fast yorker that either broke your toes or the stumps. A bloody miser with the ball who, like Ambrose, never gave you a thing. Hated conceding runs so much that if you nicked one for four he would burst into tears! If the wicket was doing a bit, his pace and bounce could make him as near to unplayable as you can get.

DENNIS LILLEE

Test debut: 1971 v England at Adelaide. *Tests:* 70. *Runs:* 905. *HS:* 73 n.o. *Ave:* 13.71. *Wickets:* 355. *Ave:* 23.92. *BB:* 7 for 83. *Five wickets:* 23. *Ten wickets:* 7.

The best fast bowler I ever played against. A wonderful craftsman. He had everything.

ABDUL QADIR

Test debut: 1977 v England at Lahore. *Tests:* 67. *Runs:* 1029. *HS:* 61. *Ave:* 15.59. *Wickets:* 236. *Ave:* 32.80. *BB:* 9 for 56. *Five wickets:* 15. *Ten wickets:* 5.

Comfortably the best leg-spinner I played against. He had exquisite control and wonderful variation, including three or four different types of googly. On a turning pitch an absolute nightmare.

So there you have it – the Best Of England to face the Best Of The World. The outcome? That's up to you.

CAST OF CHARACTERS

The following are just some of the characters appearing in this book (and the names have *not* been changed to protect the innocent!) . . .

THE FAMILY

Kath Don't tell her, but she takes all the credit for keeping us and the family together for the best part of twenty years. Last spotted advancing towards me with a rolling pin (only joking, luv).

Liam The oldest of my three children, born August 1977. Cheeky bugger who reckons he is going to be better than his old man.

Sarah The sensible one of the three Botham off-spring. Quietly assertive.

Becky The youngest (and silliest), born during the first Leukaemia Research Walk in 1985. Knows her own mind.

Les My dad, who left the services to work at Westland Helicopters in Yeovil. A gentle giant who taught me to play in the right spirit.

Marie Mum ran around in circles trying to keep up with a wandering toddler, and the pace quickened as I got older. Somehow she kept smiling.

Gerry Waller Kath's dad and my father-in-law. Has shared the occasional half o' shandy with me all over the world.

Jan Waller Kath's mum and a tremendous support for her over the years particularly when I have been abroad on tour.

MENTORS

Richard Hibbitt My ally at Milford Junior School. As gamesmaster, he encouraged me and never made too much fuss over the broken windows.

Tom Cartwright Warwickshire, Somerset, Glamorgan and England, 5 caps. Had faith in my bowling where others had none.

Brian Close Yorkshire, Somerset and England, 22 caps. My first captain at Somerset. Closey was Kath's godfather and dead against our marriage. That wasn't the first time he's been wrong in his life but you tell him . . . I value my health.

Ken Barrington Surrey and England, 82 caps. My first batting hero and a lovely man. Great influence on me when I took on the England captaincy but his death, aged 50, left a huge hole.

Mike Brearley Middlesex and England, 39 caps. The best captain I ever played with or against. A man who could read me through and through.

LORD'S GROUNDSTAFF

Len Muncer Middlesex and Glamorgan. Lord's ground-staff coach. A disciplinarian who rated my bowling as worse than useless. We did not see eye to eye.

Harry Sharp Middlesex. Lord's groundstaff coach. Much more my cup of tea, the 'Admiral' encouraged me to play by instinct if it worked.

Rodney Ontong Glamorgan. South African contemporary who shared many close shaves and income-boosting scams.

THE AUSSIES

Allan Border Friend and foe as skipper of the Aussies and Queensland. Occasionally lived up to his nickname of 'Captain Grumpy'.

Dennis Lillee Australian fast bowler, 70 Tests 1970–83. Just the man for a crisis, whether batting, bowling or getting you out of jail! The best fast bowler I ever faced.

Greg Ritchie Australian batsman, 30 Tests 1982–86. Larger than life in more ways than one, 'Fatcat' and I shared many thrills and spills.

Ian Chappell Aussie batsman, 75 Tests 1964–80. Not a drinking buddy, nor ever likely to be one after our clash in a Melbourne bar. A great player, though.

Greg Chappell Aussie batsman, 87 Tests 1970–83. My first Test scalp, and one of the best batsmen of all time. We had problems at Queensland.

Rodney Hogg Australian fast bowler, 38 Tests 1978–84. The victim of our alleged punch-up in Sydney which never took place. A great friend.

CRICKET SELECTORS

Alec Bedser The chairman of selectors who chose me for England, gave me the England captaincy and then took it away again.

Ossie Wheatley Apparently he was the chairman of the TCCB cricket committee in 1989. I say apparently because I had never heard of him before or since.

Ted Dexter Chairman of selectors 1989–93 and a master of placing both feet in his mouth at the same time. Great player, terrible astrologer.

Micky Stewart Sergeant Major and England team manager in late 1980s and early 1990s. Too much theory *and* too much practice.

A. C. Smith Chief executive of the TCCB who handled the death of Kenny Barrington and the Jackman affair in Guyana as well as anyone.

Peter May Dexter's predecessor as chairman of selectors, who presided over the appointment of four England skippers in a single series.

Ray Illingworth Appointed chairman of selectors in 1994. Replaced as coach after England's disastrous showing in the 1996 World Cup.

COUNTY CRICKETERS

Dennis Breakwell Northamptonshire and Somerset. My first flat-mate in Taunton. We shared no light, no heat, no toilet, but plenty of laughs.

Trevor Gard Somerset wicket-keeper. The bloke who made sure my feet stayed as near to the ground as possible.

Viv Richards Somerset and West Indies. A blood-brother to me but a fierce rival as well.

Joel Garner Somerset and West Indies. 'Big Bird' was silent but deadly.

Peter Roebuck Somerset. Deadly. The man I believed was responsible for the sackings of Joel and Viv that led to my leaving the club.

Vic Marks Somerset and England. From public school, but approachable nonetheless. His laugh sounds like a machine gun fired at slow speed.

Graham Dilley Kent, Worcestershire and England. The man who inspired me to turn the tables at Headingley in 1981. But for injury, may well have become a world-class fast bowler.

Geoff Cook Northamptonshire and Durham. Director of cricket who I believe never wanted me there in the first place.

David Graveney Gloucestershire and Durham. Appointed Durham skipper after I had been offered the job as an inducement to go to the club.

ENGLAND CRICKETERS

Bob Willis Surrey and Warwickshire. Fought off a stream of injuries to become the only world-class fast bowler in my time as an England player.

Geoff Boycott Yorkshire and England. 108 Tests 1964–82. Self-effacing cricketer with a wide range of interests. And then I woke up.

Mike Gatting Middlesex and England. 74 Tests 1977–93. British bulldog with a healthy appetite for food, err, runs.

Graham Gooch Essex and England. 118 Tests before retiring from international cricket in 1995. Improved with age as a batsman, but his captaincy was one-dimensional.

David Gower Leicestershire, Hampshire and England. 117 Tests 1978–92. Found his talents as captain and batsman misunderstood by those hooked on sweat.

Allan Lamb Northamptonshire and England. 79 Tests 1982–92. Gritty South African who kept me on the straight and narrow path (to the nearest bar).

LEUKAEMIA WALKERS

Chris Lander *Daily Mirror* cricket writer. 'Crash' intended to walk for a couple of days on the first Leukaemia trip but has not missed a day since.

Phil Rance Manchester businessman who trod every step of that first walk from John O'Groats, and then jumped into the sea at Land's End.

. . . AND OTHERS

Dave Roberts Physio for Worcestershire, England and Beefy's feet. Known as the 'Rooster' for his unique dancing style.

Tim Hudson Also known as Walter Mitty. The ex-DJ who took over as my manager in 1984 and seemed intent on controlling my mind.

Reg Hayter My first agent and a loyal and trusted friend.

Alan Herd The 'weasel'. Long-time solicitor and friend.

Robin Askwith Panto co-star and friend. Hired a plane to fly 'Gower and Morris are Innocent' banner over the Adelaide Oval in 1991. Sensible man.

Max Boyce Musician, actor and the man who provided the pantomime break in *Jack and the Beanstalk*. Welsh, apparently.

David English Former record company boss, actor and musician. Seagull fancier who devised the Bunbury cartoon characters and charity cricket XI.

Bill Beaumont Rival skipper on *Question of Sport* who delights in correcting my wrong answers to cricket questions.

David Coleman Host of *Question of Sport* . . . errrr . . . remarkable!

Imran Khan Sussex and Pakistan. 88 Tests 1976–91. Man who admitted to breaking the laws on ball tampering yet insisted he wasn't cheating.

Dickie Bird Arrived on earth from the planet Loony to become the best and fairest of all umpires. Great bloke, completely bonkers.

Don Oslear Had the guts to speak out over ball tampering. Lost his job as TCCB umpire soon afterwards.

Elton John Rock star, friend, father-confessor and babysitter.

Malcolm Marshall just pipped by Lilley for my ranking of the best quick bowler I ever faced. A charming man, a fiercesome but dignified opponent and a good friend. He will be sorely missed.

. . . PLUS A CAST OF THOUSANDS.

CAREER STATISTICS

Compiled by Wendy Wimbush

A	Australia	Q	Queensland
I	India	SL	Sri Lanka
NZ	New Zealand	WI	West Indies
P	Pakistan	Z	Zimbabwe

Summary of all First-Class Matches

Season	Venue	M	I	NO	HS	Runs	Avge	100
1974		18	29	3	59	441	16.96	–
1975		22	36	4	65	584	18.25	–
1976		20	35	5	167 *	1022	34.06	1
1977		17	27	3	114	738	30.75	1
1977–78	P/NZ	9	12	4	126 *	397	49.62	2
1978		17	20	0	108	538	26.90	2
1978–79	A	9	14	0	74	361	25.78	–
1979		15	20	1	137	731	38.47	2
1979–80	A/I	6	10	1	119 *	331	36.77	2
1980		18	27	0	228	1149	42.55	2
1980–81	WI	8	14	0	40	197	14.07	–
1981		16	24	2	149 *	925	42.04	3
1981–82	I/SL	11	15	1	142	760	54.28	2
1982		17	29	1	208	1241	44.32	3
1982–83	A	9	18	0	65	434	24.11	–
1983		14	21	0	152	852	40.57	3
1983–84	NZ/P	7	10	0	138	409	40.90	1
1984		17	26	1	90	797	31.88	–
1985		19	27	5	152	1530	69.54	5
1985–86	WI	8	16	0	70	379	23.68	–
1986		13	20	2	139	863	47.94	2
1986–87	A	8	14	2	138	481	40.08	1
1987		16	22	2	126 *	598	29.90	1
1987–88	Q	11	19	0	70	646	34.00	–
1988		4	4	0	7	18	4.50	–
1989		17	24	1	73	419	18.21	–
1990		13	18	1	113	595	35.00	1
1990–91	Zim	1	1	1	33 *	33	-	–
1991		13	21	3	161	785	43.61	2
1991–92	NZ	2	2	0	15	16	8.00	–
1992		17	25	2	105	713	31.00	1
1993		10	17	1	101	416	26.00	1
Totals		402	617	46	228	19399	33.97	38

50	Ct	Balls	Runs	W	Avge	BB	5w	10w
1	15	1746	739	30	24.63	5–59	1	–
2	18	3633	1704	62	27.48	5–69	1	–
6	16	3382	1880	66	28.48	6–16	4	1
5	15	3995	1983	88	22.53	6–50	6	1
1	7	1684	691	35	19.74	7–58	3	1
1	11	3632	1640	100	16.40	8–34	10	1
3	14	1915	848	44	19.27	5–51	2	–
1	21	2620	1318	46	28.65	6–81	3	–
–	5	1452	532	34	15.64	7–48	4	2
6	24	2721	1387	40	34.67	4–38	–	–
–	8	1346	790	23	34.34	4–77	–	–
4	19	3446	1712	67	25.55	6–90	4	1
5	7	1904	928	25	37.12	5–61	1	–
7	7	2950	1517	66	22.98	5–46	4	–
2	17	1918	1033	29	35.62	4–43	–	–
2	10	1394	728	22	33.09	5–38	1	–
2	8	1163	589	16	36.81	5–59	1	–
7	7	2698	1562	59	26.47	8–103	4	–
9	17	2438	1376	44	31.27	5–109	1	–
1	6	1085	671	15	44.73	5–71	1	–
5	8	1867	1043	25	41.72	6–125	1	–
2	11	1093	496	18	27.55	5–41	1	–
2	10	1560	883	21	42.04	3–51	–	–
7	18	1871	805	29	27.75	3–12	–	–
–	4	258	125	1	125.00	1–40	–	–
1	14	2980	1417	56	25.30	7–85	3	1
4	7	1168	614	21	29.23	4–65	–	–
–	–	102	38	2	19.00	2–17	–	–
4	12	2107	1077	44	24.47	7–54	3	–
–	1	228	116	5	23.20	2–23	–	–
4	9	2076	1144	26	44.00	4–72	–	–
3	8	1115	516	13	39.69	4–11	–	–
97	354	63547	31902	1172	27.22	8–34	59	8

Test Match Summary

Season	Venue	M	I	NO	HS	Runs	Avge	100
1977	A	2	2	0	25	25	12.50	–
1977–78	NZ	3	5	1	103	212	53.00	1
1978	P	3	3	0	108	212	70.66	2
1978–79	A	6	10	0	74	291	29.10	–
1979	I	4	5	0	137	244	48.80	1
1979–80	A	3	6	1	119*	187	37.40	1
1979–80	I	1	1	0	114	114	114.00	1
1980	WI	5	9	0	57	169	18.77	–
1980	A	1	1	0	0	0	–	–
1980–81	WI	4	7	0	26	73	10.42	–
1981	A	6	12	0	149*	399	36.27	2
1981–82	I	6	8	0	142	440	55.00	1
1981–82	SL	1	1	0	13	13	13.00	–
1982	I	3	3	0	208	403	134.33	2
1982	P	3	6	0	69	163	27.16	–
1982–83	A	5	10	0	58	270	27.00	–
1983	NZ	4	8	0	103	282	35.25	1
1983–84	NZ	3	4	0	138	226	56.50	1
1983–84	P	1	2	0	22	32	16.00	–
1984	WI	5	10	0	81	347	34.70	–
1984	SL	1	1	0	6	6	6.00	–
1985	A	6	8	0	85	250	31.25	–
1985–86	WI	5	10	0	38	168	16.80	–
1986	NZ	1	1	1	59*	59	–	–
1986–87	A	4	6	0	138	189	31.50	1
1987	P	5	8	1	51*	232	33.14	–
1989	A	3	4	0	46	62	15.50	–
1991	WI	1	2	1	31	35	35.00	–
1991	SL	1	1	0	22	22	22.00	–
1991–92	NZ	1	2	0	15	16	8.00	–
1992	P	2	2	0	6	8	4.00	–
	A	36	59	2	149*	1673	29.35	4
	WI	20	38	1	81	792	21.40	–
	NZ	15	23	2	138	846	40.28	3
	I	14	17	0	208	1201	70.64	5
	P	14	21	1	108	647	32.35	2
	SL	3	3	0	22	41	13.66	–
Home		59	89	4	208	2969	34.92	8
Overseas		43	72	2	142	2231	31.87	6
Totals		102	161	6	208	5200	33.54	14

50	Ct	Balls	Runs	W	Avge	BB	5w	10w
–	1	438	202	10	20.20	5–21	2	–
1	5	808	311	17	18.29	5–73	2	–
–	4	455	209	13	16.07	8–34	1	–
2	11	1268	567	23	24.65	4–42	–	–
–	10	1074	472	20	23.60	5–35	2	–
–	3	1039	371	19	19.52	6–78	2	1
–	–	293	106	13	8.15	7–48	2	1
1	2	786	385	13	29.61	3–50	–	–
–	–	188	132	1	132.00	1–43	–	–
–	5	872	492	15	32.80	4–77	–	–
1	12	1635	700	34	20.58	6–95	3	1
4	3	1443	660	17	38.82	5–61	1	–
–	–	149	65	3	21.66	3–28	–	–
1	1	561	320	9	35.55	5–46	1	–
2	1	905	478	18	26.55	5–74	1	–
1	9	1283	729	18	40.50	4–75	–	–
1	3	677	340	10	34.00	4–50	–	–
1	3	658	354	7	50.57	5–59	1	–
–	4	180	90	2	45.00	2–90	–	–
3	5	980	667	19	35.10	8–103	2	–
–	–	336	204	7	29.14	6–90	1	–
2	8	1510	855	31	27.58	5–109	1	–
–	4	809	535	11	48.63	5–71	1	–
1	–	156	82	3	27.33	3–82	–	–
–	10	638	296	9	32.88	5–41	1	–
1	3	807	433	7	61.85	3–217	–	–
–	3	480	241	3	80.33	2–63	–	–
–	3	162	67	3	22.33	2–40	–	–
–	2	96	41	1	41.00	1–26	–	–
–	1	132	76	3	25.33	2–23	–	–
–	2	144	61	0	–	–	–	–
6	57	8479	4093	148	27.65	6–78	9	2
4	19	3609	2146	61	35.18	8–103	3	–
4	14	3284	1500	64	23.43	6–34	6	1
5	14	3371	1558	59	26.40	7–48	6	1
3	14	2491	1271	40	31.77	8–34	2	–
–	2	581	310	11	28.18	6–90	1	–
13	62	12243	6226	226	27.54	8–34	17	2
9	58	9572	4652	157	29.63	7–48	10	2
22	120	21815	10878	383	28.40	8–34	27	4

County Championship Summary

Season	M	I	NO	HS	Runs	Avge	100
Somerset							
1974	16	26	3	59	400	17.39	–
1975	20	32	3	65	499	17.20	–
1976	18	31	3	167 *	944	33.71	1
1977	12	20	0	114	552	27.60	1
1978	10	14	0	86	275	19.64	–
1979	11	15	1	120	487	34.78	1
1980	10	14	0	228	875	62.50	2
1981	9	12	1	123 *	526	47.81	1
1982	11	20	1	131 *	675	35.52	1
1983	10	13	0	152	570	43.84	2
1984	11	15	1	90	444	31.71	–
1985	11	17	5	152	1211	100.91	5
1986	12	19	1	139	804	44.66	2
Total	161	248	19	228	8262	36.07	16
Worcestershire							
1987	11	14	1	126 *	366	28.15	1
1988	4	4	0	7	18	4.50	–
1989	12	18	1	73	276	16.23	–
1990	12	17	1	113	576	36.00	1
1991	10	17	2	104	567	37.80	1
Total	49	70	5	126 *	1803	27.73	3
Durham							
1992	14	23	2	105	705	33.57	1
1993	9	16	1	101	384	25.60	1
Total	23	39	3	105	1089	30.25	2
Combined total	233	357	27	228	11154	33.80	21

50	Ct	O	Runs	W	Avge	BB	5w	10w
1	13	260.3	640	27	23.70	5–59	1	–
2	18	541.2	1527	58	26.32	5–69	1	–
5	15	503.1	1645	60	27.41	6–16	4	1
3	7	498.5	1502	65	23.10	6–50	4	1
1	5	369.5	1051	58	18.12	7–61	5	–
1	11	257.4	846	26	32.53	6–81	1	–
4	18	224	736	18	40.88	3–34	–	–
3	6	279.5	976	31	31.48	6–90	1	–
4	5	247.2	719	39	18.43	5–48	2	–
1	7	119.3	388	12	32.33	5–38	1	–
4	2	230.2	691	33	20.93	5–57	1	–
6	5	130.4	464	11	42.18	4–63	–	–
4	8	285.1	961	22	43.68	6–125	1	–
39	120	3948.1	12146	460	26.40	6–16	22	2
1	7	125.3	450	14	32.14	3–51	–	–
–	4	43	125	1	125.00	1–40	–	–
1	7	386.4	1122	51	22.00	7–85	3	1
4	7	174.4	546	17	32.11	4–65	–	–
4	7	279.1	886	38	23.31	7–54	3	–
10	32	1009	3129	121	25.85	7–54	6	1
4	7	303	1010	24	42.08	4–72	–	–
3	8	168.5	450	13	34.61	4–11	–	–
7	15	471.5	1460	37	39.45	4–11	–	–
56	167	5429	16735	618	27.07	7–54	28	3

First-Class Summary by Team and Venue

	M	I	NO	HS	Runs	Avge	100
England	59	89	4	208	2969	34.92	8
MCC	4	5	2	53 *	115	38.33	–
Somerset	172	264	23	228	8686	36.04	16
Worcestershire	53	74	5	161	2064	29.91	4
Durham	25	40	3	105	1121	30.29	2
UK/HOME	313	472	37	228	14955	34.37	30
England XI							
in Australia	31	55	3	138	1493	28.71	2
in New Zealand	14	20	3	138	1493	28.71	2
in India	11	15	1	142 *	861	61.50	3
in Pakistan	4	4	1	22 *	54	18.00	–
in West Indies	16	30	0	70	576	19.20	–
in Sri Lanka	1	1	0	13	13	13.00	–
Queensland	11	19	0	70	646	34.00	–
Worcs in Zimbabwe	1	1	1	33 *	33	–	–
OVERSEAS	89	145	9	142	4444	32.67	8
CAREER	402	617	46	228	19399	33.97	38

50	Ct	Balls	Runs	W	Avge	BB	5w	10w
13	62	12243	6226	226	27.54	8–34	17	2
1	6	615	236	14	16.85	5–43	1	–
43	133	25353	12970	489	26.52	6–16	22	2
10	36	6528	3334	129	25.84	7–54	6	1
7	15	3047	1599	39	41.00	4–11	–	–
74	252	47786	24365	897	27.16	6–16	46	5
7	47	6085	2803	112	25.02	6–78	5	1
7	47	6085	2803	112	25.02	6–78	5	1
5	7	2048	969	35	27.68	7–48	3	1
–	6	508	243	6	40.50	2–31	–	–
1	14	2431	1461	38	38.44	5–71	1	–
–	–	149	65	3	21.66	3–28	–	–
7	18	1871	805	29	27.75	3–12	–	–
–	–	102	38	2	19.00	2–17	–	–
23	102	15761	7357	275	27.40	7–48	13	3
97	354	63547	31902	1172	27.22	8–34	59	8

Test Match Analysis

Series	Opponents	T	Venue	Result	NO	R	HO
Batting and Fielding						**Batting 1st**	
1977	Australia	3	Nottingham[1]	W–7w	8	25	b
		4	Leeds	W–I&85	8	0	b
1977–78	New Zealand	1	Wellington	L–72r	7	7	c
		2	Christchurch	W–174r	7	103	cw
		3	Auckland	D	6	53	cw
1978	Pakistan	1	Birmingham	W–I&57	7	100	c
		2	Lord's[2]	W–I&120	7	108	b
		3	Leeds	D	8	4	lbw
1978	New Zealand	1	Oval	W–7w	7	22	c
		2	Nottingham[3]	W–I&119	6	8	c
		3	Lord's[4]	W–7w	6	21	cw
1978–79	Australia	1	Brisbane	W–7w	7	49	cw
		2	Perth	W–166r	6	11	lbw
		3	Melbourne	L–103r	6	22	c
		4	Sydney	W–93r	6	59	cw
		5	Adelaide	W–205r	6	74	cw
		6	Sydney	W–9w	6	23	c
1979	India	1	Birmingham	W–I&83	6	33	b
		2	Lord's[5]	D	6	36	b
		3	Leeds	D	6	137	c
		4	Oval[6]	D	6	38	s
1979–80	Australia	1	Perth	L–138r	7	15	c
		2	Sydney	L–6w	7	27	c
		3	Melbourne	L–8w	6	8	cw
1979–80	India		Bombay	W–10w	6	114	lbw
1980	West Indies	C1	Nottingham	L–2w	6	57	c
		C2	Lord's	D	6	8	lbw
		C3	Manchester	D	6	8	cw
		C4	Oval[7]	D	8	9	lbw
		C5	Leeds[8]	D	6	37	c
1980	Australia	C	Lord's	D	6	0	c
1980–81	West Indies	C1	Port-of-Spain	L–I&79	6	0	lbw
		C3	Bridgetown	L–298r	6	26	cw
		C4	St John's	D	6	1	c
		C5	Kingston	D	7	13	c
1981	Australia	C1	Nottingham	L–4w	7	1	b

	Batting 2nd			Bowling 1st				Bowling 2nd			
NO	R	HO	Ct	O	M	R	W	O	M	R	W
–	–	–	1	20	5	74	5	25	5	60	–
–	–	–	–	11	3	21	5	17	3	47	–
6	19	c	1	12.6	2	27	2	9.3	3	13	2
4	30*	–	3	24.7	6	73	5	7	1	38	3
–	–	–	1	34	4	109	5	13	1	51	–
–	–	–	1	15	4	52	1	17	3	47	–
–	–	–	2	5	2	17	–	20.5	8	34	8
–	–	–	1	18	2	59	4	–			
–	–	–	–	22	7	58	1	19	2	46	3
–	–	–	2	21	9	34	6	24	7	59	3
–	–	–	–	38	13	101	6	18.1	4	39	5
–	–	–	–	12	1	40	3	26	5	95	3
6	30	c	1	11	2	46	–	11	1	54	–
6	10	cw	1	20.1	4	68	3	15	4	41	3
6	6	c	5	28	3	87	2	–			
6	7	c	–	11.4	–	42	4	14	4	37	1
–	–	–	4	9.7	1	57	4	–			
–	–	–	3	26	4	86	2	29	8	70	5
–	–	–	1	19	9	35	5	35	13	80	1
–	–	–	2	13	3	39	–	–			
6	0	RO	4	28	7	65	4	29	5	97	3
7	18	cw	–	35	9	78	6	45.5	14	98	5
7	0	c	1	17	7	29	4	23.3	12	43	–
6	119*	–	2	39.5	15	105	3	12	5	18	1
–	–	–	–	22.5	7	58	6	26	7	48	7
6	4	c	1	20	6	50	3	16.4	6	48	1
–	–	–	–	37	7	145	3	–			
6	35	lbw	1	20	6	64	3	–			
8	4	c	–	18.2	8	47	2	–			
6	7	lbw	–	19	8	31	1	–			
–	–	–	–	22	2	89	–	9.2	1	43	1
6	16	c	2	28	6	113	2	–			
6	1	c	2	25.1	5	77	4	29	5	102	3
–	–	–	–	37	6	127	4	–			
7	16	c	1	26.1	9	73	2	–			
7	33	c	1	16.5	6	34	2	10	1	34	1

Series	Opponents	T	Venue	Result	NO	R	HO
		C2	Lord's[9]	D	8	0	lbw
		3	Leeds	W–18r	7	50	cw
		4	Birimngham	W–29r	7	26	b
		5	Manchester[10]	W–103r	7	0	c
		6	Oval[11]	D	7	3	c
1981–82	India	1	Bombay[12]	L–138r	6	7	c
		2	Bangalore	D	7	55	c
		3	Delhi	D	6	66	c
		4	Calcutta	D	6	58	c
		5	Madras	D	5	52	cw
		6	Kanpur[13]	D	5	142	s
1981–82	Sri Lanka		Colombo Sara	W–7w	6	13	b
1982	India	1	Lord's	W–7w	5	67	c
		2	Manchester[14]	D	5	128	b
		3	Oval[15]	D	5	208	c
1982	Pakistan	1	Birmingham	W–113r	5	2	b
		2	Lord's	L–10w	5	31	c
		3	Leeds	W–3w	6	57	c
1982–83	Australia	1	Perth[16]	D	5	12	cw
		2	Brisbane	L–7w	5	40	c
		3	Adelaide[17]	L–8w	5	35	c
		4	Melbourne	W–3r	6	27	c
		5	Sydney	D	6	5	c
1983	New Zealand	1	Oval	W–189r	5	15	b
		2	Leeds	L–5w	5	38	c
		3	Lord's	W–127r	6	8	lbw
		4	Nottingham[18]	W–165r	6	103	lbw
1983–84	New Zealand	1	Wellington	D	6	138	c
		2	Christchurch	L–I&132	6	18	c
		3	Auckland	D	7	70	RO
1983–84	Pakistan	1	Karachi[19]	L–3w	6	22	c
1984	West Indies	1	Birmingham	L–I&180	6	64	c
		2	Lord's[20]	L–9w	6	30	c
		3	Leeds	L–8w	6	45	cw
		4	Manchester	L–I&64	6	6	c
		5	Oval[21]	L–172r	7	14	cw
1984	Sri Lanka		Lord's	D	6	6	c
1985	Australia	1	Leeds	W–5w	6	60	b

NO	R	HO	Ct	O	M	R	W	O	M	R	W
6	0	c	1	26	8	71	2	8	3	10	1
7	149*	–	2	39.2	11	95	6	7	3	14	1
7	3	cw	1	20	1	64	1	14	9	11	5
7	118	cw	4	6.2	1	28	3	36	16	86	2
7	16	lbw	3	47	13	125	6	42	9	128	4
6	29	c	–	28	6	72	4	22.3	3	61	5
–	–	–		47	9	137	2	–			
–	–	–		41	7	122	2	–			
5	31	c	1	27	8	63	2	11	3	26	–
–	–	–	2	31	10	83	1	8	1	29	–
–	–	–		25	6	67	1	–			
–	–	–		12.5	1	28	3	12	1	37	–
–	–	–		19.4	3	46	5	31.5	7	103	1
–	–	–		19	4	86	1	–			
–	–	–	1	19	2	73	2	4	–	12	–
6	0	lbw	–	24	1	86	2	21	7	70	4
5	69	c	–	44	8	148	3	7	–	30	–
6	4	c	1	24.5	9	70	4	30	8	74	5
5	0	b	–	40	10	121	2	6	1	17	–
5	15	cw	1	22	1	105	3	15.5	1	70	–
5	58	c	3	36.5	5	112	4	10	2	45	1
6	46	c	–	18	3	69	1	25.1	4	80	2
6	32	lbw	5	30	8	75	4	10	–	35	1
5	26	RO	2	16	2	62	4	4	–	17	–
5	4	c	–	26	9	81	–	0.1	–	4	–
6	61	c	1	20.4	6	50	4	7	2	20	1
6	27	c	–	14	4	33	1	25	4	73	–
–	–	–	1	27.4	8	59	5	36	6	137	1
6	0	c	1	17	1	88	1	–			
–	–	–	1	29	10	70	–	–			
6	10	b	4	30	5	90	2	–			
6	38	lbw	–	34	7	127	1	–			
6	81	lbw	–	27.4	6	103	8	20.1	2	117	–
6	14	cw	2	7	–	45	–	–			
6	1	c	1	29	5	100	2	–			
6	54	c	2	23	8	72	5	22.3	2	103	3
–	–	–	–	29	6	114	1	27	6	90	6
6	12	b	2	29.1	8	86	3	33	7	107	4

Series	Opponents	T	Venue	Result	NO	R	HO
		2	Lord's	L–4w	6	5	c
		3	Nottingham	D	6	38	c
		4	Manchester	D	6	20	c
		5	Birmingham	W–I&118	6	18	c
		6	Oval	W–I&94	7	12	cw
1985–86	West Indies	1	Kingston	L–10w	6	15	c
		2	Port-of-Spain	L–7w	6	2	c
		3	Bridgetown	L–I&30	6	14	cw
		4	Port-of-Spain[22]	L–10w	6	38	b
		5	St John's	L–240r	7	10	c
1986	New Zealand	3	Oval[23]	D	6	59*	–
1986–87	Australia	1	Brisbane[24]	W–7w	6	138	c
		2	Perth[25]	D	6	0	c
		4	Melbourne[26]	W–I&14	6	29	c
		5	Sydney	L–55r	6	16	c
1987	Pakistan	1	Manchester	D	7	48	c
		2	Lord's	D	7	6	c
		3	Leeds	L–I&18	6	26	cw
		4	Birmingham	D	7	37	c&b
		5	Oval[27]	D	6	34	b
1989	Australia	3	Birmingham[28]	D	6	46	b
		4	Manchester	L–9w	6	0	b
		5	Nottingham[29]	L–I&180	9	12	c
1991	West Indies	5	Oval	W–5w	7	31	HW
1991	Sri Lanka		Lord's	W–137r	6	22	c
1991–92	New Zealand	3	Wellington[30]	D	8	15	c
1992	Pakistan	1	Birmingham	D	–	–	–
		2	Lord's[31]	L–2w	6	2	b

[1] Age: 21 years, 246 days
[2] BB in any Lord's Test
[3] 50 wickets (R J Hadlee)
[4] 500 runs
[5] 100 wickets (Gavaskar) 2 yrs, 9 days
[6] 1000 runs Double – 21 Tests (Record)
[7] 150 wickets (Richards)
[8] 1500 runs
[9] Pair – RESIGNED CAPTAINCY
[10] 50th catch (Yallop)
[11] 200 wickets (Marsh)
[12] 2000 runs 3rd all-rounder
[13] 50 wickets v India (3rd England)
[14] 2500 runs
[15] Highest Test score
[16] 3000 runs 250 wickets (Border)

NO	R	HO	Ct	O	M	R	W	O	M	R	W
8	85	c	–	24	2	109	5	15	–	49	2
–	–	–	1	34.2	3	107	3	–			
–	–	–	1	23	4	79	4	15	3	50	–
–	–	–	1	27	1	108	1	14.1	2	52	3
–	–	–	3	20	3	64	3	17	3	44	3
6	29	b	–	19	4	67	2	–			
6	1	cw	1	9.4	–	68	1	–			
6	21	cw	2	24	3	80	1	–			
6	25	c	1	24.1	3	71	5	3	–	24	–
8	13	b	–	40	6	147	2	15	0	78	–
–	–	–	–	25	4	75	3	1	–	7	–
–	–	–	–	16	1	58	2	12	–	34	1
6	6	c	4	22	4	72	1	7.2	4	13	–
–	–	–	3	16	4	41	5	7	1	19	–
6	0	c	3	23	10	42	–	3	–	17	–
–	–	–	–	14	7	29	1	–			
–	–	–	–					–			
8	24	c	–	–				–			
4	6	c	2	48	13	121	1	20.3	3	66	2
6	51*	–	1	52	7	217	3	–			
–	–	–	2	26	5	75	1	–			
6	4	lbw	–	24	6	63	2	–			
absent injured			1	30	4	103	–	–			
7	4*	–	3	11	4	27	1	16	4	40	2
–	–	–	2	10	3	26	1	6	2	15	–
7	1	lbw	1	14	4	53	1	8	1	23	2
–	–	–	–	19	6	52	–	–			
7	6	lbw	2	5	2	9	–				

[17] 1000 v Aus 1022 runs in 1982
[18] 3500 runs
[19] Knee injury – returned to UK
[20] 4000 runs
[21] 300 wickets (Dujon)
[22] 350 wickets (Holding) 4500 runs
[23] Wicket (Edgar) with 1st ball back
[24] 22 of one over M G Hughes
[25] 100 catches (Boon)
[26] 50 catches v Australia (Waugh)
[27] 5000 runs
[28] Top score in total 242
[29] Dislocated finger
[30] 13th player 100 Tests
[31] 120 catches (Moin Khan)=Cowdrey

Championship Hundreds

For Somerset (16)

† 167 *	Nottinghamshire	Trent Bridge	1976
114	Hampshire	Taunton	1977
120	Glamorgan	Swansea	1979
126	Warwickshire	Edgbaston	1980
228	Gloucestershire	Taunton	1980
123 *	Glamorgan	Swansea	1981
† 131 *	Warwickshire	Taunton	1982
107	Worcestershire	Worcester	1983
152	Leicestershire	Leicester	1983
112	Glamorgan	Taunton	1985
149	Hampshire	Taunton	1985
† 138 *	Warwickshire	Edgbaston	1985
152	Essex	Taunton	1985
134	Northamptonshire	Weston-super-Mare	1985
104 *	Worcestershire	Weston-super-Mare	1986
139	Lancashire	Old Trafford	1986

For Worcestershire (3)

126 *	Somerset	Taunton	1987
113	Surrey	Oval	1990
104	Lancashire	Worcester	1991

For Durham (2)

† 105	Leicestershire	Durham University	1992
† 101	Worcestershire	Stockton-on-Tees	1993

†2nd innings   *not out

Championship Five Wickets/Innings

For Somerset (22)

5–59	Leicestershire	Weston-super-Mare	1974
5–69	Lancashire	Old Trafford	1975
6–25	Gloucestershire	Taunton	1976
†5–125	Gloucestershire	Taunton	1976
5–74	Yorkshire	Taunton	1976
6–16	Hampshire	Bournemouth	1976
5–71	Glamorgan	Taunton	1977
†6–50	Sussex	Hove	1977
6–58	Sussex	Taunton	1977
5–76	Warwickshire	Edgbaston	1977
†6–66	Glamorgan	Taunton	1978
5–53	Gloucestershire	Taunton	1978
7–61	Glamorgan	Cardiff	1978
6–43	Warwickshire	Weston-super-Mare	1978
6–86	Worcestershire	Worcester	1978
6–81	Surrey	Taunton	1979
6–90	Sussex	Taunton	1981
5–48	Hampshire	Bath	1982
†5–50	Worcestershire	Taunton	1982
5–38	Leicestershire	Leicester	1983
5–57	Kent	Taunton	1984
6–125	Leicestershire	Leicester	1986

For Worcestershire (6)

6–99	Northamptonshire	Northampton	1989
†5–76	Northamptonshire	Northampton	1989
7–85	Sussex	Hove	1989
5–125	Gloucestershire	Worcester	1991
†7–54	Warwickshire	Worcester	1991
5–67	Surrey	Worcester	1991

†2nd innings

County Championship Ten Wickets/Match

For Somerset (2)

11–150	Gloucestershire	Taunton	1976
10–161	Sussex	Hove	1977

For Worcestershire (1)

11–175	Northamptonshire	Northampton	1989

Non-Test Match or County Championship Hundreds

For England XI (2)

† 126 *	Canterbury	Christchurch	1977–78
122	Central Zone	Indore	1981–82

For Worcestershire (1)

161	West Indians	Worcester	1991

Non-Test Match or County Championship Ten Wickets/Match

For England XI (1)

10–91	Otago	Dunedin	1977–78

The Great All-Rounders

	T	I	Runs	Avge	100
G StA Sobers	93	160	8032	57.78	26
I T Botham	102	161	5200	33.54	14
Kapil Dev	131	184	5248	31.05	8
Imran Khan	88	126	3807	37.69	6
Sir Richard Hadlee	86	134	3124	27.16	2

Non-Test Match or County Championship Five Wickets/Innings

For England XI (3)

† 7–58	Otago	Dunedin	1977–78
† 5–51	New South Wales	Sydney	1978–79
† 5–70	Queensland	Brisbane	1978–79

For MCC (1)

5–43	Middlesex	Lord's	1978

(including a hat-trick)

Tours

Australia	1978–79, 1979–80, 1982–83, 1986–87
West Indies	1980–81 (c), 1985–86
New Zealand	1977–78, 1983–84, 1991–92
India	1979–80, 1981–82
Pakistan	1977–78, 1983–84
Sri Lanka	1981–82
Zimbabwe (Worcs)	1990–91

For limited-overs internationals only:

Australia	1991–92 World Cup
New Zealand	1982–83

W	Avge	BB	5wI	10wI	S/R
235	34.03	6–73	6	–	91.91
383	28.40	8–34	27	4	56.95
434	29.64	9–83	23	2	63.91
362	22.81	8–58	23	6	53.75
431	22.29	9–52	36	9	50.85

International Limited-Overs Matches Summary

Season		M	I	NO	HS	Runs	Avge
1976	WI	2	2	0	21	21	10.50
1977–78	Pak	3	3	2	17 *	43	43.00
1978	Pak	2	2	0	31	32	16.00
1978	NZ	2	2	0	34	37	18.50
1978–79	Aus	4	2	0	31	44	22.00
1979	W Cup	5	4	1	22	65	21.66
1979–80	WSC in Aus	9	9	0	37	114	12.66
1980	WI	2	2	1	42 *	72	72.00
1980	Aus	2	2	0	4	6	3.00
1980–81	WI	2	2	0	60	87	43.50
1981	Aus	3	3	1	24	42	21.00
1981–82	Ind	3	3	1	52	82	41.00
1981–82	SL	2	2	0	60	73	36.50
1982	Ind	2	1	0	4	4	4.00
1982	Pak	2	2	1	49	59	59.00
1982–83	WSC in Aus	10	9	0	65	205	22.77
1982–83	NZ	3	3	0	15	30	10.00
1983	W Cup	7	4	0	22	40	10.00
1983–84	NZ	3	3	0	18	34	11.33
1983–84	Pak	1	1	1	18 *	18	–
1984	WI	3	3	0	22	39	13.00
1985	Aus	3	2	0	72	101	50.50
1985–86	WI	3	3	0	29	51	17.00
1986–87	Perth Chall.	4	4	1	68	112	37.33
1986–87	WSC in Aus	10	10	1	71	252	28.00
1987	Pak	3	3	1	24	30	15.00
1989	Aus	3	3	1	25 *	37	18.50
1991	WI	1	1	0	8	8	8.00
1991–92	NZ	2	2	0	79	107	53.50
1991–92	W Cup	10	10	1	53	192	21.33
1992	Pak	5	4	2	40	76	38.00
	A	33	30	3	72	678	25.11
	WI	25	25	2	60	438	19.04
	NZ	19	18	0	79	396	22.00
	I	7	6	1	52	101	20.20
	P	23	20	9	49	319	29.00
	SL	5	4	0	60	120	30.00
	Z	1	1	0	18	18	18.00
	SA	2	2	0	22	43	21.50
	CAN	1	–				–
Home		47	40	8	72	669	20.90
Overseas		69	66	7	79	1444	24.47
Totals		116	106	15	79	2113	23.21

100	50	Ct	Balls	Runs	W	Avge	BB	4w
–	–	–	36	57	2	28.50	1–26	–
–	–	–	167	101	4	25.25	3–39	–
–	–	–	114	53	3	17.66	2–17	–
–	–	1	108	67	2	33.50	1–24	–
–	–	2	144	104	4	26.00	3–16	–
–	–	2	318	168	6	28.00	2–38	–
–	–	2	492	290	12	24.16	3–33	–
–	–	2	132	116	3	38.66	2–45	–
–	–	–	120	69	–	–	–	–
–	1	–	90	56	1	56.00	1–32	–
–	–	–	198	125	5	25.00	2–39	–
–	1	–	150	101	4	25.25	2–20	–
–	1	1	108	74	4	18.50	2–29	–
–	–	3	120	78	5	15.60	4–56	1
–	–	1	118	97	4	24.25	3–57	–
–	1	3	410	364	17	21.41	3–29	–
–	–	2	120	103	4	25.75	2–40	–
–	–	4	480	288	8	36.00	2–12	–
–	–	1	127	54	5	10.80	2–7	–
–	–	–	42	43	–	–	–	–
–	–	1	168	125	3	41.66	2–67	–
–	1	2	174	106	4	26.50	2–38	–
–	–	1	132	122	3	40.66	2–39	–
–	1	1	240	147	6	24.50	3–29	–
–	1	1	594	387	7	55.28	3–26	–
–	–	–	174	103	–	–	–	–
–	–	–	193	113	2	56.50	1–28	–
–	–	–	66	45	4	11.25	4–45	1
–	1	–	78	63	2	31.50	1–27	–
–	1	4	534	306	16	19.12	4–31	1
–	–	2	324	214	5	42.80	2–45	–
–	4	5	1747	1172	35	33.48	4–31	1
–	1	8	1338	938	31	30.25	4–45	1
–	2	8	897	624	28	22.28	3–40	–
–	1	4	396	246	12	20.50	4–56	1
–	–	7	1377	856	27	31.70	3–29	–
–	1	3	294	179	7	25.57	2–12	–
–	–	–	60	23	3	7.66	3–23	–
–	–	–	108	89	1	89.00	1–52	–
–	1	54	12	1		12.00	1–12	–
–	1	18	2843	1824	56	32.57	4–45	2
–	8	18	3428	2315	89	26.01	4–31	1
–	9	36	6271	4139	145	28.54	4–31	3

Domestic Limited-Overs Summary

Season	M	I	NO	HS	Runs	Avge	100
Sunday matches 1973–93							
Somerset	138	124	21	175 *	3185	30.92	3
Worcestershire	45	43	4	125 *	1350	34.61	1
Durham	21	20	1	67	497	26.15	–
Totals	204	187	26	175 *	5032	31.25	4
Benson & Hedges 1974–93							
Somerset	59	48	7	126 *	1039	25.34	1
Worcestershire	23	20	4	138 *	483	30.18	1
Durham	6	6	1	86	237	47.40	–
Totals	88	74	12	138 *	1759	28.37	2
Gillette Cup & NatWest Trophy 1974–93							
Somerset	33	28	6	96 *	825	37.50	–
Worcestershire	9	6	2	101	267	66.75	1
Durham	4	4	1	63 *	156	52.00	–
Totals	46	38	9	101	1248	43.03	1
Somerset	230	200	34	175 *	5049	30.41	4
Worcestershire	77	69	10	138 *	2100	35.59	3
Durham	31	30	3	86	890	32.96	–
Totals	338	299	47	175 *	8039	31.90	7

Fifties in Limited-Overs Internationals

60	West Indies	Arnos Vale	1980–81
52	India	Cuttack	1981–82
60	Sri Lanka	Colombo, SSC	1981–82
65	New Zealand	Adelaide	1982–83
72	Australia	Old Trafford	1985
68	Australia	Perth	1986–87
71	Australia	Melbourne	1986–87
79	New Zealand	Christchurch	1991–92
53	Australia	Sydney	1991–92

50	Ct	O	R	W	Avge	BB	4w
11	57	899	3965	171	23.18	4–10	4
8	15	295.4	1520	62	24.51	5–27	2
3	6	159.5	688	23	29.91	3–22	–
22	78	1354.3	6173	256	24.11	5–27	6
2	32	554	1890	88	21.47	4–16	4
–	17	219.4	754	39	19.33	5–41	2
2	3	56	171	5	34.20	2–21	–
4	52	829.4	2815	132	21.32	5–41	6
5	16	341.3	1162	41	28.34	4–20	1
2	4	88.1	376	18	20.88	5–51	2
2	–	36	156	2	78.00	1–53	–
9	20	465.4	1694	61	27.77	5–51	3
18	105	1794.3	7017	300	23.39	4–10	9
0	36	603.3	2650	119	22.26	5–27	6
7	9	251.5	1015	30	33.83	3–22	–
35	150	2649.5	10682	449	23.79	5–27	15

International Limited-Overs Matches

Four-Wicket Innings (3)

4–56	India	Headingley	1982
4–45	West Indies	Edgbaston	1991
4–31	Australia	Sydney	1991–92

Hundreds in Domestic Limited-Overs Matches

For Somerset (4)

106	Hampshire	Taunton	1981	JPL
105	Derbyshire	Taunton	1982	JPL
175*	Northamptonshire	Wellingborough	1986	JPL
126*	Glamorgan	Taunton	1986	B&H

For Worcestershire (3)

125*	Essex	Worcester	1987	JPL
138*	Gloucestershire	Bristol	1990	B&H
101	Devon	Worcester	1987	NW

Four-Wicket Innings in Domestic Limited-Overs Matches

For Somerset (9)

4–41	Middlesex	Bath	1976	JPL
4–10	Yorkshire	Scarborough	1979	JPL
4–47	Surrey	Bath	1982	JPL
4–22	Hampshire	Taunton	1983	JPL
4–16	Combined Universities	Taunton	1978	B&H
4–52	Kent	Canterbury	1982	B&H
4–27	Hampshire	Taunton	1983	B&H
4–51	Glamorgan	Swansea	1984	B&H
4–20	Sussex	Hove	1983	NW

For Worcestershire (6)

5–27	Gloucestershire	Gloucester	1987	JPL
4–25	Essex	Worcester	1990	Ref
5–41	Yorkshire	Worcester	1988	B&H
4–44	Surrey	Oval	1989	B&H
4–62	Derbyshire	Worcester	1989	NW
5–51	Lancashire	Worcester	1989	NW

INDEX